I0003738

SQL Server 2012

Database Design

Kalman Toth

SQL Server 2012 Database Design

Copyright © 2012 by Kalman Toth

Trademark Notices

Microsoft is a trademark of Microsoft Corporation.
SQL Server 2012 is a program product of Microsoft Corporation.
SQL Server 2008 is a program product of Microsoft Corporation.
SQL Server 2005 is a program product of Microsoft Corporation.
SQL Server 2000 is a program product of Microsoft Corporation.
SQL Server Management Studio (SSMS) is a program product of Microsoft Corporation.
SQL Server Data Tools (SSDT) is a program product of Microsoft Corporation.
Microsoft Help Viewer is a program product of Microsoft Corporation.
SQL Server Analysis Services (SSAS) is a program product of Microsoft Corporation.
SQL Server Integration Services (SSIS) is a program product of Microsoft Corporation.
SQL Server Reporting Services (SSRS) is a program product of Microsoft Corporation.
SQL Azure is a program product of Microsoft Corporation.
Office Visio is a program product of Microsoft Corporation.
Exam 70-461 is an exam product of Microsoft Corporation.
ORACLE is a trademark of ORACLE Corporation.
Java is a trademark of ORACLE Corporation.
DB2 is a trademark of IBM Corporation.
SYBASE is a trademark of Sybase Corporation.
McAfee is a trademark of McAfee Corporation.

Warning and Disclaimer

Every effort has been made to ensure accuracy, however, no warranty or fitness implied. The information & programs are provided on an "as is" basis.

SQL Server 2012 Database Design

Contents at a Glance

About the Author

Kalman Toth has been working with relational database technology since 1990 when one day his boss, at a commodity brokerage firm in Greenwich, Connecticut, had to leave early and gave his SQL Server login & password to Kalman along with a small SQL task. Kalman was a C/C++ developer fascinated by SQL, therefore, he studied a Transact-SQL manual 3 times from start to end "dry", without any server access. His boss was satisfied with the execution of SQL task and a few days later Kalman's dream came true: he got his very own SQL Server login. His relational database career since then includes database design, database development, database administration, OLAP architecture and Business Intelligence development. Applications included enterprise-level general ledger & financial accounting, bond funds auditing, international stock market feeds processing, broker-dealer firm risk management, derivative instruments analytics, consumer ecommerce database management for online dating, personal finance, physical fitness, diet and health. Currently he is Principal Trainer at www.sqlusa.com. His MSDN forum participation in the Transact-SQL and SQL Server Tools was rewarded with the Microsoft Community Contributor award. Kalman has a Master of Arts degree in Physics from Columbia University and a Master of Philosophy degree in Computing Science also from Columbia. Microsoft certifications in database administration, development and Business Intelligence. The dream SQL career took him across United States & Canada as well as South America & Europe. SQL also involved him in World History. At one time he worked for Deloitte & Touche on the 96th floor of World Trade Center North. On September 11, 2001, he was an RDBMS consultant at Citibank on 111 Wall Street. After escaping at 10:30 on that fateful Tuesday morning in the heavy dirt smoke, it took 10 days before he could return to his relational database development job just 1/2 mile from the nearly three thousand victims buried under steel. What Kalman loves about SQL is that the same friendly, yet powerful, commands can process 2 records or 2 million records or 200 million records the same easy way. His current interest is Artificial Intelligence. He is convinced that machine intelligence will not only replace human intelligence but surpass it million times in the near future. His hobby is flying gliders & vintage fighter planes.
Accessibility: @dbdesign1 at Twitter; http://twitter.com/dbdesign1, http://twitter.com/sqlusa, http://www.sqlusa.com/contact2005/.

CONTENTS

This page is intentionally left blank.

INTRODUCTION

Developers across the world are facing database issues daily. While they are immersed in procedural languages with loops , RDBMS forces them to think in terms of sets without loops. It takes transition. It takes training. It takes experience. Developers are exposed also to Excel worksheets or spreadsheets as they were called in the not so distant past. So if you know worksheets how hard databases can be? After all worksheets look pretty much like database tables? The big difference is connections among well-designed tables. A database is a set of connected tables which represent entities in the real world. A database can be 100 connected tables or 3000. The connection is very simple: row A in table Alpha has affiliated data with row B in table Beta. But even with 200 tables and 300 connections (FOREIGN KEY references), it takes a good amount of time to familiarize to the point of acceptable working knowledge.

"The Cemetery of Computer Languages" is expanding. You can see tombstones like PL/1, Forth, Ada, Pascal, LISP, RPG, APL, SNOBOL, JOVIAL, Algol and the list goes on. For some, the future is in question: PowerBuilder, ColdFusion, FORTRAN & COBOL. SQL on the other hand running strong after 3 decades of glorious existence. What is the difference? The basic difference is that SQL can handle large datasets in a consistent manner based on mathematical foundations. You can throw together a computer language easy: assignment statements, looping, if-then conditional, 300 library functions, and voila! Here is the new language: Mars/1, named after the red planet to be fashionable with NASA's new Mars robot. But can Mars/1 JOIN a table of 1 million rows with a table of 10 million rows in a second? The success of SQL language is so compelling that other technologies are tagged onto it like XML/XQuery which deals with semi-structured information objects.

In SQL you are thinking at a high level. In C# or Java, you are dealing with details, lots of them. That is the big difference. Why is so much of the book dedicated to database design? Why not plunge into SQL coding and sooner or later the developer will get a hang of the design? Because high level thinking requires thinking at the database design level. A farmer has 6 mules, how do we mode it in the database? We design the Farmer and FarmAnimal tables, then connect them with FarmerID FOREIGN KEY in FarmAnimal referencing the FarmerID PRIMARY KEY in the Farmer table. What is the big deal about it, looks so simple? In fact, how about just calling the tables Table1 & Table2 to be more generic? Ouch... meaningful naming is the very basis of good database design. Relational database design is truly simple for simple well-understood models. The challenge starts in modeling complex objects such as financial derivative instruments, airplane passenger scheduling or social network website. When you need to add 5 new tables to a 1000 tables database and hook them in (define FOREIGN KEY references) correctly, it is a huge challenge. To begin with, some of the 5 new tables may already be redundant, but you don't know that until you understand what the 1000 tables are really storing. Frequently, learning the application area is the biggest challenge for a developer when starting a new job.

The SQL language is simple to program and read even if when touching 10 tables. Complexities are abound though. The very first one: does the SQL statement touch the right data set? 999 records and 1000 or 998? T-SQL statements are turned into Transact-SQL scripts, stored procedures, user-defined functions and triggers, server-side database objects. They can be 5 statements or 1000 statements long programs. The style of Transact-SQL programming is different from the style in procedural programming languages. There are no arrays, only tables or table variables. Typically there is no looping, only set-based operations. Error control is different. Testing & debugging is relatively simple in Transact-SQL due to the interactive environment and the magic of selecting & executing a part without recompiling the whole.

WHO THIS BOOK IS FOR

Developers, programmers and systems analysts who are new to relational database technology. Also developers, designers and administrators, who know some SQL programming and database design, wish to expand their RDBMS design & development technology horizons. Familiarity with other computer language is assumed. The book has lots of queries, lots of T-SQL scripts, plenty to learn. The best way to learn it is to type in the query in your own SQL Server copy and test it, examine it, change it. Wouldn't it be easier just to copy & paste it? It would but the learning value would diminish. You need to feel the SQL language in your fingers. SQL queries must "pour" out from your fingers into the keyboard. Why is that so important? After everything can be found on the web and just copy & paste? Well not exactly. If you want to be an expert, it has to be in your head not on the web. Second, when your supervisor is looking over your shoulder, "Charlie, can you tell me what is the total revenue for March?", you have to be able to type in the query without SQL forum search and provide the results to your superior promptly.

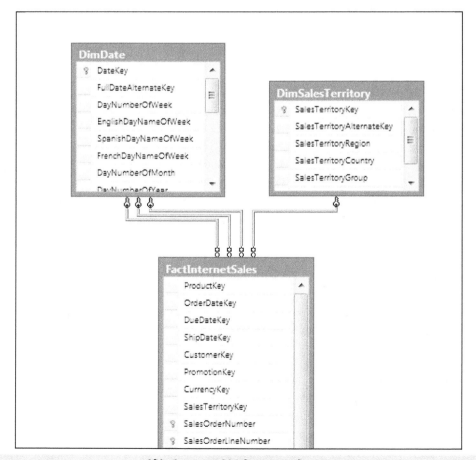

ABOUT THIS BOOK

Beginning relational database design and beginning Transact-SQL programming. It is not a reference manual, rather learn by examples: there are over 1,100 SELECT queries in the book. Instead of imaginary tables, the book uses the SQL Server sample databases for explanations and examples: pubs (PRIMARY KEYs 9, FOREIGN KEYs 10), Northwind (PRIMARY KEYs 13, FOREIGN KEYs 13) and the AdventureWorks family. Among them: AdventureWorks, AdventureWorks2008, AdventureWorks2012 (PRIMARY KEYs 71, FOREIGN KEYs 90), & AdventureWorksDW2012 (PRIMARY KEYs 27, FOREIGN KEYs 44). The book introduces relational database design concepts, then reinforces them again and again, not to bore the reader, rather indoctrinate with relational database design principles. Light weight SQL starts at the beginning of the book, because working with database metadata (not the content of the database, rather data which describes the database) is essential for understanding database design. By the time the reader gets to T-SQL programming, already knows basic SQL programming from the database design section of the book. The book was designed to be readable in any environment, even on the beach laptop around or no laptop in sight at all. All queries are followed by results row count and /or full/partial results listing in tabular (grid) format. For full benefits though, the reader should try out the T-SQL queries and scripts as he progresses from page to page, topic to topic. Example for SQL Server 2012 T-SQL query and results presentation.

```
SELECT          V.Name                              AS Vendor,
                FORMAT(SUM(POH.TotalDue), 'c', 'en-US')  AS [Total Purchase],
                FORMAT(AVG(POH.TotalDue), 'c', 'en-US')  AS [Average Purchase]
FROM AdventureWorks.Purchasing.Vendor AS V
    INNER JOIN AdventureWorks.Purchasing.PurchaseOrderHeader AS POH
        ON V.VendorID = POH.VendorID
GROUP BY V.Name  ORDER BY Vendor;
-- (79 row(s) affected) - Partial results.
```

Vendor	Total Purchase	Average Purchase
Advanced Bicycles	$28,502.09	$558.86
Allenson Cycles	$498,589.59	$9,776.27
American Bicycles and Wheels	$9,641.01	$189.04
American Bikes	$1,149,489.84	$22,539.02

CONVENTIONS USED IN THIS BOOK

The Transact-SQL queries and scripts (sequence of statements) are shaded.

The number of resulting rows is displayed as a comment line: -- (79 row(s) affected) .

The results of the queries is usually displayed in grid format.

Less frequently the results are enclosed in comment markers: /*...... */ .

When a query is a trivial variation of a previous query, no result is displayed.

While the intention of the book is database design & database development, SQL Server installation and some database administration tasks are included.

"Apparatus Intelligentia

vincet

Humanum Intelligentia"

Dedicated to

Edgar Frank "Ted" Codd

This page is intentionally left blank.

CHAPTER 1: SQL Server Sample & System Databases

AdventureWorks Series of OLTP Databases

AdventureWorks sample On Line Transaction Processing (OLTP) database has been introduced with SQL Server 2005 to replace the previous sample database Northwind, a fictional gourmet food items distributor. The intent of the AdventureWorks sample database s to support the business operations of AdventureWorks Cycles, a fictitious mountain, touring and road bike manufacturer. The company sells through dealer network and online on the web. In addition to bikes, it sells frames and parts as well as accessories such as helmets, biking clothes and water bottles. The AdventureWorks2012 database image of Touring-1000 Blue, 50 bike in Production.ProductPhoto table.

T-SQL query to generate the list of tables of AdventureWorks2012 in 5 columns. The core query is simple. Presenting the results in 5 columns instead of 1 column adds a bit of complexity.

```
;WITH cteTableList  AS (        SELECT CONCAT(SCHEMA_NAME(schema_id), '.', name)                AS  TableName,
  (( ROW_NUMBER() OVER( ORDER BY CONCAT(SCHEMA_NAME(schema_id),'.', name)) ) % 5)      AS  Remainder,
  (( ROW_NUMBER() OVER( ORDER BY CONCAT(SCHEMA_NAME(schema_id),'.', name)) - 1 )/ 5)    AS  Quotient
                        FROM AdventureWorks2012.sys.tables),
CTE AS (SELECT TableName, CASE WHEN Remainder=0 THEN 5 ELSE Remainder END AS Remainder, Quotient
        FROM cteTableList)
SELECT    MAX(CASE WHEN Remainder = 1 THEN TableName END),
        MAX(CASE WHEN Remainder = 2 THEN TableName END),
        MAX(CASE WHEN Remainder = 3 THEN TableName END),
        MAX(CASE WHEN Remainder = 4 THEN TableName END),
        MAX(CASE WHEN Remainder = 5 THEN TableName END)
FROM  CTE GROUP  BY Quotient ORDER  BY Quotient;
GO
```

CHAPTER 1: SQL Server Sample & System Databases

The query result set in grid format: tables in AdventureWorks2012

dbo.AWBuildVersion	dbo.DatabaseLog	dbo.ErrorLog	HumanResources.Department	HumanResources.Employee
HumanResources.EmployeeDepartmentHistory	HumanResources.EmployeePayHistory	HumanResources.JobCandidate	HumanResources.Shift	Person.Address
Person.AddressType	Person.BusinessEntity	Person.BusinessEntityAddress	Person.BusinessEntityContact	Person.ContactType
Person.CountryRegion	Person.EmailAddress	Person.Password	Person.Person	Person.PersonPhone
Person.PhoneNumberType	Person.StateProvince	Production.BillOfMaterials	Production.Culture	Production.Document
Production.Illustration	Production.Location	Production.Product	Production.ProductCategory	Production.ProductCostHistory
Production.ProductDescription	Production.ProductDocument	Production.ProductInventory	Production.ProductListPriceHistory	Production.ProductModel
Production.ProductModelIllustration	Production.ProductModelProductDescriptionCulture	Production.ProductPhoto	Production.ProductProductPhoto	Production.ProductReview
Production.ProductSubcategory	Production.ScrapReason	Production.TransactionHistory	Production.TransactionHistoryArchive	Production.UnitMeasure
Production.WorkOrder	Production.WorkOrderRouting	Purchasing.ProductVendor	Purchasing.PurchaseOrderDetail	Purchasing.PurchaseOrderHeader
Purchasing.ShipMethod	Purchasing.Vendor	Sales.CountryRegionCurrency	Sales.CreditCard	Sales.Currency
Sales.CurrencyRate	Sales.Customer	Sales.PersonCreditCard	Sales.SalesOrderDetail	Sales.SalesOrderHeader
Sales.SalesOrderHeaderSalesReason	Sales.SalesPerson	Sales.SalesPersonQuotaHistory	Sales.SalesReason	Sales.SalesTaxRate
Sales.SalesTerritory	Sales.SalesTerritoryHistory	Sales.ShoppingCartItem	Sales.SpecialOffer	Sales.SpecialOfferProduct
Sales.Store	NULL	NULL	NULL	NULL

CHAPTER 1: SQL Server Sample & System Databases

Diagram of Person.Person & Related Tables

Database diagram displays the Person.Person and related tables. PRIMARY KEYs are marked with a gold (in color display) key. The "oo------->" line is interpreted as many-to-one relationship. For example a person (one) can have one or more (many) credit cards. The "oo" side is the table with **FOREIGN KEY** referencing the gold key side table with the **PRIMARY KEY**.

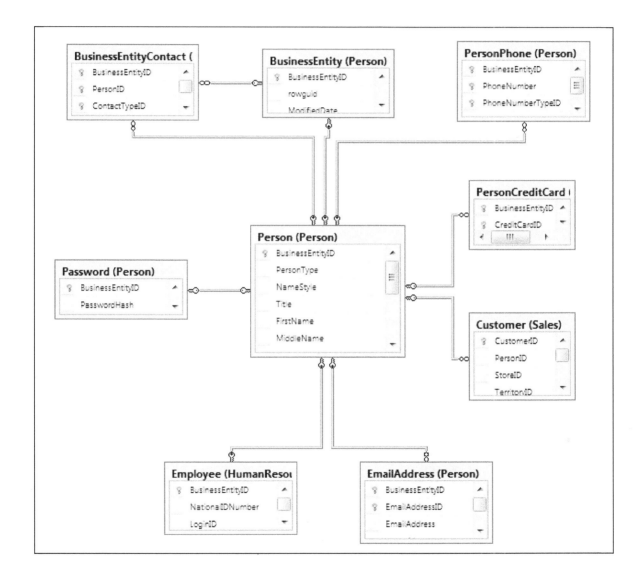

Diagram of Sales.SalesOrderHeader and Related Tables

Database diagram displays Sales.SalesOrderHeader and all tables related with **FOREIGN KEY** constraints. The SalesOrderHeader table stores the general information about each order. Line items, e.g. 5 Helmets at $30 each, are stored in the SalesOrderDetail table.

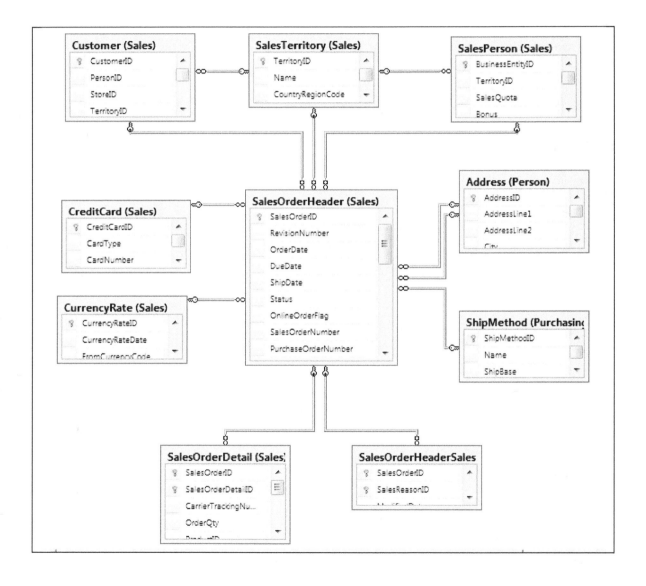

SELECT Query Basics

We have to use "light-weight" SQL (Structured Query Language) in the database design lessons. The reason is that rather difficult to discuss any database related topic without demonstration T-SQL scripts, in fact it would not make sense. **Relational database** and the **SQL language** are "married" to each other forever and ever.

The Simplest SELECT Statement

The simplest SELECT statement is "SELECT * FROM TableNameX" as demonstrated following. The "*" means wildcard inclusion of all columns in the table. Since there is no any other clause in the SELECT statement, it means also to retrieve all rows in the **table in no particular order**. Small tables which were populated in order are usually retrieved in order even though there is no ORDER BY clause. But this behaviour is purely coincidental. **Only ORDER BY clause can guarantee a sorted output.**

SELECT * FROM AdventureWorks2012.HumanResources.Department;
-- (16 row(s) affected)

DepartmentID	Name	GroupName	ModifiedDate
1	Engineering	Research and Development	2002-06-01 00:00:00.000
2	Tool Design	Research and Development	2002-06-01 00:00:00.000
3	Sales	Sales and Marketing	2002-06-01 00:00:00.000
4	Marketing	Sales and Marketing	2002-06-01 00:00:00.000
5	Purchasing	Inventory Management	2002-06-01 00:00:00.000
6	Research and Development	Research and Development	2002-06-01 00:00:00.000
7	Production	Manufacturing	2002-06-01 00:00:00.000
8	Production Control	Manufacturing	2002-06-01 00:00:00.000
9	Human Resources	Executive General and Administration	2002-06-01 00:00:00.000
10	Finance	Executive General and Administration	2002-06-01 00:00:00.000
11	Information Services	Executive General and Administration	2002-06-01 00:00:00.000
12	Document Control	Quality Assurance	2002-06-01 00:00:00.000
13	Quality Assurance	Quality Assurance	2002-06-01 00:00:00.000
14	Facilities and Maintenance	Executive General and Administration	2002-06-01 00:00:00.000
15	Shipping and Receiving	Inventory Management	2002-06-01 00:00:00.000
16	Executive	Executive General and Administration	2002-06-01 00:00:00.000

When tables are JOINed, SELECT * returns all the columns with all the data in the participant tables.

SELECT TOP 3 * FROM Sales.SalesOrderHeader H
          INNER JOIN Sales.SalesOrderDetail D
             ON H.SalesOrderID = D.SalesOrderID;
-- 121,317 rows in the JOIN

CHAPTER 1: SQL Server Sample & System Databases

Query Result Set In Text Format

If no grid format available, text format can be used. While it works, it is a challenge to read it, but computer geeks are used to this kind of data dump.

```
/* SalesOrderID RevisionNumber OrderDate          DueDate          ShipDate          Status
OnlineOrderFlag SalesOrderNumber       PurchaseOrderNumber      AccountNumber CustomerID
SalesPersonID TerritoryID BillToAddressID ShipToAddressID ShipMethodID CreditCardID
CreditCardApprovalCode CurrencyRateID SubTotal       TaxAmt          Freight          TotalDue
Comment                                                                  rowguid
ModifiedDate          SalesOrderID SalesOrderDetailID CarrierTrackingNumber   OrderQty ProductID
SpecialOfferID UnitPrice          UnitPriceDiscount   LineTotal        rowguid          ModifiedDate
----------- -------------- ----------------------- ----------------------- ----------------------- ------ -------------- ----------------
------ ----------------------- ----------------- ------------- ----------- ------------- ---------- --------------- --------------- ----------- ----------
- ----------------------- --------------- ----------------- ----------------------- ---------------------- -------------- ---------------
--------------------------------------------------- ------------------------
---------- ----------------------- -------------- ----------------------- ----------------- -------- ---------- ------------- -------------
-------- ----------------------- ----------------- --------------- ----------------------- ------------------------

43735     3          2005-07-10 00:00:00.000 2005-07-22 00:00:00.000 2005-07-17 00:00:00.000 5     1
SO43735            NULL            10-4030-016522 16522     NULL     9     25384      25384
1     6526     1034619Vi33896     119     3578.27          286.2616          89.4568
3953.9884          NULL                                                      98F80245-
C398-4562-BDAF-EA3E9A0DDFAC 2005-07-17 00:00:00.000 43735     391          NULL          1
749     1          3578.27          0.00          3578.270000          74838EF7-FDEB-4EB3-8978-
BA310FBA82E6 2005-07-10 00:00:00.000
43736     3          2005-07-10 00:00:00.000 2005-07-22 00:00:00.000 2005-07-17 00:00:00.000 5     1
SO43736            NULL            10-4030-011002 11002     NULL     9     20336      20336
1     1416     1135092Vi7270     119     3399.99          271.9992          84.9998
3756.989          NULL                                                      C14E29E7-
DB11-44EF-943E-143925A5A9AE 2005-07-17 00:00:00.000 43736     392          NULL          1
773     1          3399.99          0.00          3399.990000          3A0229FA-0A03-4126-
97CE-C3425968B670 2005-07-10 00:00:00.000
43737     3          2005-07-11 00:00:00.000 2005-07-23 00:00:00.000 2005-07-18 00:00:00.000 5     1
SO43737            NULL            10-4030-013261 13261     NULL     8     29772      29772
1     NULL     NULL            136     3578.27          286.2616          89.4568          3953.9884
NULL                                                      0B3E274D-E5A8-4E8C-A417-
0EAFABCFF162 2005-07-18 00:00:00.000 43737     393          NULL          1     750     1
3578.27          0.00          3578.270000          65AFCCE8-CA28-41C4-9A07-0265FB2DA5C8
2005-07-11 00:00:00.000                    (3 row(s) affected)   */
```

```sql
SELECT MatchingRows = COUNT(*) FROM AdventureWorks2012.Sales.SalesOrderHeader H
  INNER JOIN AdventureWorks2012.Sales.SalesOrderDetail D
       ON H.SalesOrderID = D.SalesOrderID;   -- INNER JOIN MatchingRows 121317
```

```sql
SELECT AllRowsInDetail = COUNT(*) FROM AdventureWorks2012.Sales.SalesOrderDetail
-- AllRowsInDetail 121317
```

CHAPTER 1: SQL Server Sample & System Databases

SELECT Query with WHERE Clause Predicate

Query to demonstrate how can we be selective with columns, furthermore, filter returned rows (WHERE clause) and sort them (ORDER BY clause).

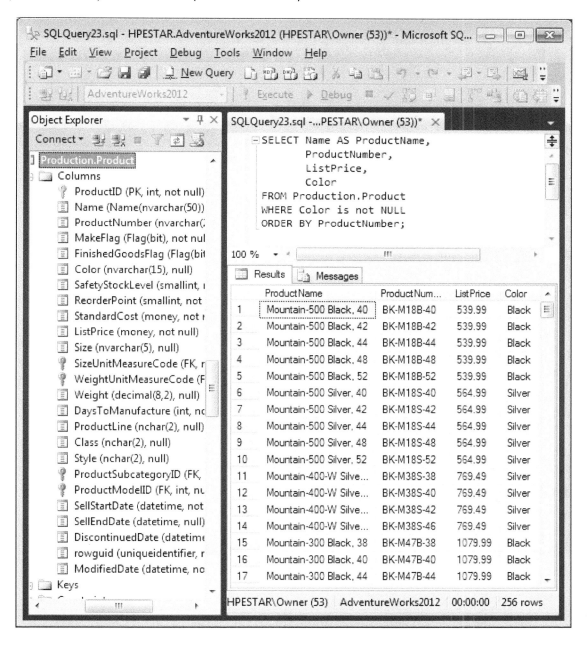

Aggregating Data with GROUP BY Query

The second basic query is GROUP BY aggregation which creates a **summary** of detail data.
GROUP BY query can be used to preview, review, survey , assess, and analyze data at a high
level.

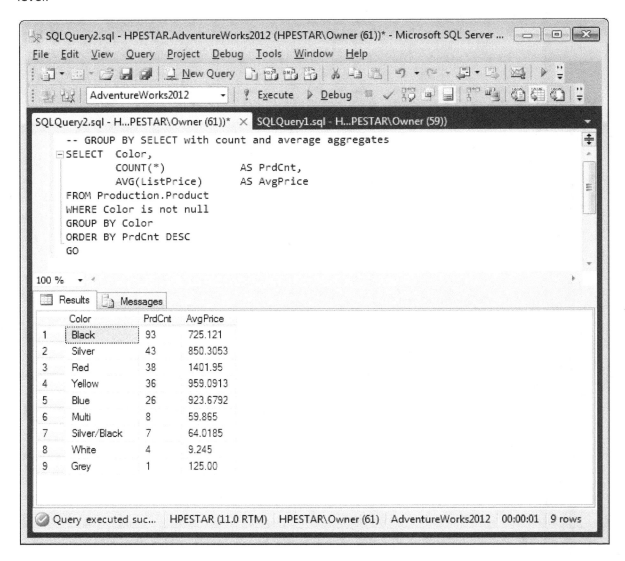

NOTE
GROUP BY aggregate queries can efficiently "fingerprint" (profile) data in tables, even millions of rows.
GROUP BY aggregates form the computational base of Business Intelligence.

GROUP BY Query with 2 Tables & ORDER BY for Sorting

JOINing two tables on matching KEYs, FOREIGN KEY to PRIMARY KEY, to combine the data contents in a consistent fashion.

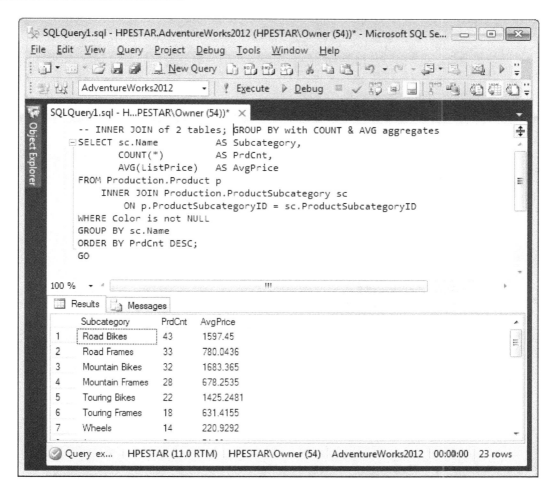

LEN(), DATALENGTH(), LTRIM() & RTRIM() Functions

The LEN() function counts characters without the trailing spaces. DATALENGTH() counts storage bytes including trailing spaces. LTRIM() trims leading spaces, RTRIM() trims trailing spaces.

```
DECLARE @W varchar(32)= CHAR(32)+'Denver'+CHAR(32);
DECLARE @UW nvarchar(32) = CHAR(32)+N'MEGŐRZÉSE'+CHAR(32);  -- UNICODE 2 bytes per character
SELECT Length=LEN(@W), DLength=DATALENGTH (@W);                                    -- 7  8
SELECT Length=LEN(@UW), DLength=DATALENGTH (@UW);                                  -- 10  22
SELECT Length=LEN(LTRIM(RTRIM(@W))), DLength=DATALENGTH (LTRIM(RTRIM(@W)));        -- 6  6
SELECT Length=LEN(LTRIM(RTRIM(@UW))), DLength=DATALENGTH (LTRIM(RTRIM(@UW)));      -- 9  18
```

CHAPTER 1: SQL Server Sample & System Databases

Finding All Accessories in Production.Product Table

Query to list all accessories (a category) for sale.

USE AdventureWorks2012;

```
SELECT          UPPER(PC.Name) AS Category, PSC.Name              AS Subcategory,
                P.Name AS Product, FORMAT(ListPrice, 'c', 'en-US')      AS ListPrice,
                FORMAT(StandardCost, 'c', 'en-US')          AS StandardCost
FROM Production.Product AS P
   INNER JOIN Production.ProductSubcategory AS PSC
            ON PSC.ProductSubcategoryID = P.ProductSubcategoryID
   INNER JOIN Production.ProductCategory AS PC
            ON PC.ProductCategoryID = PSC.ProductCategoryID
WHERE PC.Name = 'Accessories'
ORDER BY Category, Subcategory, Product;
```

Category	Subcategory	Product	ListPrice	StandardCost
ACCESSORIES	Bike Racks	Hitch Rack - 4-Bike	$120.00	$44.88
ACCESSORIES	Bike Stands	All-Purpose Bike Stand	$159.00	$59.47
ACCESSORIES	Bottles and Cages	Mountain Bottle Cage	$9.99	$3.74
ACCESSORIES	Bottles and Cages	Road Bottle Cage	$8.99	$3.36
ACCESSORIES	Bottles and Cages	Water Bottle - 30 oz.	$4.99	$1.87
ACCESSORIES	Cleaners	Bike Wash - Dissolver	$7.95	$2.97
ACCESSORIES	Fenders	Fender Set - Mountain	$21.98	$8.22
ACCESSORIES	Helmets	Sport-100 Helmet, Black	$34.99	$13.09
ACCESSORIES	Helmets	Sport-100 Helmet, Blue	$34.99	$13.09
ACCESSORIES	Helmets	Sport-100 Helmet, Red	$34.99	$13.09
ACCESSORIES	Hydration Packs	Hydration Pack - 70 oz.	$54.99	$20.57
ACCESSORIES	Lights	Headlights - Dual-Beam	$34.99	$14.43
ACCESSORIES	Lights	Headlights - Weatherproof	$44.99	$18.56
ACCESSORIES	Lights	Taillights - Battery-Powered	$13.99	$5.77
ACCESSORIES	Locks	Cable Lock	$25.00	$10.31
ACCESSORIES	Panniers	Touring-Panniers, Large	$125.00	$51.56
ACCESSORIES	Pumps	Minipump	$19.99	$8.25
ACCESSORIES	Pumps	Mountain Pump	$24.99	$10.31
ACCESSORIES	Tires and Tubes	HL Mountain Tire	$35.00	$13.09
ACCESSORIES	Tires and Tubes	HL Road Tire	$32.60	$12.19
ACCESSORIES	Tires and Tubes	LL Mountain Tire	$24.99	$9.35
ACCESSORIES	Tires and Tubes	LL Road Tire	$21.49	$8.04
ACCESSORIES	Tires and Tubes	ML Mountain Tire	$29.99	$11.22
ACCESSORIES	Tires and Tubes	ML Road Tire	$24.99	$9.35
ACCESSORIES	Tires and Tubes	Mountain Tire Tube	$4.99	$1.87
ACCESSORIES	Tires and Tubes	Patch Kit/8 Patches	$2.29	$0.86
ACCESSORIES	Tires and Tubes	Road Tire Tube	$3.99	$1.49
ACCESSORIES	Tires and Tubes	Touring Tire	$28.99	$10.84
ACCESSORIES	Tires and Tubes	Touring Tire Tube	$4.99	$1.87

How Can SQL Work without Looping?

Looping is implicit in the SQL language. The commands are set oriented and carried out for each member of the set be it 5 or 500 millions in an unordered manner.

SELECT * FROM AdventureWorks2012.Sales.SalesOrderDetail;   (121317 row(s) affected)

SQL Server database engine looped through internally on all rows in SalesOrderDetail table in an unordered way. In fact the database engine may have used some ordering for efficiency, but that behaviour is a blackbox as far as programming concerned. Implicit looping makes SQL statements so simple, yet immensely powerful for information access from low level to high level.

Single-Valued SQL Queries

Single-valued SQL queries are very important because **we can use them where ever the T-SQL syntax requires a single value just by enclosing the query in parenthesis**. The next T-SQL query returns a single value, a cell from the table which is the intersection of a row and a column.

SELECT ListPrice FROM AdventureWorks2012.Production.Product WHERE ProductID = 800;
-- (1 row(s) affected)

ListPrice
1120.49

The ">" comparison operator requires a single value on the right hand side so we plug in the single-valued query. The WHERE condition is evaluated for each row (implicit looping).

SELECT ProductID, Name AS ProductName, ListPrice
FROM AdventureWorks2012.Production.Product   -- 504 rows
WHERE ListPrice > 2 *   (
            SELECT ListPrice FROM AdventureWorks2012.Production.Product
            WHERE ProductID = 800
)
ORDER BY ListPrice DESC, ProductName;   -- (35 row(s) affected) - Partial results.

ProductID	ProductName	ListPrice
750	Road-150 Red, 44	3578.27
751	Road-150 Red, 48	3578.27
752	Road-150 Red, 52	3578.27
753	Road-150 Red, 56	3578.27
749	Road-150 Red, 62	3578.27
771	Mountain-100 Silver, 38	3399.99

CHAPTER 1: SQL Server Sample & System Databases

Data Dictionary Description of Tables in the Sales Schema

It is not easy to understand a database with 70 tables, even harder with 2,000 tables.
Documentation is very helpful, if not essential, for any database. SQL Server provides Data
Dictionary facility for documenting tables and other objects in the database. Data which
describes the design & structure of a database is called **metadata**. Here is the high level
documentation of tables in the Sales schema using the fn_listextendedproperty system
function.

```
SELECT
        CONCAT('Sales.', objname COLLATE DATABASE_DEFAULT)      AS TableName,
        value                                                   AS [Description]
FROM fn_listextendedproperty (NULL, 'schema', 'Sales', 'table', default, NULL, NULL)
ORDER BY TableName;
```

TableName	Description
Sales.ContactCreditCard	Cross-reference table mapping customers in the Contact table to their credit card information in the CreditCard table.
Sales.CountryRegionCurrency	Cross-reference table mapping ISO currency codes to a country or region.
Sales.CreditCard	Customer credit card information.
Sales.Currency	Lookup table containing standard ISO currencies.
Sales.CurrencyRate	Currency exchange rates.
Sales.Customer	Current customer information. Also see the Individual and Store tables.
Sales.CustomerAddress	Cross-reference table mapping customers to their address(es).
Sales.Individual	Demographic data about customers that purchase Adventure Works products online.
Sales.SalesOrderDetail	Individual products associated with a specific sales order. See SalesOrderHeader.
Sales.SalesOrderHeader	General sales order information.
Sales.SalesOrderHeaderSalesReason	Cross-reference table mapping sales orders to sales reason codes.
Sales.SalesPerson	Sales representative current information.
Sales.SalesPersonQuotaHistory	Sales performance tracking.
Sales.SalesReason	Lookup table of customer purchase reasons.
Sales.SalesTaxRate	Tax rate lookup table.
Sales.SalesTerritory	Sales territory lookup table.
Sales.SalesTerritoryHistory	Sales representative transfers to other sales territories.
Sales.ShoppingCartItem	Contains online customer orders until the order is submitted or cancelled.
Sales.SpecialOffer	Sale discounts lookup table.
Sales.SpecialOfferProduct	Cross-reference table mapping products to special offer discounts.
Sales.Store	Customers (resellers) of Adventure Works products.
Sales.StoreContact	Cross-reference table mapping stores and their employees.

NULL Values in Tables & Query Results

NULL means no value. If so why do we capitalize it? We don't have to. Somehow, it became a custom in the RDBMS industry, nobody knows anymore how it started. Since the U.S. default collation for server and databases are case insensitive, we can just use "null" as well. **NULL value is different from empty string (") or 0 (zero) which can be tested by the "=" or "!=" operators.** If a database table does not have a value in a cell for whatever reason, it is marked (flagged) as NULL by the database engine. When a value is entered, the NULL marking goes away. **NULL values can be tested by "IS NULL" or "IS NOT NULL" operators, but not the "=" or "!=" operators.**

The likelihood is high that the color attribute is not applicable to items like tire tube, that is the reason that some cell values were left unassigned (null).

```
SELECT TOP 5   Name                          AS ProductName,
               ProductNumber,
               ListPrice,
               Color
FROM AdventureWorks2012.Production.Product
WHERE Color IS NULL  ORDER BY ProductName DESC;
```

ProductName	ProductNumber	ListPrice	Color
Water Bottle - 30 oz.	WB-H098	4.99	NUL_
Touring Tire Tube	TT-T092	4.99	NUL_
Touring Tire	TI-T723	28.99	NUL_
Touring Rim	RM-T801	0.00	NUL_
Touring End Caps	EC-T209	0.00	NUL_

We can do random selection as well and get a mix of products with color and null value.

```
SELECT TOP 5   Name AS ProductName,
               ProductNumber,
               ListPrice,
               Color
FROM AdventureWorks2012.Production.Product  ORDER BY NEWID();    -- Random sort
```

ProductName	ProductNumber	ListPrice	Color
Touring-1000 Yellow, 46	BK-T79Y-46	2384.07	Yellow
HL Spindle/Axle	SD-9872	0.00	NU_L
ML Mountain Tire	TI-M602	29.99	NU_L
Road-650 Red, 60	BK-R50R-60	782.99	Rec
Pinch Bolt	PB-6109	0.00	NU_L

CHAPTER 1: SQL Server Sample & System Databases

NULL Values Generated by Queries

NULL values can be generated by queries as well. Typically, LEFT JOIN, RIGHT JOIN and some functions generate NULLs. The meaning of OUTER JOINs: include no-match rows from the left or right table in addition to the matching rows.

```
SELECT TOP 5
            PS.Name                      AS Category,
            P.Name                       AS ProductName,
            ProductNumber,
            ListPrice,
            Color
FROM AdventureWorks2012.Production.Product P
  RIGHT JOIN AdventureWorks2012.Production.ProductSubcategory PS
        ON    PS.ProductSubcategoryID = P.ProductSubcategoryID
              AND ListPrice >= 3500.0
ORDER BY newid();
GO
```

Category	ProductName	ProductNumber	ListPrice	Color
Road Bikes	Road-150 Red, 62	BK-R93R-62	3578.27	Red
Road Bikes	Road-150 Red, 52	BK-R93R-52	3578.27	Red
Bib-Shorts	NULL	NULL	NULL	NULL
Socks	NULL	NULL	NULL	NULL
Cranksets	NULL	NULL	NULL	NULL

Some system functions, like the brand new TRY_CONVERT(), can generate NULL values as well. If the PostalCode cannot be converted into an integer, TRY_CONVERT() returns NULL.

```
SELECT TOP 5    ConvertedZip = TRY_CONVERT(INT, PostalCode),
            AddressLine1,
            City,
            PostalCode
FROM Person.Address  ORDER by newid();
```

ConvertedZip	AddressLine1	City	PostalCode
91945	5979 El Pueblo	Lemon Grove	91945
NULL	7859 Green Valley Road	London	W1V 5RN
3220	6004 Peabody Road	Geelong	3220
NULL	6713 Eaker Way	Burnaby	V3J 6Z3
NULL	5153 Hackamore Lane	Shawnee	V8Z 4N5

The SOUNDEX() Function to Check Sound Alikes

The soundex() function is very interesting for testing different spelling of words such as names.

```
USE AdventureWorks2012;
GO

SELECT DISTINCT LastName
FROM Person.Person
WHERE soundex(LastName)  = soundex('Steel');
GO
```

LastName
Seidel
Sotelo
Stahl
Steel
Steele

```
SELECT DISTINCT LastName
FROM Person.Person
WHERE soundex(LastName) = soundex('Brown');
```

LastName
Bourne
Brian
Brown
Browne
Bruno

```
SELECT DISTINCT FirstName FROM Person.Person
WHERE soundex(FirstName) = soundex('Mary');
```

FirstName
Mari
Maria
María
Mariah
Marie
Mario
Mary
Mary Lou
Mayra

CHAPTER 1: SQL Server Sample & System Databases

Building an FK-PK Diagram in AdventureWorks2012

The **FOREIGN KEY - PRIMARY KEY** diagram of AdventureWorks2012 database with over 70 tables can be built just by adding the tables to the diagram. The FK-PK lines are automatically drawn. An FK-PK line represents a predefined referential constraint.

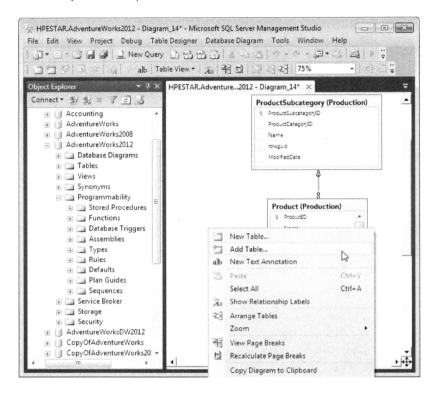

While all tables are important in a database, tables with the most connections play central roles, in a way analogous to the Sun with planets around it.

```
-- PRIMARY KEY tables with the most FOREIGN KEY references
SELECT          schema_name(schema_id)          AS SchemaName,
                o.name                          AS PKTable,
                count(*)                        AS FKCount
FROM sys.sysforeignkeys s    INNER JOIN sys.objects o       ON s.rkeyid = o.object_id
GROUP BY schema_id, o.name    HAVING count(*) >= 5    ORDER BY FKCount DESC;
```

SchemaName	PKTable	FKCount
Production	Product	14
Person	Person	7
HumanResources	Employee	6
Person	BusinessEntity	5
Sales	SalesTerritory	5

CHAPTER 1: SQL Server Sample & System Databases

AdventureWorksDW2012 Data Warehouse Database

AdventureWorksDW series contain second hand data only since they are Data Warehouse databases. All data originates from other sources such as the AdventureWorks OLTP database & Excel worksheets. Tables in the data warehousing database are divided into two groups: dimension tables & fact tables.

Simple data warehouse query.

```
SELECT        D.CalendarYear AS [Year], C.SalesTerritoryCountry AS [Country],
              FORMAT(SUM(S.SalesAmount),'c0','en-US') AS TotalSales
FROM FactInternetSales AS S  INNER JOIN DimDate AS D ON S.OrderDateKey = D.DateKey
        INNER JOIN DimSalesTerritory AS C ON S.SalesTerritoryKey = C.SalesTerritoryKey
GROUP BY D.CalendarYear, C.SalesTerritoryCountry  ORDER BY Year DESC, SUM(S.SalesAmount) DESC;
```

Year	Country	TotalSales
2008	United States	$3,324,031
2008	Australia	$2,563,884
2008	United Kingdom	$1,210,286
2008	Germany	$1,076,891
2008	France	$922,179

CHAPTER 1: SQL Server Sample & System Databases

Diagram of a Star Schema in AdventureWorksDW2012

The high level star schema diagram in AdventureWorksDW2012 Data Warehouse database with FactResellerSales fact table and related dimension tables. The temporal dimension table DimDate plays a central role in Business Intelligence data analytics.

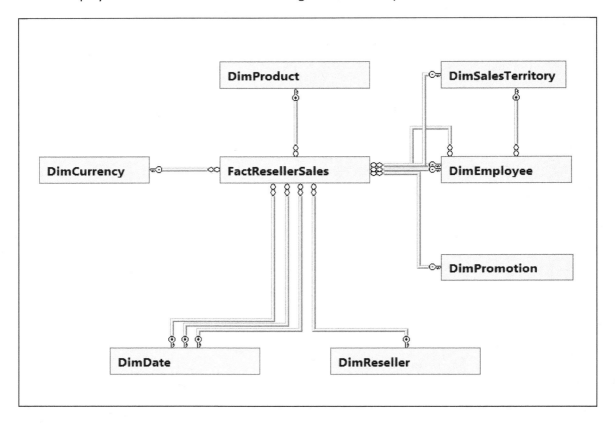

Distribution of **PRIMARY KEY - FOREIGN KEY** relationships can be generated from metadata (system views) for the entire Data Warehouse.

```
SELECT   schema_name(schema_id) AS SchemaName, o.name AS PKTable,  count(*) AS FKCount
FROM sys.sysforeignkeys s   INNER JOIN sys.objects o    ON s.rkeyid = o.object_id
GROUP BY schema_id, o.name  HAVING COUNT(*) > 2 ORDER BY FKCount DESC;
```

SchemaName	PKTable	FKCount
dbo	DimDate	12
dbo	DimCurrency	4
dbo	DimSalesTerritory	4
dbo	DimEmployee	3
dbo	DimProduct	3

AdventureWorks2008 Sample Database

There were substantial changes made from the prior version of the sample database. Among them demonstration use of the **hierarchyid** data type which has been introduced with SS 2008 to support sophisticated tree hierarchy processing. In addition employee, customer and dealer PRIMARY KEYs are pooled together and called BusinessEntityID.

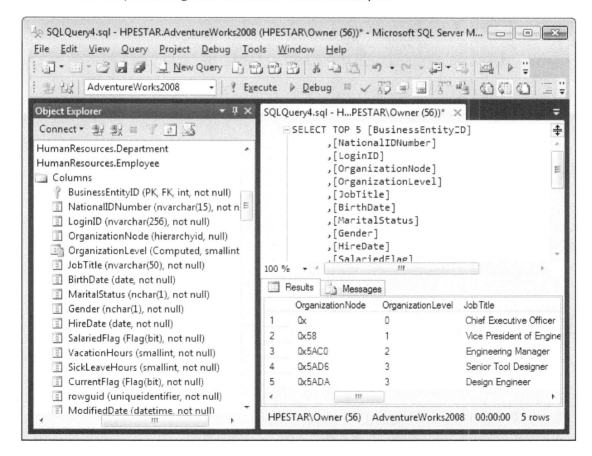

CHAPTER 1: SQL Server Sample & System Databases

AdventureWorks2012 Sample Database

There were no apparent design changes made from the prior version of the sample database. A significant content change: dates were advanced 4 years. An OrderDate (Sales.SalesOrderHeader table) of 2004-02-01 in previous versions is now 2008-02-01.

The OrderDate statistics in the two sample databases.

```
SELECT [Year]          = YEAR(OrderDate),    OrderCount    = COUNT(*)
FROM AdventureWorks2008.Sales.SalesOrderHeader GROUP BY YEAR(OrderDate)
ORDER BY [Year];
```

Year	OrderCount
2001	1379
2002	3692
2003	12443
2004	13951

```
SELECT [Year]          = YEAR(OrderDate),    OrderCount    = COUNT(*)
FROM AdventureWorks2012.Sales.SalesOrderHeader GROUP BY YEAR(OrderDate)
ORDER BY [Year];
```

Year	OrderCount
2005	1379
2006	3692
2007	12443
2008	13951

Starting with SQL Server 2012, numeric figures, among others, can be formatted with the FORMAT function.

```
SELECT  [Year]          = YEAR(OrderDate),
        OrderCount      = FORMAT(COUNT(*), '###,###')
FROM AdventureWorks2012.Sales.SalesOrderHeader
GROUP BY YEAR(OrderDate)  ORDER BY [Year];
```

Year	OrderCount
2005	1,379
2006	3,692
2007	12,443
2008	13,951

Production.Product and Related Tables

The Product table is the "center" of the database. The reason is that AdventureWorks Cycles is a product base company selling through dealers and directly to consumers through the internet. You may wonder why are we pushing **FOREIGN KEY - PRIMARY KEY** relationship so vehemently? Because there is nothing else to a database just **well-designed tables and their connections which are FK-PK constraints**.

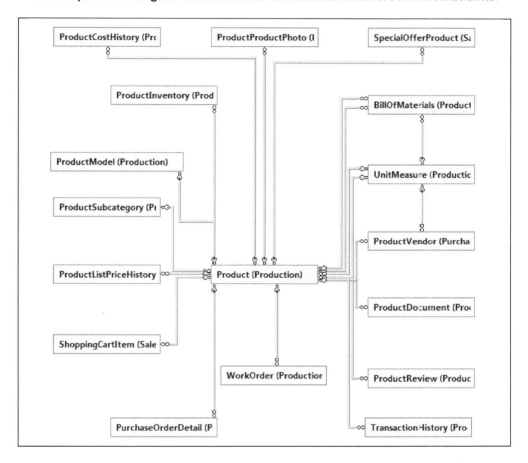

Simple OLTP query.

```
SELECT Color, WOCount=COUNT(*)  FROM Production.WorkOrder W
       INNER JOIN Production.Product P    ON W.ProductID = P.ProductID  WHERE Color != ''
GROUP BY Color ORDER BY WOCount DESC;
```

Color	WOCount
Black	18952
Silver	6620
Yellow	5231
Red	4764
Blue	2319

CHAPTER 1: SQL Server Sample & System Databases

Descriptions of Columns in Production.Product Table

Queries to list the description of table and columns from Extended Property (data dictionary).

```
USE AdventureWorks2012;
SELECT          objname AS TableName, value   AS [Description]
FROM fn_listextendedproperty( NULL, 'schema', 'Production', 'table', 'Product', NULL, NULL);
```

TableName	Description
Product	Products sold or used in the manfacturing of sold products.

```
SELECT          'Production.Product'          AS TableName,              -- String literal
                objname                       AS ColumnName,
                value                         AS [Description]
FROM fn_listextendedproperty( NULL, 'schema', 'Production', 'table',
                              'Product', 'column', default);
```

TableName	ColumnName	Description
Production.Product	ProductID	Primary key for Product records.
Production.Product	Name	Name of the product.
Production.Product	ProductNumber	Unique product identification number.
Production.Product	MakeFlag	0 = Product is purchased, 1 = Product is manufactured in-house.
Production.Product	FinishedGoodsFlag	0 = Product is not a salable item. 1 = Product is salable.
Production.Product	Color	Product color.
Production.Product	SafetyStockLevel	Minimum inventory quantity.
Production.Product	ReorderPoint	Inventory level that triggers a purchase order or work order.
Production.Product	StandardCost	Standard cost of the product.
Production.Product	ListPrice	Selling price.
Production.Product	Size	Product size.
Production.Product	SizeUnitMeasureCode	Unit of measure for Size column.
Production.Product	WeightUnitMeasureCode	Unit of measure for Weight column.
Production.Product	Weight	Product weight.
Production.Product	DaysToManufacture	Number of days required to manufacture the product.
Production.Product	ProductLine	R = Road, M = Mountain, T = Touring, S = Standard
Production.Product	Class	H = High, M = Medium, L = Low
Production.Product	Style	W = Womens, M = Mens, U = Universal
Production.Product	ProductSubcategoryID	Product is a member of this product subcategory. Foreign key to ProductSubCategory.ProductSubCategoryID.
Production.Product	ProductModelID	Product is a member of this product model. Foreign key to ProductModel.ProductModelID.
Production.Product	SellStartDate	Date the product was available for sale.
Production.Product	SellEndDate	Date the product was no longer available for sale.
Production.Product	DiscontinuedDate	Date the product was discontinued.
Production.Product	rowguid	ROWGUIDCOL number uniquely identifying the record. Used to support a merge replication sample.
Production.Product	ModifiedDate	Date and time the record was last updated.

Mountain Bikes in Production.Product Table

Query to list all mountain bikes offered for sale by AdventureWorks Cycles with category, subcategory, list price and standard cost information.

```
USE AdventureWorks2012;
SELECT  UPPER(PC.Name) AS Category, PSC.Name AS Subcategory,
        P.Name AS Product, FORMAT(ListPrice, 'c', 'en-US') AS ListPrice,
        FORMAT(StandardCost, 'c', 'en-US') AS StandardCost
FROM Production.Product AS P
  INNER JOIN Production.ProductSubcategory AS PSC
           ON PSC.ProductSubcategoryID = P.ProductSubcategoryID
  INNER JOIN Production.ProductCategory AS PC
           ON PC.ProductCategoryID = PSC.ProductCategoryID
WHERE PSC.Name = 'Mountain Bikes'
ORDER BY Category, Subcategory, Product;
```

Category	Subcategory	Product	ListPrice	StandardCost
BIKES	Mountain Bikes	Mountain-100 Black, 38	$3,374.99	$1,893.09
BIKES	Mountain Bikes	Mountain-100 Black, 42	$3,374.99	$1,893.09
BIKES	Mountain Bikes	Mountain-100 Black, 44	$3,374.99	$1,893.09
BIKES	Mountain Bikes	Mountain-100 Black, 48	$3,374.99	$1,893.09
BIKES	Mountain Bikes	Mountain-100 Silver, 38	$3,399.99	$1,912.15
BIKES	Mountain Bikes	Mountain-100 Silver, 42	$3,399.99	$1,912.15
BIKES	Mountain Bikes	Mountain-100 Silver, 44	$3,399.99	$1,912.15
BIKES	Mountain Bikes	Mountain-100 Silver, 48	$3,399.99	$1,912.15
BIKES	Mountain Bikes	Mountain-200 Black, 38	$2,294.99	$1,251.98
BIKES	Mountain Bikes	Mountain-200 Black, 42	$2,294.99	$1,251.98
BIKES	Mountain Bikes	Mountain-200 Black, 46	$2,294.99	$1,251.98
BIKES	Mountain Bikes	Mountain-200 Silver, 38	$2,319.99	$1,265.62
BIKES	Mountain Bikes	Mountain-200 Silver, 42	$2,319.99	$1,265.62
BIKES	Mountain Bikes	Mountain-200 Silver, 46	$2,319.99	$1,265.62
BIKES	Mountain Bikes	Mountain-300 Black, 38	$1,079.99	$598.44
BIKES	Mountain Bikes	Mountain-300 Black, 40	$1,079.99	$598.44
BIKES	Mountain Bikes	Mountain-300 Black, 44	$1,079.99	$598.44
BIKES	Mountain Bikes	Mountain-300 Black, 48	$1,079.99	$598.44
BIKES	Mountain Bikes	Mountain-400-W Silver, 38	$769.49	$419.78
BIKES	Mountain Bikes	Mountain-400-W Silver, 40	$769.49	$419.78
BIKES	Mountain Bikes	Mountain-400-W Silver, 42	$769.49	$419.78
BIKES	Mountain Bikes	Mountain-400-W Silver, 46	$769.49	$419.78
BIKES	Mountain Bikes	Mountain-500 Black, 40	$539.99	$294.58
BIKES	Mountain Bikes	Mountain-500 Black, 42	$539.99	$294.58
BIKES	Mountain Bikes	Mountain-500 Black, 44	$539.99	$294.58
BIKES	Mountain Bikes	Mountain-500 Black, 48	$539.99	$294.58
BIKES	Mountain Bikes	Mountain-500 Black, 52	$539.99	$294.58
BIKES	Mountain Bikes	Mountain-500 Silver, 40	$564.99	$308.22
BIKES	Mountain Bikes	Mountain-500 Silver, 42	$564.99	$308.22
BIKES	Mountain Bikes	Mountain-500 Silver, 44	$564.99	$308.22
BIKES	Mountain Bikes	Mountain-500 Silver, 48	$564.99	$308.22
BIKES	Mountain Bikes	Mountain-500 Silver, 52	$564.99	$308.22

Prior SQL Server Sample Databases

There are two other sample databases used in the releases of SQL Server: **Northwind** and **pubs**. Northwind has been introduced with SQL Server 7.0 in 1998. That SQL Server version had very short lifetime, replaced with SQL Server 2000 in year 2000. The pubs sample database originates from the time Microsoft & Sybase worked jointly on the database server project around 1990. Despite the relative simplicity of pre-2005 sample databases, they were good enough to demonstrate basic RDBMS SQL queries.

Book sales summary GROUP BY aggregation query.

```
USE pubs;
SELECT pub_name          AS Publisher,
    au_lname             AS Author,
    title                AS Title,
    SUM(qty)             AS SoldQty
FROM   authors
    INNER JOIN titleauthor
        ON authors.au_id = titleauthor.au_id
    INNER JOIN titles
        ON titles.title_id = titleauthor.title_id
    INNER JOIN publishers
        ON publishers.pub_id = titles.pub_id
    INNER JOIN sales
        ON sales.title_id = titles.title_id
GROUP  BY      pub_name,
               au_lname,
               title
ORDER BY Publisher, Author, Title;
-- (23 row(s) affected) - Partial results.
```

Publisher	Author	Title
Algodata Infosystems	Bennet	The Busy Executive's Database Guide
Algodata Infosystems	Carson	But Is It User Friendly?
Algodata Infosystems	Dull	Secrets of Silicon Valley
Algodata Infosystems	Green	The Busy Executive's Database Guide
Algodata Infosystems	Hunter	Secrets of Silicon Valley
Algodata Infosystems	MacFeather	Cooking with Computers: Surreptitious Balance Sheets
Algodata Infosystems	O'Leary	Cooking with Computers: Surreptitious Balance Sheets
Algodata Infosystems	Straight	Straight Talk About Computers
Binnet & Hardley	Blotchet-Halls	Fifty Years in Buckingham Palace Kitchens
Binnet & Hardley	DeFrance	The Gourmet Microwave

Northwind Sample Database

The Northwind database contains well-prepared sales data for a fictitious company called Northwind Traders, which imports & exports specialty gourmet foods & drinks from wholesale suppliers around the world. The company's sales offices are located in Seattle & London. Among gourmet food item products: Carnarvon Tigers, Teatime Chocolate Biscuits, Sir Rodney's Marmalade, Sir Rodney's Scones, Gustaf's Knäckebröd, Tunnbröd & Guaraná Fantástica.

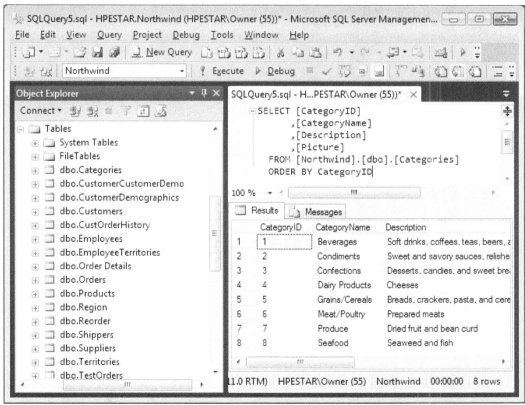

CHAPTER 1: SQL Server Sample & System Databases

Diagram of Northwind Database

The basic diagram of Northwind database excluding a few ancillary tables. The Orders table is central since the business is wholesale distribution (reselling) of high-end food products.

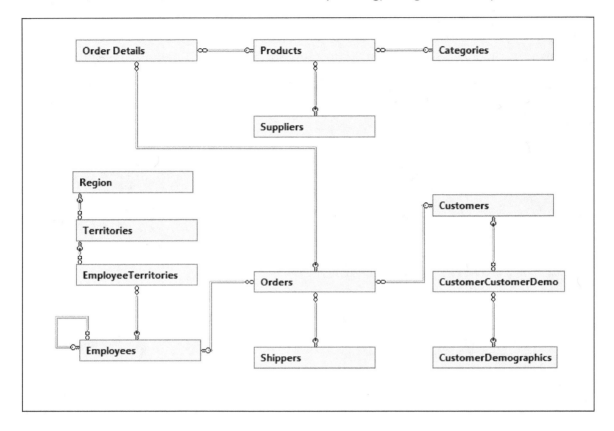

CHAPTER 1: SQL Server Sample & System Databases

pubs Sample Database

The pubs database is a very small and simple publishing database, yet it demonstrates the main features of database design such as PRIMARY KEYs, FOREIGN KEYs, and junction table reflecting many-to-many relationship. The main entities (tables) are: (book) titles, authors, titleauthor (junction table), publishers, sales & royalties.

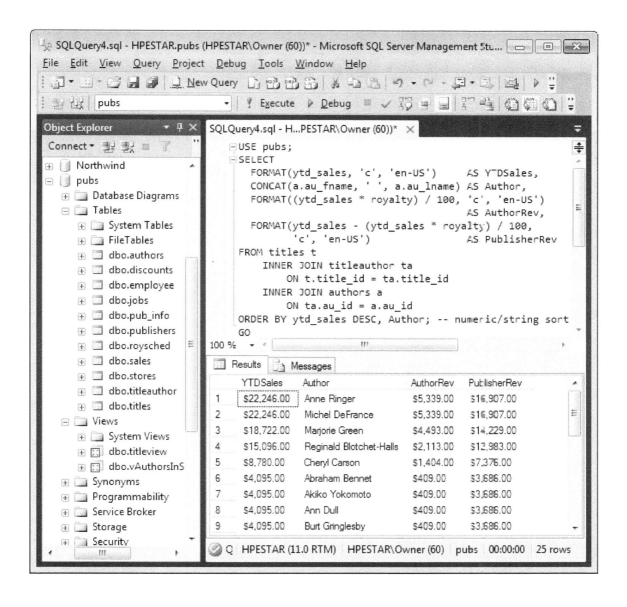

Book Titles in pubs Database

The titles table has the most interesting content in the pubs database as demonstrated by the following T-SQL query.

```
SELECT  TOP 4 title_id AS TitleID, title AS Title, type          AS Type,
        pub_id AS PubID, FORMAT(price, 'c','en-US')               AS Price,
        FORMAT(advance, 'c','en-US')                              AS  Advance,
        FORMAT(royalty/100.0, 'p') AS Royalty, FORMAT(ytd_sales, 'c', 'en-US')  AS YTDSales,
        Notes
FROM pubs.dbo.titles
ORDER BY title;
```

TitleID	Title	Type	PubID	Price	Advance	Royalty	YTDSales	Notes
PC1035	But Is It User Friendly?	popular_comp	1389	$22.95	$7,000.00	16.00 %	$8,780.00	A survey of software for the naive user, focusing on the 'friendliness' of each.
PS1372	Computer Phobic AND Non-Phobic Individuals: Behavior Variations	psychology	0877	$21.59	$7,000.00	10.00 %	$375.00	A must for the specialist, this book examines the difference between those who hate and fear computers and those who don't.
BU1111	Cooking with Computers: Surreptitious Balance Sheets	business	1389	$11.95	$5,000.00	10.00 %	$3,876.00	Helpful hints on how to use your electronic resources to the best advantage.
PS7777	Emotional Security: A New Algorithm	psychology	0736	$7.99	$4,000.00	10.00 %	$3,336.00	Protecting yourself and your loved ones from undue emotional stress in the modern world. Use of computer and nutritional aids emphasized.

Diagram of pubs Database

Since pubs is a small database, the diagram conveniently fits on a page.

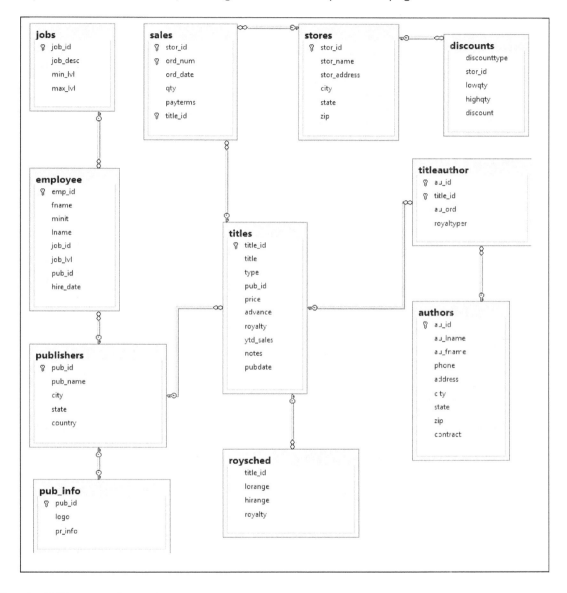

Simple JOIN on non-key columns.

```
USE pubs; SELECT p.*, a.* FROM authors AS a
INNER JOIN publishers AS p ON a.city = p.city ORDER BY p.city, a.au_lname;
```

pub_id	pub_name	city	state	country	au_id	au_lname	au_fname	phone	address	city	state	zip	contract
1389	Algodata Infosystems	Berkeley	CA	USA	409-56-7008	Bennet	Abraham	415 658-9932	6223 Bateman St.	Berkeley	CA	94705	1
1389	Algodata Infosystems	Berkeley	CA	USA	238-95-7766	Carson	Cheryl	415 548-7723	589 Darwin Ln.	Berkeley	CA	94705	1

CHAPTER I: SQL Server Sample & System Databases

SQL Server System Databases

The master, model, tempdb and msdb are system databases for special database server operations purposes. SSMS Object Explorer drill-down listing of system databases.

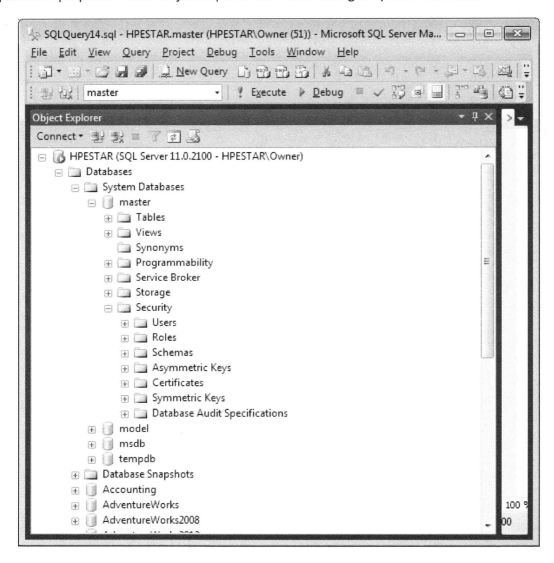

Query to create a new table in tempdb for development purposes.

```
SELECT * INTO tempdb.dbo.Product
FROM AdventureWorks2012.Production.Product
WHERE ListPrice > 0.0;
-- (304 row(s) affected)
```

CHAPTER 1: SQL Server Sample & System Databases

The master Database

The master system database is the nerve center of SQL Server. It contains tables and db objects essential for server operations. System tables are accessible only through read-only views. System tables cannot be changed by users. A subset of the system views are called Dynamic Management Views (DMV) which return server state information for monitoring the operational aspects of a SQL Server instance, diagnosing problems, and performance tuning. Dynamic Management Functions (DMF) are applied in conjunction with DMVs.

```
SELECT TOP 5     ST.text,
                 EQS.*
FROM master.sys.dm_exec_query_stats AS EQS                    -- DMV
CROSS APPLY master.sys.dm_exec_sql_text(EQS.sql_handle) as ST  -- DMF
ORDER BY last_worker_time DESC;
```

SQL Server Management Studio Object Explorer display of some objects in the master database and a query listing all databases.

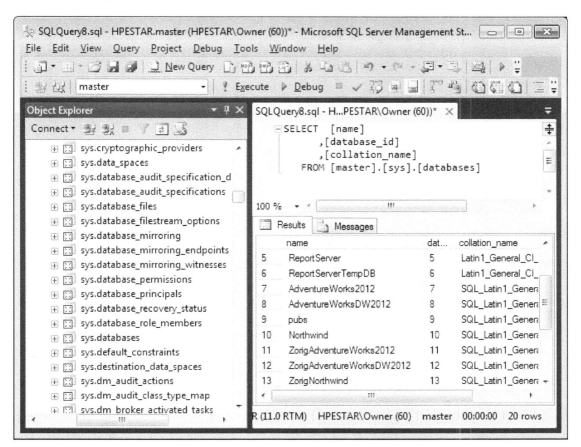

CHAPTER 1: SQL Server Sample & System Databases

An Important System View In master Database: sys.databases

```
SELECT TOP (10) name, database_id
FROM master.sys.databases
ORDER BY database_id;
```

name	database_id
master	1
tempdb	2
model	3
msdb	4
ReportServer	5
ReportServerTempDB	6
AdventureWorks2012	7
AdventureWorksDW2012	8
pubs	9
Northwind	10

spt_values table in master database can be used for integer sequence with a range of 0 - 2047.

```
-- End of the range - BOTTOM
SELECT TOP 5 number FROM master.dbo.spt_values WHERE TYPE='P'
ORDER BY number DESC;
```

number
2047
2046
2045
2044
2043

Example for using the sequence in spt_values to generate DATE and MONTH sequences.

```
SELECT TOP 5 number,   dateadd(day, number, '20000101')     AS "Date",
                       dateadd(mm, number, '20000101')      AS "Month"
FROM master.dbo.spt_values  WHERE type = 'P'  ORDER BY number;
```

number	Date	Month
0	2000-01-01 00:00:00.000	2000-01-01 00:00:00.000
1	2000-01-02 00:00:00.000	2000-02-01 00:00:00.000
2	2000-01-03 00:00:00.000	2000-03-01 00:00:00.000
3	2000-01-04 00:00:00.000	2000-04-01 00:00:00.000
4	2000-01-05 00:00:00.000	2000-05-01 00:00:00.000

The model Database

The model database serves as prototype for a new database. The model database is also the prototype for tempdb when the SQL Server instance started. Upon server shutdown or restart everything is wiped out of tempdb, it starts with a clean slate as a copy of the model database. Therefore we should only place objects into the tempdb can be purged any time.

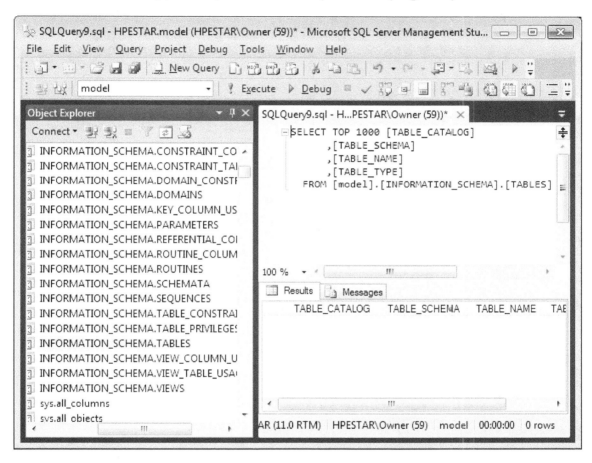

CHAPTER 1: SQL Server Sample & System Databases

The msdb Database

The msdb database is used for server internal operations such as support for SQL Server Agent job scheduling facility or keeping track of database the all important backups and restores.

Database backup history query using table in msdb database.

```
SELECT  s.name AS Name, CONVERT(DATE,MAX(b.backup_finish_date)) AS LastGoodBackup,
     b.type AS Type
FROM master.dbo.sysdatabases AS s
LEFT OUTER JOIN msdb.dbo.backupset AS b ON s.name = b.database_name
GROUP BY s.name, b.type ORDER BY Name, Type;
```

Name	LastGoodBackup	Type
Accounting	2016-11-29	D
AdventureWorks	2016-11-29	D
AdventureWorks2008	2016-11-29	D
AdventureWorks2012	2016-11-29	D

The tempdb Database

The tempdb serves as temporary database for system operations such as sorting. Temporary tables (#temp1) and global temporary tables (##globaltemp1) are stored in the tempdb as well. "Permanent" tables can be created in tempdb with a short lifetime which lasts till shutdown or restart.

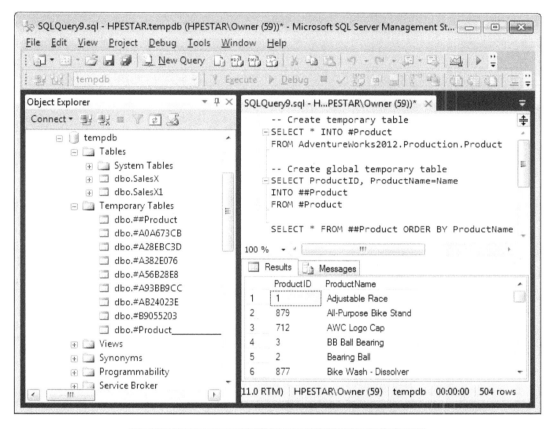

CHAPTER 1: SQL Server Sample & System Databases

Sudden Death in tempdb When Server Restarts

Even though a temporary table and a global temporary table are created and queried in the context setting for AdventureWorks2012 database, they are placed into tempdb automatically. Same consideration when a temporary table is created from a stored procedure which is compiled in an application database. Upon server restart everything is wiped out of tempdb, rebirth follows as a copy of model db. We should not place anything into tempdb we cannot afford to lose. tempdb is also used by SQL Server engine for operations such as version control, sorting and more.

> Instead of GUI & mouse use T-SQL scripts which can be saved as .sql disk files.

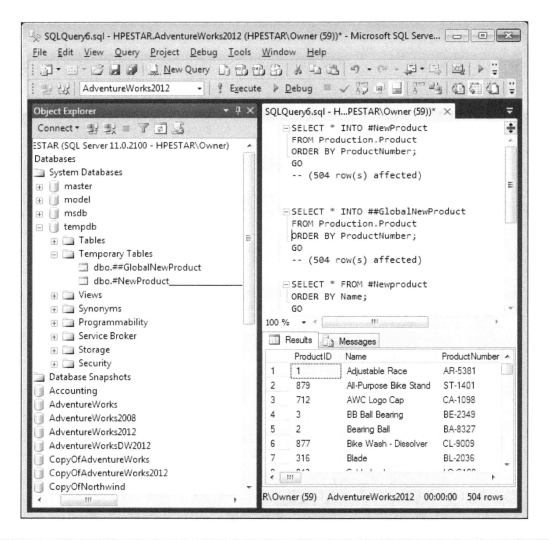

CHAPTER 2: Structure of the SELECT Statement

The SELECT Clause

The SELECT clause is the only required clause in a SELECT statement, all the other clauses are optional. The SELECT columns can be literals (constants), expressions, table columns and even subqueries. Lines can be commented with "--".

```
SELECT 15 * 15;                                           -- 225

SELECT Today = convert(DATE, getdate());                  -- 2016-07-27    -- getdate() T-
SQL only
SELECT Today = convert(DATE, CURRENT_TIMESTAMP);          -- 2016-07-27    -- ANSI SQL


SELECT          Color,
                ProdCnt             = COUNT(*),
                AvgPrice            = FORMAT(AVG(ListPrice),'c','en-US')
FROM AdventureWorks2012.Production.Product p
WHERE Color is not null
GROUP BY Color
        HAVING count(*) > 10
ORDER BY AvgPrice DESC;
```

Color	ProdCnt	AvgPrice
Yellow	36	$959.09
Blue	26	$923.68
Silver	43	$850.31
Black	93	$725.12
Red	38	$1,401.95

```
-- Equivalent with column aliases on the right
SELECT          Color,
                COUNT(*)                            AS ProdCnt,
                FORMAT(AVG(ListPrice),'c','en-US')  AS AvgPrice
FROM AdventureWorks2012.Production.Product p  WHERE Color is not null
GROUP BY Color HAVING count(*) > 10  ORDER BY AvgPrice DESC;
GO
```

CHAPTER 2: Structure of the SELECT Statement

SELECT with Search Expression

SELECT statement can have complex expressions for text or numbers as demonstrated in the next T-SQL query for finding the street name in AddressLine1 column.

```
SELECT AddressID,
       SUBSTRING(AddressLine1, CHARINDEX(' ', AddressLine1+' ', 1) +1,
       CHARINDEX(' ', AddressLine1+' ', CHARINDEX(' ', AddressLine1+' ', 1) +1) -
       CHARINDEX(' ', AddressLine1+' ', 1) -1)                                    AS StreetName,
       AddressLine1,
       City
FROM AdventureWorks2012.Person.Address
WHERE ISNUMERIC (LEFT(AddressLine1,1))=1
  AND City = 'Seattle'
ORDER BY AddressLine1;
-- -- (141 row(s) affected)- Partial results.
```

AddressID	StreetName	AddressLine1	City
13079	boulevard	081, boulevard du Montparnasse	Seattle
859	Oak	1050 Oak Street	Seattle
110	Slow	1064 Slow Creek Road	Seattle
113	Ravenwood	1102 Ravenwood	Seattle
95	Bradford	1220 Bradford Way	Seattle
32510	Steven	1349 Steven Way	Seattle
118	Balboa	136 Balboa Court	Seattle
32519	Mazatlan	137 Mazatlan	Seattle
25869	Calle	1386 Calle Verde	Seattle
114	Yorba	1398 Yorba Linda	Seattle
15657	Book	151 Book Ct	Seattle
105	Stillman	1619 Stillman Court	Seattle
18002	Carmel	1635 Carmel Dr	Seattle
19813	Acardia	1787 Acardia Pl.	Seattle
16392	Orchid	1874 Orchid Ct	Seattle
18053	Green	1883 Green View Court	Seattle
13035	Mt.	1887 Mt. Diablo St	Seattle
29864	Valley	1946 Valley Crest Drive	Seattle
13580	Hill	2030 Hill Drive	Seattle
106	San	2144 San Rafael	Seattle

```
-- Search for Crest in the middle of AddessLine1
SELECT * FROM AdventureWorks2012.Person.Address
WHERE AddressLine1 LIKE '% Crest %';
-- (21 row(s) affected)
```

CHAPTER 2: Structure of the SELECT Statement

SELECT Statement with Subquery

Two Northwind category images, Beverages & Dairy Products, from the dbo.Categories table.

The following SELECT statement involves a subquery which is called a derived table. It also demonstrates that INNER JOIN can be performed with a GROUP BY subquery as well not only with another table or view.

```
USE Northwind;
SELECT        c.CategoryName                      AS Category,
              cnum.NoOfProducts                    AS CatProdCnt,
              p.ProductName                        AS Product,
              FORMAT(p.UnitPrice,'c', 'en-US')     AS UnitPrice
FROM    Categories c
              INNER JOIN Products p      ON c.CategoryID = p.CategoryID
              INNER JOIN (    SELECT         c.CategoryID,
                                             NoOfProducts = count(* )
                       FROM    Categories c
                              INNER JOIN Products p
                              ON c.CategoryID = p.CategoryID
                              GROUP BY c.CategoryID
                     ) cnum                                 -- derived table
              ON c.CategoryID = cnum.CategoryID
ORDER BY Category, Product;       -- (77 row(s) affected) - Partial results.
```

Category	CatProdCnt	Product	UnitPrice
Dairy Products	10	Mozzarella di Giovanni	$34.80
Dairy Products	10	Queso Cabrales	$21.00
Dairy Products	10	Queso Manchego La Pastora	$38.00
Dairy Products	10	Raclette Courdavault	$55.00
Grains/Cereals	7	Filo Mix	$7.00
Grains/Cereals	7	Gnocchi di nonna Alice	$38.00
Grains/Cereals	7	Gustaf's Knäckebröd	$21.00
Grains/Cereals	7	Ravioli Angelo	$19.50
Grains/Cereals	7	Singaporean Hokkien Fried Mee	$14.00
Grains/Cereals	7	Tunnbröd	$9.00

CHAPTER 2: Structure of the SELECT Statement

Creating Delimited String List (CSV) with XML PATH

The XML PATH clause , the text() function and correlated subquery is used to create a comma delimited string within the SELECT columns. Note: it cannot be done using traditional (without XML) SQL single statement, it can be done with multiple SQL statements only. STUFF() string function is applied to replace the leading comma with an empty string.

```
USE AdventureWorks;

SELECT  Territory        = st.[Name],
        SalesYTD =  FORMAT(floor(SalesYTD), 'c', 'en-US'), -- currency format
        SalesStaffAssignmentHistory =

            STUFF((SELECT CONCAT(', ', c.FirstName, SPACE(1), c.LastName)        AS [text()]
                FROM   Person.Contact c
                INNER JOIN Sales.SalesTerritoryHistory sth
                ON c.ContactID = sth.SalesPersonID
                WHERE  sth.TerritoryID =   st.TerritoryID
                ORDER  BY StartDate
                FOR XML Path ('')), 1, 1, SPACE(0))

FROM   Sales.SalesTerritory st
ORDER  BY SalesYTD DESC;
GO
```

Territory	SalesYTD	SalesStaffAssignmentHistory
Southwest	$8,351,296.00	Shelley Dyck, Jauna Elson
Canada	$6,917,270.00	Carla Eldridge, Michael Emanuel, Gail Erickson
Northwest	$5,767,341.00	Shannon Elliott, Terry Eminhizer, Martha Espinoza
Central	$4,677,108.00	Linda Ecoffey, Maciej Dusza
France	$3,899,045.00	Mark Erickson
Northeast	$3,857,163.00	Maciej Dusza, Linda Ecoffey
United Kingdom	$3,514,865.00	Michael Emanuel
Southeast	$2,851,419.00	Carol Elliott
Germany	$2,481,039.00	Janeth Esteves
Australia	$1,977,474.00	Twanna Evans

```
-- Comma delimited list of column names
SELECT CONCAT(',', c.name)  AS [text()]
FROM  sys.columns c   WHERE c.[object_id] = OBJECT_ID('Purchasing.PurchaseOrderDetail')
ORDER BY column_id FOR XML PATH('');
```

CHAPTER 2: Structure of the SELECT Statement

Logical Processing Order of the SELECT Statement

The results from the previous step will be available to the next step. The logical processing order for a SELECT statement is the following. Actual processing by the database engine may be different due to performance and other considerations.

1.	FROM
2.	ON
3.	JOIN
4.	WHERE
5.	GROUP BY
6.	WITH CUBE or WITH ROLLUP
7.	HAVING
8.	SELECT
9.	DISTINCT
10.	ORDER BY
11.	TOP

As an example, it is logical to filter with the WHERE clause prior to applying GROUP BY. It is also logical to sort when the final result set is available.

SELECT Color, COUNT(*) AS ColorCount FROM AdventureWorks2012.Production.Product
WHERE Color is not NULL GROUP BY Color ORDER BY ColorCount DESC;

Color	ColorCount
Black	93
Silver	43
Red	38
Yellow	36
Blue	26
Multi	8
Silver/Black	7
White	4
Grey	1

CHAPTER 2: Structure of the SELECT Statement

The TOP Clause

The TOP clause filters results according the sorting specified in an ORDER BY clause, otherwise random filtering takes place.

Simple TOP usage to return 10 rows only.

SELECT TOP 10 SalesOrderID, OrderDate, TotalDue
FROM AdventureWorks2012.Sales.SalesOrderHeader ORDER BY TotalDue DESC;

SalesOrderID	OrderDate	TotalDue
51131	2007-07-01 00:00:00.000	187487.825
55282	2007-10-01 00:00:00.000	182018.6272
46616	2006-07-01 00:00:00.000	170512.6689
46981	2006-08-01 00:00:00.000	166537.0808
47395	2006-09-01 00:00:00.000	165028.7482
47369	2006-09-01 00:00:00.000	158056.5449
47355	2006-09-01 00:00:00.000	145741.8553
51822	2007-08-01 00:00:00.000	145454.366
44518	2005-11-01 00:00:00.000	142312.2199
51858	2007-08-01 00:00:00.000	140042.1209

TOP function usage: not known in advance how many rows will be returned due to "TIES".

```
SELECT   TOP 1 WITH TIES  coalesce(Color, 'N/A')          AS Color,
            FORMAT(ListPrice, 'c', 'en-US')               AS ListPrice,
            Name                                          AS ProductName,
            ProductID
FROM    AdventureWorks2012.Production.Product
ORDER BY ROW_NUMBER() OVER(PARTITION BY Color ORDER BY ListPrice DESC);
```

Color	ListPrice	ProductName	ProductID
N/A	$229.49	HL Fork	804
Black	$3,374.99	Mountain-100 Black, 38	775
Red	$3,578.27	Road-150 Red, 62	749
Silver	$3,399.99	Mountain-100 Silver, 38	771
Blue	$2,384.07	Touring-1000 Blue, 46	966
Grey	$125.00	Touring-Panniers, Large	842
Multi	$89.99	Men's Bib-Shorts, S	855
Silver/Black	$80.99	HL Mountain Pedal	937
White	$9.50	Mountain Bike Socks, M	709
Yellow	$2,384.07	Touring-1000 Yellow, 46	954

The DISTINCT Clause to Omit Duplicates

The DISTINCT clause returns only unique results, omitting duplicates in the result set.

```
USE AdventureWorks2012;
SELECT DISTINCT Color FROM Production.Product
WHERE Color is not NULL
ORDER BY Color;
GO
```

Color
Black
Blue
Grey
Multi
Red
Silver
Silver/Black
White
Yellow

```
SELECT DISTINCT ListPrice
FROM Production.Product
 WHERE ListPrice > 0.0
ORDER BY ListPrice DESC;
GO
-- (102 row(s) affected) - Partial results.
```

ListPrice
3578.27
3399.99
3374.99
2443.35

```
-- Using DISTINCT in COUNT - NULL is counted
SELECT          COUNT(*)                  AS TotalRows,
                COUNT(DISTINCT Color)     AS ProductColors,
                COUNT(DISTINCT Size)      AS ProductSizes
FROM AdventureWorks2012.Production.Product;
```

TotalRows	ProductColors	ProductSizes
504	9	18

CHAPTER 2: Structure of the SELECT Statement

The CASE Conditional Expression

The CASE conditional expression evaluates to a **single value of the same data type**, therefore **it can be used anywhere in a query where a single value is required.**

```
SELECT          CASE ProductLine
                        WHEN 'R' THEN 'Road'
                        WHEN 'M' THEN 'Mountain'
                        WHEN 'T' THEN 'Touring'
                        WHEN 'S' THEN 'Other'
                        ELSE 'Parts'
                END                             AS Category,
                Name                            AS ProductName,
                ProductNumber
FROM AdventureWorks2012.Production.Product
ORDER BY ProductName;
GO
-- (504 row(s) affected) - Partial results.
```

Category	ProductName	ProductNumber
Touring	Touring-3000 Blue, 62	BK-T18U-62
Touring	Touring-3000 Yellow, 44	BK-T18Y-44
Touring	Touring-3000 Yellow, 50	BK-T18Y-50
Touring	Touring-3000 Yellow, 54	BK-T18Y-54
Touring	Touring-3000 Yellow, 58	BK-T18Y-58
Touring	Touring-3000 Yellow, 62	BK-T18Y-62
Touring	Touring-Panniers, Large	PA-T100
Other	Water Bottle - 30 oz.	WB-H098
Mountain	Women's Mountain Shorts, L	SH-W890-L

Query to return different result sets for repeated execution due to newid().

```
SELECT   TOP 3 CompanyName,   City=CONCAT(City, ', ', Country),          PostalCode,
         [IsNumeric] =   CASE    WHEN PostalCode like '[0-9][0-9][0-9][0-9][0-9]'
                                 THEN '5-Digit Numeric'    ELSE 'Other'  END
FROM     Northwind.dbo.Suppliers
ORDER BY NEWID();                        -- random sort
GO
```

CompanyName	City	PostalCode	IsNumeric
PB Knäckebröd AB	Göteborg, Sweden	S-345 67	Other
Gai pâturage	Annecy, France	74000	5-Digit Numeric
Heli Süßwaren GmbH & Co. KG	Berlin, Germany	10785	5-Digit Numeric

Same query as above expanded with ROW_NUMBER() and another CASE expression column.

```
SELECT          ROW_NUMBER() OVER (ORDER BY Name)                AS RowNo,
                CASE ProductLine
                  WHEN 'R' THEN 'Road'
                  WHEN 'M' THEN 'Mountain'
                  WHEN 'T' THEN 'Touring'
                  WHEN 'S' THEN 'Other'
                  ELSE 'Parts'
                END                              AS Category,
                Name                             AS ProductName,
                CASE WHEN Color is null THEN 'N/A'
                       ELSE Color END            AS Color,
                ProductNumber
FROM Production.Product    ORDER BY ProductName;
-- (504 row(s) affected) - Partial results.
```

RowNo	Category	ProductName	Color	ProductNumber
1	Parts	Adjustable Race	N/A	AR-5381
2	Mountain	All-Purpose Bike Stand	N/A	ST-1401
3	Other	AWC Logo Cap	Multi	CA-1098
4	Parts	BB Ball Bearing	N/A	BE-2349
5	Parts	Bearing Ball	N/A	BA-8327
6	Other	Bike Wash - Dissolver	N/A	CL-9009
7	Parts	Blade	N/A	BL-2036
8	Other	Cable Lock	N/A	LO-C100
9	Parts	Chain	Silver	CH-0234
10	Parts	Chain Stays	N/A	CS-2812

Testing PostalCode with ISNUMERIC and generating a flag with CASE expression.

```
SELECT  TOP (4) AddressID,   City,    PostalCode                      AS Zip,
        CASE WHEN ISNUMERIC(PostalCode) = 1 THEN 'Y'  ELSE 'N'  END    AS IsZipNumeric
FROM    AdventureWorks2008.Person.Address  ORDER BY NEWID();
```

AddressID	City	Zip	IsZipNumeric
16704	Paris	75008	Y
26320	Grossmont	91941	Y
27705	Matraville	2036	Y
18901	Kirkby	KB9	N

CHAPTER 2: Structure of the SELECT Statement

The OVER Clause

The OVER clause defines the partitioning and sorting of a rowset (intermediate result set) preceding the application of an associated window function, such as ranking. Window functions are also dubbed as ranking functions.

```
USE AdventureWorks2012;
-- Query with three different OVER clauses
SELECT  ROW_NUMBER() OVER ( ORDER BY SalesOrderID, ProductID)            AS RowNum
        ,SalesOrderID, ProductID, OrderQty
        ,RANK() OVER(PARTITION BY SalesOrderID ORDER BY OrderQty DESC)    AS Ranking
        ,SUM(OrderQty) OVER(PARTITION BY SalesOrderID)                    AS TotalQty
        ,AVG(OrderQty) OVER(PARTITION BY SalesOrderID)                    AS AvgQty
        ,COUNT(OrderQty) OVER(PARTITION BY SalesOrderID)  AS "Count"  -- T-SQL keyword, use "" or []
        ,MIN(OrderQty) OVER(PARTITION BY SalesOrderID)                    AS "Min"
        ,MAX(OrderQty) OVER(PARTITION BY SalesOrderID)                    AS "Max"
FROM Sales.SalesOrderDetail
WHERE SalesOrderID BETWEEN 61190 AND 61199
ORDER BY RowNum;
-- (143 row(s) affected) - Partial results.
```

RowNum	SalesOrderID	ProductID	OrderQty	Ranking	TotalQty	AvgQty	Count	Min	Max
1	61190	707	4	13	159	3	40	1	17
2	61190	708	3	18	159	3	40	1	17
3	61190	711	5	8	159	3	40	1	17
4	61190	712	12	2	159	3	40	1	17
5	61190	714	3	18	159	3	40	1	17
6	61190	715	5	8	159	3	40	1	17
7	61190	716	5	8	159	3	40	1	17
8	61190	858	4	13	159	3	40	1	17
9	61190	859	7	6	159	3	40	1	17
10	61190	864	8	4	159	3	40	1	17
11	61190	865	3	18	159	3	40	1	17
12	61190	870	9	3	159	3	40	1	17
13	61190	876	4	13	159	3	40	1	17
14	61190	877	5	8	159	3	40	1	17
15	61190	880	1	34	159	3	40	1	17
16	61190	881	5	8	159	3	40	1	17
17	61190	883	2	26	159	3	40	1	17
18	61190	884	17	1	159	3	40	1	17
19	61190	885	3	18	159	3	40	1	17
20	61190	886	1	34	159	3	40	1	17
21	61190	889	2	26	159	3	40	1	17
22	61190	892	4	13	159	3	40	1	17
23	61190	893	3	18	159	3	40	1	17
24	61190	895	1	34	159	3	40	1	17

FROM Clause: Specifies the Data Source

The FROM clause specifies the source data sets for the query such as tables, views, derived tables and table-valued functions. Typically the tables are JOINed together. The most common JOIN is INNER JOIN which is based on equality between FOREIGN KEY and PRIMARY KEY values in the two tables.

```
PERFORMANCE NOTE
All FOREIGN KEYs should be indexed. PRIMARY KEYs are indexed automatically with unique index.
```

```
USE AdventureWorks2012;
GO
SELECT
  ROW_NUMBER() OVER(ORDER BY SalesYTD DESC)                          AS RowNo,
  ROW_NUMBER() OVER(PARTITION BY PostalCode ORDER BY SalesYTD DESC)  AS SeqNo,
          CONCAT(p.FirstName, SPACE(1), p.LastName)         AS SalesStaff,
          FORMAT(s.SalesYTD,'c','en-US')                    AS YTDSales,
          City,
          a.PostalCode                                      AS ZipCode
FROM Sales.SalesPerson AS s
  INNER JOIN Person.Person AS p
    ON s.BusinessEntityID = p.BusinessEntityID
  INNER JOIN Person.Address AS a
    ON a.AddressID = p.BusinessEntityID
WHERE TerritoryID IS NOT NULL   AND SalesYTD <> 0 ORDER BY ZipCode, SeqNo;
```

RowNo	SeqNo	SalesStaff	YTDSales	City	ZipCode
1	1	Linda Mitchell	$4,251,368.55	Issaquah	98027
3	2	Michael Blythe	$3,763,178.18	Issaquah	98027
4	3	Jillian Carson	$3,189,418.37	Issaquah	98027
8	4	Tsvi Reiter	$2,315,185.61	Issaquah	98027
12	5	Garrett Vargas	$1,453,719.47	Issaquah	98027
14	6	Pamela Ansman-Wolfe	$1,352,577.13	Issaquah	98027
2	1	Jae Pak	$4,116,871.23	Renton	98055
5	2	Ranjit Varkey Chudukatil	$3,121,616.32	Renton	98055
6	3	José Saraiva	$2,604,540.72	Renton	98055
7	4	Shu Ito	$2,458,535.62	Renton	98055
9	5	Rachel Valdez	$1,827,066.71	Renton	98055
10	6	Tete Mensa-Annan	$1,576,562.20	Renton	98055
11	7	David Campbell	$1,573,012.94	Renton	98055
13	8	Lynn Tsoflias	$1,421,810.92	Renton	98055

CHAPTER 2: Structure of the SELECT Statement

The WHERE Clause to Filter Records (Rows)

The WHERE clause filters the rows generated by the query. Only rows satisfying (TRUE) the WHERE clause predicates are returned.

PERFORMANCE NOTE
All columns in WHERE clause should be indexed.

USE AdventureWorks2012;

String equal match predicate - equal is TRUE, not equal is FALSE.

```
SELECT ProductID, Name, ListPrice, Color
FROM Production.Product  WHERE Name = 'Mountain-100 Silver, 38' ;
```

ProductID	Name	ListPrice	Color
771	Mountain-100 Silver, 38	3399.99	Silver

```
-- Function equality predicate
SELECT * FROM Sales.SalesOrderHeader WHERE YEAR(OrderDate) = 2008;
-- (13951 row(s) affected)
```

PERFORMANCE NOTE
When a column is used as a parameter in a function (e.g. YEAR(OrderDate)), index (if any) usage is voided.
Instead of random SEEK, all rows are SCANned in the table. The predicate is not SARGable.

```
-- String wildcard match predicate
SELECT ProductID, Name, ListPrice, Color
FROM Production.Product  WHERE Name LIKE ('%touring%');
```

```
-- Integer range predicate
SELECT ProductID, Name, ListPrice, Color
FROM Production.Product  WHERE ProductID >= 997 ;
```

```
-- Double string wildcard match predicate
SELECT ProductID, Name, ListPrice, Color
FROM Production.Product  WHERE Name LIKE ('%bike%')  AND Name LIKE ('%44%');
```

```
-- String list match predicate
SELECT ProductID, Name, ListPrice, Color  FROM Production.Product
WHERE Name IN ('Mountain-100 Silver, 44', 'Mountain-100 Black, 44');
```

The GROUP BY Clause to Aggregate Results

The GROUP BY clause is applied to partition the rows and calculate aggregate values. An extremely powerful way of looking at the data from a summary point of view.

```
SELECT
            V.Name                                   AS Vendor,
            FORMAT(SUM(TotalDue), 'c', 'en-US')      AS TotalPurchase,
            A.City,
            SP.Name                                  AS State,
            CR.Name                                  AS Country
FROM Purchasing.Vendor AS V
   INNER JOIN Purchasing.VendorAddress AS VA
            ON VA.VendorID = V.VendorID
   INNER JOIN Person.Address AS A
            ON A.AddressID = VA.AddressID
   INNER JOIN Person.StateProvince AS SP
            ON SP.StateProvinceID =   A.StateProvinceID
   INNER JOIN Person.CountryRegion AS CR
            ON CR.CountryRegionCode = SP.CountryRegionCode
   INNER JOIN Purchasing.PurchaseOrderHeader POH
            ON POH.VendorID = V.VendorID
GROUP BY  V.Name, A.City, SP.Name, CR.Name
ORDER BY SUM(TotalDue) DESC,  Vendor;   -- TotalPurchase does a string sort instead of numeric
GO
-- (79 row(s) affected) - Partial results.
```

Vendor	TotalPurchase	City	State	Country
Superior Bicycles	$5,034,266.74	Lynnwood	Washington	United States
Professional Athletic Consultants	$3,379,946.32	Burbank	California	United States
Chicago City Saddles	$3,347,165.20	Daly City	California	United States
Jackson Authority	$2,821,333.52	Long Beach	California	United States
Vision Cycles, Inc.	$2,777,684.91	Glendale	California	United States
Sport Fan Co.	$2,675,889.22	Burien	Washington	United States
Proseware, Inc.	$2,593,901.31	Lebanon	Oregon	United States
Crowley Sport	$2,472,770.05	Chicago	Illinois	United States
Greenwood Athletic Company	$2,472,770.05	Lemon Grove	Arizona	United States
Mitchell Sports	$2,424,284.37	Everett	Washington	United States
First Rate Bicycles	$2,304,231.55	La Mesa	New Mexico	United States
Signature Cycles	$2,236,033.80	Coronado	California	United States
Electronic Bike Repair & Supplies	$2,154,773.37	Tacoma	Washington	United States
Vista Road Bikes	$2,090,857.52	Salem	Oregon	United States
Victory Bikes	$2,052,173.62	Issaquah	Washington	United States
Bicycle Specialists	$1,952,375.30	Lake Oswego	Oregon	United States

The HAVING Clause to Filter Aggregates

The HAVING clause is similar to the WHERE clause filtering but applies to GROUP BY aggregates.

```
USE AdventureWorks;
SELECT
            V.Name                              AS Vendor,
            FORMAT(SUM(TotalDue), 'c', 'en-US') AS TotalPurchase,
            A.City,
            SP.Name                             AS State,
            CR.Name                             AS Country
FROM Purchasing.Vendor AS V
   INNER JOIN Purchasing.VendorAddress AS VA
            ON VA.VendorID = V.VendorID
   INNER JOIN Person.Address AS A
            ON A.AddressID = VA.AddressID
   INNER JOIN Person.StateProvince AS SP
            ON SP.StateProvinceID =  A.StateProvinceID
   INNER JOIN Person.CountryRegion AS CR
            ON CR.CountryRegionCode = SP.CountryRegionCode
   INNER JOIN Purchasing.PurchaseOrderHeader POH
            ON POH.VendorID = V.VendorID
GROUP BY  V.Name, A.City, SP.Name, CR.Name
HAVING SUM(TotalDue) < $26000   -- HAVING clause predicate
ORDER BY SUM(TotalDue) DESC,  Vendor;
```

Vendor	TotalPurchase	City	State	Country
Speed Corporation	$25,732.84	Anacortes	Washington	United States
Gardner Touring Cycles	$25,633.64	Altadena	California	United States
National Bike Association	$25,513.90	Sedro Woolley	Washington	United States
Australia Bike Retailer	$25,060.04	Bellingham	Washington	United States
WestAmerica Bicycle Co.	$25,060.04	Houston	Texas	United States
Ready Rentals	$23,635.06	Kirkland	Washington	United States
Morgan Bike Accessories	$23,146.99	Albany	New York	United States
Continental Pro Cycles	$22,960.07	Long Beach	California	United States
American Bicycles and Wheels	$9,641.01	West Covina	California	United States
Litware, Inc.	$8,553.32	Santa Cruz	California	United States
Business Equipment Center	$8,497.80	Everett	Montana	United States
Bloomington Multisport	$8,243.95	West Covina	California	United States
International	$8,061.10	Salt Lake City	Utah	United States
Wide World Importers	$8,025.60	Concord	California	United States
Midwest Sport, Inc.	$7,328.72	Detroit	Michigan	United States
Wood Fitness	$6,947.58	Philadelphia	Pennsylvania	United States
Metro Sport Equipment	$6,324.53	Lebanon	Oregon	United States
Burnett Road Warriors	$5,779.99	Corvallis	Oregon	United States
Lindell	$5,412.57	Lebanon	Oregon	United States
Consumer Cycles	$3,378.17	Torrance	California	United States
Northern Bike Travel	$2,048.42	Anacortes	Washington	United States

The ORDER BY Clause to Sort Results

The ORDER BY clause sorts the result set. It guarantees ordering according to the columns or expressions listed from major to minor keys. Unique ordering requires a set of keys which generate unique data rows. The major key, YEAR(HireDate), in the first example is not sufficient for uniqueness.

```
USE AdventureWorks2012;          -- Sort on 2 keys
SELECT BusinessEntityID AS EmployeeID, JobTitle, HireDate
FROM HumanResources.Employee  ORDER BY YEAR(HireDate) DESC, EmployeeID;
-- (290 row(s) affected) - Partial results.
```

EmployeeID	JobTitle	HireDate
285	Pacific Sales Manager	2007-04-15
286	Sales Representative	2007-07-01
288	Sales Representative	2007-07-01

```
-- Sort on CASE conditional expression
SELECT   BusinessEntityID AS SalesStaffID, CONCAT(LastName, ', ', FirstName) AS FullName,
         CASE CountryRegionName WHEN 'United States' THEN TerritoryName
              ELSE '' END AS TerritoryName, CountryRegionName
FROM Sales.vSalesPerson   WHERE TerritoryName IS NOT NULL        -- view
ORDER BY CASE WHEN CountryRegionName != 'United States' THEN  CountryRegionName
              ELSE TerritoryName  END;
```

SalesStaffID	FullName	TerritoryName	CountryRegionName
286	Tsoflias, Lynn		Australia
278	Vargas, Garrett		Canada
282	Saraiva, José		Canada

The EXCEPT & INTERSECT Set Operators

The EXCEPT operator & the INTERSECT operator require the column lists are compatible for the comparison.

```
USE tempdb;  -- Prepare two tables with 400 random(newid()) picks from the Product table
SELECT TOP (400) * INTO Prod1 FROM AdventureWorks2012.Production.Product ORDER BY NEWID();
SELECT TOP (400) * INTO Prod2 FROM AdventureWorks2012.Production.Product ORDER BY NEWID();

-- EXCEPT SET OPERATOR - no match rows
SELECT * FROM PROD1 EXCEPT SELECT * FROM PROD2;  -- (81 row(s) affected)

-- INTERSECT SET OPERATOR - matching rows
SELECT * FROM PROD1 INTERSECT SELECT * FROM PROD2;  -- (319 row(s) affected)
```

CHAPTER 2: Structure of the SELECT Statement

CTE - Common Table Expression

CTE helps with structured programming by the definition of named subqueries at the beginning of the query. It supports nesting and recursion.

```
USE AdventureWorks;
-- Testing CTE
WITH CTE (SalesPersonID, NumberOfOrders, MostRecentOrderDate)
   AS  (       SELECT SalesPersonID, COUNT(*), CONVERT(date, MAX(OrderDate))
               FROM Sales.SalesOrderHeader
               GROUP BY SalesPersonID   )
SELECT * FROM CTE;
-- (18 row(s) affected) - Partial results.
```

SalesPersonID	NumberOfOrders	MostRecentOrderDate
284	39	2004-05-01
278	234	2004-06-01
281	242	2004-06-01

```
-- Using CTE in a query
;WITH CTE (SalesPersonID, NumberOfOrders, MostRecentOrderDate)
   AS  ( SELECT SalesPersonID, COUNT(*), CONVERT(date, MAX(OrderDate))
        FROM Sales.SalesOrderHeader    GROUP BY SalesPersonID        )
-- Start of outer (main) query
 SELECT          E.EmployeeID,
                 OE.NumberOfOrders              AS EmpOrders,
                 OE.MostRecentOrderDate         AS EmpLastOrder,
                 E.ManagerID,
                 OM.NumberOfOrders              AS MgrOrders,
                 OM.MostRecentOrderDate         AS MgrLastOrder
 FROM   HumanResources.Employee AS E
         INNER JOIN CTE AS OE           ON E.EmployeeID = OE.SalesPersonID
         LEFT OUTER JOIN CTE AS OM      ON E.ManagerID = OM.SalesPersonID
ORDER BY EmployeeID;
-- (17 row(s) affected) - Partial results.
```

EmployeeID	EmpOrders	EmpLastOrder	ManagerID	MgrOrders	MgrLastOrder
268	48	2004-06-01	273	NULL	NULL
275	450	2004-06-01	268	48	2004-06-01
276	418	2004-06-01	268	48	2004-06-01
277	473	2004-06-01	268	48	2004-06-01
278	234	2004-06-01	268	48	2004-06-01

Combining Results of Multiple Queries with UNION

UNION and UNION ALL (no duplicates elimination) operators can be used to **stack result sets from two or more queries into a single result set**.

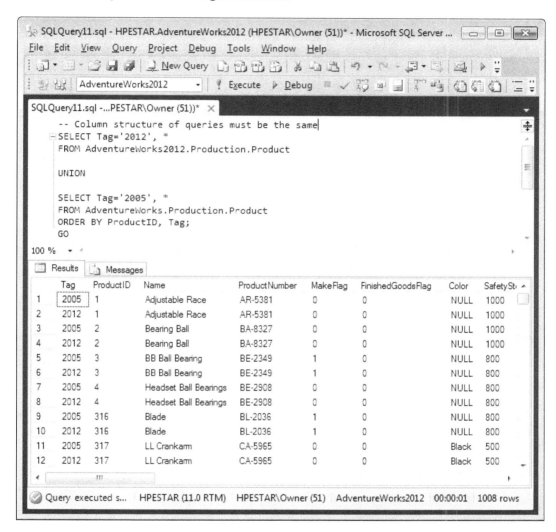

-- Combining data from OLTP & data warehouse databases
SELECT FirstName,LastName, 0 AS TotalChildren
FROM AdventureWorks2012.Person.Person
UNION ALL
SELECT FirstName,LastName, TotalChildren
FROM AdventureWorksDW2012..DimCustomer;

CHAPTER 2: Structure of the SELECT Statement

TOP n by Group Query with OVER PARTITION BY

OVER PARTITION BY method is very convenient for TOP n by group selection. List of top 3 orders placed by resellers (customers of AdventureWorks Cycles).

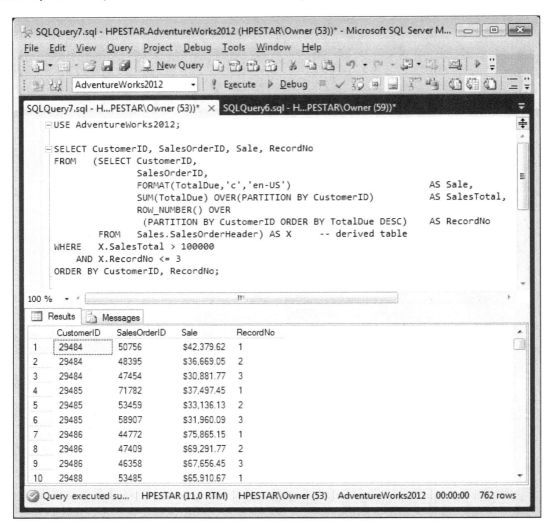

```
-- Row numbering by partitioning view results
SELECT ROW_NUMBER() OVER(PARTITION BY PhoneNumberType ORDER BY SalesYTD DESC) RN,
       CONCAT(FirstName, ' ', LastName) as Name, ROUND(SalesYTD,2,1) AS YTDSales,
       PhoneNumberType
FROM AdventureWorks2012.Sales.vSalesPerson
ORDER BY PhoneNumberType, RN;
```

CHAPTER 2: Structure of the SELECT Statement

CHAPTER 3: SQL Server Management Studio

SQL Server Programming, Administration & Management Tool

SQL Server Management Studio (SSMS) is a GUI (Graphical User Interface) tool for accessing, configuring, managing, administering, and developing all major components of SQL Server with the exception of Business Intelligence components: SSAS (Analysis Services), SSRS (Reporting Services) & SSIS (Integration Services). The two main environments in SSMS: Object Explorer and Query Editor. Object Explorer is used to access servers, databases and db objects. Query Editor is to develop and execute queries. SSMS is used by a DBA (Data Base Administrator) for administrative and programming functions. SSMS can also be used by a database developer to develop application related db objects such as stored procedures, functions and triggers. Some developers prefer to stay in Visual Studio environment which has features to support database development albeit not as extensive as Management Studio. A typical screen display of Management Studio.

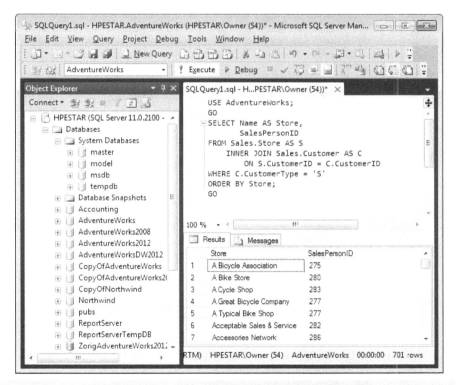

CHAPTER 3: SQL Server Management Studio

Query Editor

The Query Editor is used to type in queries, edit them and submit them for execution by the server. Queries can also be loaded from a disk file, typically with .sql extension. In addition to textual query development, a number of special tools available such as graphical query designer, debugger, execution plan display and query analysis by the Database Engine Tuning Advisor. IntelliSense provides contextual assistance with SQL syntax checking and guessing object names in a drop-down menu based on the typed prefix.

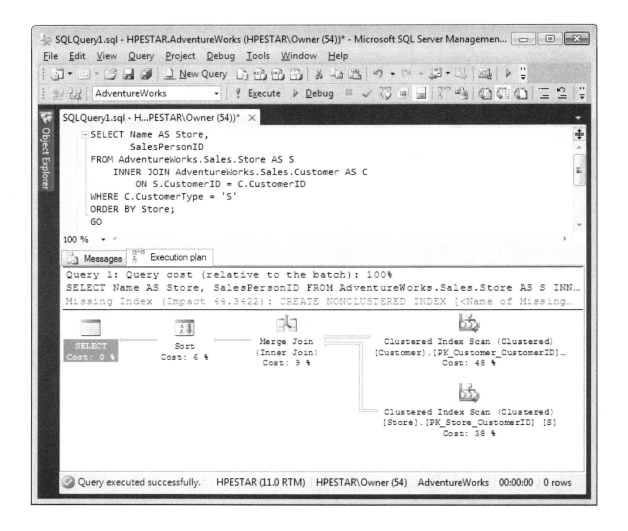

Execute All Batches in Query Editor

The entire content of the Query Editor is executed when we click on the Execute button. Batches typically separated by "GO" on a separate line.

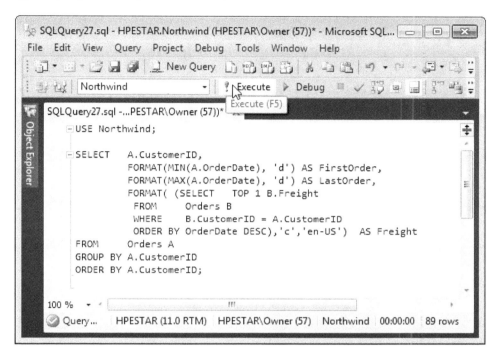

The Significance of GO in T-SQL Scripts

"GO" is not transmitted to SQL Server. "GO" indicates the end of batch to the client software such as SSMS. "GO" also indicates the end of a logical unit to the human reader. Certain statements must be the first line, or have "GO" preceding them.

```
USE AdventureWorks2012;
CREATE FUNCTION Z () RETURNS TABLE AS
RETURN  SELECT * FROM Production.ProductSubcategory;
GO    /* Msg 111, Level 15, State 1, Line 2   'CREATE FUNCTION' must be the first statement in a query batch. */

USE AdventureWorks2012;
GO
CREATE FUNCTION Z () RETURNS TABLE AS RETURN SELECT * FROM
Production.ProductSubcategory;
GO
-- Command(s) completed successfully.
```

CHAPTER 3: SQL Server Management Studio

The Results Pane contains the result rows of the query. It is currently set to Grid format.

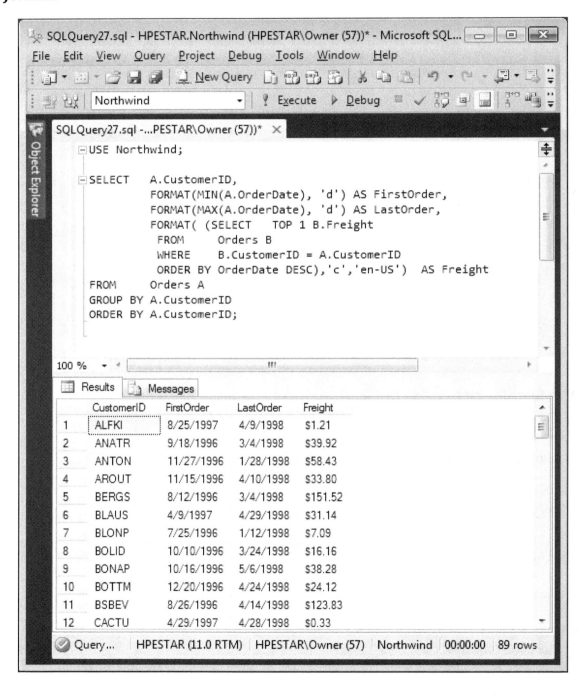

The Messages Pane gets the row count values, warning & error messages as well as the output of the PRINT & RAISERROR statements if any.

The client software also gets the same messages following query execution.

Routing Results to Grid, Text or File

Results can be routed to Grid, Text or File from the right-click menu or the Query drop-down menu.

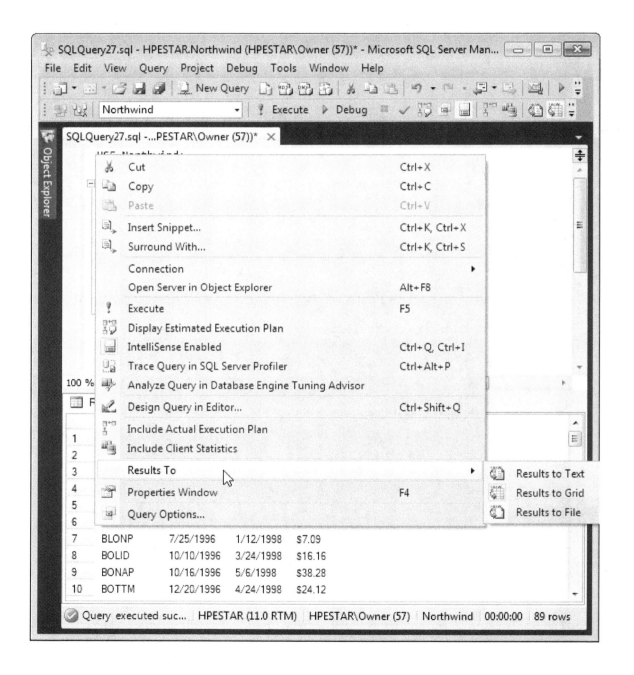

Routing Results to Text

The following screen window image displays results in text format. Messages also come to the Results window, following the results rows.

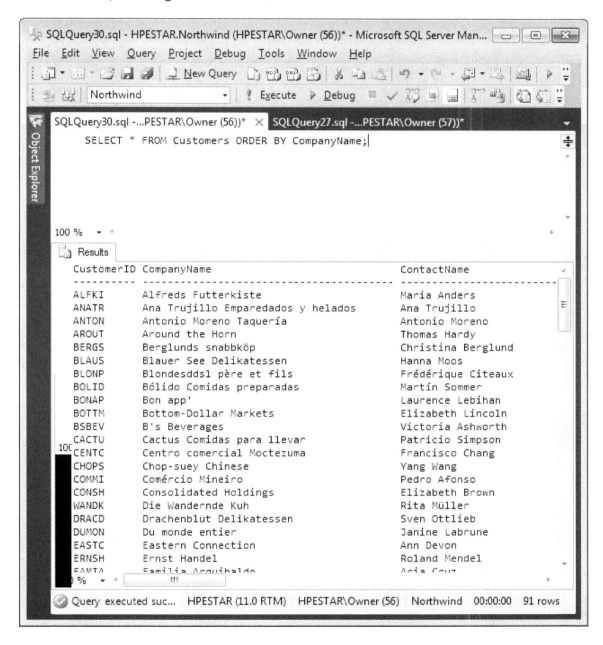

Routing Results to File

When the routing option is file, the file save window pops up upon query execution.

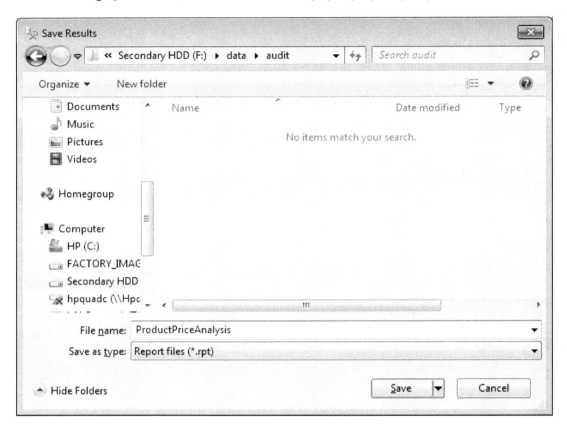

Part of the file in Notepad.

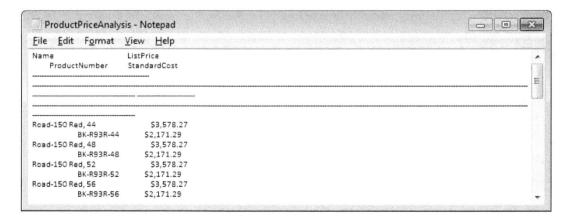

Saving Results in CSV Flat File Format

Results can also be saved in CSV (comma separated values) format which can be read by Excel and other software.

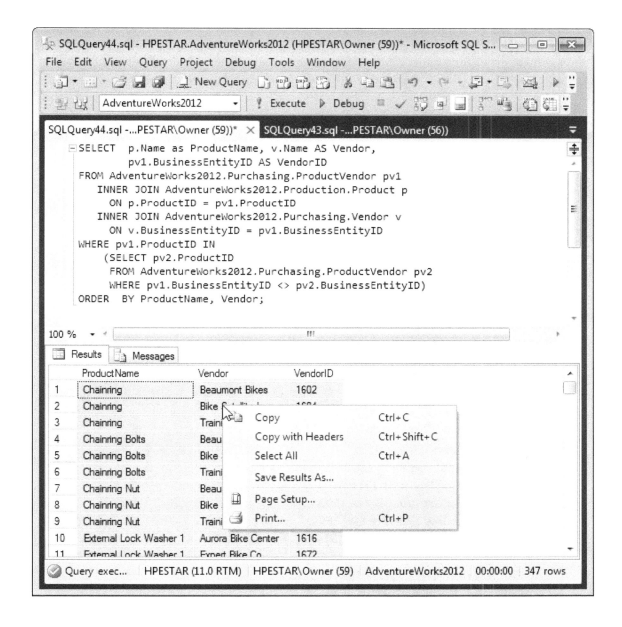

The saving file dialog box is configured automatically to csv saving.

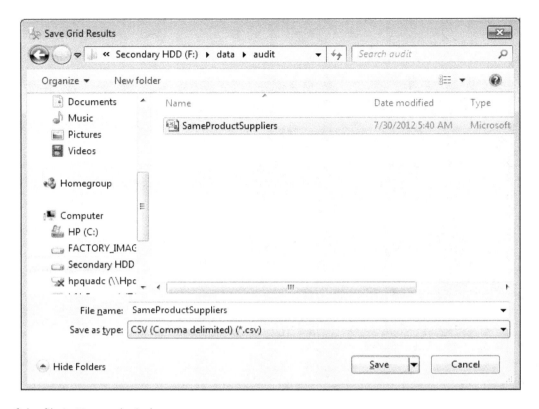

Part of the file in Notepad window.

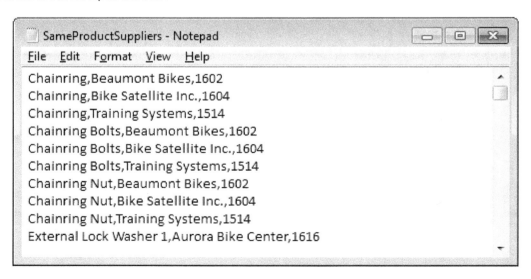

Copy & Paste Results to Excel

Using the copy / copy with headers option in SSMS result window, the query results can simply be pasted into an Excel worksheet. Excel may do implicit conversions on some columns.

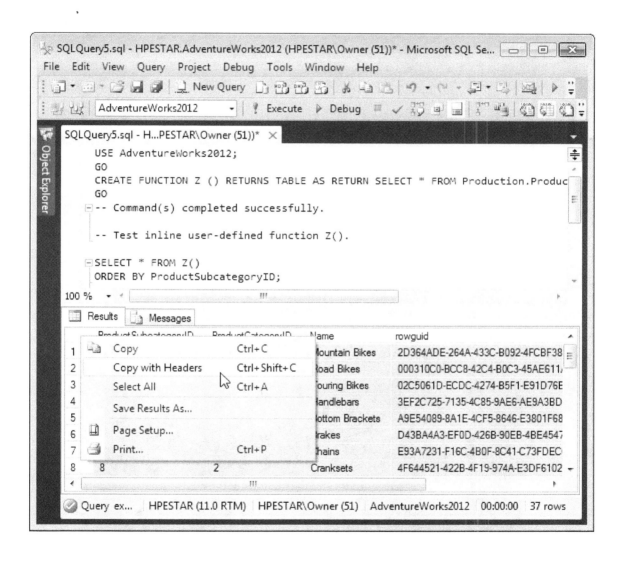

After pasting into an Excel worksheet some formatting may be necessary such as for datetime columns.

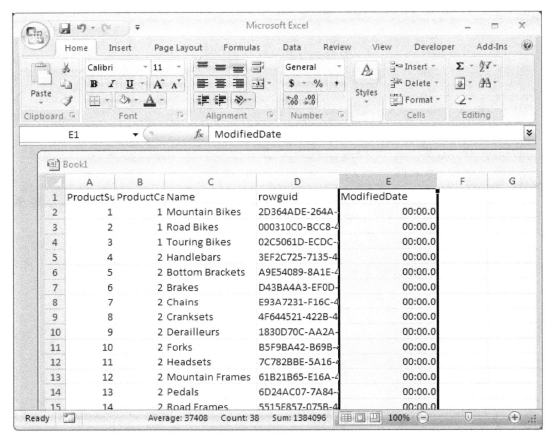

Error Handling & Debugging

Error handling and debugging is a major part of database development work. When there is an error, it is displayed in the Messages area (or returned to the application client software) which automatically becomes active. In the following example, we introduced an invalid column name which resulted in error. The error message line reference starts with the top line of the batch which is the first line after the first "GO" which indicates a new batch. The red wave-underlining comes from optional IntelliSense and not related to the execution attempt error message. IntelliSense gives warning ahead of time if it detects a potential error. Simple errors can be corrected with help from the error message. Complex errors may required web search and/or examining the query in parts.

Locating the Error Line in a Query

Position the cursor on the error and double click. The error line will be highlighted. This method does not work for all errors.

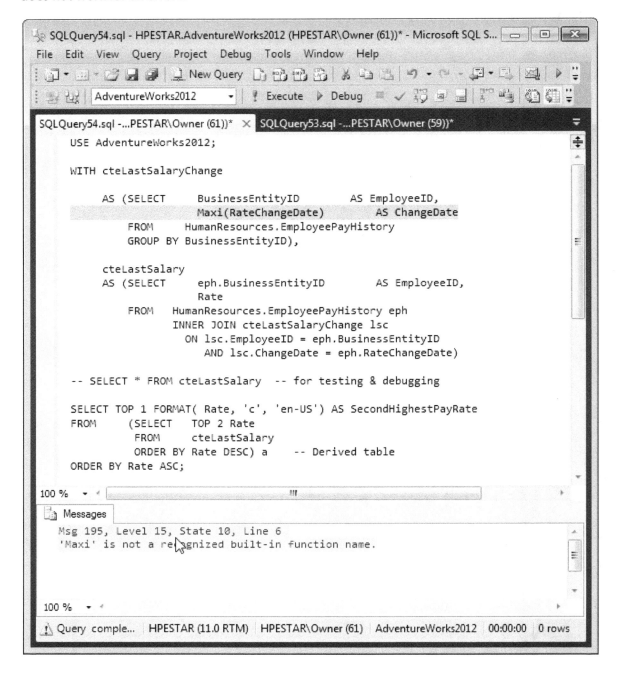

Error Message Pointing to the Wrong Line

For some errors, the first line of the query (3) is returned by the database engine not the actual error line (13). The error message is still very helpful though in this instance.

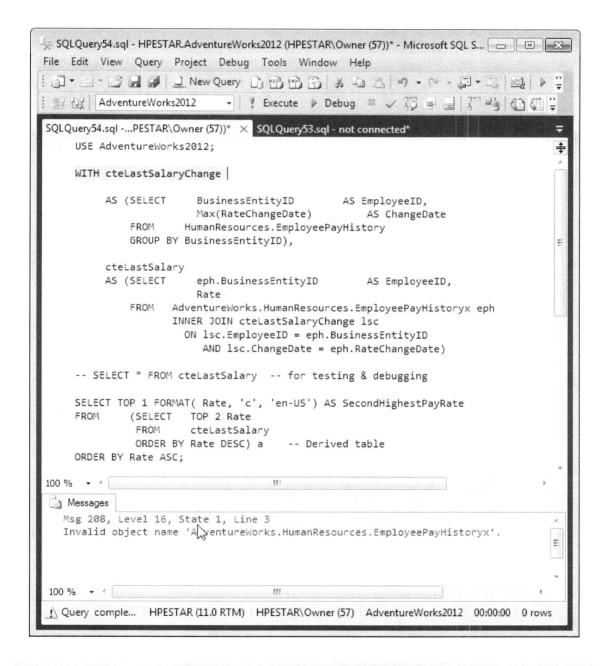

Parsing a Query for Syntax Errors

A query (or one or more batches) can be parsed for syntax errors. Parsing catches syntax errors such as using "ORDER" instead of "ORDER BY" for sorting.

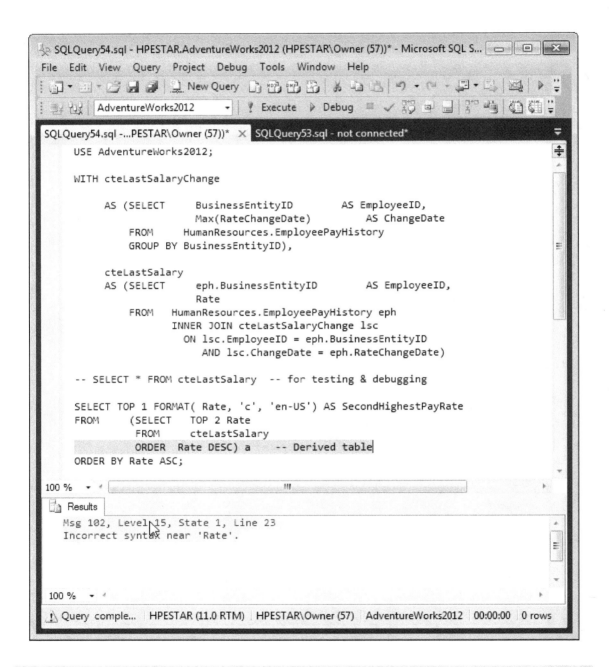

Deferred Name Resolution Process

Deferred Name Resolution Process: Only syntax errors are caught when parsed, not execution (runtime) errors as shown in the following demo which has an invalid table reference (EmployeePayHistoryx). Similarly, **stored procedures can be compiled without errors with invalid table references**. A table need not exist for stored procedure compilation, only for execution.

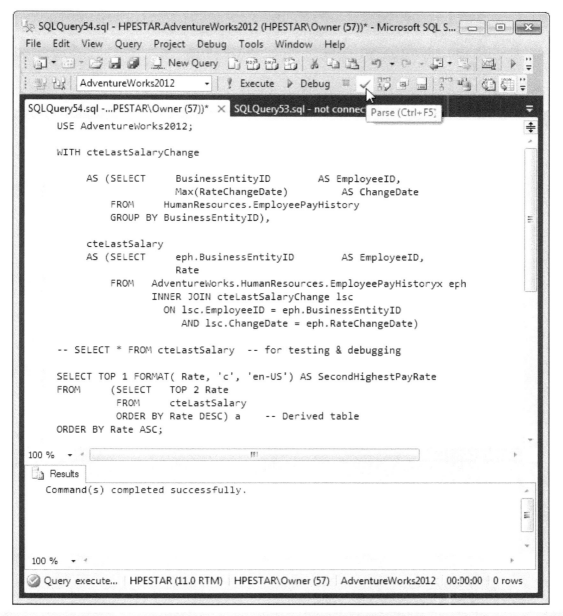

Executing Single Batch Only

A single batch can be executed by selecting (highlighting) it and clicking on Execute.

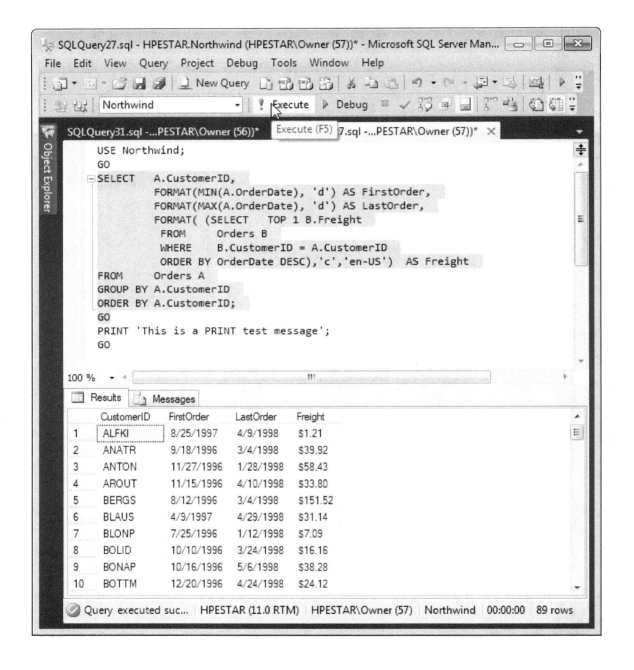

Executing Part of a Query

A part of a query can be executed as long as it is a valid query, otherwise error results. The
query part has to be selected (highlighted) and the Execute button has to be pushed. The
selected part of the query is considered a batch which is sent to the server. In this example, we
executed the subquery (inner query) in the WHERE clause predicate.

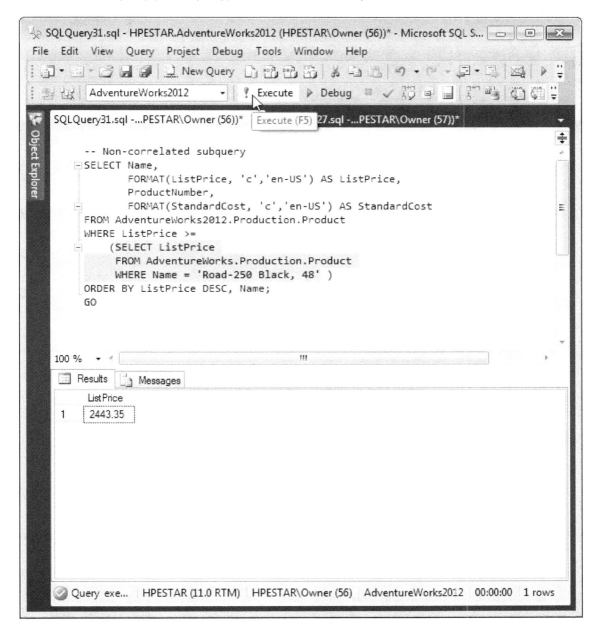

Object Explorer

SSMS Object Explorer functions as:

- ➢ A tree-based directory of all database objects
- ➢ A launching base for graphical user-interface tools
- ➢ An access way to object properties

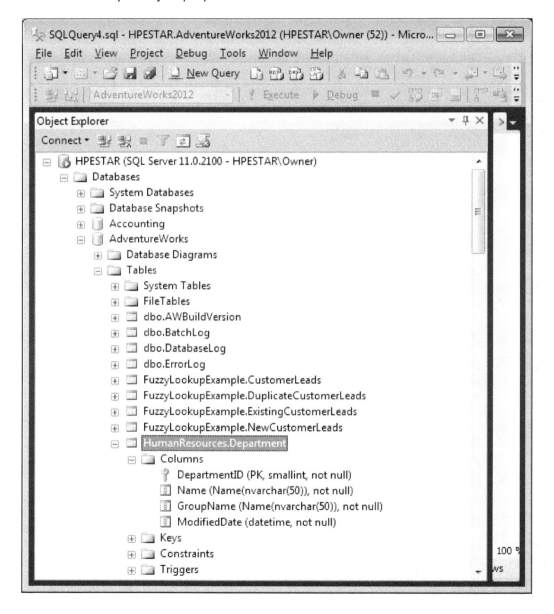

Context-Sensitive Right-Click Menu

Based on what object the cursor is on, right-click menu changes accordingly, it is context-sensitive. In the following demo the cursor is on table object when we right click on the mouse.

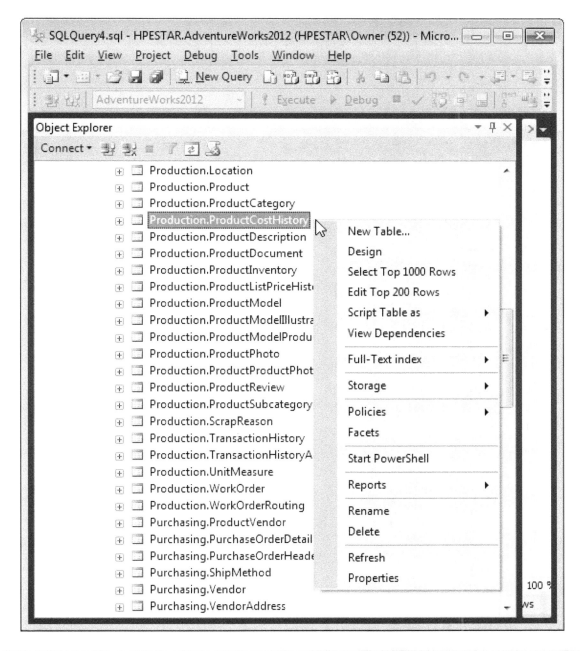

CHAPTER 3: SQL Server Management Studio

Server Administration & Management Tools

All the available SQL Server administration and management tools can be accessed from the Object Explorer. Usually the Database Administrator (DBA) uses these tools.

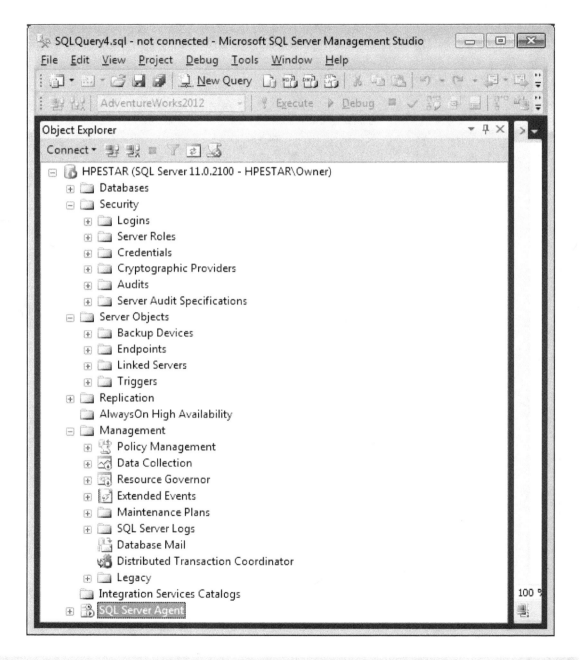

SQL Server Agent Jobs to Automate Administration Tasks

SQL Server Agent is a job creation and scheduling facility with notification features. For example, database backup job can be scheduled to execute 2:15AM every night as shown on the following dialog box. Stored procedure execution can also be setup as a job and scheduled for periodic execution.

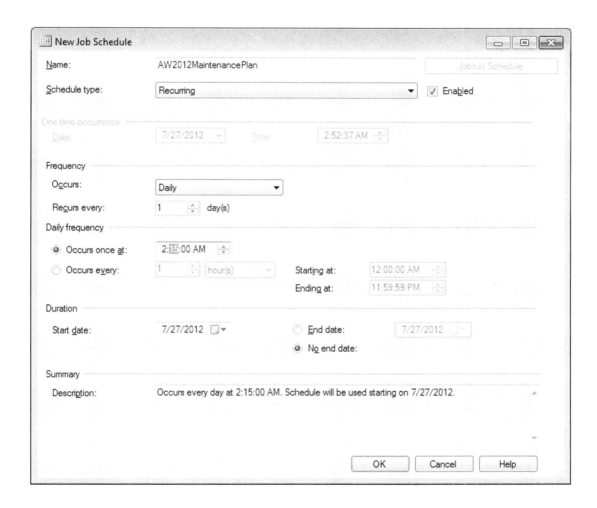

Job properties panel can be used to create and manage jobs with multiple job steps and multiple schedules.

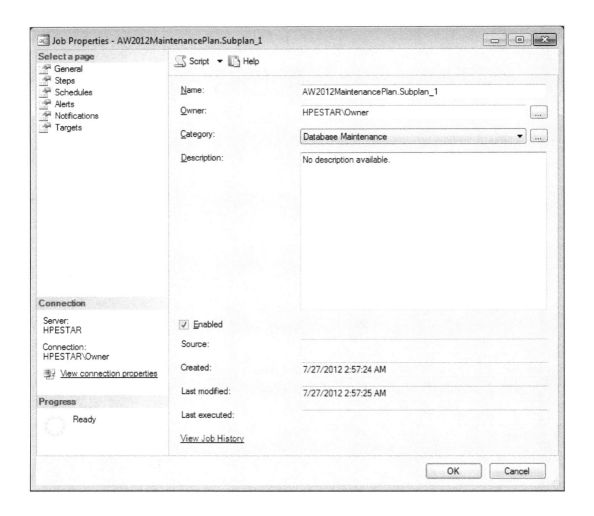

Graphical Query Designer

The Design Query in Editor entry on the Query drop-down menu launches the graphical Query Designer which can be used to design the query with GUI method and the T-SQL SELECT code will be generated automatically upon completion.

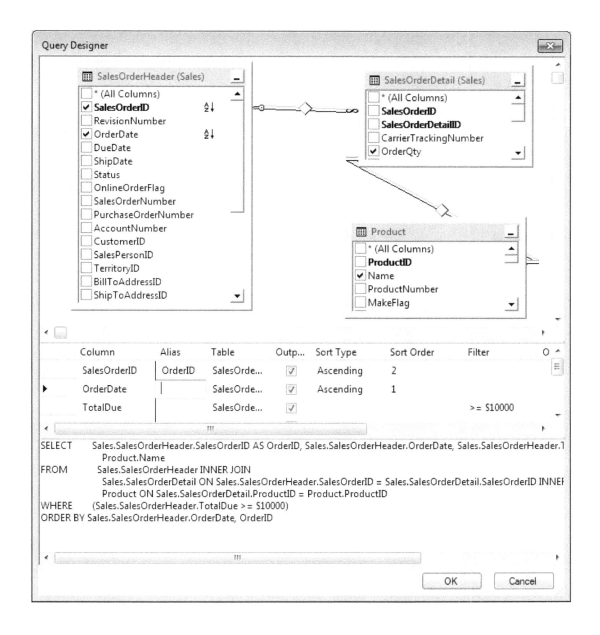

Designing a GROUP BY Query in Query Designer

Query Designer can be used to design from simple to complex queries. It can also serve as a
starter query for a more complex query. It is really easy to get the tables JOINs graphically.

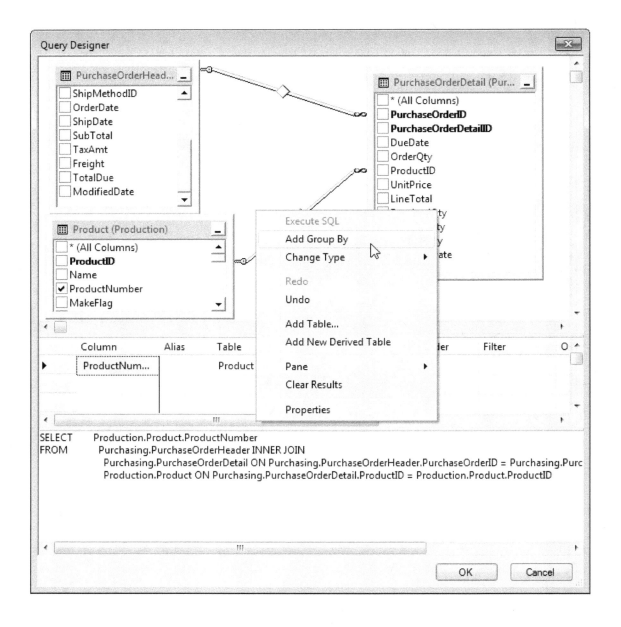

The Production.Product.Name column will also be configured as GROUP BY (drop-down default).

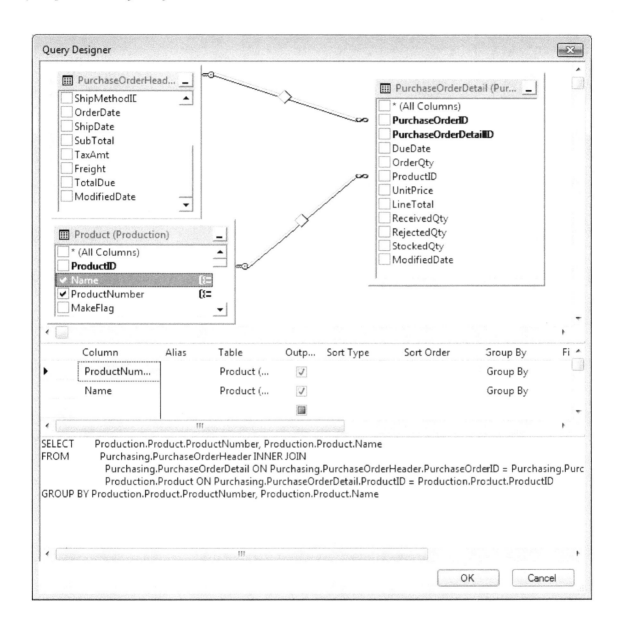

We add the TotalDue column and change the summary function to "SUM" from "Group by" and configure sorting on the first column.

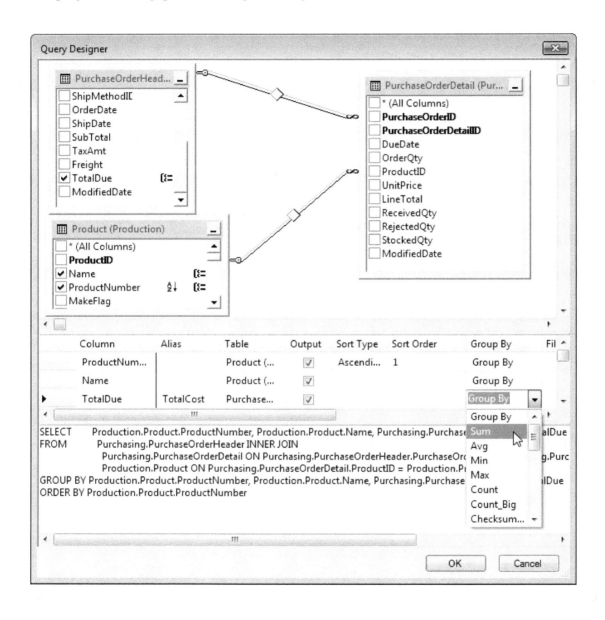

After pressing OK, the query is moved into the Query Editor window. Frequently it requires reformatting.

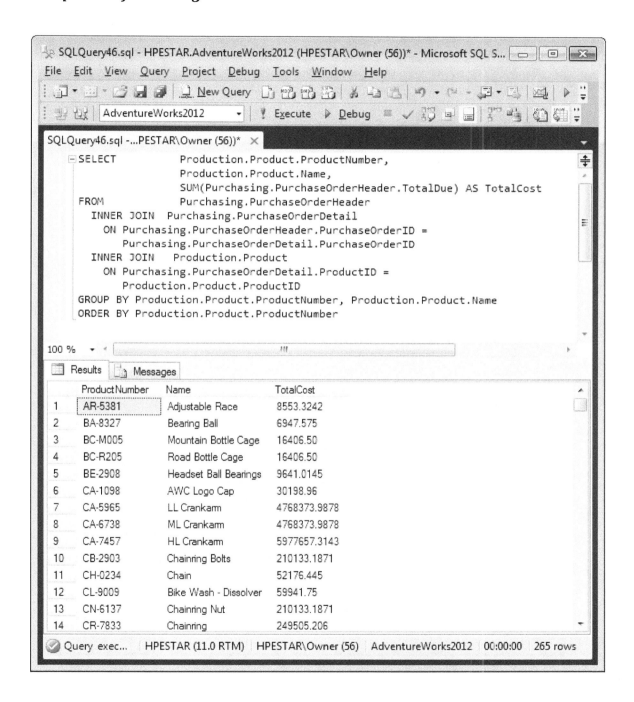

The only remaining issue with the query is the 3-part column references which is hard to read. We can change the query for readability improvement by using table aliases.

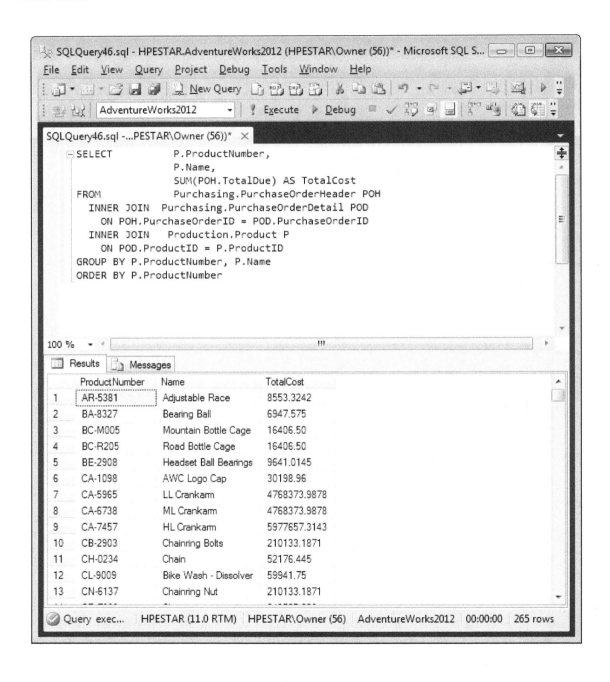

Graphically Editing of an Existing Query

An existing query, exception certain complex queries, can be uploaded into the Graphical Query Designer the following way: select (highlight) the query and right-click for the drop-down menu; click on Design Query in Editor.

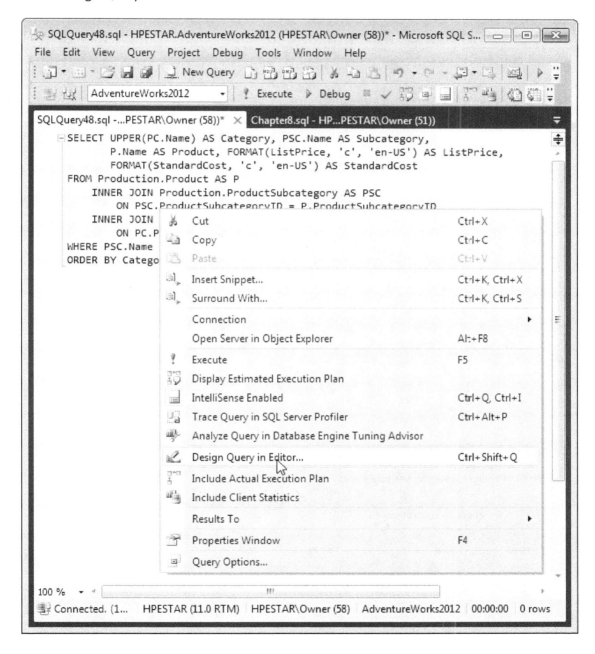

Following screen image shows the query in the Graphical Query Designer after some manual beautifying such as moving the tables for better display.

The query can be edited graphically and upon clicking on "OK", the query text is updated in the Query Editor window.

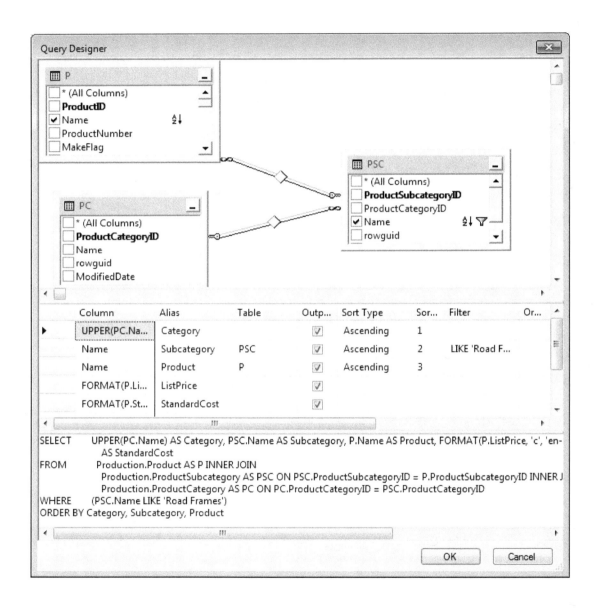

Configuring Line Numbers in Query Editor

Line numbering is an option which is off by default. Line numbers are helpful to find errors in large queries or T-SQL scripts (a sequence of T-SQL statements) when the error references a line number. Following is an example an error which includes the line number.

The Display Line Numbers option in the query editor can be activated from Options.

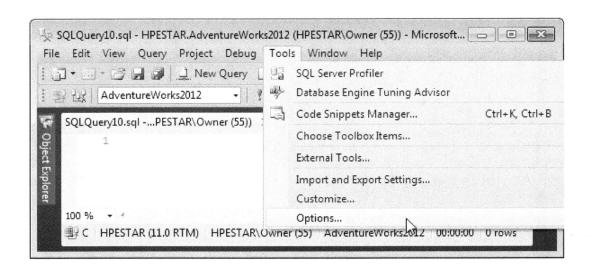

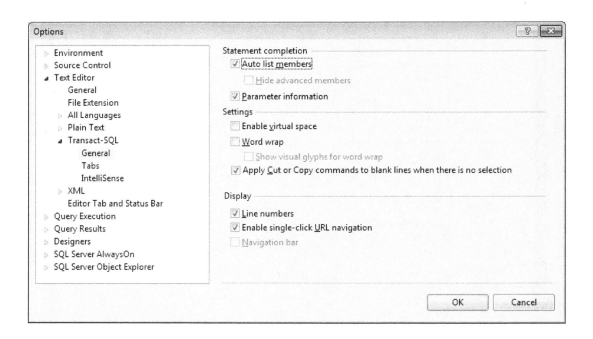

IntelliSense - Your Smart Assistant

IntelliSense is a smart agent in Query Editor. It helps completing long object names and pointing out potential errors by red wave-lining (squiggly) them.

The Options configuration screen for IntelliSense.

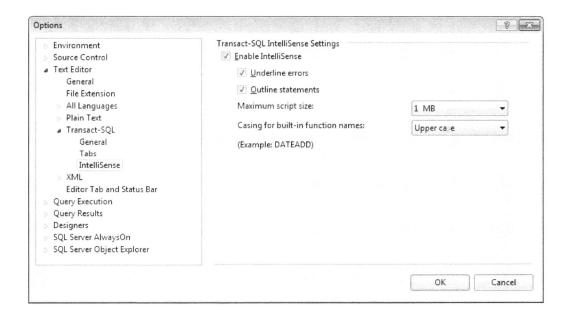

Underlining with red wave-line potential errors such as misspelling of a column name.

```
SELECT TOP 1000 [BillOfMaterialsID]
      ,[ProductAssemblyID]
      ,[ComponentID]
      ,[StartDate]
      ,[EndDate]
      ,[UnitMeasureCodex]
      ,[BOMLevel]
      ,[PerAssemblyQty]
      ,[ModifiedDate]
  FROM [AdventureWorks2012].[Production].[BillOfMaterials]
```

100 %

CHAPTER 3: SQL Server Management Studio

IntelliSense Guessing and Completing Object Names
Screenshots show IntelliSense in action when typing queries.

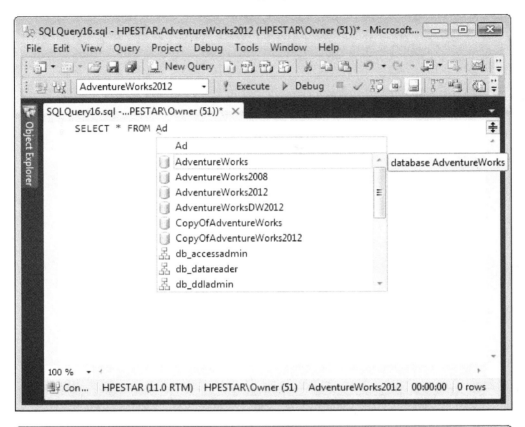

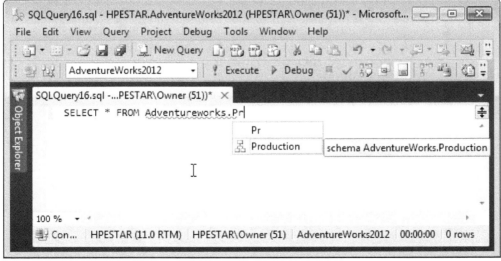

CHAPTER 3: SQL Server Management Studio

IntelliSense drop-down menu for "Prod".

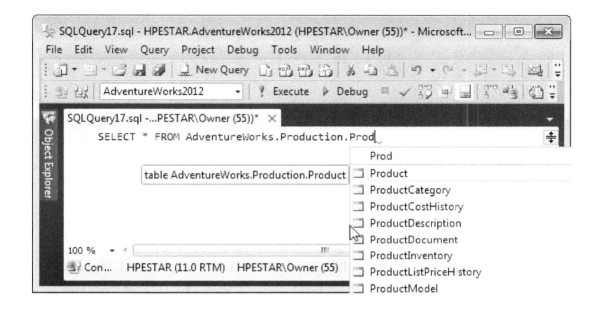

IntelliSense drop-down menu for "ProductS".

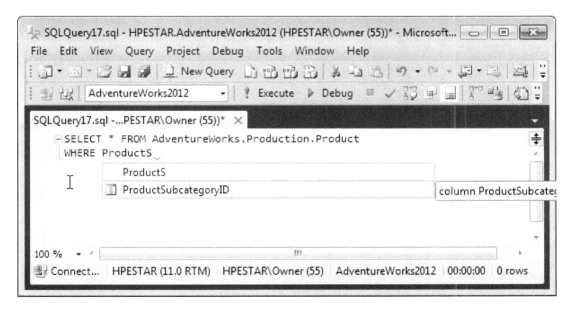

CHAPTER 3: SQL Server Management Studio

IntelliSense completion assistance for "ProductN"

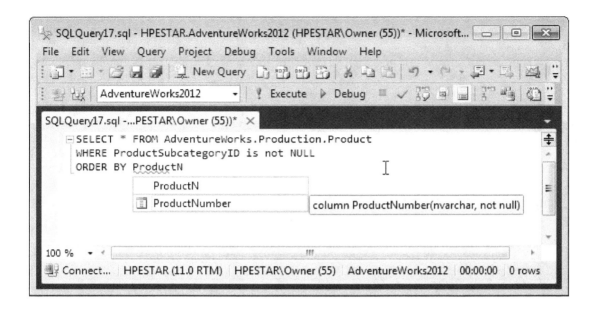

IntelliSense completion assistance for "Produ"

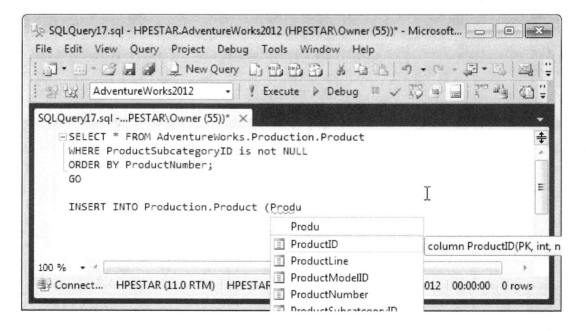

IntelliSense Assisting with User-Defined Objects

IntelliSense helps out with a user-defined stored procedure execution.

IntelliSense Smart Guessing Partial Word in Middle of Object Names

You don't have to remember how an object name starts. You just have to remember some part of the name. Looking for the system view associated with "waits".

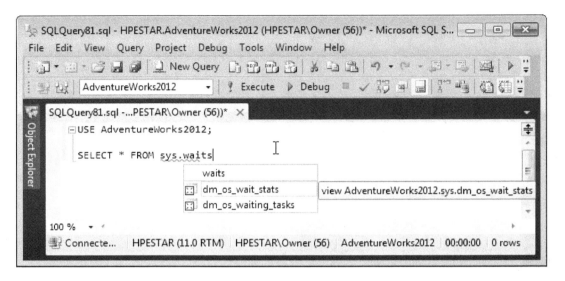

Looking for the SalesOrderHeader table but only remembering "head".

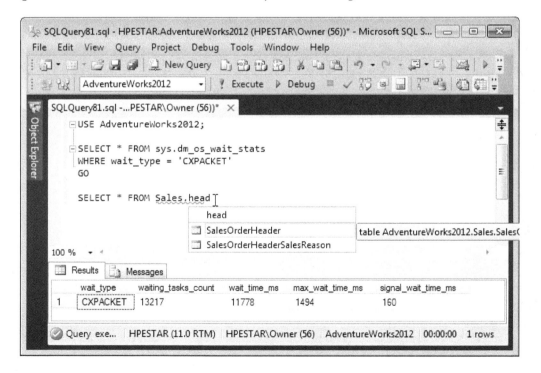

Hovering over Red Squiggly Underline Errors for Explanation

IntelliSense red wave (squiggly) underlining of errors which is caused, actually, by a single invalid table reference.

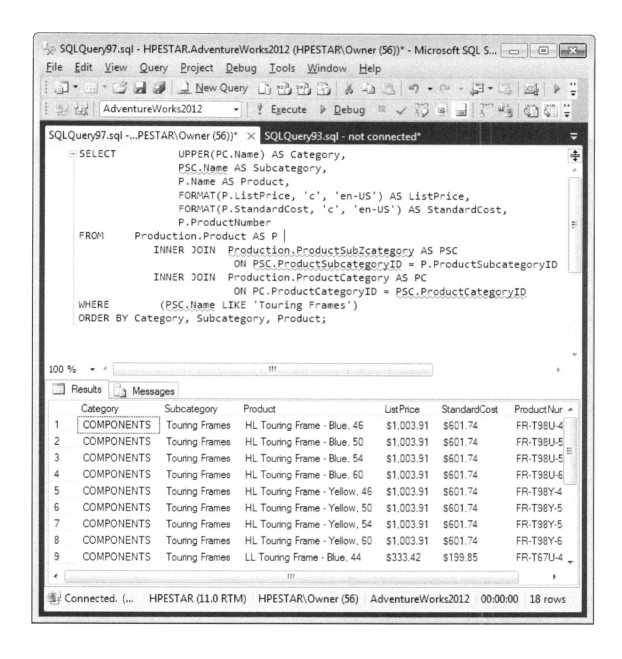

Common Error: The multi-part identifier "abc" could not be bound.

Hovering over the first error results in an explanation pop-up. This is a distant error, the kind usually the hardest to solve, because, actually, it is a secondary error caused by the primary error which is located on a different line. In this instance, there are few lines difference only, but in a large stored procedure the difference can be 200 lines as an example.

```
PSC.Name AS Subcategory,
    The multi-part identifier "PSC.Name" could not be bound.
```

Hovering over the second error yields the cause of all errors: "ProductSubZcategory".

```
Production.ProductSubZcategory AS PSC
    Invalid object name 'Production.ProductSubZcategory'.
```

The remaining error messages are all "multi-part..." caused by the solitary invalid table reference.

```
PSC.ProductSubcategoryID = P.ProductSubcategoryID
    The multi-part identifier "PSC.ProductSubcategoryID" could not be bound.
```

After fixing the table name, all errors are gone.

```
SELECT      UPPER(PC.Name)                          AS Category,
            PSC.Name                                AS Subcategory,
            P.Name                                  AS Product,
            FORMAT(P.ListPrice, 'c', 'en-US')       AS ListPrice,
            FORMAT(P.StandardCost, 'c', 'en-US')    AS StandardCost,
            P.ProductNumber
FROM        Production.Product AS P
            INNER JOIN  Production.ProductSubcategory AS PSC
                        ON PSC.ProductSubcategoryID = P.ProductSubcategoryID
            INNER JOIN  Production.ProductCategory AS PC
                        ON PC.ProductCategoryID = PSC.ProductCategoryID
WHERE       (PSC.Name LIKE 'Touring Frames')
ORDER BY Category, Subcategory, Product;
```

Refreshing IntelliSense Cache for New DB Objects

IntelliSense cache is not updated real-time. If new objects are created in another connection (session), they will not be seen until exit SSMS/reenter or IntelliSense cache is updated. No red-wave underline for the **newly created object SOD** in the same connection.

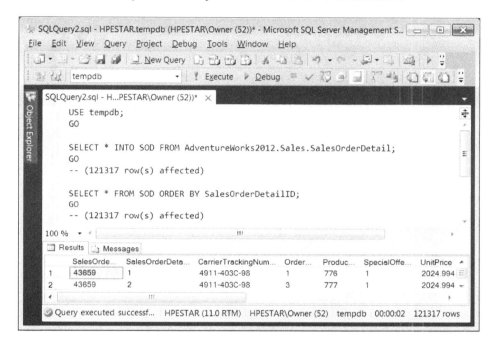

In another connection, the query works, but there are red squiggly underlining for the new table & column.

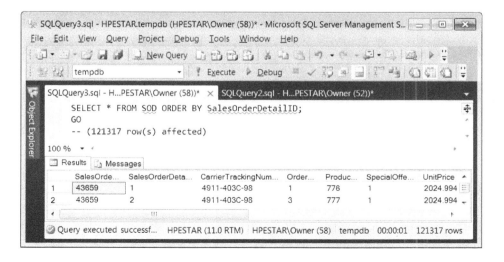

CHAPTER 3: SQL Server Management Studio

Refreshing IntelliSense Local Cache

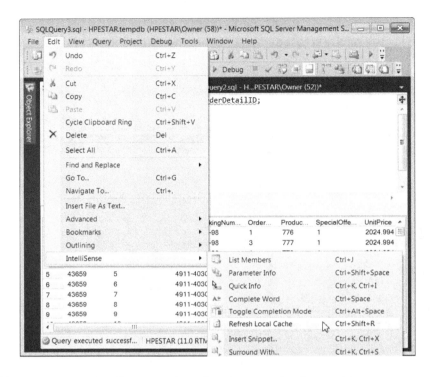

Squiggly red line goes away in all connections for the new database objects.

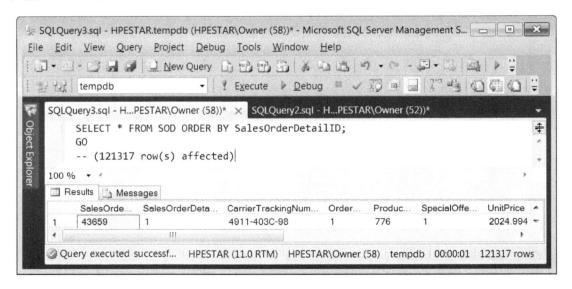

CHAPTER 3: SQL Server Management Studio

CHAPTER 4: Basic Concepts of Client-Server Computing

Client - Server Relational Database Management System

The "server" is SQL Server, operating on a powerful hardware platform, managing databases and related items. The client is application software. The real client is naturally a human user who runs the application software. Automated software which uses the database for one thing or another is also considered a "client". The client computer, in the next room or thousands of miles away, is connected to the server through communications link. The client software sends a request, a query, to SQL Server, after execution the server returns the results to the client. An example for a query sent by the client to the server:

SELECT ListPrice FROM AdventureWorks2012.Production.Product WHERE ProductID = 800;

SQL Server executes the query and returns "1120.49" to the client with a flag indicating successful query execution. A tempting analogy is a restaurant: kitchen is the server, patrons are the clients and the communications / delivery done by waiters & waitresses.

Screenshot displays SQL Server (highlighted) along with other related software such as SQL Server Agent (job scheduling facility) , SSIS (data transformation & transfer), SSRS (Reporting), SSAS (OLAP Cube) and other auxiliary software.

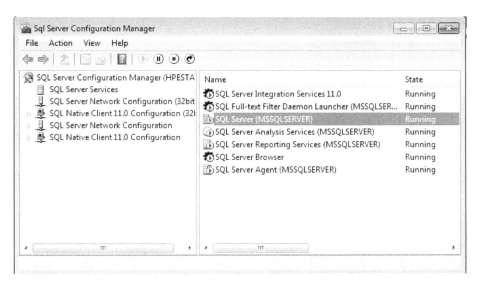

CHAPTER 4: Basic Concepts of Client-Server Computing

Database Objects on Server-Side

Screenshot of Object Explorer displays almost all important database objects with the exception of constraints, triggers and indexes.

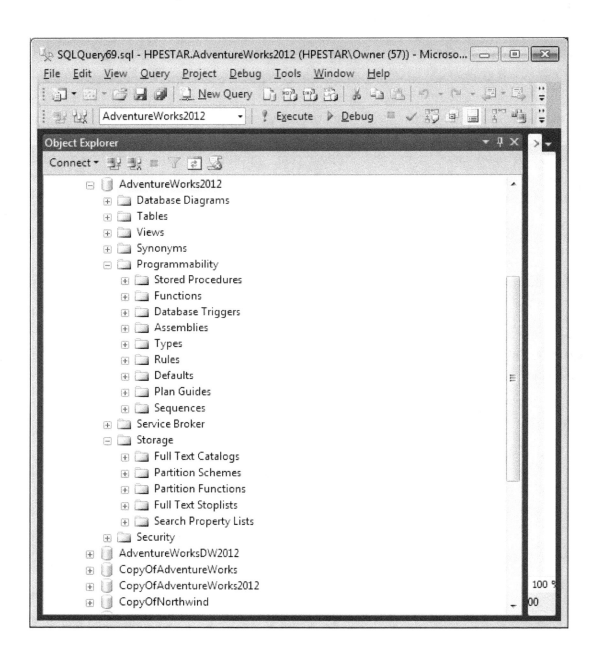

Database Related Items on Client-Side

On the client side the following items:

- ➤ SQL Server client libraries to access the server and database
- ➤ SQL queries imbedded in application programs
- ➤ Stored procedure calls imbedded in application software

Queries by themselves are not database object. To make them database objects we have to build stored procedures, functions or views around them.

The following code segment illustrates database connection and query from ASP to Inventory database. In ANSI SQL terminology catalog means database.

```
' Connect
<%
Dim StrConnInventory
Dim ConnInventory

StrConnInventory = "Provider=SQLOLEDB.1;Data Source=LONDONHEADOFFICE;Initial
Catalog=Inventory;User ID=finance;Password=fa$nAnCe#9*"

Set ConnInventory = Server.CreateObject("ADODB.Connection")

ConnInventory.ConnectionTimeout = 4000
ConnInventory.CommandTimeout = 4000
ConnInventory.Open StrConnInventory

' Query
Dim YourQuery As String = "SELECT Name, Price FROM Product"
 Dim YourCommand As New SqlCommand(YourQuery)
 YourCommand.Connection = ConnInventory
 YourConnection.Open()
 YourCommand.ExecuteNonQuery()
 Response.Write(YourCommand)
 YourCommand.Connection.Close()
%>
' Disconnect
<%
ConnInventory.Close
Set ConnInventory = Nothing
%>
```

CHAPTER 4: Basic Concepts of Client-Server Computing

SQL Server Profiler to Monitor Client-Server Communications

SQL Server Profiler, a tool in SSMS, has two modes of operations: interactive GUI and silent T-SQL script based operation. The simplest use of the Profiler is to check what queries are sent to the server (SQL Server) from the client and how long does processing take (duration). The client software sending the queries is SSMS. Even though SSMS appears as the "face of SQL Server", it is only a client software.

```
USE pubs;
GO
SELECT * FROM titles;
GO


USE Northwind;
GO
SELECT * FROM Products ORDER BY ProductName;
GO


USE AdventureWorks2012;
GO
SELECT * FROM Sales.SalesOrderHeader WHERE OrderDate='20080201';
GO
```

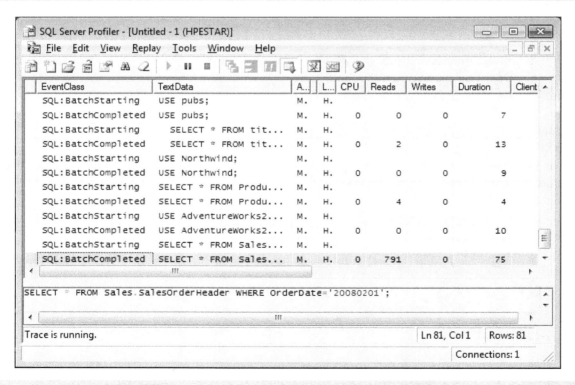

Table - Database Object

A database table holds data in tabular format by rows and columns. The main method of connecting tables is FOREIGN KEY referencing PRIMARY KEY. A set of connected tables makes up the database. Screenshot displays the structure and partial content of Northwind database Products table.

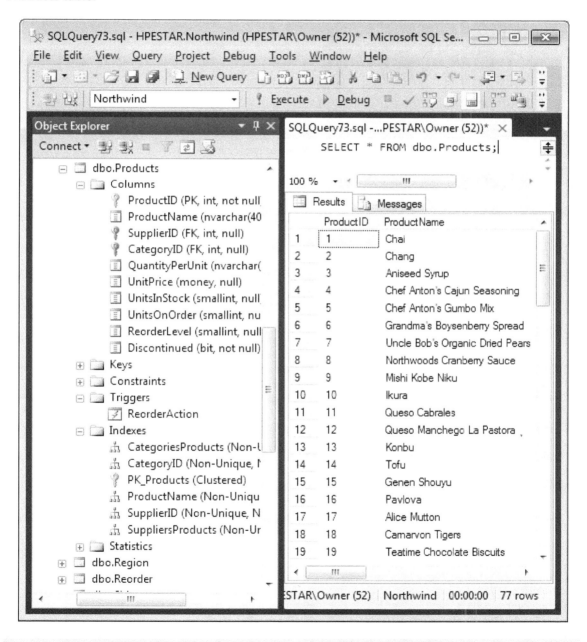

CHAPTER 4: Basic Concepts of Client-Server Computing

Tables in Production Schema

The listing and data dictionary description of tables in AdventureWorks2012 Production schema.

```
USE AdventureWorks2012;

SELECT  CONCAT('Production.', objname COLLATE DATABASE_DEFAULT) AS TableName,
        value                                              AS [Description]
FROM fn_listextendedproperty (          NULL,
                              'schema', 'Production',
                              'table', default,
                              NULL, NULL)
ORDER BY TableName;
```

TableName	Description
Production.BillOfMaterials	Items required to make bicycles and bicycle subassemblies. It identifies the hierarchical relationship between a parent product and its components.
Production.Culture	Lookup table containing the languages in which some AdventureWorks data is stored.
Production.Document	Product maintenance documents.
Production.Illustration	Bicycle assembly diagrams.
Production.Location	Product inventory and manufacturing locations.
Production.Product	Products sold or used in the manfacturing of sold products.
Production.ProductCategory	High-level product categorization.
Production.ProductCostHistory	Changes in the cost of a product over time.
Production.ProductDescription	Product descriptions in several languages.
Production.ProductDocument	Cross-reference table mapping products to related product documents.
Production.ProductInventory	Product inventory information.
Production.ProductListPriceHistory	Changes in the list price of a product over time.
Production.ProductModel	Product model classification.
Production.ProductModelIllustration	Cross-reference table mapping product models and illustrations.
Production.ProductModelProductDescriptionCulture	Cross-reference table mapping product descriptions and the language the description is written in.
Production.ProductPhoto	Product images.
Production.ProductProductPhoto	Cross-reference table mapping products and product photos.
Production.ProductReview	Customer reviews of products they have purchased.
Production.ProductSubcategory	Product subcategories. See ProductCategory table.
Production.ScrapReason	Manufacturing failure reasons lookup table.
Production.TransactionHistory	Record of each purchase order, sales order, or work order transaction year to date.
Production.TransactionHistoryArchive	Transactions for previous years.
Production.UnitMeasure	Unit of measure lookup table.
Production.WorkOrder	Manufacturing work orders.
Production.WorkOrderRouting	Work order details.

Index - Database Object

An index on a table is a B-tree based structure which speeds up random searches. **Typically PRIMARY KEY (automatic), FOREIGN KEY and WHERE clause columns have indexes.** If the index is constructed on more than one column, it is called **composite index**. If all the columns in a query are in the index, it is called **covering index**. Properties dialog box displays the PRIMARY KEY composite index of the EmployeeDepartmentHistory table.

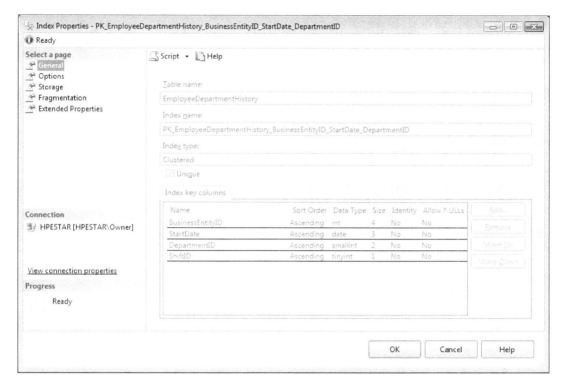

CHAPTER 4: Basic Concepts of Client-Server Computing

Diagram of EmployeeDepartmentHistory and Related Tables

EmployeeDepartmentHistory is a simple junction table with three FOREIGN KEYs to the
Employee, Shift and Department tables respectively.

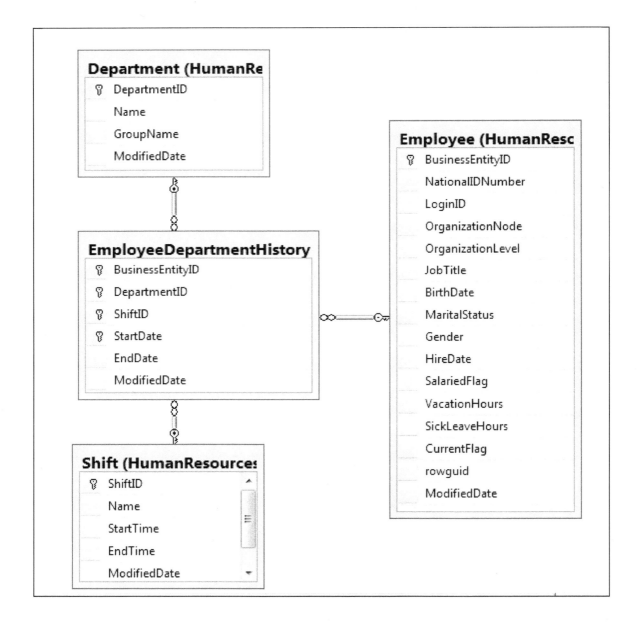

Index Description in Data Dictionary

The indexes listing for Product, SalesOrderHeader & SalesOrderDetail tables.

USE AdventureWorks2012;

```
SELECT   objtype                      AS ObjectType,
         'Sales.SalesOrderHeader'     AS TableName,
         objname                      AS ObjectName,
         value                        AS [Description]
FROM fn_listextendedproperty (NULL, 'schema', 'Sales', 'table', 'SalesOrderHeader', 'index', default)

UNION

SELECT objtype, 'Sales.SalesOrderDetail', objname, value
FROM fn_listextendedproperty (NULL, 'schema', 'Sales', 'table', 'SalesOrderDetail', 'index', default)

UNION

SELECT objtype, 'Production.Product', objname,  value
FROM fn_listextendedproperty (NULL, 'schema', 'Production', 'table', 'Product', 'index', default)
ORDER BY TableName;
GO
```

ObjectType	TableName	ObjectName	Description
INDEX	Production.Product	AK_Product_Name	Unique nonclustered index.
INDEX	Production.Product	AK_Product_ProductNumber	Unique nonclustered index.
INDEX	Production.Product	AK_Product_rowguid	Unique nonclustered index. Used to support replication samples.
INDEX	Production.Product	PK_Product_ProductID	Clustered index created by a primary key constraint.
INDEX	Sales.SalesOrderDetail	AK_SalesOrderDetail_rowguid	Unique nonclustered index. Used to support replication samples.
INDEX	Sales.SalesOrderDetail	IX_SalesOrderDetail_ProductID	Nonclustered index.
INDEX	Sales.SalesOrderDetail	PK_SalesOrderDetail_SalesOrderID_SalesOrderDetailID	Clustered index created by a primary key constraint.
INDEX	Sales.SalesOrderHeader	AK_SalesOrderHeader_rowguid	Unique nonclustered index. Used to support replication samples.
INDEX	Sales.SalesOrderHeader	AK_SalesOrderHeader_SalesOrderNumber	Unique nonclustered index.
INDEX	Sales.SalesOrderHeader	IX_SalesOrderHeader_CustomerID	Nonclustered index.
INDEX	Sales.SalesOrderHeader	IX_SalesOrderHeader_SalesPersonID	Nonclustered index.
INDEX	Sales.SalesOrderHeader	PK_SalesOrderHeader_SalesOrderID	Clustered index created by a primary key constraint.

CHAPTER 4: Basic Concepts of Client-Server Computing

Constraint - Database Object

The PRIMARY KEY constraint ensures that each row has a unique ID. The FOREIGN KEY constraint ensures that the FK points to (references) a valid PK. CHECK constraint enforces formulas (check clauses) defined for a column such as OrderQty > 0. If the formula evaluates to TRUE, the CHECK constraint satisfied, otherwise ERROR condition is generated by the database engine. SSMS screenshot shows a CHECK constraints listing query and results in the Northwind database.

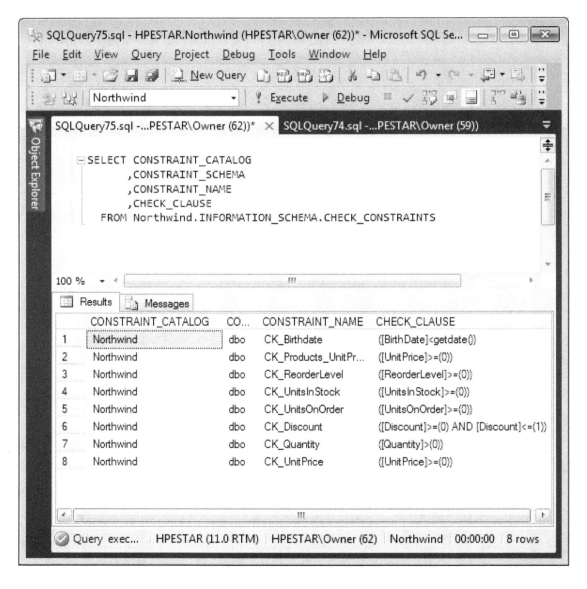

PRIMARY KEY & FOREIGN KEY Constraint Descriptions in Data Dictionary

Query to retrieve constraint descriptions (extended properties) for Product, SalesOrderHeader & SalesOrderDetail tables. Note: *description* not definition.

```
USE AdventureWorks2012;

-- UNION of 3 result sets
SELECT objtype AS ObjectType, 'Sales.SalesOrderHeader' AS TableName,
        objname as ObjectName, value AS [Description]
FROM fn_listextendedproperty (NULL, 'schema', 'Sales', 'table', 'SalesOrderHeader', 'constraint', default)
WHERE left(convert(varchar,value),7)='Foreign' or left(convert(varchar,value),7)='Primary'
UNION
SELECT objtype, 'Sales.SalesOrderDetail', objname,  value
FROM fn_listextendedproperty (NULL, 'schema', 'Sales', 'table', 'SalesOrderDetail', 'constraint', default)
WHERE left(convert(varchar,value),7)='Foreign' or left(convert(varchar,value),7)='Primary'
UNION
SELECT objtype, 'Production.Product', objname,  value
FROM fn_listextendedproperty (NULL, 'schema', 'Production', 'table', 'Product', 'constraint', default)
WHERE left(convert(varchar,value),7)='Foreign' or left(convert(varchar,value),7)='Primary'
ORDER BY TableName, ObjectName DESC;
GO
```

ObjectType	TableName	ObjectName	Description
CONSTRAINT	Production.Product	PK_Product_ProductID	Primary key (clustered) constraint
CONSTRAINT	Production.Product	FK_Product_UnitMeasure_WeightUnitMeasureCode	Foreign key constraint referencing UnitMeasure.UnitMeasureCode.
CONSTRAINT	Production.Product	FK_Product_UnitMeasure_SizeUnitMeasureCode	Foreign key constraint referencing UnitMeasure.UnitMeasureCode.
CONSTRAINT	Production.Product	FK_Product_ProductSubcategory_ProductSubcategoryID	Foreign key constraint referencing ProductSubcategory.ProductSubcategoryID.
CONSTRAINT	Production.Product	FK_Product_ProductModel_ProductModelID	Foreign key constraint referencing ProductModel.ProductModelID.
CONSTRAINT	Sales.SalesOrderDetail	PK_SalesOrderDetail_SalesOrderID_SalesOrderDetailID	Primary key (clustered) constraint
CONSTRAINT	Sales.SalesOrderDetail	FK_SalesOrderDetail_SpecialOfferProduct_SpecialOfferIDProductID	Foreign key constraint referencing SpecialOfferProduct.SpecialOfferIDProductID.
CONSTRAINT	Sales.SalesOrderDetail	FK_SalesOrderDetail_SalesOrderHeader_SalesOrderID	Foreign key constraint referencing SalesOrderHeader.PurchaseOrderID.
CONSTRAINT	Sales.SalesOrderHeader	PK_SalesOrderHeader_SalesOrderID	Primary key (clustered) constraint
CONSTRAINT	Sales.SalesOrderHeader	FK_SalesOrderHeader_ShipMethod_ShipMethodID	Foreign key constraint referencing ShipMethod.ShipMethodID.
CONSTRAINT	Sales.SalesOrderHeader	FK_SalesOrderHeader_SalesTerritory_TerritoryID	Foreign key constraint referencing SalesTerritory.TerritoryID.
CONSTRAINT	Sales.SalesOrderHeader	FK_SalesOrderHeader_SalesPerson_SalesPersonID	Foreign key constraint referencing SalesPerson.SalesPersonID.
CONSTRAINT	Sales.SalesOrderHeader	FK_SalesOrderHeader_Customer_CustomerID	Foreign key constraint referencing Customer.CustomerID.
CONSTRAINT	Sales.SalesOrderHeader	FK_SalesOrderHeader_CurrencyRate_CurrencyRateID	Foreign key constraint referencing CurrencyRate.CurrencyRateID.
CONSTRAINT	Sales.SalesOrderHeader	FK_SalesOrderHeader_CreditCard_CreditCardID	Foreign key constraint referencing CreditCard.CreditCardID.
CONSTRAINT	Sales.SalesOrderHeader	FK_SalesOrderHeader_Address_ShipToAddressID	Foreign key constraint referencing Address.AddressID.
CONSTRAINT	Sales.SalesOrderHeader	FK_SalesOrderHeader_Address_BillToAddressID	Foreign key constraint referencing Address.AddressID.

CHAPTER 4: Basic Concepts of Client-Server Computing

View - Database Object

A SELECT query, with some restrictions, can be repackaged as view and thus become a server-side object, a coveted status, from "homeless" to "mansion". The creation of view is very simple, basically a name assignment is required as shown in the following demonstration. As soon as the CREATE VIEW statement is executed successfully the query, unknown to the SQL Server so far, becomes an "official" SQL Server database object, stored in the database. A view, a virtual table, can be used just like a table in SELECT queries. A note about the query: **the column aliases FirstAuthor and SecondAuthor cannot be used in the WHERE clause, only in the ORDER BY clause if present.**

SELECT results from views require ORDER BY if sorting is desired. There is no way around it.

```
USE pubs;
GO


CREATE VIEW vAuthorsInSameCity
AS
SELECT          FirstAuthor       = CONCAT(au1.au_fname,' ', au1.au_lname),
                SecondAuthor      = CONCAT(au2.au_fname,' ', au2.au_lname),
                FirstCity         = au1.city,
                SecondCity        = au2.city
FROM    authors au1
     INNER JOIN authors au2
       ON au1.city = au2.city
WHERE   CONCAT(au1.au_fname,' ', au1.au_lname) < CONCAT(au2.au_fname,' ', au2.au_lname)
GO


SELECT * FROM vAuthorsInSameCity
ORDER BY FirstAuthor, SecondAuthor
GO
-- (13 row(s) affected) - Partial results.
```

FirstAuthor	SecondAuthor	FirstCity	SecondCity
Abraham Bennet	Cheryl Carson	Berkeley	Berkeley
Albert Ringer	Anne Ringer	Salt Lake City	Salt Lake City
Ann Dull	Sheryl Hunter	Palo Alto	Palo Alto
Dean Straight	Dirk Stringer	Oakland	Oakland
Dean Straight	Livia Karsen	Oakland	Oakland
Dean Straight	Marjorie Green	Oakland	Oakland
Dean Straight	Stearns MacFeather	Oakland	Oakland
Dirk Stringer	Livia Karsen	Oakland	Oakland

View Descriptions in Data Dictionary

Query to list view descriptions in selected schemas.

```
USE AdventureWorks2012;
SELECT   CONCAT('Sales.', objname COLLATE DATABASE_DEFAULT)              AS ViewName,
         value                                                           AS [Description]
FROM fn_listextendedproperty (NULL, 'schema', 'Sales', 'view', default, NULL, NULL)
UNION
SELECT   CONCAT('Production.', objname COLLATE DATABASE_DEFAULT),  value
FROM fn_listextendedproperty (NULL, 'schema', 'Production', 'view', default, NULL, NULL)
UNION
SELECT   CONCAT('HumanResources.', objname COLLATE DATABASE_DEFAULT),  value
FROM fn_listextendedproperty (NULL, 'schema', 'HumanResources', 'view', default, NULL, NULL)
UNION
SELECT   CONCAT('Person.', objname COLLATE DATABASE_DEFAULT),   value
FROM fn_listextendedproperty (NULL, 'schema', 'Person', 'view', default, NULL, NULL)
ORDER BY ViewName;  -- (18 row(s) affected) - Partial results.
```

ViewName	Description
HumanResources.vEmployee	Employee names and addresses.
HumanResources.vEmployeeDepartment	Returns employee name, title, and current department.
HumanResources.vEmployeeDepartmentHistory	Returns employee name and current and previous departments
HumanResources.vJobCandidate	Job candidate names and resumes.

CREATE Indexed View for Business Critical Queries

An indexed view is stored like a table unlike a standard view which is a virtual table with a query that is evaluated upon view invocation. Performance is the main benefit of an indexed view, but it comes at a cost: it slows down INSERTs and other operations in the underlying tables.

```
IF OBJECT_ID ('Sales.vSalesByDateByProduct', 'V') IS NOT NULL DROP VIEW Sales.vSalesByDateByProduct ;
GO
CREATE VIEW Sales.vSalesByDateByProduct WITH SCHEMABINDING  AS
   SELECT OrderDate, ProductNumber, SUM(LineTotal) AS TotalSales, COUNT_BIG(*) AS Items
   FROM Sales.SalesOrderDetail AS sod INNER JOIN Sales.SalesOrderHeader AS soh
     ON soh.SalesOrderID = sod.SalesOrderID   INNER JOIN Production.Product p ON sod.ProductID=p.ProductID
     GROUP BY OrderDate, ProductNumber;
GO
CREATE UNIQUE CLUSTERED INDEX idxVSalesCI ON Sales.vSalesByDateByProduct (OrderDate, ProductNumber);
GO
SELECT * FROM Sales.vSalesByDateByProduct ORDER BY OrderDate, ProductNumber;
GO  -- (26878 row(s) affected) - Partial results.
```

OrderDate	ProductNumber	TotalSales	Items
2005-07-01 00:00:00.000	BK-M82B-38	44549.868000	7
2005-07-01 00:00:00.000	BK-M82B-42	32399.904000	8
2005-07-01 00:00:00.000	BK-M82B-44	46574.862000	7

CHAPTER 4: Basic Concepts of Client-Server Computing

Graphical View Designer

A view can be designed graphically or an existing view altered by using the Design option on the
View drop-down menu in SSMS Object Explorer. First we create a view, then enter the graphical
view designer to take a look.

```
USE [Northwind];
GO
CREATE VIEW [dbo].[ListOfProducts] AS
SELECT Categories.CategoryName as Category, ProductName, CompanyName AS Supplier
FROM Categories          INNER JOIN Products  ON Categories.CategoryID = Products.CategoryID
                         INNER JOIN Suppliers  ON Suppliers.SupplierID = Products.SupplierID
WHERE (((Products.Discontinued)=0));
GO
```

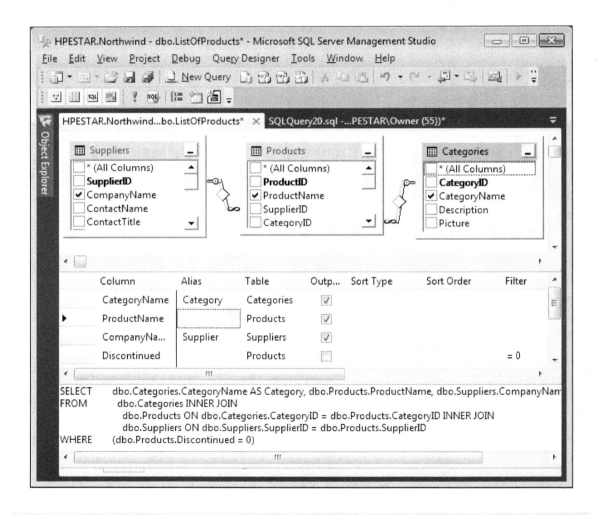

Stored Procedure: Server-Side Program

Stored procedures are T-SQL programs with optional input/output parameters. They vary from very simply to extremely complex. Following is the query which we will transform into a stored procedure, a server-side database object. Typical stored procedure returns table-like results to the client application software just like a SELECT query. That is though not a requirement.

```
USE AdventureWorks2012;
GO
SELECT        P.Name                    AS Product,
              L.Name                    AS [Inventory Location],
              SUM(PI.Quantity)          AS [Qty Available]
FROM Production.Product AS P
   INNER JOIN Production.ProductInventory AS PI
           ON P.ProductID = PI.ProductID
   INNER JOIN Production.Location AS L
           ON PI.LocationID = L.LocationID
   INNER JOIN Production.ProductSubcategory SC
           ON P.ProductSubcategoryID = SC.ProductSubcategoryID
WHERE SC.Name = 'Touring Bikes'
GROUP BY P.Name, L.Name
ORDER BY P.Name;
GO
-- (44 row(s) affected) - Partial results.
```

Product	Inventory Location	Qty Available
Touring-1000 Blue, 46	Final Assembly	85
Touring-1000 Blue, 46	Finished Goods Storage	99
Touring-1000 Blue, 50	Final Assembly	81
Touring-1000 Blue, 50	Finished Goods Storage	67
Touring-1000 Blue, 54	Final Assembly	60
Touring-1000 Blue, 54	Finished Goods Storage	73
Touring-1000 Blue, 60	Final Assembly	99
Touring-1000 Blue, 60	Finished Goods Storage	30
Touring-1000 Yellow, 46	Final Assembly	83
Touring-1000 Yellow, 46	Finished Goods Storage	65
Touring-1000 Yellow, 50	Final Assembly	62
Touring-1000 Yellow, 50	Finished Goods Storage	75
Touring-1000 Yellow, 54	Final Assembly	40
Touring-1000 Yellow, 54	Finished Goods Storage	35
Touring-1000 Yellow, 60	Final Assembly	100

Stored Procedure with Input Parameters

To make the stored procedure even more useful, we replace the literal 'Touring Bikes' with an input parameter.

```
CREATE PROC uspProductInventoryLocation @Subcategory nvarchar(50)
AS
BEGIN
SELECT          P.Name                          AS Product,
                L.Name                          AS [Inventory Location],
                SUM(PI.Quantity)                AS [Qty Available]
FROM Production.Product AS P
   INNER JOIN Production.ProductInventory AS PI
            ON P.ProductID = PI.ProductID
   INNER JOIN Production.Location AS L
            ON PI.LocationID = L.LocationID
   INNER JOIN Production.ProductSubcategory SC
            ON P.ProductSubcategoryID = SC.ProductSubcategoryID
WHERE SC.Name = @Subcategory
GROUP BY P.Name, L.Name
ORDER BY P.Name;
END
GO


-- Execute stored procedure with parameter
EXEC uspProductInventoryLocation 'Touring Bikes';
-- (44 row(s) affected)

EXEC uspProductInventoryLocation 'Mountain Bikes';        -- (64 row(s) affected) - Partial results.
```

Product	Inventory Location	Qty Available
Mountain-100 Black, 38	Final Assembly	56
Mountain-100 Black, 38	Finished Goods Storage	99
Mountain-100 Black, 42	Final Assembly	116
Mountain-100 Black, 42	Finished Goods Storage	78
Mountain-100 Black, 44	Final Assembly	100
Mountain-100 Black, 44	Finished Goods Storage	49
Mountain-100 Black, 48	Final Assembly	65
Mountain-100 Black, 48	Finished Goods Storage	88
Mountain-100 Silver, 38	Final Assembly	100
Mountain-100 Silver, 38	Finished Goods Storage	49
Mountain-100 Silver, 42	Final Assembly	65
Mountain-100 Silver, 42	Finished Goods Storage	88
Mountain-100 Silver, 44	Final Assembly	75
Mountain-100 Silver, 44	Finished Goods Storage	83
Mountain-100 Silver, 48	Final Assembly	102

Stored Procedure Descriptions in Data Dictionary

Query to list stored procedure descriptions in selected schemas.

```
USE AdventureWorks2012;

SELECT
        CONCAT('dbo.', objname COLLATE DATABASE_DEFAULT)                    AS SprocName,
        value                                                              AS [Description]
FROM fn_listextendedproperty (NULL, 'schema', 'dbo', 'procedure', default, NULL, NULL)
WHERE LEN(convert(nvarchar(max),value)) > 4
UNION
SELECT
        CONCAT('dbo.', objname COLLATE DATABASE_DEFAULT),
        value
FROM fn_listextendedproperty (NULL, 'schema', 'HumanResources', 'procedure', default, NULL, NULL)
ORDER BY SprocName;
```

SprocName	Description
dbo.uspGetBillOfMaterials	Stored procedure using a recursive query to return a multi-level bill of material for the specified ProductID.
dbo.uspGetEmployeeManagers	Stored procedure using a recursive query to return the direct and indirect managers of the specified employee.
dbo.uspGetManagerEmployees	Stored procedure using a recursive query to return the direct and indirect employees of the specified manager.
dbo.uspGetWhereUsedProductID	Stored procedure using a recursive query to return all components or assemblies that directly or indirectly use the specified ProductID.
dbo.uspLogError	Logs error information in the ErrorLog table about the error that caused execution to jump to the CATCH block of a TRY...CATCH construct. Should be executed from within the scope of a CATCH block otherwise it will return without inserting error information.
dbo.uspPrintError	Prints error information about the error that caused execution to jump to the CATCH block of a TRY...CATCH construct. Should be executed from within the scope of a CATCH block otherwise it will return without printing any error information.
dbo.uspUpdateEmployeeHireInfo	Updates the Employee table and inserts a new row in the EmployeePayHistory table with the values specified in the input parameters.
dbo.uspUpdateEmployeeLogin	Updates the Employee table with the values specified in the input parameters for the given BusinessEntityID.
dbo.uspUpdateEmployeePersonalInfo	Updates the Employee table with the values specified in the input parameters for the given EmployeeID.

Trigger: Event Fired Server-Side Program

Trigger is like a stored procedure with four differences:

- ➤ Trigger is fired by an event such as table insert not by a call like a stored procedure.
- ➤ Trigger has the deleted (old row copy) and inserted (new row copy) tables available.
- ➤ Trigger does not have input/output parameter option.
- ➤ Trigger never returns table-like results.

Trigger to synchronize data in StateTaxFreeBondArchive table if data is inserted or updated in the StateTaxFreeBond table.

```
CREATE TRIGGER trgFillInMissingCouponRate

ON [dbo].StateTaxFreeBond

FOR INSERT,UPDATE

AS

BEGIN

    UPDATE StateTaxFreeBondArchive

      SET CouponRate = isnull(i.CouponRate,m.CouponRate)

    FROM StateTaxFreeBondArchive m

      INNER JOIN inserted i

        ON m.MBCID = i.MBCID

END
GO
```

Once a trigger is compiled, it is active and working silently in the background whenever insert, update or delete event fires it up.

It is important to note that there is a downside to the trigger "stealth" operation: if a trigger is dropped , it may not be noticed as part of the day-to-day operation. This behaviour is unlike stored procedure whereby if dropped, it causes error in the calling application software which can be noticed by users.

Function: Read-Only Server-Side Program

A user-defined function is also a program like a stored procedure, however, **no database change can be performed within a function, read only**. The database can be changed both in a trigger and a stored procedure. The following T-SQL script demonstrates the creation and use of a table-valued user-defined function. The other function type is scalar-valued, returns only a single value.

```
CREATE FUNCTION dbo.ufnSplitCommaDelimitedIntegerString (@NumberList nvarchar(max))
RETURNS @SplitList TABLE ( Element INT )
AS
 BEGIN
   DECLARE @Pointer   int,
        @Element nvarchar(32)
   SET @NumberList = LTRIM(RTRIM(@NumberList))
   IF ( RIGHT(@NumberList, 1) != ',' )
    SET @NumberList=@NumberList + ','
   SET @Pointer = CHARINDEX(',', @NumberList, 1)
   IF REPLACE(@NumberList, ',', '') <> ''
    BEGIN
      WHILE ( @Pointer > 0 )
       BEGIN
         SET @Element = LTRIM(RTRIM(LEFT(@NumberList, @Pointer - 1)))
         IF ( @Element <> '' )
          INSERT INTO @SplitList
          VALUES    (CONVERT(int, @Element))
         SET @NumberList = RIGHT(@NumberList,
               LEN(@NumberList) - @Pointer  )
         SET @Pointer = CHARINDEX(',', @NumberList, 1)
       END
    END
   RETURN
 END;
GO
SELECT * FROM  dbo.ufnSplitCommaDelimitedIntegerString ('1, 2, 4, 8, 16, 32, 64, 128, 256');
```

Element
1
2
4
8
16
32
64
128
256

CHAPTER 4: Basic Concepts of Client-Server Computing

User-Defined Function Descriptions in Data Dictionary

Query to list user-defined function descriptions in the default "dbo" schema. "dbo" stands for database owner, a database role.

```
USE AdventureWorks2012;
GO

SELECT
        CONCAT('dbo.', objname COLLATE DATABASE_DEFAULT)         AS UDFName,
        value                                                     AS [Description]
FROM fn_listextendedproperty (NULL, 'schema', 'dbo', 'function', default, NULL, NULL)
WHERE LEN(convert(nvarchar(max),value)) > 4
ORDER BY UDFName;
GO
```

UDFName	Description
dbo.ufnGetAccountingEndDate	Scalar function used in the uSalesOrderHeader trigger to set the starting account date.
dbo.ufnGetAccountingStartDate	Scalar function used in the uSalesOrderHeader trigger to set the ending account date.
dbo.ufnGetContactInformation	Table value function returning the first name, last name, job title and contact type for a given contact.
dbo.ufnGetDocumentStatusText	Scalar function returning the text representation of the Status column in the Document table.
dbo.ufnGetProductDealerPrice	Scalar function returning the dealer price for a given product on a particular order date.
dbo.ufnGetProductListPrice	Scalar function returning the list price for a given product on a particular order date.
dbo.ufnGetProductStandardCost	Scalar function returning the standard cost for a given product on a particular order date.
dbo.ufnGetPurchaseOrderStatusText	Scalar function returning the text representation of the Status column in the PurchaseOrderHeader table.
dbo.ufnGetSalesOrderStatusText	Scalar function returning the text representation of the Status column in the SalesOrderHeader table.
dbo.ufnGetStock	Scalar function returning the quantity of inventory in LocationID 6 (Miscellaneous Storage)for a specified ProductID.
dbo.ufnLeadingZeros	Scalar function used by the Sales.Customer table to help set the account number

Sequence - Database Object

The INT IDENTITY(1,1) function commonly used as **SURROGATE PRIMARY KEY** is limited to the host table. Sequence object, new in SQL Server 2012, can be shared by tables and programs. T-SQL script to demonstrate how two tables can share an integer sequence.

```
USE AdventureWorks2012;
GO
CREATE SEQUENCE CustomerSequence as INT
START WITH 1  INCREMENT BY 1;
GO
CREATE TABLE LONDONCustomer
(
        CustomerID      INT PRIMARY KEY,
        Name            NVARCHAR(64) UNIQUE,
        ModifiedDate    DATE default (CURRENT_TIMESTAMP)    );
GO
CREATE TABLE NYCCustomer
(
        CustomerID      INT PRIMARY KEY,
        Name            NVARCHAR(64) UNIQUE,
        ModifiedDate    DATE default (CURRENT_TIMESTAMP)    );
GO
INSERT NYCCustomer (CustomerID, Name)
VALUES
        (NEXT VALUE FOR CustomerSequence, 'Richard Blackstone'),
        (NEXT VALUE FOR CustomerSequence, 'Anna Smithfield');
GO
SELECT * FROM NYCCustomer;
```

CustomerID	Name	ModifiedDate
1	Richard Blackstone	2016-07-18
2	Anna Smithfield	2016-07-18

```
INSERT LONDONCustomer (CustomerID, Name)
VALUES
        (NEXT VALUE FOR CustomerSequence, 'Kevin Lionheart'),
        (NEXT VALUE FOR CustomerSequence, 'Linda Wakefield');
GO

SELECT * FROM LONDONCustomer;
```

CustomerID	Name	ModifiedDate
3	Kevin Lionheart	2016-07-18
4	Linda Wakefield	2016-07-18

CHAPTER 4: Basic Concepts of Client-Server Computing

ROW_NUMBER() and Ranking Functions

Ranking functions (window functions), introduced with SQL Server 2005, provide sequencing and ranking items in a partition or all. ROW_NUMBER() (sequence) function is the most used.

```
SELECT  CustomerID,
        CONVERT(date, OrderDate)                        AS OrderDate,
        RANK() OVER (    PARTITION BY CustomerID
                         ORDER BY OrderDate DESC)        AS RankNo
FROM  AdventureWorks2012.Sales.SalesOrderHeader
ORDER  BY CustomerID,  RankNo;
GO
-- (31465 row(s) affected) - Partial results.
```

CustomerID	OrderDate	RankNo
11014	2007-11-01	1
11014	2007-09-24	2
11015	2007-07-22	1
11016	2007-08-13	1
11017	2008-04-16	1
11017	2007-07-05	2
11017	2005-07-15	3
11018	2008-04-26	1
11018	2007-07-20	2
11018	2005-07-20	3
11019	2008-07-15	1
11019	2008-07-14	2
11019	2008-06-12	3
11019	2008-06-02	4
11019	2008-06-01	5
11019	2008-04-28	6
11019	2008-04-19	7
11019	2008-03-22	8
11019	2008-03-11	9
11019	2008-02-23	10
11019	2008-01-24	11
11019	2007-11-26	12
11019	2007-11-09	13
11019	2007-10-30	14
11019	2007-09-14	15
11019	2007-09-05	16
11019	2007-08-16	17
11020	2007-07-02	1

Partition data by CustomerID and rank it OrderDate DESC (most recent orders first).

```
SELECT *
FROM   (SELECT CustomerID,
           CONVERT(date, OrderDate)          AS OrderDate,
           RANK()  OVER (
               PARTITION BY CustomerID
               ORDER BY OrderDate DESC)       AS RankNo
       FROM   AdventureWorks2012.Sales.SalesOrderHeader) x -- derived table
WHERE  RankNo  BETWEEN 1 AND 4
ORDER  BY CustomerID;
GO
-- (29383 row(s) affected)  - Partial results.
```

CustomerID	OrderDate	RankNo
11675	2007-08-13	1
11675	2006-04-27	2
11676	2008-06-11	1
11676	2008-02-21	2
11677	2008-06-02	1
11677	2008-03-24	2
11677	2008-03-17	3
11677	2008-03-07	4
11678	2007-08-09	1
11678	2006-04-12	2
11679	2008-06-01	1
11679	2008-04-15	2
11680	2008-07-22	1
11680	2008-03-04	2
11681	2008-05-28	1
11681	2007-09-08	2
11682	2008-06-11	1
11682	2008-03-08	2
11683	2007-08-11	1
11683	2006-04-07	2
11684	2008-06-14	1
11684	2008-01-02	2
11685	2008-06-15	1
11685	2007-09-12	2
11686	2007-10-26	1
11686	2007-09-09	2
11687	2007-12-23	1
11687	2007-10-14	2
11688	2007-08-18	1
11688	2006-04-04	2
11689	2008-03-05	1
11689	2008-02-27	2

CHAPTER 4: Basic Concepts of Client-Server Computing

Query to compare RANK, DENSE_RANK and NTILE.

```
USE AdventureWorks;

SELECT c.AccountNumber                          AS CustAccount,
    FLOOR(h.SubTotal / 1000)                     AS [SubTotal (Thousands $)],
    ROW_NUMBER() OVER(
        ORDER BY FLOOR(h.SubTotal /1000) DESC)    AS RowNumber,
    RANK() OVER(
        ORDER BY FLOOR(h.SubTotal /1000) DESC)   AS Rank,
    DENSE_RANK() OVER(
        ORDER BY FLOOR(h.SubTotal /1000) DESC)   AS DenseRank,
    NTILE(5) OVER(
        ORDER BY FLOOR(h.SubTotal /1000) DESC)   AS NTile
FROM   Sales.Customer c
    INNER JOIN Sales.SalesOrderHeader h
        ON c.CustomerID = h.CustomerID
    INNER JOIN Sales.SalesTerritory t
        ON h.TerritoryID = t.TerritoryID
WHERE  t.Name = 'Germany'
        AND OrderDate >= '20040101' AND OrderDate  <  DATEADD(yy, 1, '20040101' )
        AND SubTotal >= 4000.0
ORDER  BY RowNumber;
```

CustAccount	SubTotal (Thousands $)	RowNumber	Rank	DenseRank	NTile
AW00000230	100.00	1	1	1	1
AW00000230	88.00	2	2	2	1
AW00000302	77.00	3	3	3	1
AW00000320	68.00	4	4	4	1
AW00000536	68.00	5	4	4	1
AW00000536	64.00	6	6	5	1
AW00000266	58.00	7	7	6	1
AW00000302	44.00	8	8	7	2
AW00000687	43.00	9	9	8	2
AW00000482	36.00	10	10	9	2
AW00000176	36.00	11	10	9	2
AW00000464	35.00	12	12	10	2
AW00000320	35.00	13	12	10	2
AW00000176	34.00	14	14	11	2
AW00000464	34.00	15	14	11	3

CHAPTER 4: Basic Concepts of Client-Server Computing

Dynamic SQL To Soar Beyond the Limits of Static SQL

Static (regular) T-SQL syntax does not accept variables at all places in a query. With dynamic SQL we can overcome the limitation. Dynamic SQL script uses table list metadata from the INFORMATION_SCHEMA.TABLES system view to build a COUNT() query for all tables. COUNT(*) returns 4 bytes integer. For large values COUNT_BIG() returns an 8 bytes integer.

```
DECLARE @SQL nvarchar(max) = '', @Schema sysname, @Table sysname;
SELECT TOP 20 @SQL = CONCAT(@SQL , 'SELECT ''',QUOTENAME(TABLE_SCHEMA),'.',
        QUOTENAME(TABLE_NAME),'''',
        '= COUNT(*) FROM ', QUOTENAME(TABLE_SCHEMA),'.',QUOTENAME(TABLE_NAME) , ';',
CHAR(10))
FROM AdventureWorks2012.INFORMATION_SCHEMA.TABLES
WHERE TABLE_TYPE='BASE TABLE';
PRINT @SQL;          -- Test & debug - Partial results.
```

```
SELECT '[Production].[ScrapReason]'= COUNT(*) FROM [Production].[ScrapReason];
SELECT '[HumanResources].[Shift]'= COUNT(*) FROM [HumanResources].[Shift];
SELECT '[Production].[ProductCategory]'= COUNT(*) FROM [Production].[ProductCategory];
SELECT '[Purchasing].[ShipMethod]'= COUNT(*) FROM [Purchasing].[ShipMethod];
SELECT '[Production].[ProductCostHistory]'= COUNT(*) FROM [Production].[ProductCostHistory];
SELECT '[Production].[ProductDescription]'= COUNT(*) FROM [Production].[ProductDescription];
SELECT '[Sales].[ShoppingCartItem]'= COUNT(*) FROM [Sales].[ShoppingCartItem];
SELECT '[Production].[ProductDocument]'= COUNT(*) FROM [Production].[ProductDocument];
SELECT '[dbo].[DatabaseLog]'= COUNT(*) FROM [dbo].[DatabaseLog];
SELECT '[Production].[ProductInventory]'= COUNT(*) FROM [Production].[ProductInventory];
```

```
EXEC sp_executesql @SQL   -- Dynamic SQL query execution
-- Partial results.
```

```
[Production].[ScrapReason]
16

[HumanResources].[Shift]
3

[Production].[ProductCategory]
4

[Purchasing].[ShipMethod]
5
```

CHAPTER 4: Basic Concepts of Client-Server Computing

Built-in System Functions

SQL Server T-SQL language has a large collection of system functions such as date & time, string and math function. The nested REPLACE string function can be used to remove unwanted characters from a string.

```
DECLARE @text nvarchar(128) = '#1245! $99^@';
SELECT REPLACE(REPLACE(REPLACE(REPLACE(REPLACE(REPLACE(REPLACE(REPLACE(REPLACE(@text,
     '!',''),'@',''),'#',''),'$',''),'%',''),'^',''),'&',''),'*',''),' ','');      -- 124599
```

All the system function are listed in SSMS Object Explorer under the Programmability tab.

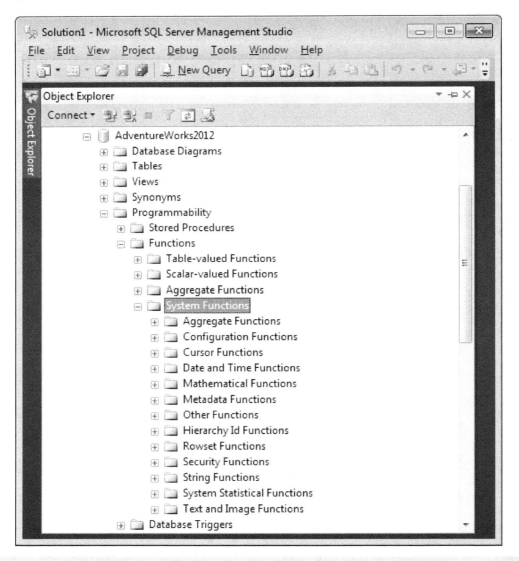

Local Variables & Table Variables in T-SQL

Local variables with different data types have scope of a batch or a stored procedure/trigger/function. Note that a "GO" in T-SQL script indicates end of batch, therefore the end of scope for local variables. Table variable is a virtual table with similar scope to local variable. Script to demonstrate local and table variables.

```
DECLARE @i INT;  SET @i = 999;

SELECT @i + @i;
-- 1998

SELECT @i = 555;  -- assignment
SELECT @i + @i;
GO
-- 1110

DECLARE @i INT = 999;              -- new in SQL Server 2008
SET @i += 1;                       -- new in SQL Server 2008

SELECT @i;
GO
-- 1000

DECLARE @OrderShipperJunction TABLE                     -- Table variable
  (
    ShipperID            SMALLINT IDENTITY ( 1, 1 ) PRIMARY KEY,
    ShipperName          NVARCHAR(64),
    PurchaseOrderID      INT,
    ShipDate             DATE DEFAULT (CURRENT_TIMESTAMP),
    FreightCost          SMALLMONEY
  ) ;
INSERT @OrderShipperJunction
    (ShipperName,
     PurchaseOrderID,
     FreightCost)
VALUES('Custom Motor Bike Distributor',      11111,     177.34)

SELECT * FROM   @OrderShipperJunction
GO
```

ShipperID	ShipperName	PurchaseOrderID	ShipDate	FreightCost
1	Custom Motor Bike Distributor	11111	2016-07-18	177.34

CHAPTER 4: Basic Concepts of Client-Server Computing

Metadata Visibility Through System Views

The system views provide SQL Server and database metadata which can be used just for viewing in SSMS Object Explorer or programmatically in T-SQL scripts. The system views are based on system tables which are no longer accessible since SQL Server 2005. The system view sys.objects contains all the basic info on each and every user objects in the database with the exception of indexes. Query to retrieve partial data form sys.objects system view.

```
select
   s.name                    as [Schema],
   o.name                    as [Name],
   o.type_desc               as [Type],
   o.create_date             as CreateDate
from   sys.objects o
         inner join sys.schemas s
           on s.schema_id = o.schema_id
where is_ms_shipped = 0
order by [Type], [Schema], [Name]
-- (722 row(s) affected)  -  Partial results.
```

Schema	Name	Type	CreateDate
HumanResources	Department	USER_TABLE	2012-03-14 13:14:19.267
HumanResources	Employee	USER_TABLE	2012-03-14 13:14:19.303
HumanResources	EmployeeDepartmentHistory	USER_TABLE	2012-03-14 13:14:19.313
HumanResources	EmployeePayHistory	USER_TABLE	2012-03-14 13:14:19.320
HumanResources	JobCandidate	USER_TABLE	2012-03-14 13:14:19.337
HumanResources	Shift	USER_TABLE	2012-03-14 13:14:19.593
Person	Address	USER_TABLE	2012-03-14 13:14:19.140
Person	AddressType	USER_TABLE	2012-03-14 13:14:19.150
Person	BusinessEntity	USER_TABLE	2012-03-14 13:14:19.183
Person	BusinessEntityAddress	USER_TABLE	2012-03-14 13:14:19.190
Person	BusinessEntityContact	USER_TABLE	2012-03-14 13:14:19.197
Person	ContactType	USER_TABLE	2012-03-14 13:14:19.207
Person	CountryRegion	USER_TABLE	2012-03-14 13:14:19.220
Person	EmailAddress	USER_TABLE	2012-03-14 13:14:19.290
Person	Password	USER_TABLE	2012-03-14 13:14:19.350
Person	Person	USER_TABLE	2012-03-14 13:14:19.357
Person	PersonPhone	USER_TABLE	2012-03-14 13:14:19.370
Person	PhoneNumberType	USER_TABLE	2012-03-14 13:14:19.377
Person	StateProvince	USER_TABLE	2012-03-14 13:14:19.623
Production	BillOfMaterials	USER_TABLE	2012-03-14 13:14:19.170
Production	Culture	USER_TABLE	2012-03-14 13:14:19.237

ariationsaratedime

Constructing T-SQL Identifiers

Identifiers are the names given to SQL Server & database objects such as linked servers, tables, views or stored procedures.

Very simple rule: **do not include any special character in an identifier other than single underscore (_). Double underscore in an identifier inevitably leads to confusion, loss of database developer productivity.**

Creating good identifiers helps with productivity in database development, administration and maintenance. Using names AccountsPayable1 and AccountsPayable2 as variations for AccountsPayable is not good because the 1,2 suffixes are meaningless. On the other hand AccountsPayableLondon & AccountsPayableNYC are good, meaningful names. The list of identifiers can be enumerated from AdventureWorks2012.sys.objects.

SELECT name FROM AdventureWorks2012.sys.objects   ORDER BY name; -- (820 row(s) affected)

Selected results with comments.

Identifier(name)	Style Comment
Account	single word
AddressType	double words CamelCase style
BillOfMaterials	CamelCase (also known as Pascal case)
BusinessEntityContact	CamelCase
CK__ImageStore__67152DD3	double underscore separator, CK prefix for CHECK CONSTRAINT
CK_Document_Status	single underscore separator
CK_EmployeeDepartmentHistory_EndDate	mixed - CamelCase and underscore
DF__ImageStor__is_sy__75634D2A	database engine (system) generated name
sp_creatediagram	old-fashioned, sp prefix for system procedure
syscscolsegments	old-fashioned with abbreviations
ufnGetProductDealerPrice	Hungarian naming, ufn stands for user(-defined) function
vSalesPersonSalesByFiscalYears	Hungarian naming, v prefix is for view

The Use of [] - Square Brackets in Identifiers

Each identifier can be enclosed in square brackets, but not required. If the identifier is the same as a T-SQL reserved keyword, then it is required. Square brackets are also required when the identifier includes a special character such as space. Double quotes can be used also but that becomes very confusing when single quotes are present. The use of brackets is demonstrated in the following T-SQL script.

```
USE Northwind;

-- Syntax error without brackets since table name has space
SELECT * FROM Order Details;
/* ERROR
Msg 156, Level 15, State 1, Line 3
Incorrect syntax near the keyword 'Order'.
*/

-- Valid statement with brackets around table name
SELECT * FROM [Order Details];
-- (2155 row(s) affected)

-- Create and populate table with SELECT INTO
-- Error since ORDER is a reserved keyword
SELECT * INTO Order FROM Orders;
/* ERROR
Msg 156, Level 15, State 1, Line 1
Incorrect syntax near the keyword 'Order'.
*/

-- With brackets, query is valid
SELECT * INTO [Order] FROM Orders;
-- (830 row(s) affected)
```

When a database object is scripted out in SSMS Object Explore, the identifiers are surrounded with square brackets even when not needed as shown in the following demonstration.

```
CREATE TABLE [dbo].[Order Details](
        [OrderID] [int] NOT NULL,
        [ProductID] [int] NOT NULL,
        [UnitPrice] [money] NOT NULL,
        [Quantity] [smallint] NOT NULL,
        [Discount] [real] NOT NULL,
CONSTRAINT [PK_Order_Details] PRIMARY KEY CLUSTERED
(       [OrderID] ASC,
        [ProductID] ASC));
```

CHAPTER 5: Fundamentals of Relational Database Design

Logical Data Modeling

Logical data modeling is the first step in database design. The task can be carried out by systems analysts, subject-matter experts, database designers or lead database developers. Small budget projects usually settle for an experienced database developer in the design role. The database design team spends time with the future users (stakeholders) cf the database to find out the expectations and requirements for the new database. As soon as the design team has some basic idea of functional requirements, the iterative process continues with discussing entities (corresponds to tables in the database) and their relationships with the users. For example the Order entity has many to many relationship to the Product entity. A Product occurs in many orders, and an Order may hold many products.

Physical Data Modeling

Physical Data Modeling is the process of translating the logical data model into actual database tables and related objects such as PRIMARY KEY and FOREIGN KEY constraints. If a software tool was used to design the logical data model then the forward engineering feature can be applied to generate SQL scripts to create tables and related database objects. **An important step in this process is the design of indexes to support SQL query performance**. Example for Data Warehouse dimension table implementation.

CHAPTER 5: Fundamentals of Relational Database Design

Column Definitions for the FactInternetSales Table

Table columns for a fact table in AdventureWorksDW2012 database. PK stands for PRIMARY KEY, FK for FOREGN KEY. The PRIMARY KEY is a composite of 2 columns: SalesOrderNumber and SalesOrderLineNumber.

The screen image is from SSMS Object Explorer.

```
□ ▦ dbo.FactInternetSales
  □ ▢ Columns
        ⚷ ProductKey (FK, int, not null)
        ⚷ OrderDateKey (FK, int, not null)
        ⚷ DueDateKey (FK, int, not null)
        ⚷ ShipDateKey (FK, int, not null)
        ⚷ CustomerKey (FK, int, not null)
        ⚷ PromotionKey (FK, int, not null)
        ⚷ CurrencyKey (FK, int, not null)
        ⚷ SalesTerritoryKey (FK, int, not null)
        ⚷ SalesOrderNumber (PK, nvarchar(20), not null)
        ⚷ SalesOrderLineNumber (PK, tinyint, not null)
        ▤ RevisionNumber (tinyint, not null)
        ▤ OrderQuantity (smallint, not null)
        ▤ UnitPrice (money, not null)
        ▤ ExtendedAmount (money, not null)
        ▤ UnitPriceDiscountPct (float, not null)
        ▤ DiscountAmount (float, not null)
        ▤ ProductStandardCost (money, not null)
        ▤ TotalProductCost (money, not null)
        ▤ SalesAmount (money, not null)
        ▤ TaxAmt (money, not null)
        ▤ Freight (money, not null)
        ▤ CarrierTrackingNumber (nvarchar(25), null)
        ▤ CustomerPONumber (nvarchar(25), null)
        ▤ OrderDate (datetime, null)
        ▤ DueDate (datetime, null)
        ▤ ShipDate (datetime, null)
```

Table Column Data Types

Exact Numerics

bigint	8 byte signed integer	-- Exact Numerics
bit	Boolean	
decimal	5 - 17 bytes decimal number with variable precision	
int	4 byte signed integer	
money	8 byte with ten-thousandth accuracy	
numeric	Same as decimal	
smallint	2 byte signed integer	
smallmoney	4 byte with ten-thousandth accuracy	
tinyint	1 byte signed integer	

Approximate Numerics

float	4 - 8 byte floating point	-- Approximate Numerics
real	4 byte floating point	

Date and Time

date	3 byte date only
datetime	8 byte date & time
datetime2	6 - 8 byte date & time
datetimeoffset	10 byte date & time with time zone
smalldatetime	4 byte date & time
time	5 byte time only

Character Strings

char	Fixed length ASCII character storage - 1 byte for each character -- Character String
text	Variable-length ASCII data with a maximum string length of 2^31-1 (deprecated)
varchar	Variable length ASCII character storage

Unicode Character Strings

nchar	Fixed length UNICODE character storage - 2 bytes for each character
ntext	Variable-length UNICODE data with a maximum string length of 2^30-1 (deprecated)
nvarchar	Variable length UNICODE character storage

Binary Strings

binary	Fixed-length binary data with maximum storage size of 2^31-1 bytes -- Binary String
image	Variable-length binary data with maximum storage size of 2^31-1 bytes (deprecated)
varbinary	Variable-length binary data with maximum storage size of 2^31-1 bytes

Other Data Types

cursor	Contains a reference to a cursor - not for column use
hierarchyid	Represents a position in a tree hierarchy, typically a few bytes up to 892 bytes
sql_variant	Stores values of various SQL Server data types, maximum length of 8016 bytes
table	Store a result set for processing at a later time, not for columns
timestamp	8 byte generated binary number, mechanism for version-stamping table rows
uniqueidentifier	16 byte GUID - Globally Unique Identifier
xml	Stores XML data up to 2GB in size

CHAPTER 5: Fundamentals of Relational Database Design

Date Type max_length, precision, scale & collation_name Listing
Database metadata on data types can be found in types system view.

```
SELECT          name, system_type_id, max_length, precision, scale,
                isnull(collation_name, SPACE(0)) AS collation_name
FROM AdventureWorks2012.sys.types WHERE schema_id = 4 ORDER BY name;
```

name	system_type_id	max_length	precision	scale	collation_name
bigint	127	8	19	0	
binary	173	8000	0	0	
bit	104	1	1	0	
char	175	8000	0	0	SQL_Latin1_General_CP1_CI_AS
date	40	3	10	0	
datetime	61	8	23	3	
datetime2	42	8	27	7	
datetimeoffset	43	10	34	7	
decimal	106	17	38	38	
float	62	8	53	0	
geography	240	-1	0	0	
geometry	240	-1	0	0	
hierarchyid	240	892	0	0	
image	34	16	0	0	
int	56	4	10	0	
money	60	8	19	4	
nchar	239	8000	0	0	SQL_Latin1_General_CP1_CI_AS
ntext	99	16	0	0	SQL_Latin1_General_CP1_CI_AS
numeric	108	17	38	38	
nvarchar	231	8000	0	0	SQL_Latin1_General_CP1_CI_AS
real	59	4	24	0	
smalldatetime	58	4	16	0	
smallint	52	2	5	0	
smallmoney	122	4	10	4	
sql_variant	98	8016	0	0	
sysname	231	256	0	0	SQL_Latin1_General_CP1_CI_AS
text	35	16	0	0	SQL_Latin1_General_CP1_CI_AS
time	41	5	16	7	
timestamp	189	8	0	0	
tinyint	48	1	3	0	
uniqueidentifier	36	16	0	0	
varbinary	165	8000	0	0	
varchar	167	8000	0	0	SQL_Latin1_General_CP1_CI_AS
xml	241	-1	0	0	

CHAPTER 5: *Fundamentals of Relational Database Design*

U.S. Default Collation SQL_Latin1_General_CP1_CI_AS

Interpretation:

- ➢ SQL collation not Windows
- ➢ Latin 1 alphabet
- ➢ Code page 1 for sorting
- ➢ Case insensitive
- ➢ Accent sensitive

SQL_Latin1_General_CP1_CI_AS is the default collation of SQL Server 2012 in the United States. Only a handful of experts around the world really understand collations. You first encounter with collation will probably be like the following error.

```
SELECT CONCAT('Production.', objname) AS TableName, value AS [Description]
FROM fn_listextendedproperty (NULL, 'schema', 'Production', 'table', default, NULL, NULL);
GO
/*  Msg 468, Level 16, State 9, Line 1
Cannot resolve the collation conflict between "SQL_Latin1_General_CP1_CI_AS" and
"Latin1_General_CI_AI" in the concat operation.
*/
```

The easiest fix in most collation error cases is placing COLLATE DATABASE_DEFAULT following the right most operator.

```
SELECT CONCAT('Production.', objname COLLATE DATABASE_DEFAULT) AS TableName,
               value AS [Description]
FROM fn_listextendedproperty (NULL, 'schema', 'Production', 'table', default, NULL, NULL);
```

There are a number of articles on the web which deal extensively with collations.

Collation is a column level property. Server and database collations are only defaults. To change the collation of a column, use ALTER TABLE.

```
-- SQL Server Change Column Collation
SELECT * INTO Product FROM AdventureWorks2012.Production.Product;
GO
ALTER TABLE Product ALTER COLUMN Name nvarchar(50) COLLATE SQL_Latin1_General_CP1_CS_AS null;
GO  -- (504 row(s) affected)
```

CHAPTER 5: Fundamentals of Relational Database Design

DATE & DATETIME Temporal Data Types

DATE data type has been introduced with SQL Server 2008. DATETIME on the other hand is around since the inception of SQL Server. A good deal of programming effort goes into supporting hundreds of different string date & time formats. Each country has its own string date formats adding more to the general confusion. As an example in the United States the mdy string date format is used. In the United Kingdom, the dmy format is used. When one looks at a date like 10/11/2015, it is not apparent which date format is it. In a globalized world the data flows freely from one country to another, frequently without adequate documentation, hence the loss of database developer productivity as related to date & time data issues. List of century (CCYY or YYYY) datetime conversions styles (stylenumber >= 100).

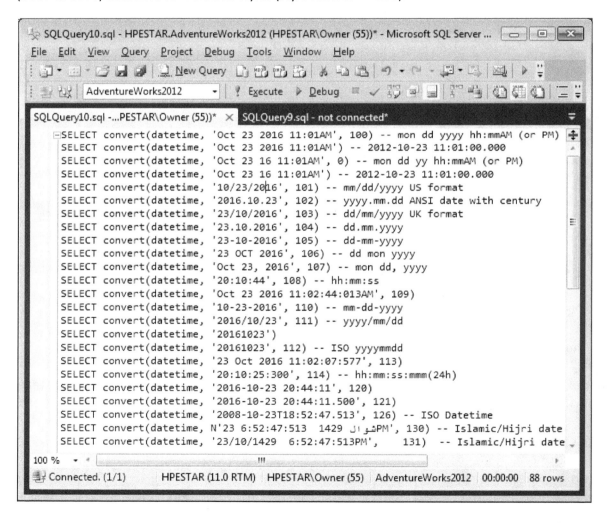

Two Ways of Commenting in T-SQL Scripts

Line comment is prefixed by "--". Multiple lines comment has to be enclosed with "/*" and "*/".

Exploring Database Schemas

A schema - introduced in SQL Server 2005 - is a single-level container of database objects to replace database object "owner" in previous SQL Server versions. **The default schema is "dbo", database owner**. Schemas can be used for functional separation of objects which may be essential in large databases with thousands of tables. The application schemas in AdventureWorks: HumanResources, Production, Purchasing, Sales, and Person. The word "schemas" also used in database terminology to mean table definition scripts or database diagram. Screenshot to display all the schemas in AdventureWorks2012 and to demonstrate the use of the CREATE SCHEMA statement. Database object reference in SQL Server 2012 is: "dbname.schemaname.objectname" like "AdventureWorks2012.Sales.SalesOrderheader".

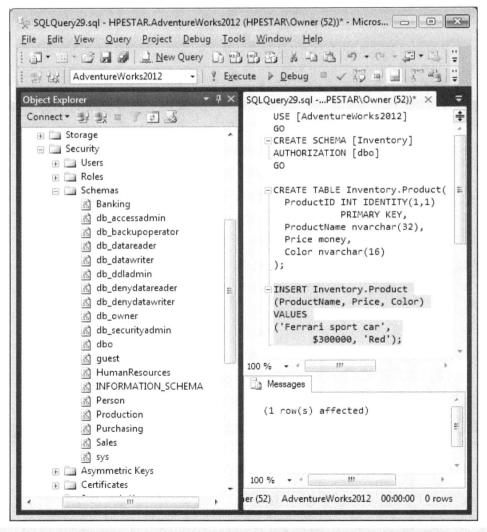

SCHEMA_NAME() Function

The SCHEMA_NAME() function can be used to obtain the name of a schema based on the schema_id parameter. Query to list all 3 database objects with the name 'Product" in 3 different schemas.

```
SELECT          CONCAT(SCHEMA_NAME(schema_id),'.',name) as ObjectName,
                name, object_id, schema_id, type, type_desc
FROM sys.objects
WHERE name = 'Product' ORDER BY ObjectName;
```

ObjectName	name	object_id	schema_id	type	type_desc
dbo.Product	Product	264388011	1	U	USER_TABLE
Inventory.Product	Product	1533964541	11	U	USER_TABLE
Production.Product	Product	1973582069	7	U	USER_TABLE

T-SQL query to display all the schemas in AdventureWorks2012.

```
SELECT s.*,  p.name as PrincipalName
FROM AdventureWorks2012.sys.schemas s
  INNER JOIN AdventureWorks2012.sys.database_principals p    ON s.principal_id = p.principal_id
ORDER BY principal_id, s.name;
```

name	schema_id	principal_id	PrincipalName
Banking	10	1	dbo
dbo	1	1	dbo
HumanResources	5	1	dbo
Inventory	11	1	dbo
Person	6	1	dbo
Production	7	1	dbo
Purchasing	8	1	dbo
Sales	9	1	dbo
guest	2	2	guest
INFORMATION_SCHEMA	3	3	INFORMATION_SCHEMA
sys	4	4	sys
db_owner	16384	16384	db_owner
db_accessadmin	16385	16385	db_accessadmin
db_securityadmin	16386	16386	db_securityadmin
db_ddladmin	16387	16387	db_ddladmin
db_backupoperator	16389	16389	db_backupoperator
db_datareader	16390	16390	db_datareader
db_datawriter	16391	16391	db_datawriter
db_denydatareader	16392	16392	db_denydatareader
db_denydatawriter	16393	16393	db_denydatawriter

CHAPTER 5: Fundamentals of Relational Database Design

Tables in HumanResources, Person & Purchasing Schemas
Query to list tables in the above schemas with data dictionary description.

```
USE AdventureWorks2012;
SELECT   CONCAT('Purchasing.', objname COLLATE DATABASE_DEFAULT)        AS TableName,
         value                                                          AS [Description]
FROM fn_listextendedproperty (NULL, 'schema', 'Purchasing', 'table', default, NULL, NULL)
UNION
SELECT   CONCAT('Person.', objname COLLATE DATABASE_DEFAULT)            AS TableName,
         value                                                          AS [Description]
FROM fn_listextendedproperty (NULL, 'schema', 'Person', 'table', default, NULL, NULL)
UNION
SELECT   CONCAT('HumanResources.', objname COLLATE DATABASE_DEFAULT) AS TableName,
         value                                                          AS [Description]
FROM fn_listextendedproperty (NULL, 'schema', 'HumanResources', 'table', default, NULL, NULL)
ORDER BY TableName;
```

TableName	Description
HumanResources.Department	Lookup table containing the departments within the Adventure Works Cycles company.
HumanResources.Employee	Employee information such as salary, department, and title.
HumanResources.EmployeeDepartmentHistory	Employee department transfers.
HumanResources.EmployeePayHistory	Employee pay history.
HumanResources.JobCandidate	Résumés submitted to Human Resources by job applicants.
HumanResources.Shift	Work shift lookup table.
Person.Address	Street address information for customers, employees, and vendors.
Person.AddressType	Types of addresses stored in the Address table.
Person.BusinessEntity	Source of the ID that connects vendors, customers, and employees with address and contact information.
Person.BusinessEntityAddress	Cross-reference table mapping customers, vendors, and employees to their addresses.
Person.BusinessEntityContact	Cross-reference table mapping stores, vendors, and employees to people
Person.ContactType	Lookup table containing the types of business entity contacts.
Person.CountryRegion	Lookup table containing the ISO standard codes for countries and regions.
Person.EmailAddress	Where to send a person email.
Person.Password	One way hashed authentication information
Person.Person	Human beings involved with AdventureWorks: employees, customer contacts, and vendor contacts.
Person.PersonPhone	Telephone number and type of a person.
Person.PhoneNumberType	Type of phone number of a person.
Person.StateProvince	State and province lookup table.
Purchasing.ProductVendor	Cross-reference table mapping vendors with the products they supply.
Purchasing.PurchaseOrderDetail	Individual products associated with a specific purchase order. See PurchaseOrderHeader.
Purchasing.PurchaseOrderHeader	General purchase order information. See PurchaseOrderDetail.
Purchasing.ShipMethod	Shipping company lookup table.
Purchasing.Vendor	Companies from whom Adventure Works Cycles purchases parts or other goods.

The CREATE TABLE Statement

Creates a table based on column name, data type & size specifications. Constraint and default information can be included as well, or alternately given as a separate ALTER TABLE statement.

Branch Banking Database with ON DELETE CASCADE

T-SQL script to create basic banking application tables. Preceding the first CREATE TABLE, we execute a CREATE SCHEMA to group the tables within one schema.

```
USE AdventureWorks2012;
GO

CREATE SCHEMA Banking;
GO


CREATE TABLE Banking.Branch
 (
   BranchID     INT IDENTITY ( 1, 1 ),
   BranchName   CHAR(32) NOT NULL UNIQUE,
   BranchCity   CHAR(32) NOT NULL,
   Assets       MONEY NOT NULL,
   ModifiedDate DATETIME DEFAULT (getdate()),
   PRIMARY KEY ( BranchID ),
 );

CREATE TABLE Banking.Account
 (
   AccountID     INT IDENTITY ( 1, 1 ) UNIQUE,
   BranchID      INT NOT NULL,
   AccountNumber CHAR(20) NOT NULL UNIQUE,
   AccountType   CHAR(12) NOT NULL CONSTRAINT ATC CHECK (AccountType IN ('C',  'S')),
   Balance       MONEY NOT NULL,
   ModifiedDate  DATETIME DEFAULT (getdate()),
   PRIMARY KEY ( AccountID ),
   FOREIGN KEY ( BranchID ) REFERENCES Banking.Branch(BranchID) ON DELETE   CASCADE
 );
```

-- T-SQL script continued

```
CREATE TABLE Banking.[Transaction]
 (
   TransactionID INT IDENTITY ( 1, 1 ) PRIMARY KEY,
   AccountID    INT NOT NULL,
   TranType     CHAR(1),
   Amount       MONEY,
   ModifiedDate  DATETIME DEFAULT (getdate()),
   UNIQUE ( AccountID, ModifiedDate),
   FOREIGN KEY ( AccountID ) REFERENCES Banking.Account(AccountID) ON DELETE    CASCADE
 );


CREATE TABLE Banking.Customer
 (
   CustomerID   INT IDENTITY ( 1, 1 ) PRIMARY KEY,
   Name       CHAR(32) NOT NULL,
   SSNo       CHAR(9) NOT NULL UNIQUE,
   [Type]     CHAR(20) NOT NULL,
   Street     VARCHAR(32) NOT NULL,
   City       CHAR(32) NOT NULL,
   [State]    CHAR(32) NOT NULL,
   Zip        CHAR(10) NOT NULL,
   Country    CHAR(32) NOT NULL,
   ModifiedDate DATETIME DEFAULT (getdate())
 );

CREATE TABLE Banking.Loan
 (
   LoanID      INT IDENTITY ( 1, 1 ) PRIMARY KEY,
   BranchID    INT NOT NULL REFERENCES Banking.Branch(BranchID) ON DELETE   CASCADE,
   LoanNumber   CHAR(20) NOT NULL UNIQUE,
   LoanType    VARCHAR(30) NOT NULL,
   Amount     MONEY NOT NULL,
   ModifiedDate DATETIME DEFAULT (getdate())
 );
```

-- T-SQL script continued

```
CREATE TABLE Banking.Depositor
 (
   CustomerID   INT NOT NULL,
   AccountID    INT NOT NULL,
   ModifiedDate DATETIME DEFAULT (getdate()),
   PRIMARY KEY ( CustomerID, AccountID ),
   FOREIGN KEY ( AccountID ) REFERENCES Banking.Account(AccountID) ON DELETE  CASCADE,
   FOREIGN KEY ( CustomerID ) REFERENCES Banking.Customer(CustomerID)
 );

CREATE TABLE Banking.Borrower
 (
   CustomerID   INT NOT NULL,
   LoanID       INT NOT NULL,
   ModifiedDate DATETIME DEFAULT (getdate()),
   PRIMARY KEY ( CustomerID, LoanID ),
   FOREIGN KEY ( CustomerID ) REFERENCES Banking.Customer(CustomerID),
   FOREIGN KEY ( LoanID ) REFERENCES Banking.Loan(LoanID)
 );
```

CHAPTER 5: Fundamentals of Relational Database Design

Temporary Tables: Workhorses of SQL Server

So much so that they even have their own database: tempdb. Temporary tables (example: #Product1) can be applied in queries just like permanent tables. The differences are:

> ➢ Temporary tables are created in tempdb.

> ➢ Temporary tables have limited life.

There are two versions:

> ➢ Temporary tables (#tempA) are multi-user automatically, cannot be shared among connections.

> ➢ Global temporary tables (##gtempB) is single-user, can be shared among connections.

Global temporary tables are used only for special purposes since they make stored procedures single user only.

Temporary tables can be created by CREATE TABLE or SELECT INTO methods.

```
USE AdventureWorks2012;
GO
-- Command(s) completed successfully.
```

```
-- Create temporary table with CREATE TABLE
CREATE TABLE #Product
 (
        ProductID INT,
        ProductName nvarchar(50),
        ListPrice money,
        Color varchar(16)
);
GO
-- Command(s) completed successfully.
```

```
INSERT INTO #Product
SELECT   ProductID,
         Name,
         ListPrice,
         Color
FROM Production.Product ORDER BY Name;
GO  --(504 row(s) affected)
```

CHAPTER 5: *Fundamentals of Relational Database Design*

Temporary Tables Are Handy When Developing Scripts Or Stored Procedures

```
SELECT TOP 10 * FROM #Product
ORDER BY ProductName;
GO
```

ProductID	ProductName	ListPrice	Color
1	Adjustable Race	0.00	NULL
879	All-Purpose Bike Stand	159.00	NULL
712	AWC Logo Cap	8.99	Multi
3	BB Ball Bearing	0.00	NULL
2	Bearing Ball	0.00	NULL
877	Bike Wash - Dissolver	7.95	NULL
316	Blade	0.00	NULL
843	Cable Lock	25.00	NULL
952	Chain	20.24	Silver
324	Chain Stays	0.00	NULL

```
DROP TABLE #Product;
GO

-- CREATE temporary table with SELECT INTO
SELECT ProductID, ProductName = Name, ListPrice, StandardCost, Color
INTO #ProductA
FROM Production.Product
ORDER BY ProductName;
GO

SELECT TOP 10 * FROM #ProductA
ORDER BY ProductName;
```

ProductID	ProductName	ListPrice	StandardCost	Color
1	Adjustable Race	0.00	0.00	NULL
879	All-Purpose Bike Stand	159.00	59.466	NULL
712	AWC Logo Cap	8.99	6.9223	Multi
3	BB Ball Bearing	0.00	0.00	NULL
2	Bearing Ball	0.00	0.00	NULL
877	Bike Wash - Dissolver	7.95	2.9733	NULL
316	Blade	0.00	0.00	NULL
843	Cable Lock	25.00	10.3125	NULL
952	Chain	20.24	8.9866	Silver
324	Chain Stays	0.00	0.00	NULL

```
DROP TABLE #ProductA;
GO
```

CHAPTER 5: Fundamentals of Relational Database Design

ALTER TABLE for Changing Table Definition

An empty table can easily be altered by ALTER TABLE. A populated table change (alter) may require additional operations such as data conversion to the new column data type. Generally increasing the size of a column is a safe change even if the table is populated. If we were to change size from 25 to 10, truncation may occur (data loss), for which we would have to plan by examining what will be lost if any. When decreasing string column size, we can use the LEFT function to truncate the string. T-SQL script to increase the size of a column from 25 to 32, then decrease it 9.

```
USE CopyOfAdventureWorks2012;
-- Sales.SalesOrderDetail columns
/*Name    Policy Health State
SalesOrderID (PK, FK, int, not null)
SalesOrderDetailID (PK, int, not null)
CarrierTrackingNumber (nvarchar(25), null) ..... */
```

```
-- Increase column size of CarrierTrackingNumber
ALTER TABLE Sales.SalesOrderDetail   ALTER COLUMN CarrierTrackingNumber nvarchar(32)  null;
```

```
/* Columns after ALTER TABLE
Name      Policy Health State
SalesOrderID (PK, FK, int, not null)
SalesOrderDetailID (PK, int, not null)
CarrierTrackingNumber (nvarchar(32), null) .....             */
```

```
SELECT TOP (1) SalesOrderID, CarrierTrackingNumber FROM  Sales.SalesOrderDetail ORDER BY SalesOrderID;
```

SalesOrderID	CarrierTrackingNumber
43659	4911-403C-98

We shall now decrease the size to 9 characters, but first truncate the extra characters. Without the UPDATE, the following error happens.
/* Msg 8152, Level 16, State 13, Line 1 String or binary data would be truncated. The statement has been terminated.*/

```
UPDATE Sales.SalesOrderDetail SET CarrierTrackingNumber = LEFT (CarrierTrackingNumber,9);
-- (121317 row(s) affected)
```

```
-- Decrease column size of CarrierTrackingNumber
ALTER TABLE Sales.SalesOrderDetail   ALTER COLUMN CarrierTrackingNumber nvarchar(9)  null;
-- Command(s) completed successfully.
```

```
SELECT TOP (1) SalesOrderID, CarrierTrackingNumber FROM  Sales.SalesOrderDetail  ORDER BY SalesOrderID;
```

SalesOrderID	CarrierTrackingNumber
43659	4911-403C

Renaming Tables & Columns with sp_rename

The system stored procedure sp_rename can be used to rename tables, columns and other user-created database objects.

```
USE tempdb;
GO


-- Create test table
SELECT * INTO Department FROM AdventureWorks2012.HumanResources.Department;
GO
-- (16 row(s) affected)

SELECT TOP 1 * FROM Department;
GO
```

DepartmentID	Name	GroupName	ModifiedDate
1	Engineering	Research and Development	2002-06-01 00:00:00.000

```
-- Rename table column
EXEC sp_rename "Department.Name", "Department";
GO

SELECT TOP 1 * FROM Department;
GO
```

DepartmentID	Department	GroupName	ModifiedDate
1	Engineering	Research and Development	2002-06-01 00:00:00.000

```
-- Rename table
EXEC sp_rename "dbo.Department", "ProfitCenter"
GO

SELECT * FROM ProfitCenter;
GO
```

DepartmentID	Department	GroupName	ModifiedDate
1	Engineering	Research and Development	2002-06-01 00:00:00.000

```
DROP TABLE tempdb.dbo.ProfitCenter;
GO
```

CHAPTER 5: Fundamentals of Relational Database Design

DROP TABLE: A Dangerous Statement

The DROP TABLE statement is to delete a table, including content, for good. It is a very
dangerous statement which we don't want to execute accidentally. Therefore, if appropriate we
should comment it out in a T-SQL script to prevent unintentional execution.

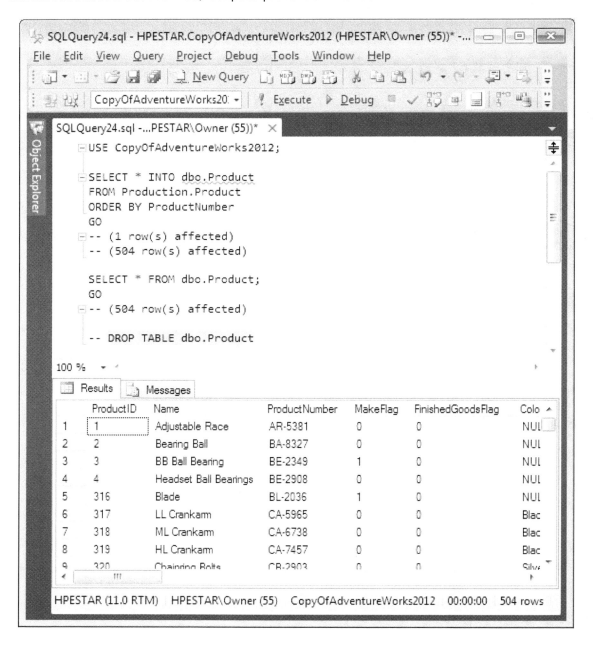

Table Constraints Inclusion in CREATE TABLE

Table constraints are user-defined database objects that restricts the behaviors of columns. PRIMARY KEY, UNIQUE KEY, FOREIGN KEY, or CHECK constraint, or a DEFAULT constraint can be included in the CREATE TABLE statement on the same line as the column or added as a separate line. In the definition of the Banking.Branch table UNIQUE and DEFAULT constraints are included in the same line while the PRIMARY KEY constraint has its own line at the end of column list. In the definition of Banking.Loan table, the PRIMARY KEY constraint is included with the column definition. FOREIGN KEY constraint definition can include ON DELETE CASCADE action option, meaning if the PRIMARY KEY is deleted all FOREIGN KEYs in the table referencing it should also be deleted.

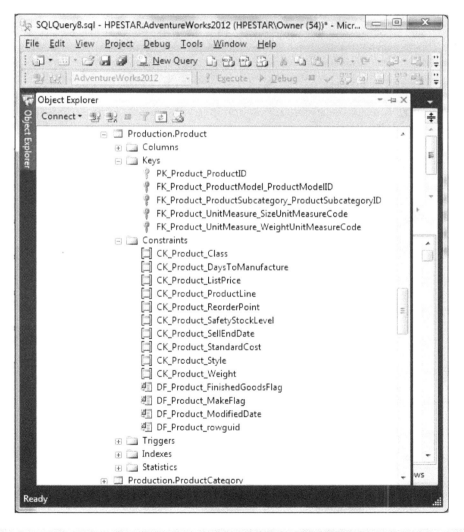

Nullability Column-Level Constraints in CREATE TABLE

The default is NULL, the column can contain NULL entries, the column is nullable. We have to specifically declare NOT NULL on the column line in CREATE TABLE if we want to add the cardinality constraint to the column. The NULL / NOT NULL constraint cannot be declared on a separate line. In the Production.Product table the Color column is nullable. The ListPrice column is not nullable instead has 0.0 price where there is no price.

PRIMARY KEY constraint on a column automatically implies NOT NULL

The UNIQUE KEY CONSTRAINT allows only one NULL entry in a column since two or more NULL entries would not be unique. Demonstration script:

```
USE tempdb;
CREATE TABLE Product     (   ProductID INT UNIQUE,
                             ProductName varchar(64) PRIMARY KEY
                         );

INSERT Product (ProductName) VALUES ('Mobile Phone xZing');
-- (1 row(s) affected)


-- One NULL is OK in ProductID column
-- Second NULL insert attempt errors out

INSERT Product (ProductName) VALUES ('Motor Bike');

/* Msg 2627, Level 14, State 1, Line 7
Violation of UNIQUE KEY constraint 'UQ__Product__B40CC6ECDF4DC6D3'.
Cannot insert duplicate key in object 'dbo.Product'.
The duplicate key value is (<NULL>).
The statement has been terminated. */


-- NULL value in PRIMARY KEY column not allowed

INSERT Product (ProductID) VALUES (2);

/* Msg 515, Level 16, State 2, Line 2
Cannot insert the value NULL into column
'ProductName', table 'tempdb.dbo.Product';
column does not allow nulls. INSERT fails.
The statement has been terminated. */

SELECT * FROM Product;
```

ProductID	ProductName
NULL	Mobile Phone xZing

The PRIMARY KEY constraint is a combination of UNIQUE and NOT NULL constraints.

CHAPTER 5: Fundamentals of Relational Database Design

PRIMARY KEY & FOREIGN KEY Constraints

The PRIMARY KEY constraint is to ensure a referenceable unique address for each row in a table. PK column value cannot be NULL. The underlying mechanism to carry out the enforcement action is a unique index which is clustered by default but in can be nonclustered. PRIMARY KEY constraint can be considered as a UNIQUE constraint with NOT NULL on the column. The typical PRIMARY KEY is the SURROGATE PRIMARY KEY INT IDENTITY(1,1) column. There can only be one PRIMARY KEY defined per table. A PRIMARY KEY can consist of multiple columns, a composite PRIMARY KEY. A PRIMARY KEY cannot be based on part of a column. Production.ProductSubcategory table PRIMARY KEY setup.

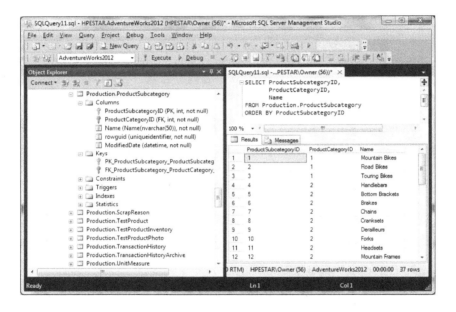

The ProductSubcategoryID is the PRIMARY KEY constraint. It is an INT IDENTITY(1,1) surrogate key. ProductCategoryID is a FOREIGN KEY referencing the Production.ProductCategory table ProductCategoryID column. "Name" is the NATURAL KEY. rowguid (used in replication) & ModifiedDate are row maintenance columns. The NATURAL KEY column Name has NOT NULL constraint and unique index defined. As such it can serve as PRIMARY KEY for the table, but we shall see why a meaningless integer number (INT IDENTITY) is better for PRIMARY KEY. Related to this topic: A heap is a table without a clustered index. The implication is if we choose nonclustered PRIMARY KEY, we have to define a clustered index on other column(s) so that the database engine can work with the table as normal. Clustered index speeds up range searches.

The SURROGATE PRIMARY KEY should not be exposed to end-users, it is for programming use only.

CHAPTER 5: Fundamentals of Relational Database Design

FOREIGN KEY constraint requires that the referenced PK value exists.
FOREIGN KEY column is nullable. FOREIGN KEY can be named differently from the referenced PRIMARY KEY, although for readability purposes usually the same. **Multiple FK columns can reference the same PK column**. In such a case only one FK column can have the same name as the PK column. Invalid FK reference results in error.

```
USE [AdventureWorks2012]
GO

INSERT INTO Production.ProductSubcategory
      (ProductCategoryID
      ,Name)
   VALUES
      (99
      ,'Inner Tube')

/*
Msg 547, Level 16, State 0, Line 2
The INSERT statement conflicted with the FOREIGN KEY constraint
"FK_ProductSubcategory_ProductCategory_ProductCategoryID".
The conflict occurred in database "AdventureWorks2012",
table "Production.ProductCategory", column 'ProductCategoryID'.
The statement has been terminated.
*/
```

DELETE attempt on a referenced PRIMARY KEY will give an error unless DELETE CASCADE is defined on the FK:

```
DELETE FROM Production.ProductSubcategory
WHERE ProductSubCategoryID = 4
GO

/* Msg 547, Level 16, State 0, Line 1
The DELETE statement conflicted with the REFERENCE constraint
"FK_Product_ProductSubcategory_ProductSubcategoryID".
The conflict occurred in database "AdventureWorks2012",
table "Production.Product", column 'ProductSubcategoryID'.
The statement has been terminated.  */
```

CHAPTER 5: Fundamentals of Relational Database Design

Single Column & Composite PRIMARY KEY List with XML PATH

Query to form delimited list for composite PRIMARY KEY columns. STUFF function deletes the leading comma.

```
-- Show composite PRIMARY KEYs as a comma-delimited list
USE AdventureWorks2012;
SELECT K.TABLE_SCHEMA,
       T.TABLE_NAME,
       PK_COLUMN_NAMES =
             STUFF(( SELECT
                           CONCAT(', ',   KK.COLUMN_NAME)              AS [text()]
                           FROM   INFORMATION_SCHEMA.KEY_COLUMN_USAGE kk
                     WHERE  K.CONSTRAINT_NAME = KK.CONSTRAINT_NAME
                     ORDER BY  KK.ORDINAL_POSITION
                     FOR XML Path ('')), 1, 1, '')
FROM    INFORMATION_SCHEMA.TABLE_CONSTRAINTS T
  INNER JOIN    INFORMATION_SCHEMA.KEY_COLUMN_USAGE K
      ON T.CONSTRAINT_NAME = K.CONSTRAINT_NAME
WHERE          T.CONSTRAINT_TYPE = 'PRIMARY KEY'
               AND K.ORDINAL_POSITION = 1
ORDER BY       K.TABLE_SCHEMA,
               T.TABLE_NAME;
-- (71 row(s) affected) - Partial results
```

TABLE_SCHEMA	TABLE_NAME	PK_COLUMN_NAMES
dbo	AWBuildVersion	SystemInformationID
dbo	DatabaseLog	DatabaseLogID
dbo	ErrorLog	ErrorLogID
HumanResources	Department	DepartmentID
HumanResources	Employee	BusinessEntityID
HumanResources	EmployeeDepartmentHistory	BusinessEntityID, StartDate, DepartmentID, ShiftID
HumanResources	EmployeePayHistory	BusinessEntityID, RateChangeDate
HumanResources	JobCandidate	JobCandidateID
HumanResources	Shift	ShiftID
Person	Address	AddressID
Person	AddressType	AddressTypeID
Person	BusinessEntity	BusinessEntityID
Person	BusinessEntityAddress	BusinessEntityID, AddressID, AddressTypeID
Person	BusinessEntityContact	BusinessEntityID, PersonID, ContactTypeID
Person	ContactType	ContactTypeID
Person	CountryRegion	CountryRegionCode
Person	EmailAddress	BusinessEntityID, EmailAddressID
Person	Password	BusinessEntityID
Person	Person	BusinessEntityID
Person	PersonPhone	BusinessEntityID, PhoneNumber, PhoneNumberTypeID

SSMS GUI Table Designer

SSMS Object Explorer includes a GUI Table Designer which can be launched the following ways for new or existing table from the right-click drop-down menus.

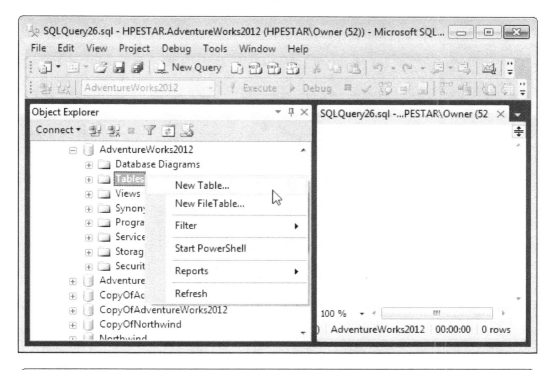

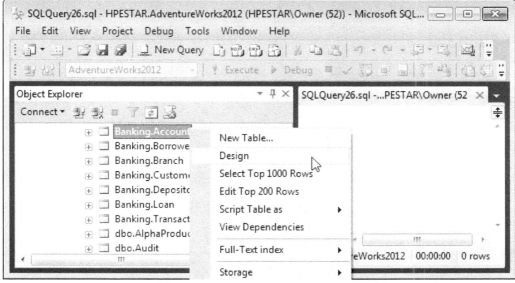

CHAPTER 5: Fundamentals of Relational Database Design

Basic GUI Table Design

The Table Designer provides line-by-line row design including all properties (bottom of dialog box) such as defaults, computed columns, identity and so on.

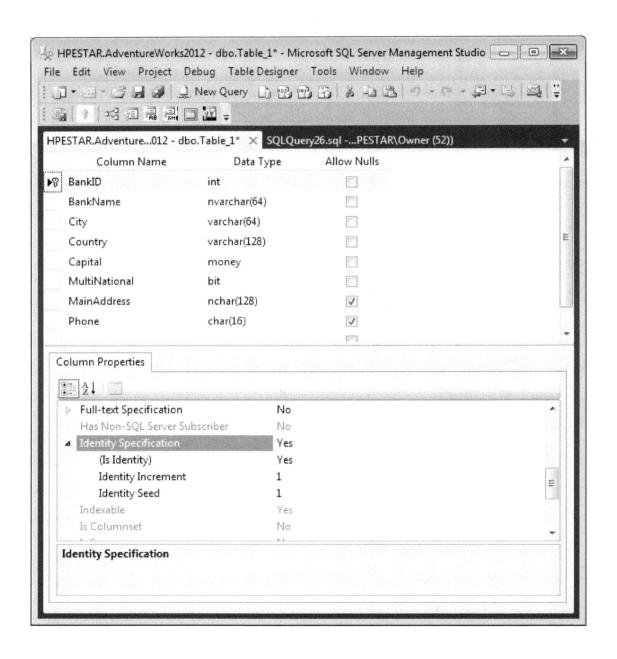

CHECK Constraint Definition

CHECK Constraint design window can be launched from toolbox icon: Manage Check Constraints or right-click drop-down menu. We create a constraint on Capital to be greater or equal to $5 billion.

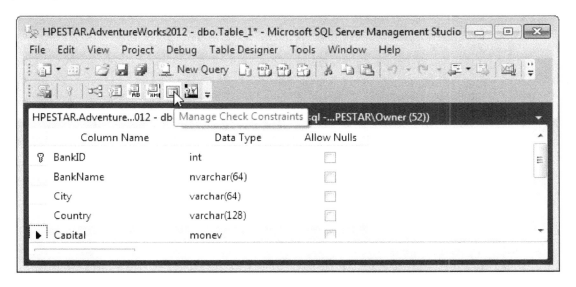

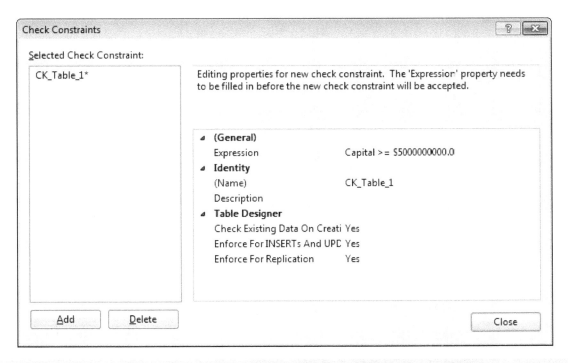

Managing Indexes and Keys

The Manage Indexes and Keys window can be launched by toolbox icon or right-click menu. We add UNIQUE KEY property to the BankName column.

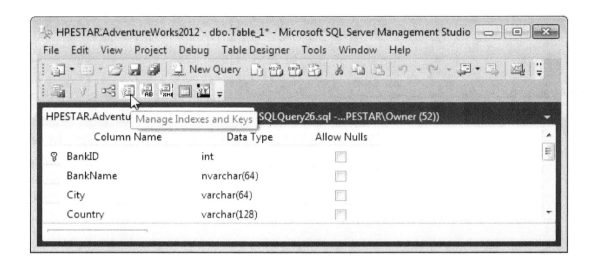

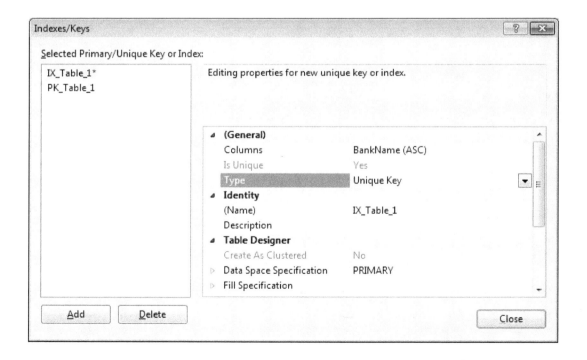

Setting PRIMARY KEY with a Single Click

PRIMARY KEY can simply be configured just by clicking on the gold key icon. A PRIMARY KEY constraint is created automatically.

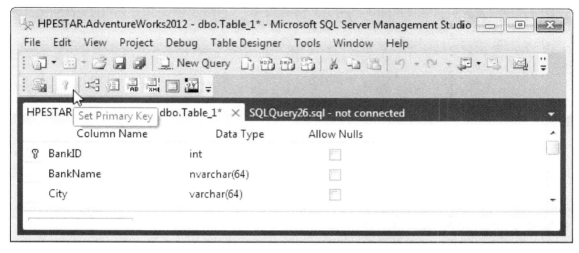

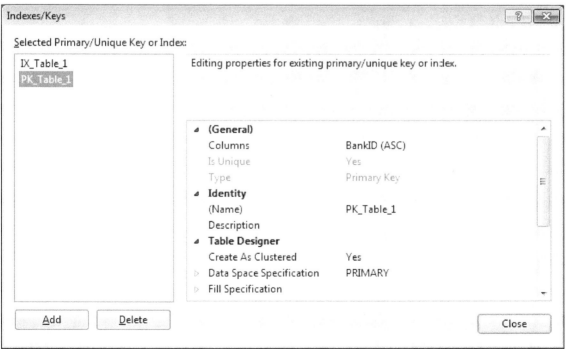

CHAPTER 5: Fundamentals of Relational Database Design

Configuring FOREIGN KEY: Declarative Referential Integrity

The Relationships facility can be used to create a FOREIGN KEY link (constraint). NOTE: demo only, BusinessEntityID column in the demo table has no relationship to AdventureWorks tables.

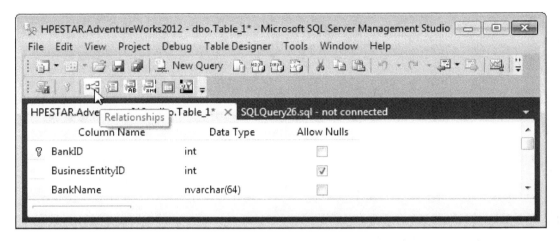

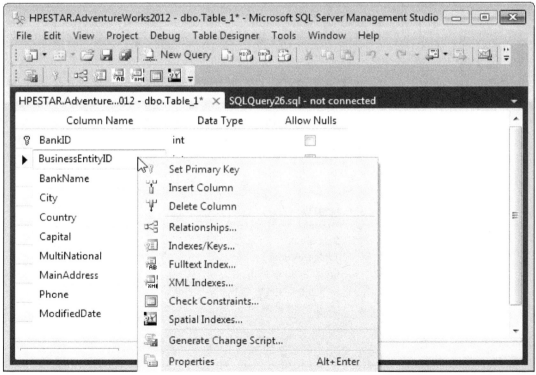

Tables And Columns Specific Tab Is To Define Mapping From FK To PK

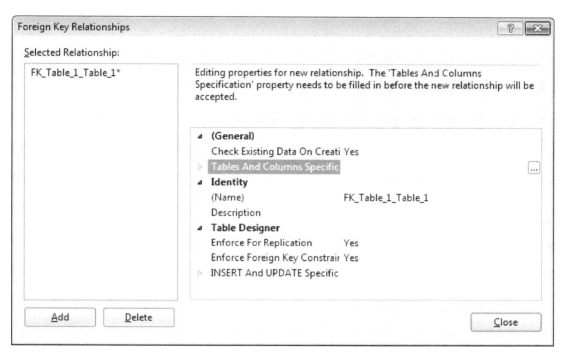

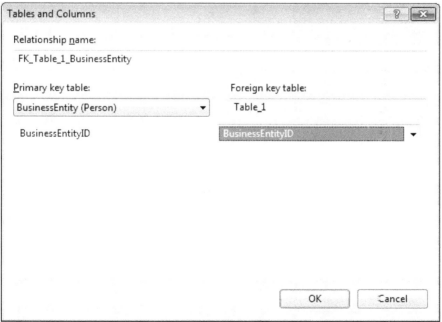

T-SQL Script Generation from GUI Table Designer

T-SQL code can be generated any time prior to saving the changes.

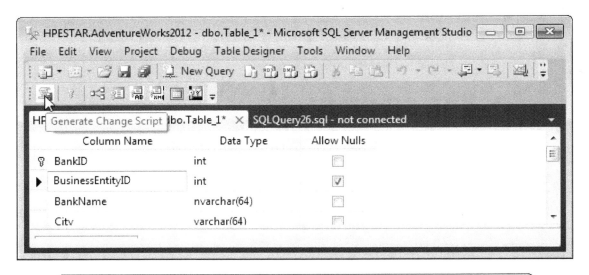

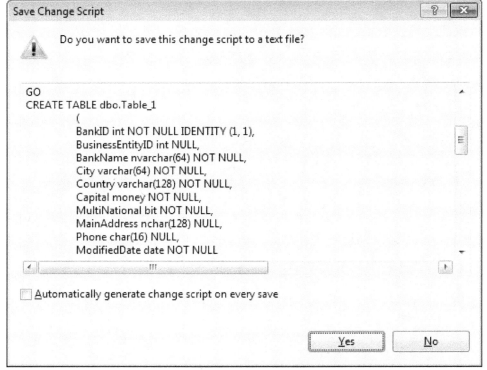

Generated CREATE TABLE & Related Objects Script

Code generated by the Table Designer.

```
/* To prevent any potential data loss issues, you should review this script in detail before running it
outside the context of the database designer.*/
BEGIN TRANSACTION
SET QUOTED_IDENTIFIER ON
SET ARITHABORT ON
SET NUMERIC_ROUNDABORT OFF
SET CONCAT_NULL_YIELDS_NULL ON
SET ANSI_NULLS ON
SET ANSI_PADDING ON
SET ANSI_WARNINGS ON
COMMIT
BEGIN TRANSACTION
GO
CREATE TABLE dbo.Table_1
        (
        BankID int NOT NULL IDENTITY (1, 1),
        BusinessEntityID int NULL,
        BankName nvarchar(64) NOT NULL,
        City varchar(64) NOT NULL,
        Country varchar(128) NOT NULL,
        Capital money NOT NULL,
        MultiNational bit NOT NULL,
        MainAddress nchar(128) NULL,
        Phone char(16) NULL,
        ModifiedDate date NOT NULL
        ) ON [PRIMARY]
GO
ALTER TABLE dbo.Table_1 ADD CONSTRAINT
        CK_Table_1 CHECK (Capital >= $5000000000.0)
GO
ALTER TABLE dbo.Table_1 ADD CONSTRAINT
        DF_Table_1_ModifiedDate DEFAULT CURRENT_TIMESTAMP FOR ModifiedDate
GO
ALTER TABLE dbo.Table_1 ADD CONSTRAINT
        PK_Table_1 PRIMARY KEY CLUSTERED
        (
        BankID
        ) WITH( STATISTICS_NORECOMPUTE = OFF, IGNORE_DUP_KEY = OFF, ALLOW_ROW_LOCKS = ON,
ALLOW_PAGE_LOCKS = ON) ON [PRIMARY]

GO
```

CHAPTER 5: Fundamentals of Relational Database Design

-- T-SQL script continues

```
ALTER TABLE dbo.Table_1 ADD CONSTRAINT
        IX_Table_1 UNIQUE NONCLUSTERED
        (
        BankName
        ) WITH( STATISTICS_NORECOMPUTE = OFF, IGNORE_DUP_KEY = OFF, ALLOW_ROW_LOCKS = ON,
ALLOW_PAGE_LOCKS = ON) ON [PRIMARY]

GO
ALTER TABLE dbo.Table_1 ADD CONSTRAINT
        FK_Table_1_Table_1 FOREIGN KEY
        (
        BankID
        ) REFERENCES dbo.Table_1
        (
        BankID
        ) ON UPDATE  NO ACTION
         ON DELETE  NO ACTION

GO
ALTER TABLE dbo.Table_1 SET (LOCK_ESCALATION = TABLE)
GO
COMMIT
```

Upon Exit or Save, a name can be assigned to the table. In this instance, the Table_1 is changed to MultiNationalBank. The Table Designer automatically replaces all the "Table_1" occurrences in the script with "MultiNationalBank".

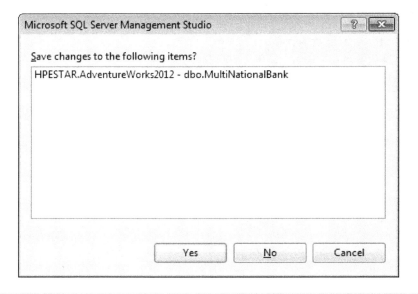

CHAPTER 5: Fundamentals of Relational Database Design

One-to-Many Relationship Implementation

The cardinality of relationship implemented with PRIMARY KEY & FOREIGN KEY constraints is one-to-many. Many FKs can reference a single PK value. In the following demo, many products map to a single subcategory value 'Touring Bike'. The matching is not done on the name between tables, rather on the surrogate PK value 3.

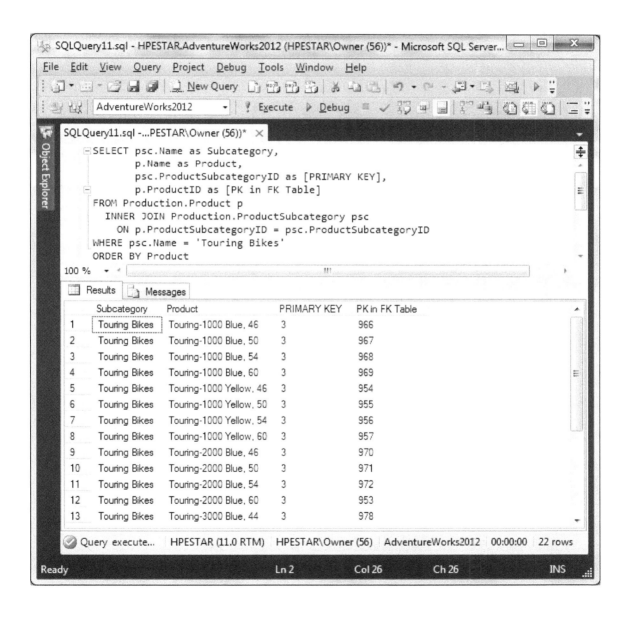

FOREIGN KEY Referencing A UNIQUE KEY

A FOREIGN KEY can reference a UNIQUE KEY or UNIQUE index column in another table in addition to the PRIMARY KEY. In the following demonstration a FOREIGN KEY is created from ProdNumber column pointing to Production.Product ProductNumber (UNIQUE index) column.

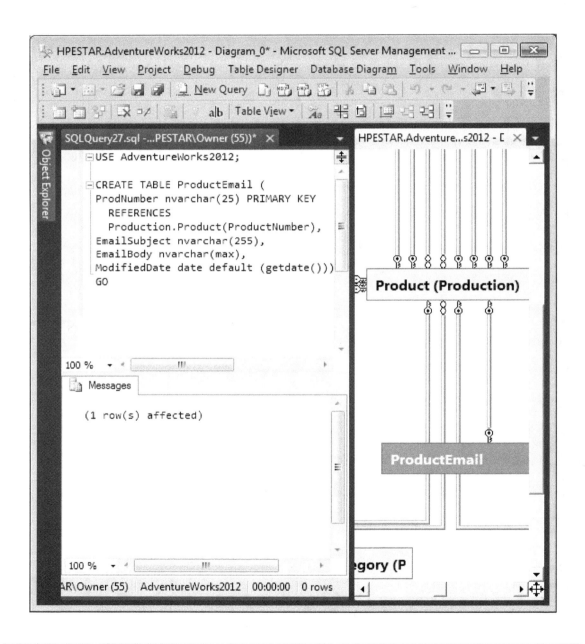

FOREIGN KEY Relationship Without Constraint

A table can have a FOREIGN KEY which is not supported by server-side constraint. In such instance the client-side application software has to ensure that the relationship is valid. Generally it is undesirable. **Whatever can be done on the server-side should be done there because it is more efficient development wise, maintenance wise and performance wise.** Demonstration to remove the FK constraint on the ProductID column in the [Order Details] table of the CopyOfNorthwind database.

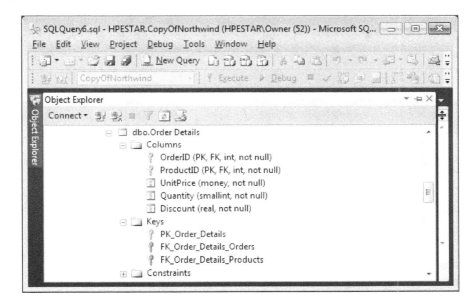

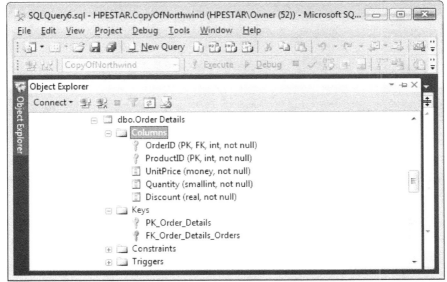

CHAPTER 5: Fundamentals of Relational Database Design

Database Diagram Design Tool in SSMS

Management Studio Object Explorer includes a diagramming tool for tables and their relationships with each other. While not as sophisticated as independent database design tools, it is excellent for working with a small number of tables.

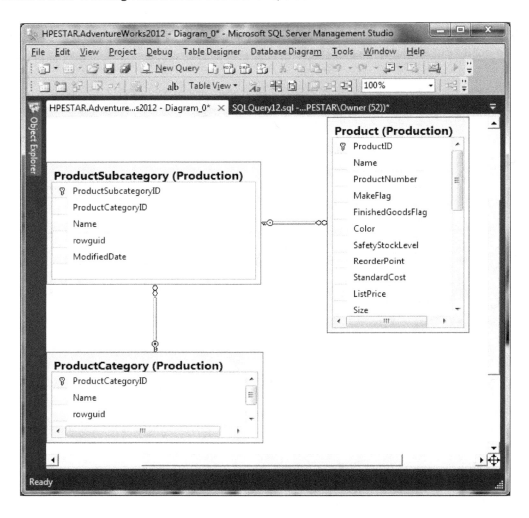

The diagramming tool has both reverse engineering and forward engineering features. **Reverse engineering**: it creates a diagram based on table and PK/FK constraints definitions. **Forward engineering**: it can change table and constraint setup in the database based on diagram changes. The Gold Key (PRIMARY KEY symbol) end of the connection line points to the PRIMARY KEY table, while the double "o" (infinite symbol in mathematics, here meaning many) end to the FOREIGN KEY table.

PRIMARY KEY & FOREIGN KEY as JOIN ON Keys

When we need data from two related tables we have to JOIN the tables. The typical JOIN keys are the PRIMARY KEY and FOREIGN KEY. In the following demonstration, we want to display the subcategory for each Touring Bike product from the Product table. Since the 'Touring Bike' subcategory value is in the ProductSubcategory table, we have to JOIN it to the Product table. The JOIN keys are: ProductSubcategoryID PRIMARY KEY in the ProductSubcategory table and ProductSubcategoryID FOREIGN KEY in the Product table. Naming the FK same as the PK is helpful with readability, therefore developer productivity.

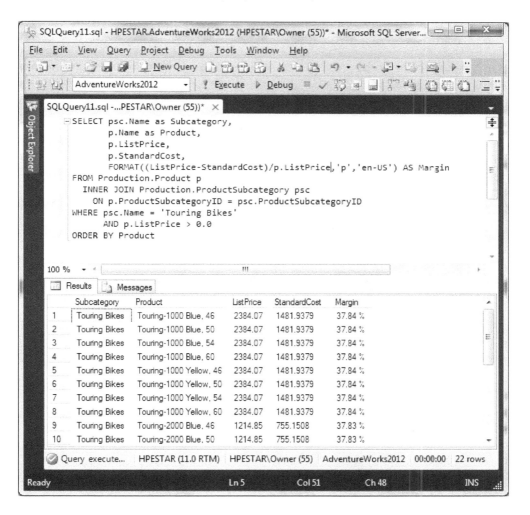

The Margin column is calculated with an expression. It is also formatted as percentage with US English culture.

CHAPTER 5: Fundamentals of Relational Database Design

Composite & Indirect FOREIGN KEY

A composite (more than one column) PRIMARY KEY requires matching composite FOREIGN KEY references. In the Sales.SalesOrderDetail table SpecialOfferID & ProductID constitute a composite FOREIGN KEY which references the SpecialOfferProduct table composite PRIMARY KEY. Thus ProductID indirectly references the Production.Product table.

NATURAL KEY is a Must in Every Table

NATURAL KEY is a unique key which can serve as PRIMARY KEY for identifying data. A product name is a natural key in a product table. A product number is also a NATURAL KEY in a product table. Note that product "number" should better be called product identification since it is frequently not a number rather it is alphanumeric like: AB342BL where BL stands for blue. The Name and ProductNumber columns are NATURAL KEYs in the Production.Product table. **Every table should have a NATURAL KEY**. If it does not, there is a definition problem. Naturally, test tables, work tables and staging tables are exceptions to this rule.

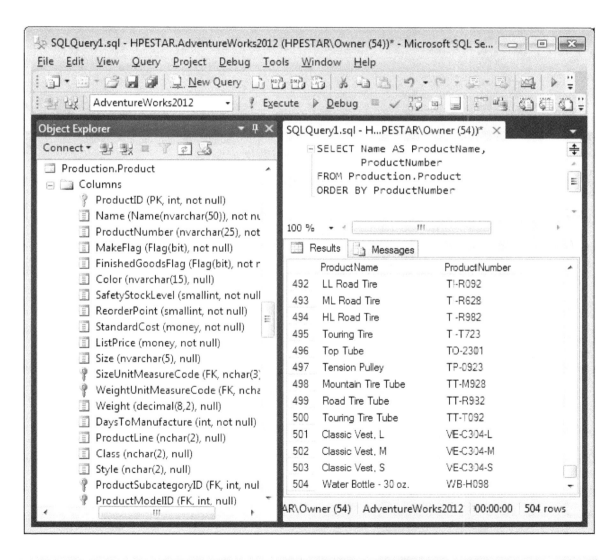

CHAPTER 5: Fundamentals of Relational Database Design

CANDIDATE KEY

A CANDIDATE KEY can be any column or a combination of columns that can qualify as UNIQUE KEY in a table with no NULL value. The ProductID, Name, ProductNumber, rowguid (16 byte random value like FA3C65CD-0A22-47E3-BDF6-53F1DC138C43, hyphens are for readability) are all CANDIDATE KEYs in the Production.Product table. Only one of them can be the PRIMARY KEY. In this instance the selected PRIMARY KEY is ProductID, a SURROGATE (to NATURAL KEY) INT IDENTITY (1,1) PRIMARY KEY.

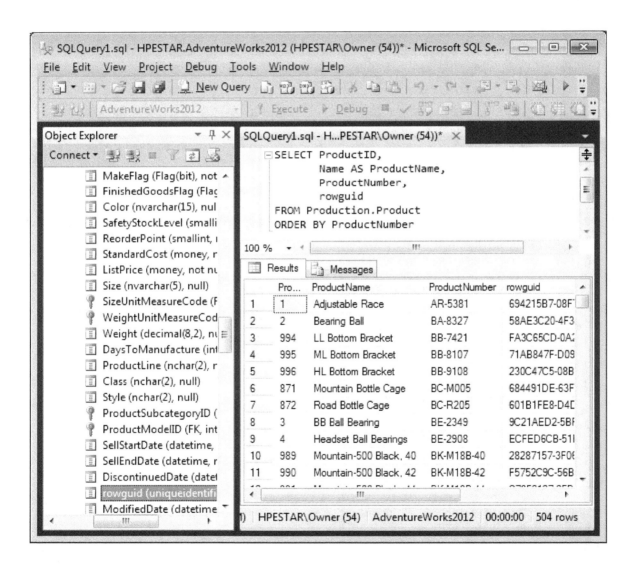

Logical Data Modeling in Visio

The following screenshots demonstrate logical / conceptual data modeling in Visio using the ORM diagram tool.

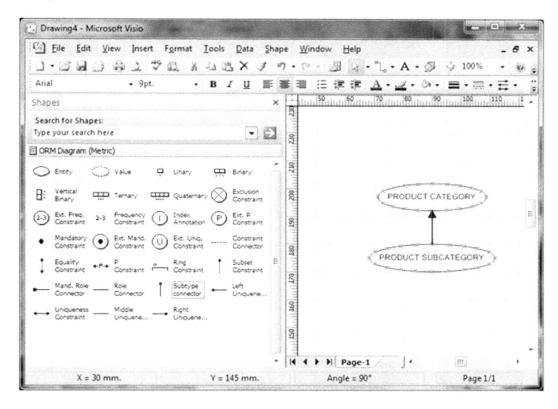

Following is the actual implementation of the above relationship.

```
CREATE TABLE [Production].[ProductCategory](
        [ProductCategoryID] [int] IDENTITY(1,1) PRIMARY KEY,
        [Name] [dbo].[Name] NOT NULL,
        [rowguid] [uniqueidentifier] ROWGUIDCOL  NOT NULL,
        [ModifiedDate] [datetime] NOT NULL          );

CREATE TABLE [Production].[ProductSubcategory](
        [ProductSubcategoryID] [int] IDENTITY(1,1) PRIMARY KEY,
        [ProductCategoryID] [int] NOT NULL REFERENCES
Production.ProductCategory(ProductCategoryID) ,
        [Name] [dbo].[Name] NOT NULL,
        [rowguid] [uniqueidentifier] ROWGUIDCOL  NOT NULL,
        [ModifiedDate] [datetime] NOT NULL          );
```

CHAPTER 5: Fundamentals of Relational Database Design

Branch Banking Conceptual Diagram Preparation In Visio ORM Diagram Tool

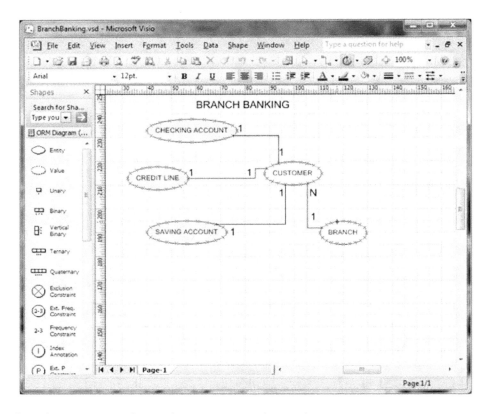

The actual implementation of Branch - Customer relationship.

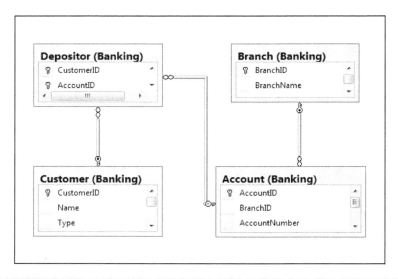

CHAPTER 5: Fundamentals of Relational Database Design

Relational Database Design with Visio

Office Visio can be used for physical database modeling and design. Another widely used database modeling tool is ERWIN.

A sample database design diagram in Visio. Lines represent FOREIGN KEY constraints, arrowheads point to the referenced table.

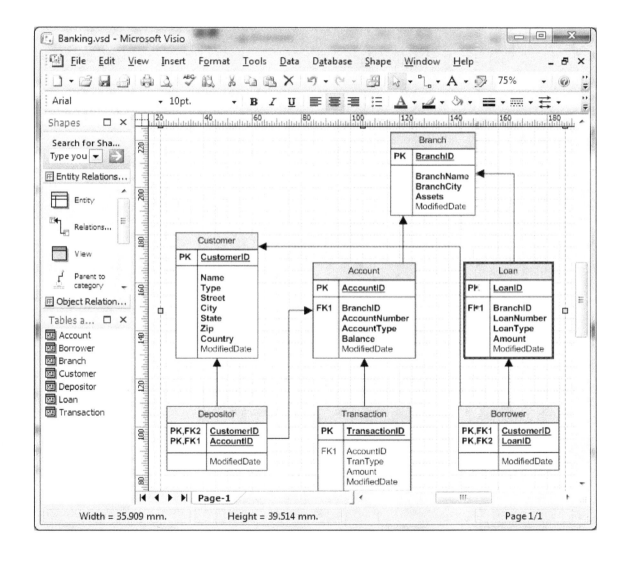

CHAPTER 5: Fundamentals of Relational Database Design

AdventureWorks Database Model in Visio

A segment of the AdventureWorks database design model in Visio. U indicates UNIQUE KEY or unique index.

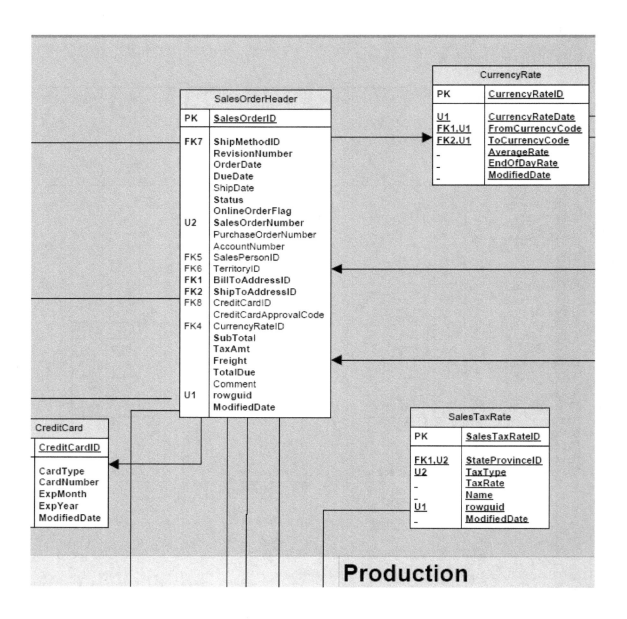

Reverse Engineering a Database with Visio

Visio can reverse engineer a database. Based on PRIMARY KEY & FOREIGN KEY constraints and table definitions, it can construct a database diagram automatically. Here are the first and an intermediate steps.

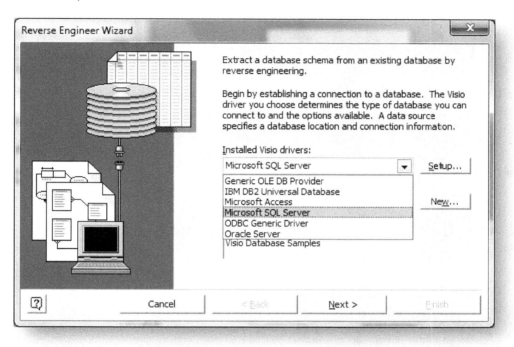

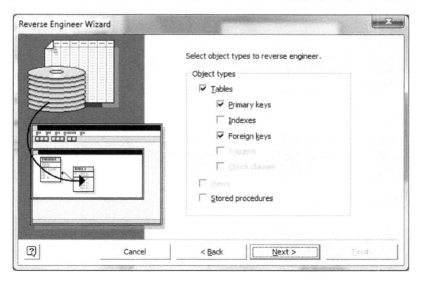

CHAPTER 5: Fundamentals of Relational Database Design

Reverse Engineered Diagram of Northwind

A section display from the reverse engineered diagram of Northwind sample database(not clear why "Discontinued" displays in bold):

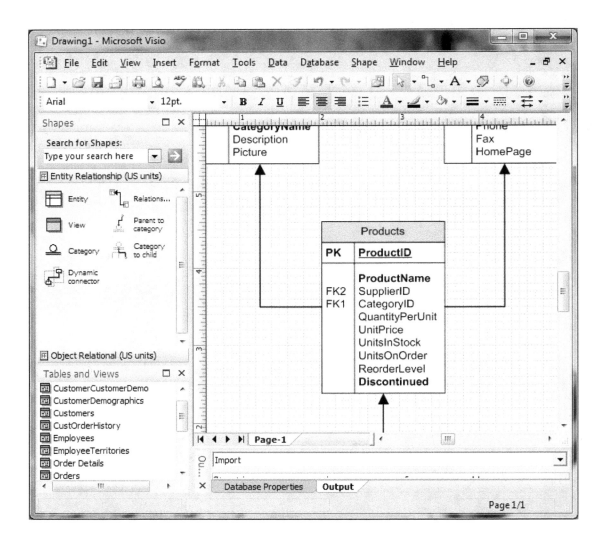

Forward Engineering a Database with Visio

Visio product itself does not have forward engineering feature. Alberto Ferrari developed an Office Addin for generating database scripts from a Visio database model diagram: Visio Forward Engineer Addin for Office 2010 (http://sqlblog.com/blogs/alberto_ferrari/archive/2010/04/16/visio-forward-engineer-addin-for-office-2010.aspx).

Codeplex blog post and free download for the same: Visio Forward Engineer Addin (http://forwardengineer.codeplex.com/).

Forward Engineering from SSMS Diagram Tool

The Database Diagram Tool in SSMS Object Explorer support graphical design and forward engineering.

Screenshot to show the creation of a new table "Automobile" in the Diagram Tool.

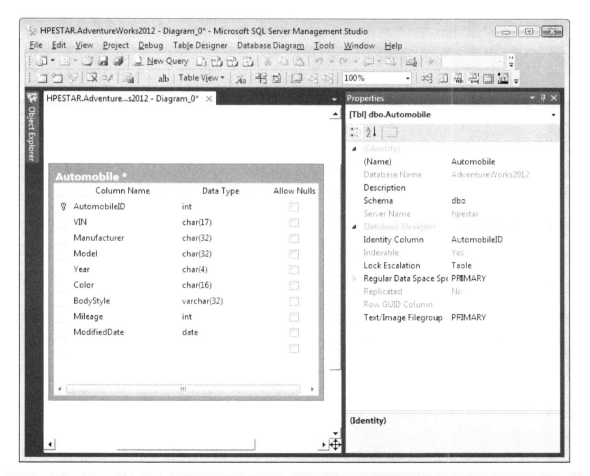

CHAPTER 5: Fundamentals of Relational Database Design

The Properties Dialog Box Allows The Individual Configuration Of Each Column

The Right Click drop-down menu has options to Add Indexes/Keys, Add XML Indexes, Add Spatial Indexes, Add Fulltext Indexes, Delete Tables from Database (DANGEROUS!), CHECK constraint and other table related database objects.

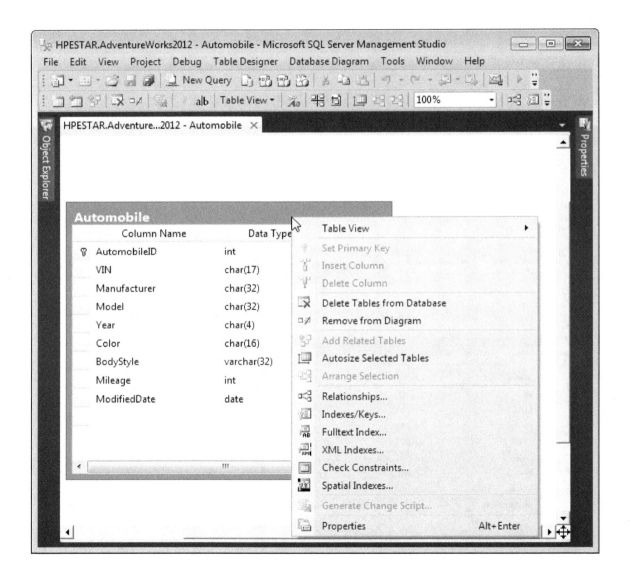

Forward Engineering Can Be Initiated By Exiting / Saving The Diagram

The save option dialog box activates automatically upon exit.

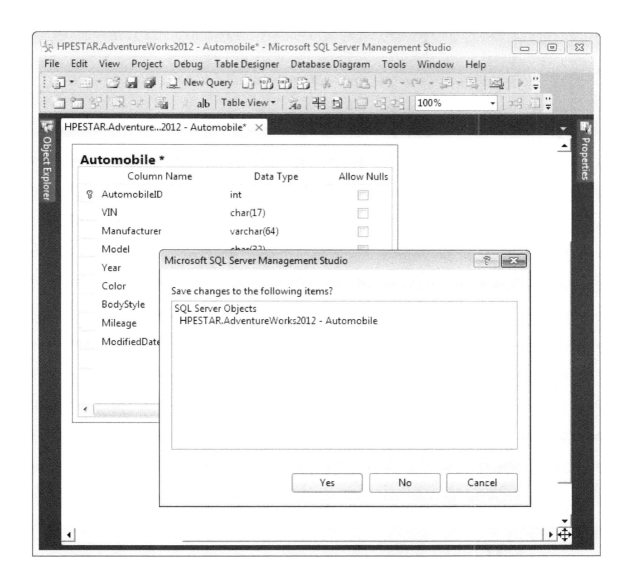

Save Change Script Panel Pops Up With The Generated T-SQL Change Script

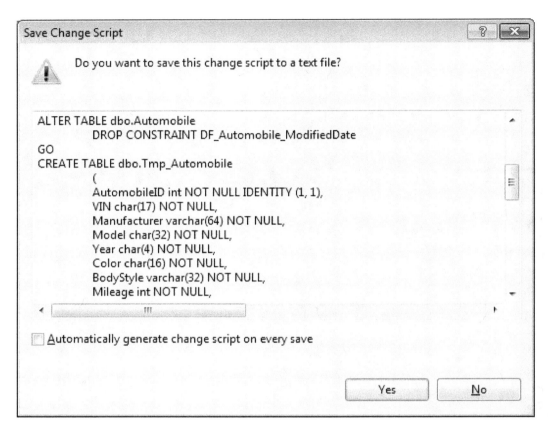

The generated T-SQL change script for changing Manufacturer data type to varchar(64).

```
/* To prevent any potential data loss issues, you should review this script in detail before running it
outside the context of the database designer.*/
BEGIN TRANSACTION
SET QUOTED_IDENTIFIER ON
SET ARITHABORT ON
SET NUMERIC_ROUNDABORT OFF
SET CONCAT_NULL_YIELDS_NULL ON
SET ANSI_NULLS ON
SET ANSI_PADDING ON
SET ANSI_WARNINGS ON
COMMIT
BEGIN TRANSACTION
GO
```

-- T-SQL script continued

```
ALTER TABLE dbo.Automobile
        DROP CONSTRAINT DF_Automobile_ModifiedDate
GO


CREATE TABLE dbo.Tmp_Automobile          (

        AutomobileID int NOT NULL IDENTITY (1, 1),
        VIN char(17) NOT NULL,
        Manufacturer varchar(64) NOT NULL,
        Model char(32) NOT NULL,
        Year char(4) NOT NULL,
        Color char(16) NOT NULL,
        BodyStyle varchar(32) NOT NULL,
        Mileage int NOT NULL,
        ModifiedDate date NOT NULL )  ON [PRIMARY]
GO
ALTER TABLE dbo.Tmp_Automobile SET (LOCK_ESCALATION = TABLE)
GO
ALTER TABLE dbo.Tmp_Automobile ADD CONSTRAINT
        DF_Automobile_ModifiedDate DEFAULT (getdate()) FOR ModifiedDate
GO
SET IDENTITY_INSERT dbo.Tmp_Automobile ON
GO
IF EXISTS(SELECT * FROM dbo.Automobile)
        EXEC('INSERT INTO dbo.Tmp_Automobile (AutomobileID, VIN, Manufacturer, Model, Year,
Color, BodyStyle, Mileage, ModifiedDate)
                SELECT AutomobileID, VIN, CONVERT(varchar(64), Manufacturer), Model, Year, Color,
BodyStyle, Mileage, ModifiedDate FROM dbo.Automobile WITH (HOLDLOCK TABLOCKX)')
GO
SET IDENTITY_INSERT dbo.Tmp_Automobile OFF
GO
DROP TABLE dbo.Automobile
GO
EXECUTE sp_rename N'dbo.Tmp_Automobile', N'Automobile', 'OBJECT'
GO
ALTER TABLE dbo.Automobile ADD CONSTRAINT
        PK_Automobile PRIMARY KEY CLUSTERED
        ( AutomobileID
        ) WITH( STATISTICS_NORECOMPUTE = OFF, IGNORE_DUP_KEY = OFF, ALLOW_ROW_LOCKS = ON,
ALLOW_PAGE_LOCKS = ON) ON [PRIMARY]
GO
COMMIT
```

CHAPTER 5: Fundamentals of Relational Database Design

Generate Change Script Option

Forward Engineering can also be initiated by the Generate Change Script option. The same option can be used when making any changes to the Diagram using the Diagram Tool.

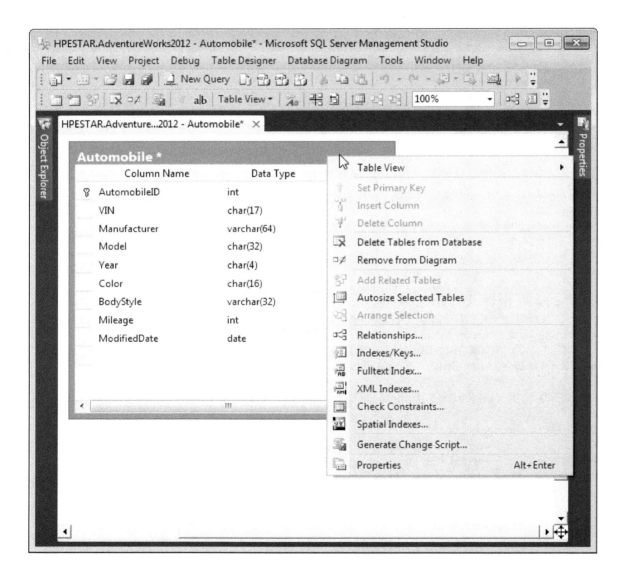

The Generated Script Of The Automobile Table By The Diagram Tool

```
USE [AdventureWorks2012]
GO

/****** Object:  Table [dbo].[Automobile]    Script Date: 7/22/2016 11:20:17 AM ******/
SET ANSI_NULLS ON
GO

SET QUOTED_IDENTIFIER ON
GO

SET ANSI_PADDING ON
GO

CREATE TABLE [dbo].[Automobile](
        [AutomobileID] [int] IDENTITY(1,1) NOT NULL,
        [VIN] [char](17) NOT NULL,
        [Manufacturer] [char](32) NOT NULL,
        [Model] [char](32) NOT NULL,
        [Year] [char](4) NOT NULL,
        [Color] [char](16) NOT NULL,
        [BodyStyle] [varchar](32) NOT NULL,
        [Mileage] [int] NOT NULL,
        [ModifiedDate] [date] NOT NULL,
 CONSTRAINT [PK_Automobile] PRIMARY KEY CLUSTERED
(
        [AutomobileID] ASC
)WITH (PAD_INDEX = OFF, STATISTICS_NORECOMPUTE = OFF, IGNORE_DUP_KEY = OFF,
ALLOW_ROW_LOCKS = ON, ALLOW_PAGE_LOCKS = ON) ON [PRIMARY]
) ON [PRIMARY]

GO

SET ANSI_PADDING ON
GO

ALTER TABLE [dbo].[Automobile] ADD  CONSTRAINT [DF_Automobile_ModifiedDate]
DEFAULT (getdate()) FOR [ModifiedDate]
GO
```

Scripting Single Database Object with Related Objects

The scripting feature works only through the graphical user interface (GUI) in SSMS Object Explorer. **There is no command to script a table.** Start with Right Click on the Banking.Account table.

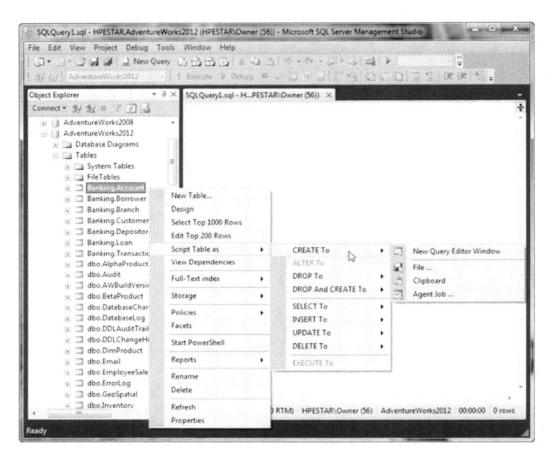

Generated script for the Banking.Account table and related objects.

```
USE [AdventureWorks2012]
GO
SET ANSI_NULLS ON
GO
SET QUOTED_IDENTIFIER ON
GO
SET ANSI_PADDING ON
GO
```

-- **T-SQL script continued**

```
CREATE TABLE [Banking].[Account](
        [AccountID] [int] IDENTITY(1,1) NOT NULL,
        [BranchID] [int] NOT NULL,
        [AccountNumber] [char](20) NOT NULL,
        [AccountType] [char](12) NOT NULL,
        [Balance] [money] NOT NULL,
        [ModifiedDate] [datetime] NULL,
PRIMARY KEY CLUSTERED
(
        [AccountID] ASC
)WITH  (PAD_INDEX  =  OFF,  STATISTICS_NORECOMPUTE  =  OFF,  IGNORE_DUP_KEY  =  OFF,
ALLOW_ROW_LOCKS = ON,
ALLOW_PAGE_LOCKS = ON) ON [PRIMARY],
UNIQUE NONCLUSTERED
(       [AccountID] ASC
)WITH  (PAD_INDEX  =  OFF,  STATISTICS_NORECOMPUTE  =  OFF,  IGNORE_DUP_KEY  =  OFF,
ALLOW_ROW_LOCKS = ON,
ALLOW_PAGE_LOCKS = ON) ON [PRIMARY],
UNIQUE NONCLUSTERED
(
        [AccountNumber] ASC
)WITH  (PAD_INDEX  =  OFF,  STATISTICS_NORECOMPUTE  =  OFF,  IGNORE_DUP_KEY  =  OFF,
ALLOW_ROW_LOCKS = ON,
ALLOW_PAGE_LOCKS = ON) ON [PRIMARY]   ) ON [PRIMARY]
GO
SET ANSI_PADDING ON
GO
ALTER TABLE [Banking].[Account] ADD  DEFAULT (getdate()) FOR [ModifiedDate]
GO

ALTER TABLE [Banking].[Account]  WITH CHECK ADD FOREIGN KEY([BranchID])
REFERENCES [Banking].[Branch] ([BranchID])
ON DELETE CASCADE
GO

ALTER TABLE [Banking].[Account]  WITH CHECK ADD  CONSTRAINT [ATC]
CHECK  (([AccountType]='S' OR [AccountType]='C'))
GO
```

CHAPTER 5: Fundamentals of Relational Database Design

Scripting DB Objects With Script Wizard

The Script Wizard is a sophisticated tool for scripting out multiple objects, in fact all objects can be scripted in a single setup and execution. The generated script can be saved to single/multiple files, new query window or the Clipboard. The launching sequence of menus starts with Right Click on the database.

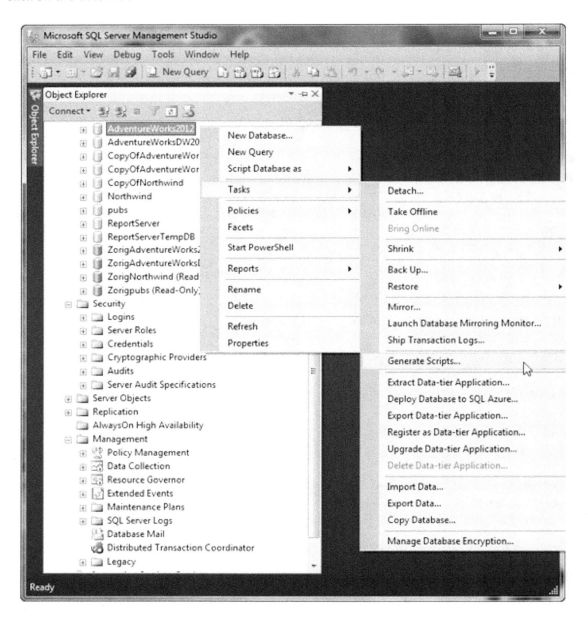

Script Wizard Optional Description Page

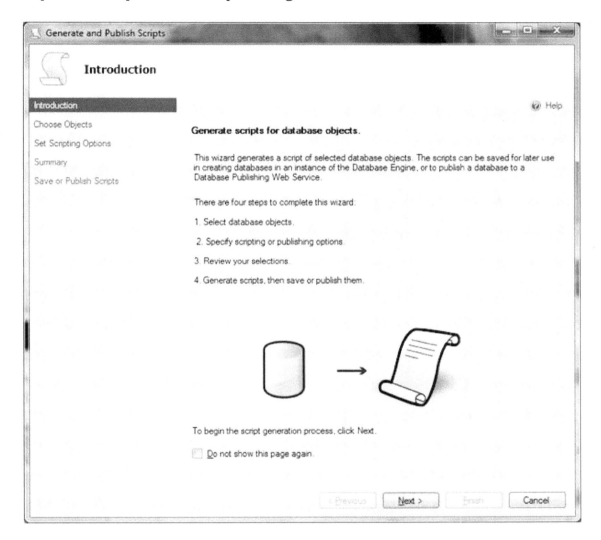

Object Selection Panel For Scripting

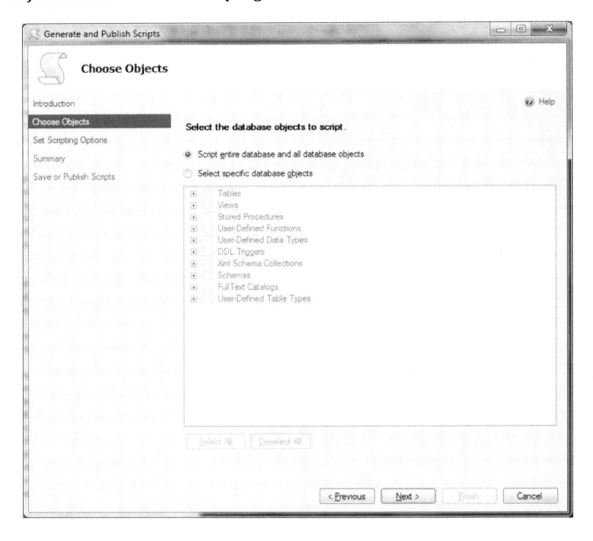

A number of options can be set for generation, including scripting of related objects.

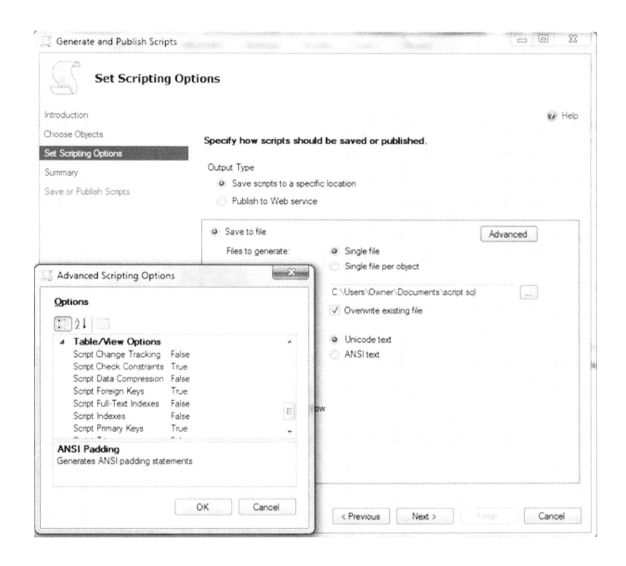

The script generated by the Script Wizard for the Banking.Loan table and related objects

```
USE [AdventureWorks2012]
GO
SET ANSI_NULLS ON
GO
SET QUOTED_IDENTIFIER ON
GO
SET ANSI_PADDING ON
GO
CREATE TABLE [Banking].[Loan](
        [LoanID] [int] IDENTITY(1,1) NOT NULL,
        [BranchID] [int] NOT NULL,
        [LoanNumber] [char](20) NOT NULL,
        [LoanType] [varchar](30) NOT NULL,
        [Amount] [money] NOT NULL,
        [ModifiedDate] [datetime] NULL,
PRIMARY KEY CLUSTERED
(       [LoanID] ASC
)WITH (PAD_INDEX = OFF, STATISTICS_NORECOMPUTE = OFF, IGNORE_DUP_KEY = OFF,
ALLOW_ROW_LOCKS = ON, ALLOW_PAGE_LOCKS = ON) ON [PRIMARY],
UNIQUE NONCLUSTERED
(
        [LoanID] ASC
)WITH (PAD_INDEX = OFF, STATISTICS_NORECOMPUTE = OFF, IGNORE_DUP_KEY = OFF,
ALLOW_ROW_LOCKS = ON, ALLOW_PAGE_LOCKS = ON) ON [PRIMARY],
UNIQUE NONCLUSTERED
(
        [LoanNumber] ASC
)WITH (PAD_INDEX = OFF, STATISTICS_NORECOMPUTE = OFF, IGNORE_DUP_KEY = OFF,
ALLOW_ROW_LOCKS = ON, ALLOW_PAGE_LOCKS = ON) ON [PRIMARY]
) ON [PRIMARY]

GO
SET ANSI_PADDING ON
GO
ALTER TABLE [Banking].[Loan] ADD  DEFAULT (getdate()) FOR [ModifiedDate]
GO
ALTER TABLE [Banking].[Loan]  WITH CHECK ADD FOREIGN KEY([BranchID])
REFERENCES [Banking].[Branch] ([BranchID])
ON DELETE CASCADE
GO
```

CHAPTER 5: Fundamentals of Relational Database Design

SEQUENCE Objects

Sequence objects are new in SQL Server 2012. They are similar to the INT IDENTITY(1,1) sequence, however, there is a big difference: they don't "live" inside a table. They are table independent database objects. T-SQL demonstration script displays the flexibility of the new method for sequence number management.

```
-- Create a sequence object similar to INT IDENTITY(1,1)
CREATE SEQUENCE seqPurchaseOrder
AS INT
START WITH 1   INCREMENT BY 1;
GO

SELECT NEXT VALUE FOR seqPurchaseOrder;
GO 50
/* 1  2  3  .... 50 */

SELECT NEXT VALUE FOR seqPurchaseOrder;
GO
-- 51

SELECT NextOrderNo = NEXT VALUE FOR seqPurchaseOrder;
-- 52

SELECT NEXT VALUE FOR seqPurchaseOrder as NextOrderNo;
-- 54

EXEC sp_help seqPurchaseOrder;
```

Name	Owner	Type	Created_datetime
seqPurchaseOrder	dbo	sequence object	2016-06-27 09:14:32.940

```
DECLARE @List TABLE (id int identity(1,1) primary key, i int);
INSERT @List(i) SELECT NEXT VALUE FOR seqPurchaseOrder;
INSERT @List(i) SELECT NEXT VALUE FOR seqPurchaseOrder;
INSERT @List(i) SELECT NEXT VALUE FOR seqPurchaseOrder;
INSERT @List(i) SELECT NEXT VALUE FOR seqPurchaseOrder;
INSERT @List(i) VALUES (NEXT VALUE FOR seqPurchaseOrder);
SELECT * FROM @List
```

id	i
1	55
2	56
3	57
4	58
5	59

CHAPTER 5: Fundamentals of Relational Database Design

SEQUENCE Object Sharing

SEQUENCE is visible in other connections/session as well not only now but until it exists.

Create a new connection to test NEXT VALUE for seqPurchaseOrder.

```
-- Check current value
SELECT current_value
FROM sys.sequences
WHERE name = 'seqPurchaseOrder';
-- 58
```

```
-- Check metadata
SELECT name, object_id, schema_name(schema_id) as SchemaName, type
FROM sys.sequences;
```

name	object_id	SchemaName	type
seqPurchaseOrder	1338487847	dbo	SO

```
DECLARE @List TABLE (id int identity(1,1) primary key,
            i int default (NEXT VALUE FOR seqPurchaseOrder));
INSERT @List(i) DEFAULT VALUES;
INSERT @List(i) DEFAULT VALUES;
INSERT @List(i) DEFAULT VALUES;
INSERT @List(i) DEFAULT VALUES;
INSERT @List(i)DEFAULT VALUES;
SELECT * FROM @List
```

id	i
1	59
2	60
3	61
4	62
5	63

```
DROP SEQUENCE seqPurchaseOrder;
GO
```

```
SELECT NEXT VALUE FOR seqPurchaseOrder;
```

```
/* Error Message:  Msg 208, Level 16, State 1, Line 2

Invalid object name 'seqPurchaseOrder'.  */
```

CHAPTER 5: Fundamentals of Relational Database Design

Cyclical Sequence Objects

We can create cyclical sequence objects as well for enumerating cyclical temporal objects such as weekdays or months.

```
CREATE SEQUENCE seqCycleSeven
AS TINYINT
START WITH 1  INCREMENT BY 1  MINVALUE  1  MAXVALUE  7  CYCLE
GO

CREATE TABLE #Weekdays ( ID INT IDENTITY(1,1) PRIMARY KEY, Weekday nchar(20));
GO

-- Populate table with days progressing by addition of cycle number to current day
INSERT INTO #Weekdays
SELECT DATENAME(dw, dateadd(dd,NEXT VALUE for seqCycleSeven,CURRENT_TIMESTAMP));
GO 20

SELECT * FROM #Weekdays ORDER BY ID;
GO
```

ID	Weekday
1	Tuesday
2	Wednesday
3	Thursday
4	Friday
5	Saturday
6	Sunday
7	Monday
8	Tuesday
9	Wednesday
10	Thursday
11	Friday
12	Saturday
13	Sunday
14	Monday
15	Tuesday
16	Wednesday
17	Thursday
18	Friday
19	Saturday
20	Sunday

```
DROP SEQUENCE seqCycleSeven;  DROP TABLE #Weekdays;
```

CHAPTER 5: Fundamentals of Relational Database Design

Getting the Source Code with sp_helptext

The sp_helptext system procedure can be applied to get the source code for some objects, but not all. **Table source code can only be obtained with GUI scripting in Object Explorer.**

```
EXEC sp_helptext 'sp_who'
GO
-- Command(s) completed successfully. - 94 rows - Partial results.


CREATE PROCEDURE sys.Sp_who --- 1995/11/28 15:48
 @loginame SYSNAME = NULL --or 'active'
AS
  DECLARE @spidlow  INT,
       @spidhigh INT,
       @spid    INT,
       @sid     VARBINARY(85)

  SELECT @spidlow = 0,
     @spidhigh = 32767

  IF ( @loginame IS NOT NULL
     AND Upper(@loginame COLLATE latin1_general_ci_as) = 'ACTIVE' )
   BEGIN
     SELECT spid,
         ecid,
         status,
         loginame=Rtrim(loginame),
         hostname,
         blk=CONVERT(CHAR(5), blocked),
         dbname = CASE
              WHEN dbid = 0 THEN NULL
              WHEN dbid <> 0 THEN Db_name(dbid)
            END,
         cmd,
         request_id
     FROM   sys.sysprocesses_ex
     WHERE  spid >= @spidlow
        AND spid <= @spidhigh
        AND Upper(cmd) <> 'AWAITING COMMAND'

     RETURN ( 0 )
   END
```

CHAPTER 6: Normal Forms & Database Normalization

The Goals of Database Normalizaton

Database normalization is the design technique of logically organizing data in a database:

> ➤ Data should uniquely be addressable in a database by table, row and column identification - like x, y, z coordinates in 3D space.

> ➤ Data redundancy (storing the same data in more than one table) should be avoided.

> ➤ Data dependency (a property is fully dependent on the PRIMARY KEY) should ensure that a piece of data gets into the right table or if there is none, a new one is created.

The first goal is relatively easy to achieve yet data duplication in a table is a constant issue plaguing database installations. The second goal is simple as well yet it conflicts with deep-seated human insecurity of not seeing all the data together. The third goal on the other hand requires careful design considerations, it can be challenging for complex data relationships or if the database designer is not familiar with the application. If an OLTP database with many data access points is not normalized, the result is inefficiency in database application development and maintenance which can be quite costly to a company for years to come. Metadata query to list all FOREIGN KEYs in NorthWind followed by a high level database diagram.

```
select     fkschema = fk.constraint_schema, fktable = fk.table_name, fkcolumn = fk.column_name,
           pkcolumn = pk.column_name,  pktable = pk.table_name, pkschema = pk.table_schema,
           fkname = rc.constraint_name
from  northwind.information_schema.referential_constraints rc
        inner join northwind.information_schema.key_column_usage fk
              on fk.constraint_name = rc.constraint_name
        inner join northwind.information_schema.key_column_usage pk
              on pk.constraint_name = rc.unique_constraint_name
where   fk.ordinal_position = pk.ordinal_position order by fkschema, fktable, fkcolumn;
```

fkschema	fktable	fkcolumn	pkcolumn	pktable	pkschema	fkname
dbo	CustomerCustomerDemo	CustomerID	CustomerID	Customers	dbo	FK_CustomerCustomerDemo_Customers
dbo	CustomerCustomerDemo	CustomerTypeID	CustomerTypeID	CustomerDemographics	dbo	FK_CustomerCustomerDemo
dbo	Employees	ReportsTo	EmployeeID	Employees	dbo	FK_Employees_Employees
dbo	EmployeeTerritories	EmployeeID	EmployeeID	Employees	dbo	FK_EmployeeTerritories_Employees
dbo	EmployeeTerritories	TerritoryID	TerritoryID	Territories	dbo	FK_EmployeeTerritories_Territories
dbo	Order Details	OrderID	OrderID	Orders	dbo	FK_Order_Details_Orders
dbo	Order Details	ProductID	ProductID	Products	dbo	FK_Order_Details_Products
dbo	Orders	CustomerID	CustomerID	Customers	dbo	FK_Orders_Customers
dbo	Orders	EmployeeID	EmployeeID	Employees	dbo	FK_Orders_Employees
dbo	Orders	ShipVia	ShipperID	Shippers	dbo	FK_Orders_Shippers
dbo	Products	CategoryID	CategoryID	Categories	dbo	FK_Products_Categories
dbo	Products	SupplierID	SupplierID	Suppliers	dbo	FK_Products_Suppliers
dbo	Territories	RegionID	RegionID	Region	dbo	FK_Territories_Region

CHAPTER 6: Normal Forms & Database Normalization

Orders & Related Tables Diagram in Northwind

The database diagram clearly shows the central role of the Orders table at a company which is a reseller not a manufacturer.

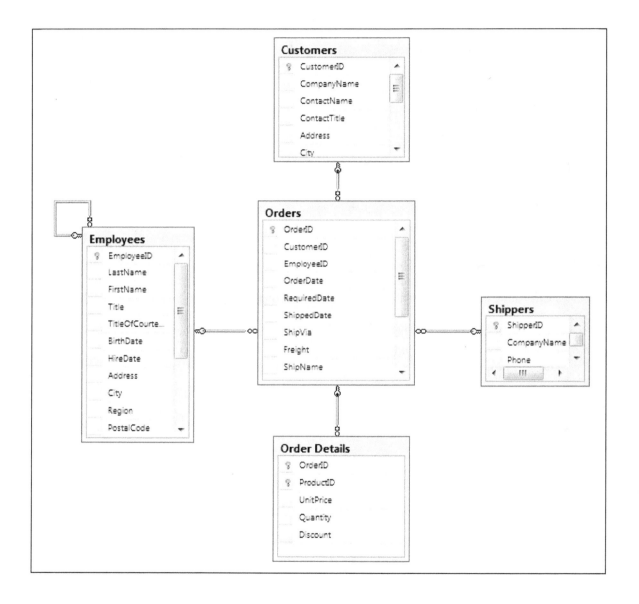

First Normal Form (1NF)

The first normal form establishes RDBMS basics. The rules make common sense.

➢ Each group of related data (entity) should have its own table (no piggybacking data).

➢ Each column should be identified with a unique name in a table.

➢ Each row should be identified with a unique column or set of columns (PRIMARY KEY).

Selected tables (entities) in Northwind database.

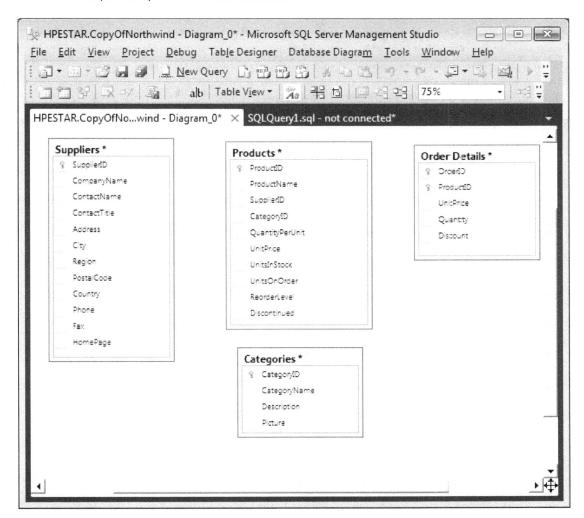

CHAPTER 6: Normal Forms & Database Normalization

Second Normal Form (2NF)

The Second Normal Form addresses the issue of piggybacking data on a related table.

> ➢ Tables are in First Normal Form.

> ➢ Remove subsets of data that apply to multiple rows of a table and create a separate table for them.

> ➢ Create relationships between these new tables and their predecessors through the use of FOREIGN KEYs.

The tacit assumption here that there was no logical data modeling or that had a mistake. The database designer has created a set of tables and now taking a second look to see if all data belong to that table. Frequently the design starts with lead database developer preparing a first version of the design. Only big companies can afford the "luxury" of logical data modeling and professional database designer. That has to be qualified with a little known fact. Even a small company can hire a professional database designer for a month, surely money well spent. Categories table can easily piggyback on the Products table. Being a separate table increases the usefulness, flexibility and expandability of the design.

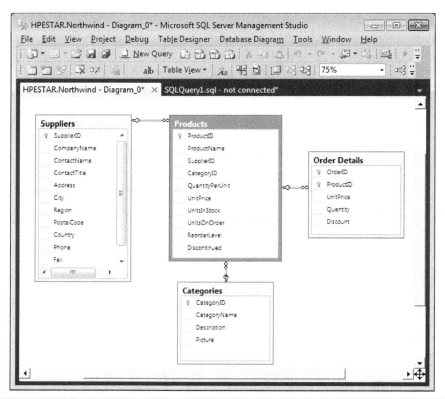

Third Normal Form (3NF)

The Third Normal Form addresses the issue of storing the data in the appropriate table.

➢ Tables are in Second Normal Form.

➢ Remove columns that are not dependent upon the PRIMARY KEY and move them to the correct table.

The royalty and ytd_sales columns are not fully dependent on the title_id PRIMARY KEY. In fact royalty schedule is specified in the roysched table and the dependency includes quantity sold. A view (virtual table) can be setup to return the current royalties based on books sold and the royalty schedule. A more appropriate table for ytd_sales would be saleshist (SalesHistory). The inclusion of the time dependent dynamic ytd_sales column is suspicious right off the bat since all the other columns are static.

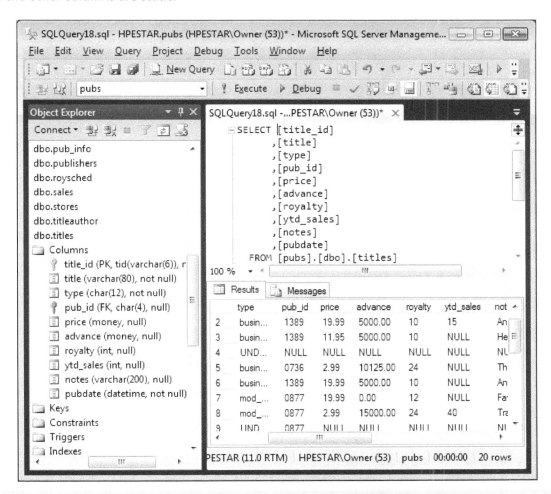

CHAPTER 6: Normal Forms & Database Normalization

Fourth Normal Form (4NF)

The Fourth Normal Form addresses the issue of subtle data dependency:

> ➢ Tables are in Third Normal Form.

> ➢ A relation should not have multi-valued dependencies.

If we look at "Road-650 Black, 44" and "Road-650 Red, 44" bikes in Production.Product we see
that they are the same bike with different color. So it would be sufficient to store only a single
row "Road-650, 44" and setup a junction table between the Product table and the (new) Color
table to indicate the color variations and other dependent information. We can see that the
color occurs in 3 columns: Name, ProductNumber (first letter of color) and Color. By doing 4NF
normalization we can remove the color reference from the Name and ProductNumber columns.

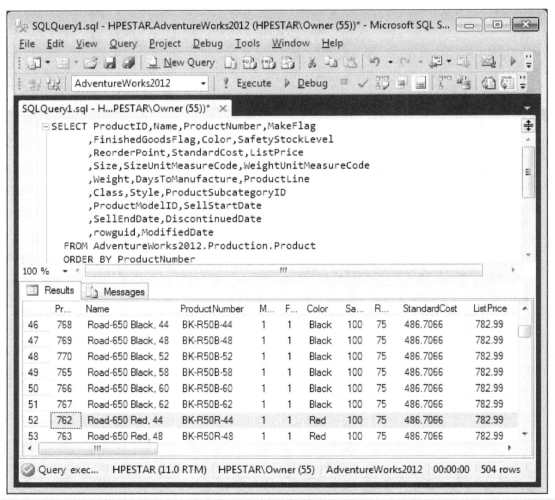

Database Denormalizaton

Database denormalization is a technique to reduce the number of tables in a normalized database. The author personally disagrees with this process: why would you go into the trouble and expense of creating a normalized database and then ruin it? Regardless of the author's opinion, denormalization is an accepted notion in the database industry. Too many tables require too many JOINs, that is the underlying justification. The trouble with this process is two-fold:

➢ There is no guideline when to stop with denormalization, 10% table reduction, 50%?

➢ Also, there are no guidelines as to which tables to eliminate when denormalizing.

If you eliminate too many tables you may just end up with a messy database instead of the original neat & efficient 3NF database thus creating a potential disaster for your employer. Typically you would look at the small static tables as candidates for elimination which are not FOREIGN KEY referenced from many tables. There are precise guidelines now to achieve a normalized database. It is a scientific process. Denormalization is not. Performance is another reason mentioned for denormalization, but that is generally not a valid claim. There are much better ways to achieve good performance than denormalizing a well-designed database system. Hypothetically, let's take a look at low population tables in AdventureWorks2012, as candidates for denormalization.

```
SELECT  TOP 10 SCHEMA_NAME(schema_id)+'.'+o.name AS TableName, max(i.rows) AS Rows
FROM    sys.sysobjects o INNER JOIN sys.sysindexes i   ON o.id = i.id
    INNER JOIN sys.objects oo     ON o.id = oo.object_id
WHERE   xtype = 'u' AND OBJECTPROPERTY(o.id,N'IsUserTable') = 1
GROUP BY schema_id, o.name ORDER BY Rows ASC;
```

TableName	Rows
dbo.ErrorLog	0
dbo.AWBuildVersion	1
Person.PhoneNumberType	3
HumanResources.Shift	3
Sales.ShoppingCartItem	3
Production.ProductCategory	4
Production.ProductReview	4
Production.Illustration	5
Purchasing.ShipMethod	5
Person.AddressType	6

Tables like PhoneNumberType, Shift, Shipmethod and SalesReason can likely be eliminated without dire consequences. However, why ruin a well-designed 3NF database such as AdventureWorks2012 just to decrease the number of JOINs with one or two? Is it annoying to have 10 JOINs in a query? Not really. That is how SQL works. Is SQL Server going to be much faster with 8 JOINs as opposed to 10 JOINs? No, there is no such a rule in query optimization.

CHAPTER 6: Normal Forms & Database Normalization

Better Alternative to Denormalization

The best alternative is to use views for frequently used queries to avoid building JOINs again and again. The results of SELECT from a view must be sorted with ORDER BY just like the case for tables. There is no way around it. Demonstration of the powerful method.

```
USE AdventureWorks;
SELECT
            V.Name                                          AS Vendor,
            CONCAT(C.LastName, ', ', C.FirstName)           AS Contact,
            CT.Name                                         AS Title
FROM Person.Contact AS C
   INNER JOIN Purchasing.VendorContact VC
            ON C.ContactID = VC.ContactID
   INNER JOIN Person.ContactType CT
            ON CT.ContactTypeID = VC.ContactTypeID
   INNER JOIN Purchasing.Vendor V
            ON V.VendorID = VC.VendorID
ORDER BY Vendor, Contact;
-- (156 row(s) affected)
```

```
CREATE VIEW vVendorContact
AS
SELECT
            V.Name                                          AS Vendor,
            CONCAT(C.LastName, ', ', C.FirstName)           AS Contact,
            CT.Name                                         AS Title
FROM Person.Contact AS C
   INNER JOIN Purchasing.VendorContact VC        ON C.ContactID = VC.ContactID
   INNER JOIN Person.ContactType CT              ON CT.ContactTypeID = VC.ContactTypeID
   INNER JOIN Purchasing.Vendor V                ON V.VendorID = VC.VendorID
GO
```

```
SELECT TOP 5 * FROM vVendorContact ORDER BY Vendor, Contact;
```

Vendor	Contact	Title
A. Datum Corporation	Pellow, Frank	Assistant Sales Agent
A. Datum Corporation	Wilkie, Jay	Sales Agent
A. Datum Corporation	Yu, Wei	Sales Manager
Advanced Bicycles	Moeller, Jonathan	Sales Associate
Advanced Bicycles	Wilson, James	Sales Manager

We have created from the 4 tables JOIN, a very simple to use, very easy to remember view.

CHAPTER 6: Normal Forms & Database Normalization

Ten Most Common Database Design Mistakes

Along his database career the author found the following list of common design issues:

➢ Not involving systems analysts and/or subject matter experts in conceptual design.

➢ Not employing accomplished database designer / lead developer to implement 3NF design standards.

➢ Denormalizing a well-designed database.

➢ Not having NATURAL KEY in addition to INT IDENTITY(1,1) SURROGATE PRIMARY KEY.

➢ Poor documentation & lack of naming convention for the project.

➢ Not using PRIMARY KEY, FOREIGN KEY, UNIQUE , CHECK & DEFAULT constraints to protect data integrity.

➢ Using client programs for data management instead of server side stored procedures, functions & views.

➢ Using triggers to fix design or client software problems.

➢ Not following the solution implementation hierarchy: constraints -> stored procedures -> triggers -> client SW.

➢ Lack of formal Quality Assurance process.

Working for a Company with Messy Database Design

In your career you may work for companies with proper 3NF design databases, companies with messy databases or somewhere in the middle. It is a joy to work in 3NF environment. On the other hand, if the database is badly designed, or more accurately lacks design, you have to be careful in criticizing it because you can pick up enemies quickly or even get fired. Badly designed database usually becomes an IT department political issue instead of remaining a technical issue. Most companies don't want to invest in redesigning the database properly. In such a situation you have to accept working with poorly designed databases, enjoy your nice paycheck and wait for an opportunity when new tables or database is needed to create proper 3NF design.

Query to List All Table Sizes in a Database

T-SQL script to list all table sizes in AdventureWorks2012 database. Note: the tables are uniquely named in AdventureWorks databases, so there are no duplicates if the schema name is not used. This assumption though not true generally. Objects can be named the same in different schemas.

```
declare @TableSpace table (TableName sysname, RowsK varchar(32), -- table variable
       ReservedMB varchar(32), DataMB varchar(32),
       IndexMB varchar(32), UnusedMB varchar(32));

insert @TableSpace
exec sp_MSforeachtable @command1="exec sp_spaceused '?';" -- undocumented system procedure

update @TableSpace set RowsK = CONVERT(varchar,  1+convert(int, RowsK)/1024)
update @TableSpace set ReservedMB = CONVERT(varchar,
           1+convert(int,LEFT(ReservedMB, charindex(' K', ReservedMB,-1)))/1024);
update @TableSpace set DataMB = CONVERT(varchar,
           1+convert(int,LEFT(DataMB, charindex(' K', DataMB,-1)))/1024);
update @TableSpace set IndexMB = CONVERT(varchar,
           convert(int,LEFT(IndexMB, charindex(' K', IndexMB,-1)))/1024);
update @TableSpace set UnusedMB = CONVERT(varchar,
           convert(int,LEFT(UnusedMB, charindex(' K', UnusedMB,-1)))/1024);

select * from @TableSpace order by convert(int,DataMB) desc;
go
-- (71 row(s) affected) -- Partial results.
```

TableName	RowsK	ReservedMB	DataMB	IndexMB	UnusedMB
Person	20	84	30	51	2
SalesOrderDetail	119	18	10	6	1
DatabaseLog	2	7	7	0	0
TransactionHistory	111	11	7	3	0
WorkOrderRouting	66	8	6	1	0
SalesOrderHeader	31	9	6	2	0
WorkOrder	71	7	5	2	0
TransactionHistoryArchive	88	9	5	3	0
ProductPhoto	1	3	3	0	0
Address	20	6	3	2	0
CreditCard	19	3	2	0	0
EmailAddress	20	4	2	1	0
Password	20	2	2	0	0
PersonPhone	20	3	2	0	0
SalesTerritory	1	1	1	0	0
PhoneNumberType	1	1	1	0	0
Product	1	1	1	0	0
SalesTerritoryHistory	1	1	1	0	0
SalesPersonQuotaHistory	1	1	1	0	0
Employee	1	1	1	0	0

CHAPTER 7: Functional Database Design

Types of Table Relationships

The most frequent relationship is one-to-many (or many-to-one) indicating many FOREIGN KEY references to a single PRIMARY KEY table row. Example: Products & ProductCategories; A product category may have 50 different products. The next most popular one is many-to-many relationship indicating that a single row in Table Alpha can reference multiple rows in Table Beta. Example: Classes & Students at a college; A class may have 20 students and a student may take 5 different classes. In the following pubs table relationship diagram we can see:

> many-to-many relationship (oo - oo connectors): titleauthor table
> one-to-one relationship (2 gold keys): publishers & pub_info tables
> one-to-many: the remaining relationships

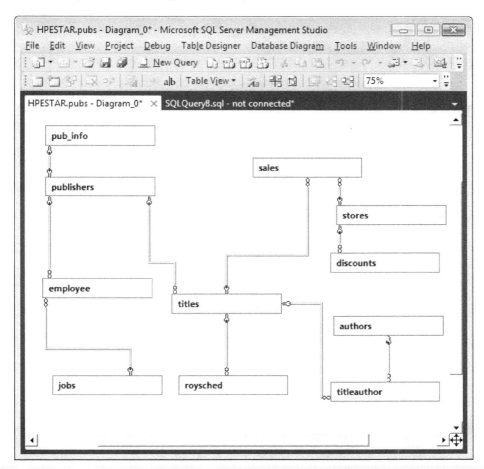

CHAPTER 7: Functional Database Design

One-To-Many Relationship - FOREIGN KEY Reference

Northwind example shows that each product belongs to a category. CategoryID column in the Products table (FOREIGN KEY) references CategoryID in Categories table (PRIMARY KEY). One category can have 0 to many products. FK name can be different from PK name. However, if possible, PK name is the best choice for FK name. When multiple FK-s referencing the same PK, we have to choose different names for FK-s.

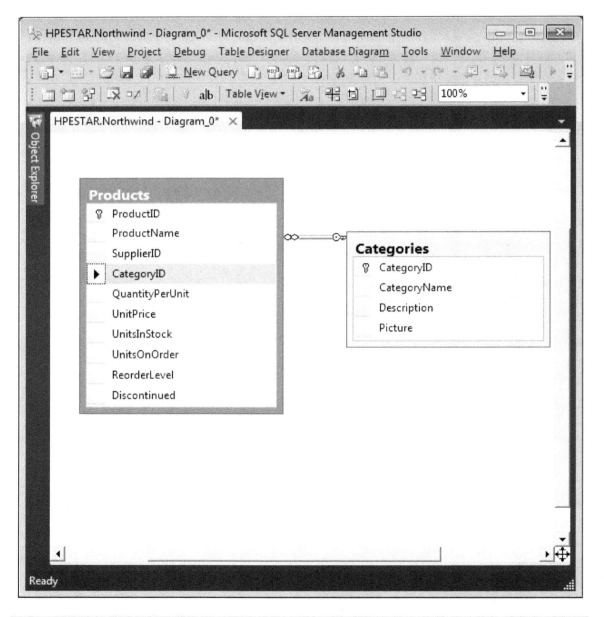

CategoryID in the Products table is a FOREIGN KEY (a pointer) to a PRIMARY KEY in the Categories table

Therefore, we can safely JOIN the two tables using the two ON KEYs.

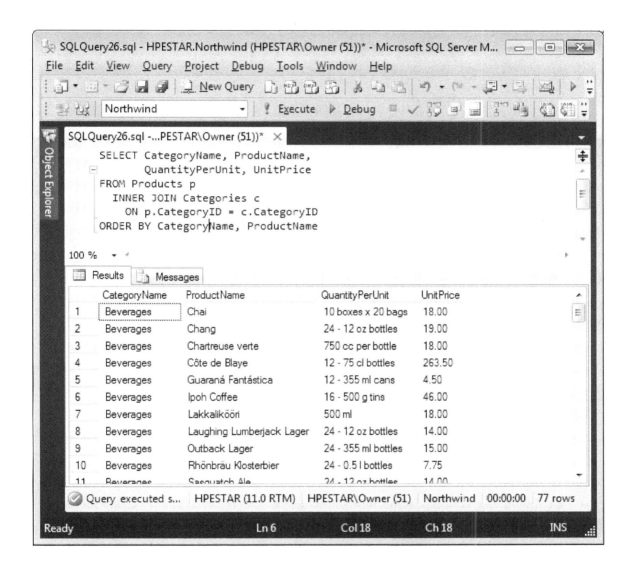

The PRIMARY KEY and FOREIGN KEY should not be exposed to the database application user

The Business Intelligence consumer needs meaningful information not meaningless numbers. The software engineer can see the PK and FK values as part of his work.

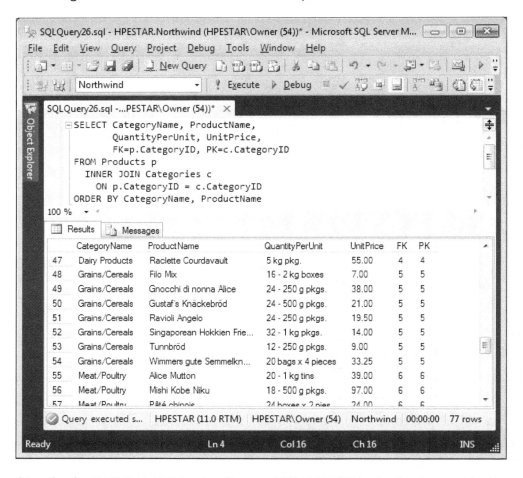

We could make the NATURAL KEY ProductName a PRIMARY KEY in the Products table. However, that is a string field (column) nvarchar(40) which can be 80 bytes in size (each UNICODE character is 2 bytes). That would present increased space use and decreased performance in JOINs. It would also present increased maintenance cost if we have to change a product name, for example, "Ravioli Angelo" to "Ravioli Los Angeles". The change would have to be performed in the PRIMARY KEY table and each FOREIGN KEY table. The 4-byte integer SURROGATE PRIMARY KEY ProductID solves all the problems above. Minimal space use, fast in JOINs and since a meaningless number (a database pointer), we never have to change it. If the ProductName changes, it is just a single UPDATE in the PRIMARY KEY table.

CHAPTER 7: Functional Database Design

Composite PRIMARY KEY

A composite PRIMARY KEY consists of two or more columns. Junction tables typical y apply composite PRIMARY KEYs. An example is the Production.ProductProductPhoto junction table.

> ProductID (PK, FK, int, not null)
> ProductPhotoID (PK, FK, int, not null)
> Primary (Flag(bit), not null)
> ModifiedDate (datetime, not null

The PRIMARY KEY is the composite of two FOREIGN KEYs: ProductID and ProductPhotoID.

T-SQL script definition of the above composite PRIMARY KEY.

```
USE [AdventureWorks2012];
GO

ALTER TABLE [Production].[ProductProductPhoto]
ADD  CONSTRAINT [PK_ProductProductPhoto_ProductID_ProductPhotoID]
PRIMARY KEY NONCLUSTERED
(
        [ProductID] ASC,
        [ProductPhotoID] ASC
);
```

A FOREIGN KEY referencing a composite PRIMARY KEY must have the same column structure. Query to display all the data in the table.

```
SELECT  ProductID
        ,ProductPhotoID
        ,[Primary]
        ,ModifiedDate
  FROM AdventureWorks2012.Production.ProductProductPhoto;
-- (504 row(s) affected) - Partial results.
```

ProductID	ProductPhotoID	Primary	ModifiedDate
813	1	1	2006-06-01 00:00:00.000
814	1	1	2006-06-01 00:00:00.0C0
815	160	1	2006-06-01 00:00:00.0C0
816	160	1	2006-06-01 00:00:00.0C0
817	160	1	2006-06-01 00:00:00.0C0
818	160	1	2006-06-01 00:00:00.000

> NOTE
> Use composite UNIQUE KEY and INT SURROGATE PRIMARY KEY in base tables.
> Composite PRIMARY KEY requires composite FOREIGN KEY!

CHAPTER 7: Functional Database Design

Parent-Child Hierarchy

When an employee's record includes the manager's ID, it is called self-reference since the manager is an employee also. A simple organizational chart (tree structure) can be established by self-referencing FOREIGN KEYs.

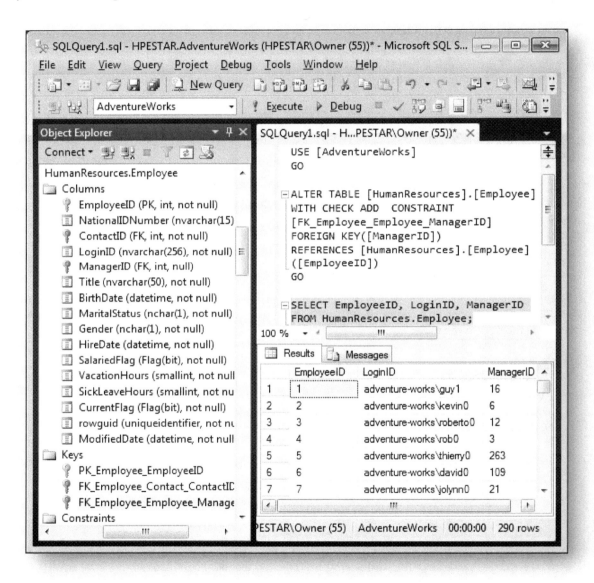

Reading the table: david0 is the supervisor of kevin0, and roberto0 is the supervisor of rob0.

Hierarchical Relationship - Multi-Level with FOREIGN KEYs

Product, ProductSubcategory and ProductCategory in AdventureWorks represent multi-level hierarchy which can be implemented with FOREIGN KEYs. To get the hierarchical information, we need to INNER JOIN the tables on the FOREIGN KEYS and PRIMARY KEYS. Column aliases are used to create meaningful column names from the 3 "Name"-s.

Tree Hierarchy Representation with hierarchyid

An alternate to using self-referencing FOREIGN KEY is the application of hierarchyid data type introduced with SQL Server 2008.

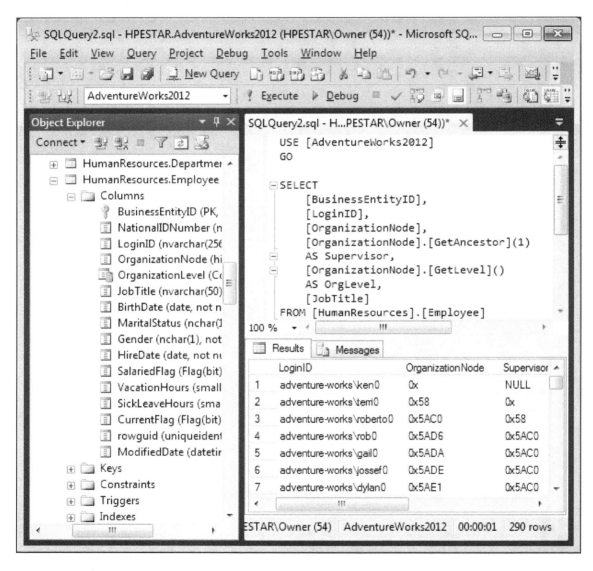

We can read from the table that ken0 (Ken Sanchez, CEO) is the supervisor of terri0 who in turn is the supervisor of roberto0 who is the supervisor of rob0.

Many-To-Many Relationship - Junction Table

Junction tables have many names, most popular among them are junction table, cross-reference table and bridge table. The titleauthor table in the pubs database is a junction table: a title (book) can have many authors and an author can write many titles. The PR MARY KEY is a composite of two FOREIGN KEYs referencing the titles and authors tables.

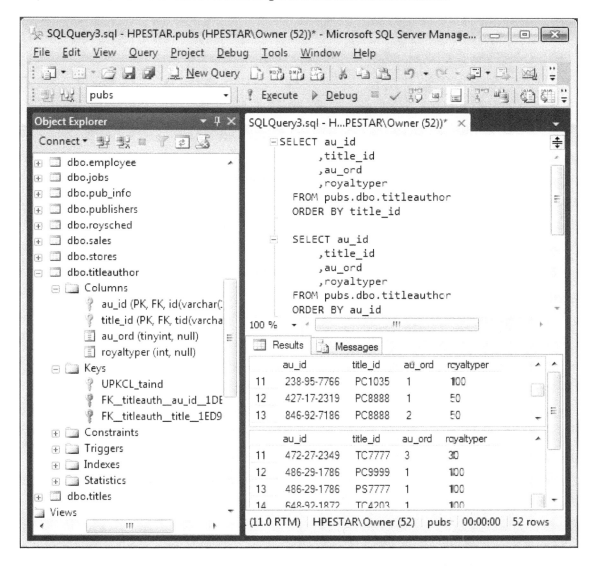

Reading the author - title junction table: book title PC8888 has multiple (two) authors, while author 486-29-1786 wrote multiple (two) books.

CHAPTER 7: Functional Database Design

Parent-Child or Master-Detail Tables Design

In the AdventureWorks series of sample databases, Sales.SalesOrderHeader and
Sales.SalesOrderDetail tables are implemented as master-detail tables. Similarly for
Purchasing.PurchaseOrderHeader and Purchasing.PurchaseOrderDetail. The PRIMARY KEY of
SalesOrderHeader is SalesOrderID (INT IDENTITY(1,1)). The PRIMARY KEY of SalesOrderDetail is
composite of SalesOrderID FOREIGN KEY and SalesOrderDetailID (INT IDENTITY(1,1)). The
business meaning is that an order from a bicycle reseller can have many line items such
mountain bikes, helmets, touring frames and jerseys.

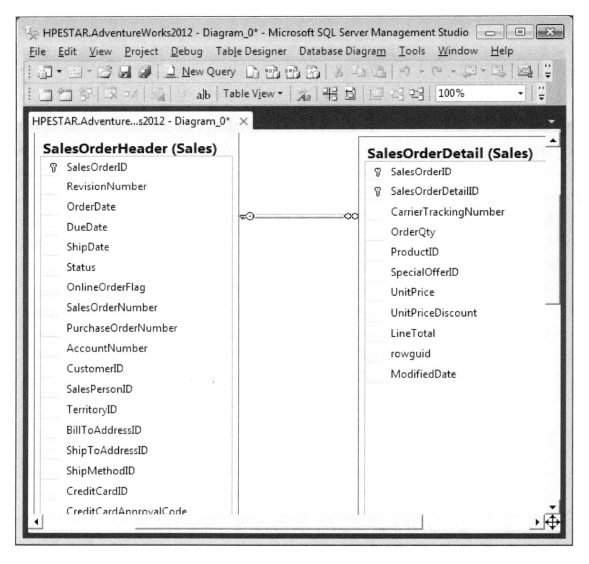

Column Descriptions of SalesOrderHeader & SalesOrderDetail Tables

UNION query to lists the column descriptions for the above master-detail tables from the data dictionary.

```
SELECT  'Sales.SalesOrderHeader' AS TableName, objname    AS ColumnName,
        value                                             AS [Description]
FROM fn_listextendedproperty (NULL, 'schema', 'Sales', 'table', 'SalesOrderHeader', 'Column', default)

UNION

SELECT  'Sales.SalesOrderDetail' AS TableName, objname    AS ColumnName,
        value                                             AS [Description]
FROM fn_listextendedproperty (NULL, 'schema', 'Sales', 'table', 'SalesOrderDetail', 'Column', default)

ORDER BY TableName DESC, ColumnName;
```

TableName	ColumnName	Description
Sales.SalesOrderHeader	AccountNumber	Financial accounting number reference.
Sales.SalesOrderHeader	BillToAddressID	Customer billing address. Foreign key to Address.AddressID.
Sales.SalesOrderHeader	Comment	Sales representative comments.
Sales.SalesOrderHeader	CreditCardApprovalCode	Approval code provided by the credit card company.
Sales.SalesOrderHeader	CreditCardID	Credit card identification number. Foreign key to CreditCard.CreditCardID.
Sales.SalesOrderHeader	CurrencyRateID	Currency exchange rate used. Foreign key to CurrencyRate.CurrencyRateID.
Sales.SalesOrderHeader	CustomerID	Customer identification number. Foreign key to Customer.BusinessEntityID.
Sales.SalesOrderHeader	DueDate	Date the order is due to the customer.
Sales.SalesOrderHeader	Freight	Shipping cost.
Sales.SalesOrderHeader	ModifiedDate	Date and time the record was last updated.
Sales.SalesOrderHeader	OnlineOrderFlag	0 = Order placed by sales person. 1 = Order placed online by customer.
Sales.SalesOrderHeader	OrderDate	Dates the sales order was created.
Sales.SalesOrderHeader	PurchaseOrderNumber	Customer purchase order number reference.
Sales.SalesOrderHeader	RevisionNumber	Incremental number to track changes to the sales order over time.
Sales.SalesOrderHeader	rowguid	ROWGUIDCOL number uniquely identifying the record. Used to support a merge replication sample.
Sales.SalesOrderHeader	SalesOrderID	Primary key.
Sales.SalesOrderHeader	SalesOrderNumber	Unique sales order identification number.
Sales.SalesOrderHeader	SalesPersonID	Sales person who created the sales order. Foreign key to SalesPerson.BusinessEntityID.
Sales.SalesOrderHeader	ShipDate	Date the order was shipped to the customer.
Sales.SalesOrderHeader	ShipMethodID	Shipping method. Foreign key to ShipMethod.ShipMethodID.
Sales.SalesOrderHeader	ShipToAddressID	Customer shipping address. Foreign key to Address.AddressID.
Sales.SalesOrderHeader	Status	Order current status. 1 = In process; 2 = Approved; 3 = Backordered; 4 = Rejected; 5 = Shipped; 6 = Cancelled
Sales.SalesOrderHeader	SubTotal	Sales subtotal. Computed as SUM(SalesOrderDetail.LineTotal)for the appropriate SalesOrderID.
Sales.SalesOrderHeader	TaxAmt	Tax amount.
Sales.SalesOrderHeader	TerritoryID	Territory in which the sale was made. Foreign key to SalesTerritory.SalesTerritoryID.
Sales.SalesOrderHeader	TotalDue	Total due from customer. Computed as Subtotal + TaxAmt + Freight.
Sales.SalesOrderDetail	CarrierTrackingNumber	Shipment tracking number supplied by the shipper.
Sales.SalesOrderDetail	LineTotal	Per product subtotal. Computed as UnitPrice * (1 - UnitPriceDiscount) * OrderQty.
Sales.SalesOrderDetail	ModifiedDate	Date and time the record was last updated.
Sales.SalesOrderDetail	OrderQty	Quantity ordered per product.
Sales.SalesOrderDetail	ProductID	Product sold to customer. Foreign key to Product.ProductID.
Sales.SalesOrderDetail	rowguid	ROWGUIDCOL number uniquely identifying the record. Used to support a merge replication sample.
Sales.SalesOrderDetail	SalesOrderDetailID	Primary key. One incremental unique number per product sold.
Sales.SalesOrderDetail	SalesOrderID	Primary key. Foreign key to SalesOrderHeader.SalesOrderID.
Sales.SalesOrderDetail	SpecialOfferID	Promotional code. Foreign key to SpecialOffer.SpecialOfferID.
Sales.SalesOrderDetail	UnitPrice	Selling price of a single product.
Sales.SalesOrderDetail	UnitPriceDiscount	Discount amount.

Diagram of PurchaseOrderHeader and Related Tables

Database diagram to display the special relationship to the child table PurchaseOrderDetail and PK-FK relationships to other tables.

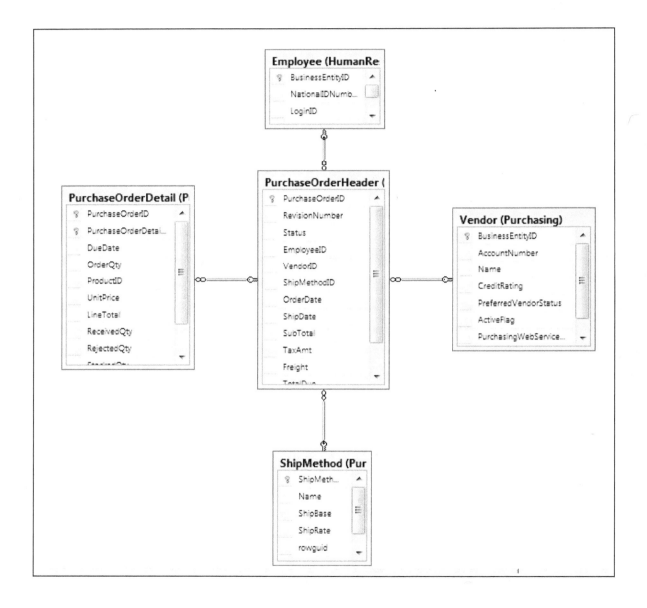

Multiple FOREIGN KEYs from One Table to Another

Database diagram to illustrate the double FOREIGN KEYs from BillOfMaterials table to the Product table. The FOREIGN KEYs are named **ComponentID and ProductAssemblyID**. In the Product table **SizeUnitMeasureCode & WeightUnitMeasureCode** are double FOREIGN KEYs to the UnitMeasure table.

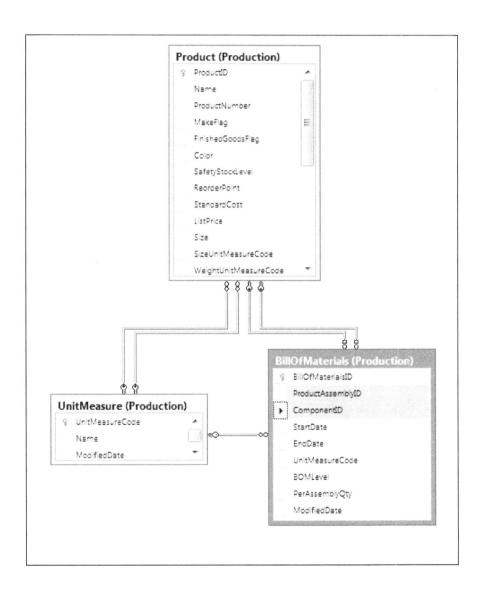

Parent - Multiple Children Table Design

Database design & diagram to represent a parent table with two children table. Notice that in the children table the PRIMARY KEY is a FOREIGN KEY simultaneously.

```
CREATE TABLE Security  (
    Symbol              CHAR(7)  PRIMARY KEY,
    SecurityName        NVARCHAR(64),
    CUSIP               CHAR(9),
    ModifiedDate        DATETIME DEFAULT (CURRENT_TIMESTAMP)   );


CREATE TABLE Stock  (
    Symbol              CHAR(7)  PRIMARY KEY REFERENCES Security ON DELETE CASCADE,
    AuthShares          BIGINT,
    IssuedShares        BIGINT,
    ClosingPrice        DECIMAL(14, 2),
    ModifiedDate        DATETIME DEFAULT (CURRENT_TIMESTAMP)   );


CREATE TABLE Bond   (
    Symbol              CHAR(7)  PRIMARY KEY REFERENCES Security ON DELETE CASCADE,
    Rate                DECIMAL(14, 6),
    FaceValue           DECIMAL(14, 2),
    MaturityDate        DATE,
    ClosingPrice        DECIMAL(14, 2),
    ModifiedDate        DATETIME DEFAULT (CURRENT_TIMESTAMP)   );
```

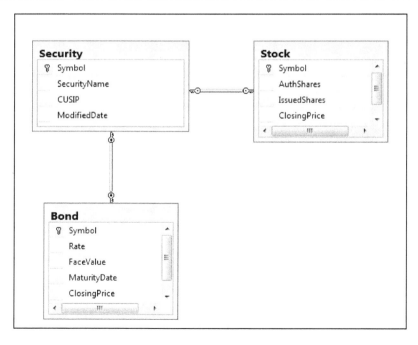

LookupHeader & Lookup Tables for Storing All Lookups

T-SQL script to demonstrate a simple implementation of LookupHeader & Lookup (detail) tables
to prevent database "pollution" by many small lookup (code/translate) tables.

```
USE AdventureWorks2012;

CREATE TABLE LookupHeader
 (
        LookupHeaderID          INT IDENTITY(1, 1)      PRIMARY KEY,
        [Type]                  VARCHAR(80)             UNIQUE,
        ModifiedDate            DATETIME                default ( CURRENT_TIMESTAMP)
 );
go


CREATE TABLE Lookup
 (
        LookupID                INT IDENTITY(1,1) PRIMARY KEY nonclustered,
        LookupHeaderID          INT NOT NULL REFERENCES LookupHeader(LcokupHeaderID),
        Code                    VARCHAR(6) NOT NULL,
        [Description]           VARCHAR(255),
        ModifiedDate            DATETIME default ( CURRENT_TIMESTAMP)
 );
go


-- composite PRIMARY KEY
ALTER TABLE dbo.Lookup
        ADD CONSTRAINT uq_lookup UNIQUE CLUSTERED ( LookupHeaderID, Code );
go


INSERT LookupHeader  ([Type]) VALUES ('Country');
INSERT LookupHeader  ([Type]) VALUES ('Department');

SELECT * FROM   LookupHeader ;
go
```

LookupHeaderID	Type	ModifiedDate
1	Country	2016-08-08 07:34:59.C77
2	Department	2016-08-08 07:34:59.113

```
-- Populate department code
INSERT INTO LookUp (LookupHeaderID, Code, Description)  VALUES   (2, '1', 'Human Resources');
INSERT INTO LookUp (LookupHeaderID, Code, Description)  VALUES   (2, '2', 'Accounting');
INSERT INTO LookUp (LookupHeaderID, Code, Description)  VALUES   (2, '3', 'Engineering');
GO
```

CHAPTER 7: Functional Database Design

-- T-SQL script continued

```
-- Populate country code lookup
INSERT INTO LookUp (LookupHeaderID, Code, Description)
SELECT 1, [CountryRegionCode],[Name]
 FROM [AdventureWorks2012].[Person].[CountryRegion]
ORDER BY CountryRegionCode;
go

-- Check lookup table content
SELECT * FROM   Lookup ORDER  BY LookupHeaderID, Code;
```

Partial display of the Lookup table content.

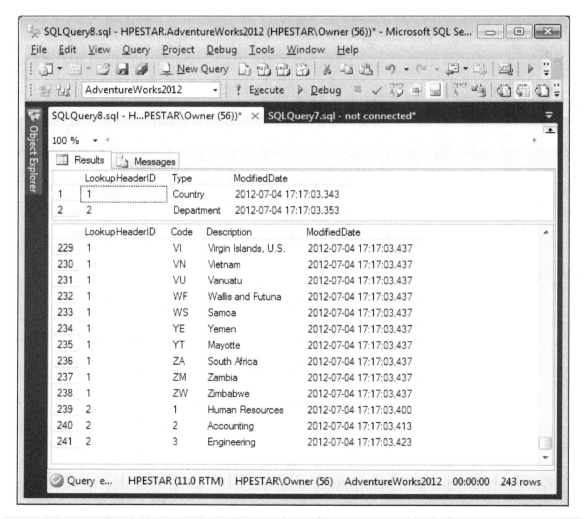

History Table Design

AdventureWorks2012 EmployeeDepartmentHistory table follows the career of an employee from department to department each with StartDate and EndDate. If EndDate is NULL, that is the employee's current department. For employee ID 250 (BusinessEntityID) the current department is 5. The PRIMARY KEY is composite of BusinessEntityID (employee ID), DepartmentID, ShiftID and StartDate. The first 3 columns in the PRIMARY KEY are FOREIGN KEYs also. BusinessEntityID references (points to) the Employee table, DepartmentID the Department table and ShiftID the Shift table.

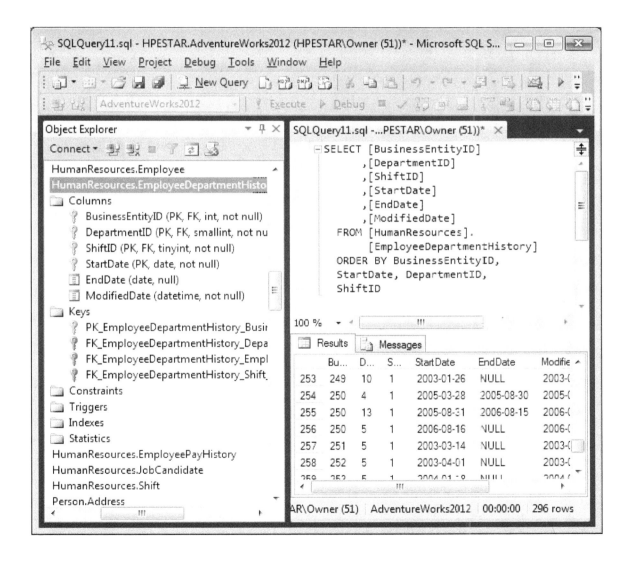

Implementing One-To-One Relationship

In a one-to-one relationship, a row in the main table can have no more than one matching row in the secondary table, and vice versa. **A one-to-one relationship requires that both of the related columns are primary keys.** One-to-one relationship tables are not very common because most of the time a single table is used. Nonetheless, we might use a one-to-one relationship tables to: Vertically partition a table with many columns; Vertically divide a table to a narrow and wide part for performance reasons - example: email header & email body; Isolate sensitive columns in a table for security reasons; Store information that applies only to a subset of the main table thus avoiding lots of NULLs in the rows. Demonstration to show the one-to-one relationship between Product and ProductInventory tables.

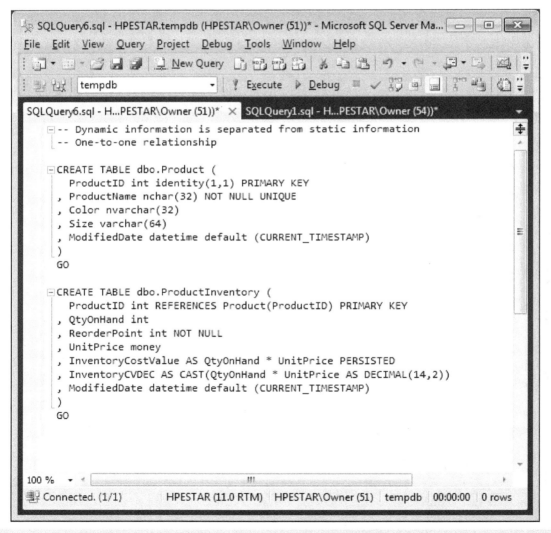

One-To-One Relationship between publisher & pub_info Tables

The intent of the database designer was to separate the bulk data (logo image, PR description) from the regular size columns which likely are more frequently used as well. The implementation: pub_id in pub_info table is PRIMARY KEY and FOREIGN KEY to publishers pub_id.

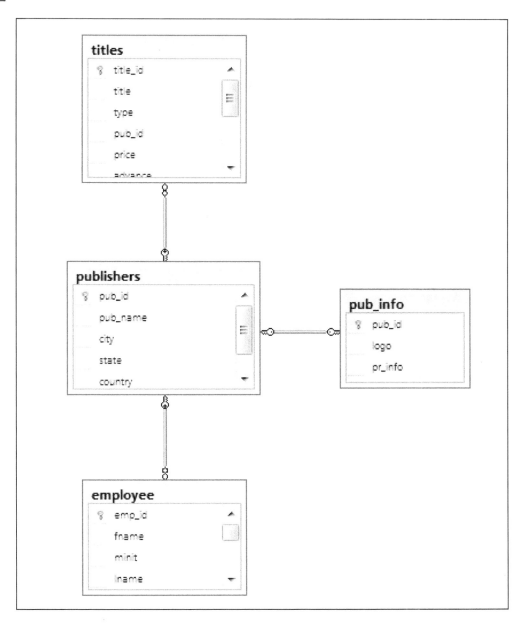

Tables with Computed Columns

A column can be automatically generated by a formula/expression involving other columns. The generation is "on the fly" when needed. To persist the column the PERSISTED property must be used. That is a requirement for some use such as indexing. All computed columns can be listed by a simple query.

```
SELECT object_name(object_id) as TableName, name AS ComputedColumn,
        definition AS Expression FROM sys.computed_columns ORDER BY name;
```

The demonstration introduces 2 computed columns into the ProductInventory table.

```
USE tempdb;

CREATE TABLE dbo.Product (
        ProductID int identity(1,1) PRIMARY KEY
        , ProductName nchar(32) NOT NULL UNIQUE
        , Color nvarchar(32)
        , Size varchar(64)
        , ModifiedDate datetime default (CURRENT_TIMESTAMP) );

-- Table with two computed columns
CREATE TABLE dbo.ProductInventory (
        ProductID int REFERENCES Product(ProductID) PRIMARY KEY
        , QtyOnHand int
        , ReorderPoint int NOT NULL
        , UnitPrice money
        , InventoryCostValue AS QtyOnHand * UnitPrice PERSISTED
        , InventoryCVDEC AS CAST(QtyOnHand * UnitPrice AS DECIMAL(14,0))
        , ModifiedDate datetime default (CURRENT_TIMESTAMP) );
GO


INSERT Product(ProductName, Color, Size) SELECT 'MusicMobile', 'White', '2" x 3"';
INSERT Product(ProductName, Color, Size) SELECT 'ReaderMobile',  'Black', '5" x 9"';
INSERT Product(ProductName, Color, Size) SELECT 'PhoneMobile',  'Blue', '2 1/2" x 4"';
INSERT Product(ProductName, Color, Size) SELECT 'DELTA laptop', 'Gray', '12" x 16" x 2"';
GO

SELECT * from dbo.Product;
```

ProductID	ProductName	Color	Size	ModifiedDate
1	MusicMobile	White	2" x 3"	2016-07-08 10:05:53.943
2	ReaderMobile	Black	5" x 9"	2016-07-08 10:05:53.947
3	PhoneMobile	Blue	2 1/2" x 4"	2016-07-08 10:05:53.947
4	DELTA laptop	Gray	12" x 16" x 2"	2016-07-08 10:05:53.947

-- T-SQL script continued

INSERT ProductInventory (ProductID, QtyOnHand, ReorderPoint, UnitPrice) SELECT 1, 105, 30, $99.99;
INSERT ProductInventory (ProductID, QtyOnHand, ReorderPoint, UnitPrice) SELECT 2, 105, 40, $299.99;
INSERT ProductInventory (ProductID, QtyOnHand, ReorderPoint, UnitPrice) SELECT 3, 208, 30, $399.99;
INSERT ProductInventory (ProductID, QtyOnHand, ReorderPoint, UnitPrice) SELECT 4, 103, 30, $599.99;
GO

SELECT * FROM ProductInventory;
GO

ProductID	QtyOnHand	ReorderPoint	UnitPrice	InventoryCostValue	InventoryCVDEC
1	105	30	99.99	10498.95	10499
2	105	40	299.99	31498.95	31499
3	208	30	399.99	83197.92	83198
4	103	30	599.99	61798.97	61799

Combination query with INNER JOIN and formatting.

```
SELECT          ProductName                             AS [Product Name],
                QtyOnHand                               AS [Quantity On Hand],
                ReorderPoint                            AS [Reorder Point],
                FORMAT(UnitPrice,'c','en-US')           AS [Unit Price],
                FORMAT(InventoryCostValue, 'c','en-US') AS [ Inventory Cost Value],
                FORMAT(InventoryCVDEC, 'c','en-US')     AS [Inventory Cost Rounded]
FROM Product P
        INNER JOIN ProductInventory PI
                ON P.ProductID = PI.ProductID
ORDER BY ProductName;
GO
```

Product Name	Quantity On Hand	Reorder Point	Unit Price	Inventory Cost Value	Inventory Cost Rounded
DELTA laptop	103	30	$599.99	$61,798.97	$61,799.00
MusicMobile	105	30	$99.99	$10,498.95	$10,499.00
PhoneMobile	208	30	$399.99	$83,197.92	$83,198.00
ReaderMobile	105	40	$299.99	$31,498.95	$31,499.00

-- Cleanup - FOREIGN KEY table must be dropped first
DROP TABLE tempdb.dbo.ProductInventory;
DROP TABLE tempdb.dbo.Product;

CHAPTER 7: Functional Database Design

Building the Data Dictionary

The best way to build the data dictionary is the same time when the database objects are created. It can also be done in the final phases of the database development project when changes are rare to the object designs.

GUI Data Dictionary Maintenance

As an example, right click on a table column name and choose Properties.

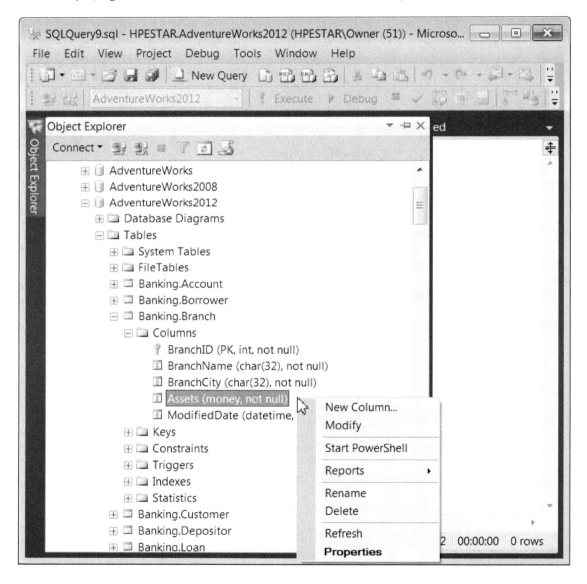

Extended Properties page can be used for Data Dictionary entry

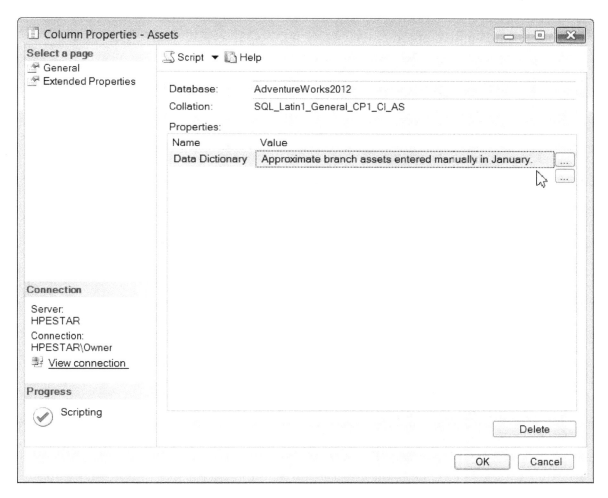

Check the new entry in the Data Dictionary with a query.

SELECT *
FROM fn_listextendedproperty (NULL, 'schema', 'Banking', 'table', 'Branch', 'Column', NULL);
GO

objtype	objname	name	value
COLUMN	Assets	Data Dictionary	Approximate branch assets entered manually in January.

CHAPTER 7: Functional Database Design

Data Dictionary Maintenance with T-SQL Scripts

The advantage of using T-SQL scripts for Data Dictionary maintenance is that the script can be saved as a .sql file and rerun when necessary as is or after editing. BOL Data Dictionary web page: http://msdn.microsoft.com/en-us/library/ms124438(v=sql.100).aspx .

```
USE [AdventureWorks2012];
GO


-- Delete Data Dictionary entry
EXEC sys.sp_dropextendedproperty @name=N'Data Dictionary' ,
        @level0type=N'SCHEMA',@level0name=N'Banking',
        @level1type=N'TABLE',@level1name=N'Branch',
        @level2type=N'COLUMN',@level2name=N'Assets';
GO


-- Add Data Dictionary entry
EXEC sys.sp_addextendedproperty @name=N'Data Dictionary',
        @value=N'Approximate branch assets entered manually in January each year.' ,
        @level0type=N'SCHEMA',@level0name=N'Banking', @level1type=N'TABLE',
        @level1name=N'Branch', @level2type=N'COLUMN',@level2name=N'Assets';
GO


-- Check new Data Dictionary entry
SELECT *
FROM fn_listextendedproperty (NULL, 'schema', 'Banking', 'table', 'Branch', 'Column', NULL);
```

objtype	objname	name	value
COLUMN	Assets	Data Dictionary	Approximate branch assets entered manually in January each year.

```
-- Data Dictionary entry for BranchName
EXEC sys.sp_addextendedproperty @name=N'Data Dictionary',
        @value=N'Name of the branch. Updated by supervisor only.' ,
        @level0type=N'SCHEMA',@level0name=N'Banking', @level1type=N'TABLE',
        @level1name=N'Branch', @level2type=N'COLUMN',@level2name=N'BranchName';
GO
```

CHAPTER 7: Functional Database Design

Updating an Existing Data Dictionary Entry

```
-- Update Data Dictionary entry
EXEC sys.sp_updateextendedproperty @name=N'Data Dictionary',
@value=N'Approximate branch assets entered in January each year by an automated process.' ,
@level0type=N'SCHEMA',@level0name=N'Banking',
@level1type=N'TABLE',@level1name=N'Branch',
@level2type=N'COLUMN',@level2name=N'Assets'
GO


SELECT *
FROM fn_listextendedproperty (NULL, 'schema', 'Banking', 'table', 'Branch', 'Column', NULL);
GO
```

objtype	objname	name	value
COLUMN	Assets	Data Dictionary	Approximate branch assets entered in January each year by an automated process.

```
-- Data Dictionary entry for BranchCity
EXEC sys.sp_addextendedproperty @name=N'Data Dictionary',
          @value=N'City & State where branch is located.' ,
          @level0type=N'SCHEMA',@level0name=N'Banking', @level1type=N'TABLE',
          @level1name=N'Branch', @level2type=N'COLUMN',@level2name=N'BranchCity';
GO


-- Listing all Data Dictionary entries for table
SELECT *
FROM fn_listextendedproperty (NULL, 'schema', 'Banking', 'table', 'Branch', 'Column', NULL)
ORDER BY objname;
```

objtype	objname	name	value
COLUMN	Assets	Data Dictionary	Approximate branch assets entered in January each year by an automated process.
COLUMN	BranchCity	Data Dictionary	City & State where branch is located.
COLUMN	BranchName	Data Dictionary	Name of the branch. Updated by supervisor only.

CHAPTER 7: Functional Database Design

Lead Developer as Database Designer

A senior database developer should be able to design a modest business application database. The reason is that he worked with a number of databases so well-familiar with the concept of 3NF relational database design. Naturally if the lead developer is not familiar with the business, then it is rather difficult, there is a steep learning curve. But then it is difficult also for a professional database designer. Getting a systems analyst on board is the best approach to work with the database designer.

Database Design Team at Big Budget Projects

Large companies for important projects may setup the following design team:

> ➤ 1-2 database designers
> ➤ 1-3 systems analysts
> ➤ 1-4 subject matter experts

Hiring Database Design Consultant where Resources Are Limited

Even a small company or a small project at large company should consider hiring a professional database designer on a consulting basis for a month or so to design the database. A well-designed 3NF database may reduce development from 50 man-months to 35 man-months, thus the payback may start before the project is completed. The payback continues after production deployment due to lower cost of future application software development and database maintenance. Once this author was consulting in stored procedure development at a small organization which was the fund raiser for a Connecticut seminary. Only one full-time manager/dba/developer, with consultants help. Quite shockingly, the database was excellent 3NF design. Only big-budget places can afford such a good 3NF design so goes the common wisdom. The manager explained that he hired a consultant expert database designer for a month. An excellent choice indeed.

Database System Solution Implementation Hierarchy

Frequently solutions can be implemented more than one way in a relational database system. For example, the constraint OrderQty > 0 can be implemented as CHECK constraint, stored procedure, trigger and as code in application software. There are great advantages to implement a solution at the lowest possible level of the following hierarchy.

> ➤ Table design
> ➤ Constraint
> ➤ Stored procedure
> ➤ Trigger
> ➤ Client software

List All Default Constraints with Definition

T-SQL metadata query to enumerate all column defaults with definition using a system view.

```
SELECT   SCHEMA_NAME(schema_id)                              AS SCHEMA_NAME,
         OBJECT_NAME(PARENT_OBJECT_ID)                       AS TABLE_NAME,
         COL_NAME (PARENT_OBJECT_ID, PARENT_COLUMN_ID)       AS COLUMN_NAME,
         Definition                                          AS DEFAULT_DEFINITION,
         NAME                                                AS DEFAULT_CONSTRAINT_NAME
FROM AdventureWorks2012.SYS.DEFAULT_CONSTRAINTS
ORDER BY 1, 2;  -- column numbers
-- (152 row(s) affected) - Partial results.
```

SCHEMA_NAME	TABLE_NAME	COLUMN_NAME	DEFAULT_DEFINITION	DEFAULT_CONSTRAINT_NAME
dbo	AWBuildVersion	ModifiedDate	(getdate())	DF_AWBuildVersion_ModifiedDate
dbo	ErrorLog	ErrorTime	(getdate())	DF_ErrorLog_ErrorTime
HumanResources	Department	ModifiedDate	(getdate())	DF_Department_ModifiedDate
HumanResources	Employee	SalariedFlag	((1))	DF_Employee_SalariedFlag
HumanResources	Employee	VacationHours	((0))	DF_Employee_VacationHours
HumanResources	Employee	SickLeaveHours	((0))	DF_Employee_SickLeaveHours
HumanResources	Employee	CurrentFlag	((1))	DF_Employee_CurrentFlag
HumanResources	Employee	rowguid	(newid())	DF_Employee_rowguid
HumanResources	Employee	ModifiedDate	(getdate())	DF_Employee_ModifiedDate
HumanResources	EmployeeDepartmentHistory	ModifiedDate	(getdate())	DF_EmployeeDepartmentHistory_ModifiedDate
HumanResources	EmployeePayHistory	ModifiedDate	(getdate())	DF_EmployeePayHistory_ModifiedDate
HumanResources	JobCandidate	ModifiedDate	(getdate())	DF_JobCandidate_ModifiedDate
HumanResources	Shift	ModifiedDate	(getdate())	DF_Shift_ModifiedDate
Person	Address	rowguid	(newid())	DF_Address_rowguid
Person	Address	ModifiedDate	(getdate())	DF_Address_ModifiedDate
Person	AddressType	rowguid	(newid())	DF_AddressType_rowguid
Person	AddressType	ModifiedDate	(getdate())	DF_AddressType_ModifiedDate
Person	BusinessEntity	rowguid	(newid())	DF_BusinessEntity_rowguid
Person	BusinessEntity	ModifiedDate	(getdate())	DF_BusinessEntity_ModifiedDate

The sp_helpconstraints system procedure to list all constraints (including default) on a table.

Partitioning Query via Pure SQL - Ye Olde Way

Add new sequence numbering column for subsets(partition by OrderID) with standard SQL only. Note that the old way is not very efficient, the ROW_NUMBER() OVER PARTITION is better performing.

```
USE Northwind;
SELECT   OD.OrderID,
         SeqNo                                            AS LineItem,
         OD.ProductID,
         UnitPrice,
         Quantity                                         AS Qty,
         CONVERT(NUMERIC(3, 2), Discount)                 AS Discount,
         CONVERT(NUMERIC(12, 2), UnitPrice * Quantity * ( 1.0 - Discount ))   AS LineTotal
FROM   [Order Details] OD
     INNER JOIN (SELECT count(*) SeqNo,   a.OrderID,   a.ProductID
         FROM   [Order Details] A
             INNER JOIN [Order Details] B
                 ON A.ProductID >= B.ProductID   AND A.OrderID = B.OrderID
         GROUP  BY A.OrderID,
                 A.ProductID) a
         ON OD.OrderID = a.OrderID
         AND OD.ProductID = a.ProductID
WHERE  OD.OrderID < 10300
ORDER  BY OD.OrderID,  OD.ProductID, SeqNo;
-- (140 row(s) affected) - Partial results.
```

OrderID	LineItem	ProductID	UnitPrice	Qty	Discount	LineTotal
10255	1	2	15.20	20	0.00	304.00
10255	2	16	13.90	35	0.00	486.50
10255	3	36	15.20	25	0.00	380.00
10255	4	59	44.00	30	0.00	1320.00
10256	1	53	26.20	15	0.00	393.00
10256	2	77	10.40	12	0.00	124.80
10257	1	27	35.10	25	0.00	877.50
10257	2	39	14.40	6	0.00	86.40
10257	3	77	10.40	15	0.00	156.00
10258	1	2	15.20	50	0.20	608.00
10258	2	5	17.00	65	0.20	884.00
10258	3	32	25.60	6	0.20	122.88
10259	1	21	8.00	10	0.00	80.00
10259	2	37	20.80	1	0.00	20.80
10260	1	41	7.70	16	0.25	92.40
10260	2	57	15.60	50	0.00	780.00
10260	3	62	39.40	15	0.25	443.25

CHAPTER 8: Advanced Database Design Concepts

FileTable - Integrating Folders with Database

Storing large number of binary files such as images was a challenge until SQL Server 2012: FileTable integrates files in a folder into the database, yet keep them accessible at Windows file system level. In the past, there were two solutions:

> ➤ Keep only the filenames in the database table.
> ➤ Keep both the filenames and binary file objects (varbinary(max)) in the table.

Using the first method, the files were not backed up with the database since they were not part of the database. Applying the second method, the binary objects were in the database, but as a deadweight, since not much can be done with them. FileTable is the best of both worlds: files are backed up / restored with the database, yet they remain visible at the file system level. So if a new file is dropped (copied) into the folder, it becomes visible to SQL Server instantaneously. FileTable requires the FILESTREAM feature as shown on the Server Properties dialog box.

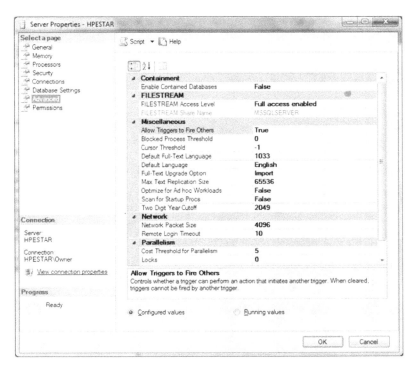

CHAPTER 8: Advanced Database Design Concepts

The CREATE TABLE statement for a FileTable

```
-- Create FileTable -- new to SQL Server 2012
CREATE TABLE ImageStore
AS FileTable
   WITH (
      FileTable_Directory = 'ImageStore',
      FileTable_Collate_Filename = database_default
      );
GO
-- (1 row(s) affected)
```

We can determine the FileTable folder name which is visible at the file system level the following way.

```
SELECT DBName=DB_NAME ( database_id ), directory_name
   FROM sys.database_filestream_options
      WHERE directory_name is not null;
GO
```

DBName	directory_name
AdventureWorks2012	FSDIR

FileTable directory(path):

\\YOURSERVER\MSSQLSERVER\FSDIR\ImageStore

CHAPTER 8: Advanced Database Design Concepts

The dialog box for database options setup as related to FILESTREAM

"hpestar" is the name of the SQL Server instance (default instance, same name as the computer).

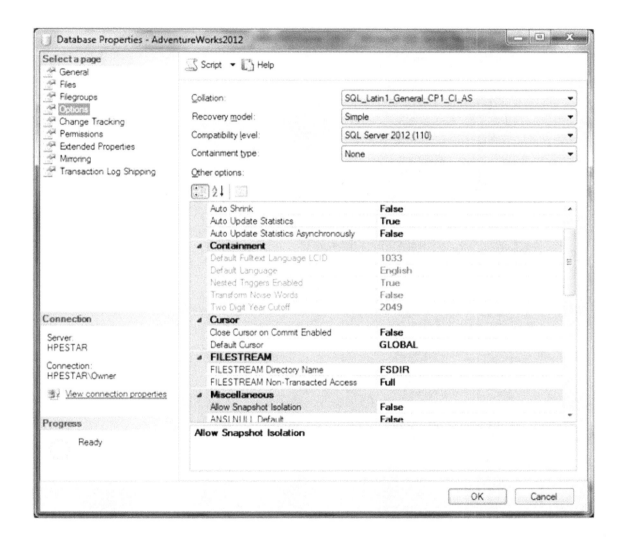

The FileTable folder is currently empty.

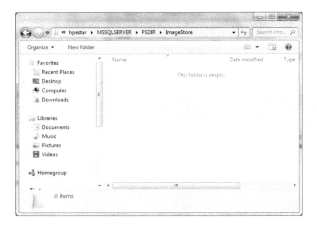

We shall now copy 3 photos in the ImageStore folder using Windows Copy & Paste operation.

The photos are "visible" from the database side as well.

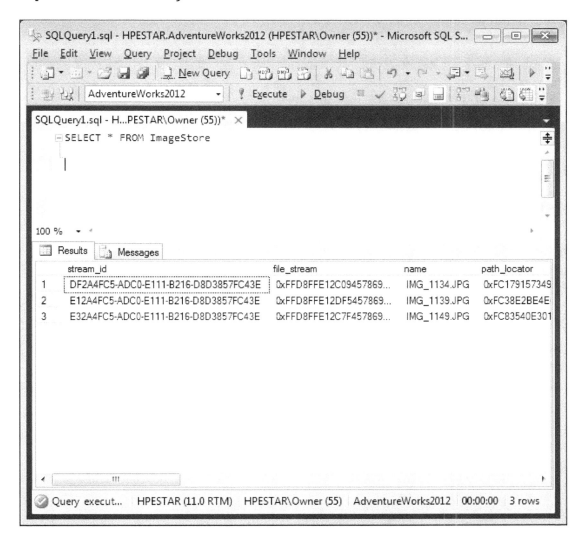

The INSERT, UPDATE and DELETE commands are operational on FileTable, however, a new column cannot be added as demonstrated in the following script:

```
SELECT * FROM ImageStore;
GO
UPDATE ImageStore SET name='RollerCoaster.jpg'
WHERE stream_id='E73EA731-AAAA-E111-9078-D8D3857FC43E';
GO
SELECT * FROM ImageStore;
```

CHAPTER 8: Advanced Database Design Concepts

Adding Files to FileTable Using T-SQL

There are two T-SQL methods available.

```
-- Adding files from T-SQL - method 1 xp_cmdshell copy
EXEC xp_cmdshell 'copy "C:\photo\000Test\xBermuda.jpg"
"\\HPESTAR\mssqlserver\FSDIR\ImageStore\xBermuda.jpg"'
GO
```

```
-- Adding files from T-SQL - method 2 OPENROWSET
INSERT INTO [dbo].[ImageStore] ([name],[file_stream])
SELECT 'Bermuda9.jpg', * FROM
     OPENROWSET(BULK N'C:\photo\2012\BERMUDA\BERMUDA\IMG_1154.jpg', SINGLE_BLOB)
                AS FileUpload
```

Deleting Files from FileTable Using T-SQL

```
SELECT * FROM ImageStore
GO
```

```
DELETE ImageStore
WHERE stream_id = '62F55342-ABAA-E111-9078-D8D3857FC43E'
GO
```

```
SELECT * FROM ImageStore
GO
```

```
-- Column(s) cannot be added to a FileTable
ALTER TABLE ImageStore
ADD AddDate smalldatetime NULL
CONSTRAINT AddDateDflt
DEFAULT CURRENT_TIMESTAMP WITH VALUES ;
GO
/* Msg 33422, Level 16, State 1, Line 2
The column 'AddDate' cannot be added to table 'ImageStore' as it is a FileTable.
Adding columns to the fixed schema of a FileTable object is not permitted.
*/
```

```
DROP TABLE ImageStore
GO
```

Data Compression: Compressed Table

The table compression option has been introduced with SQL Server 2008. Data is compressed inside a database table, and it reduces the size of the table. Performance benefit in addition to space saving: "reads" reduction; queries need to read fewer pages from the disk. Sufficient CPU resources are required for the SQL Server instance to compress and decompress table data, when data is read (SELECT) or written (INSERT, UPDATE, MERGE). Analysis is required to ensure that table compression has no adverse effect on business critical query performance. Data compression may not be available in all editions of SQL Server. In the demonstration, first we create a new table for testing.

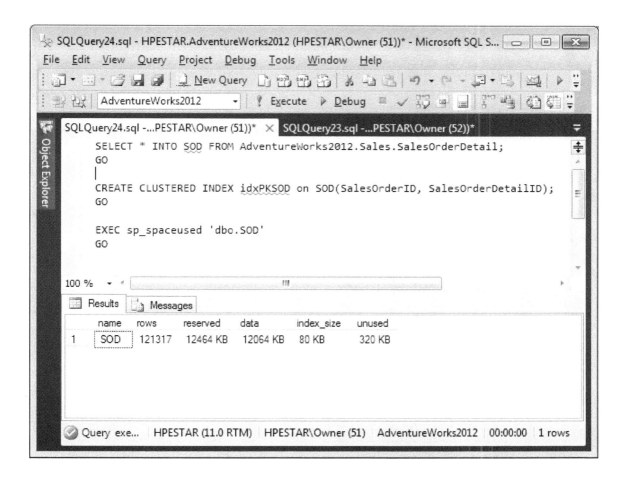

Switching to PAGE-LEVEL Compression

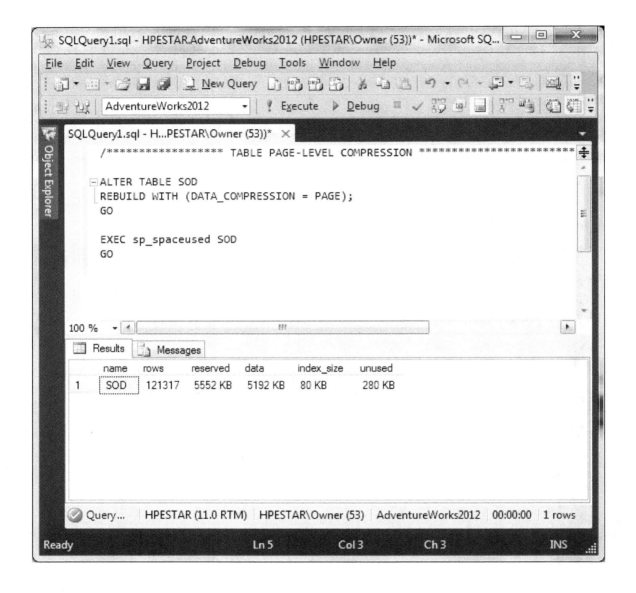

Data storage size decreased from around 12 MB to around 5 MB.

Testing ROW-LEVEL Compression

We can see the space reduction from 12MB to around 7.5MB.

Space reduction can be estimated with a system stored procedure.

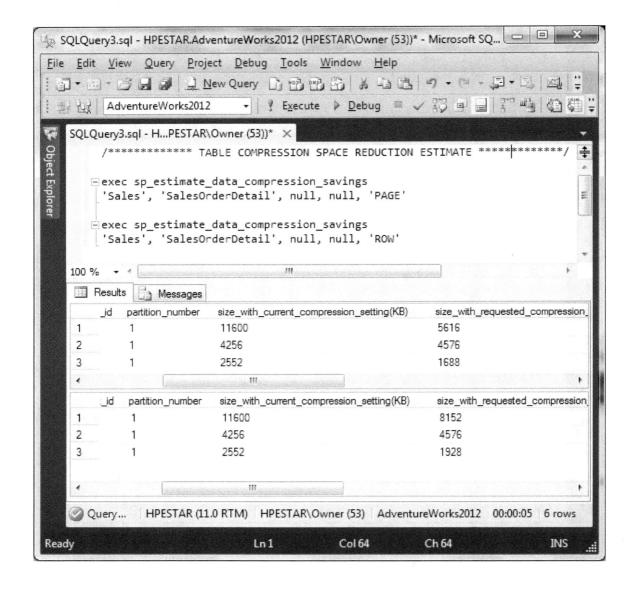

Careful and extensive considerations are required to decide to apply row, page or no compression to a table.

Query To Check How Many Rows Are Stored In An 8K Page In The Original Non-Compressed Table

Query to check the same for the compressed table SOD

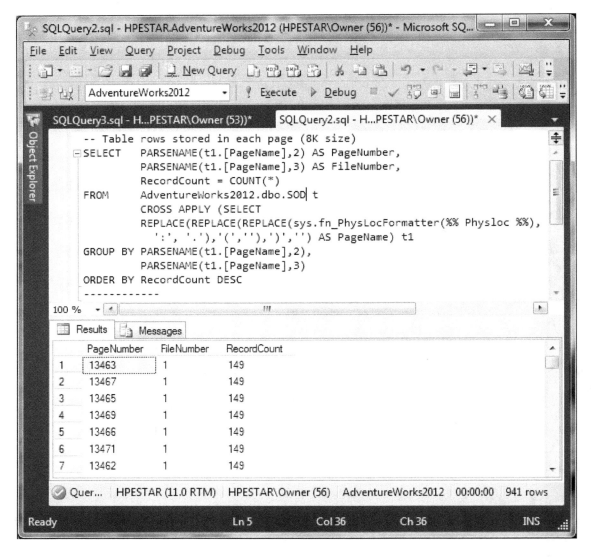

We can see that the best record (rows) count is 149 per page as opposed to 102 when the rows are not compressed. Since compression and decompression are processing intensive, we are trading CPU load vs. disk load. Which one to choose? PAGE compression is the true compression with maximum space saving. Choose PAGE compression for best disk IO reduction. As mentioned earlier careful preparation is required to make sure there are no undesirable side effects.

Data Compression: Compressed Index

Index can also be compressed. The following script creates and compresses an index with included columns.

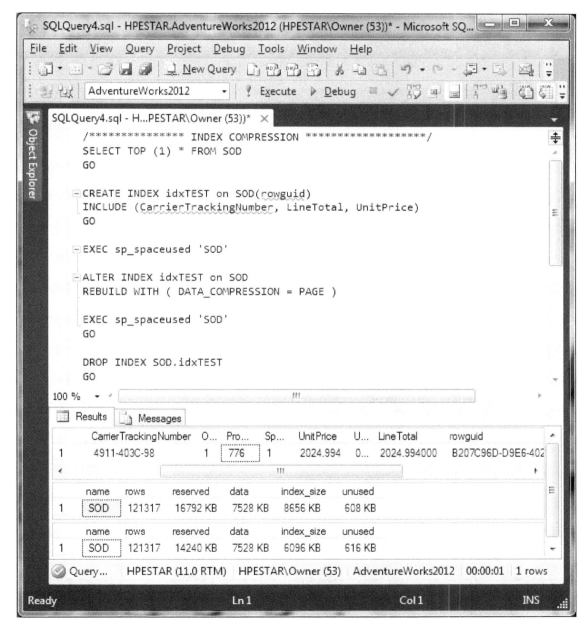

We can observe the index size reduction. Note that index_size includes all indexes.

CHAPTER 8: Advanced Database Design Concepts

The GUI Data Compression Wizard

The wizard can be started with Right Click on the table in SSMS Object Explorer.

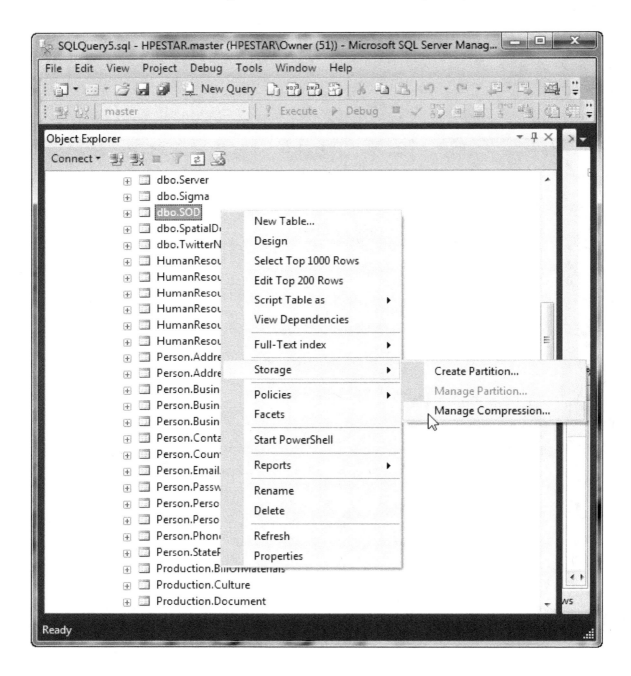

Space Saving Calculation Wizard Page
The figures include table & indexes total size.

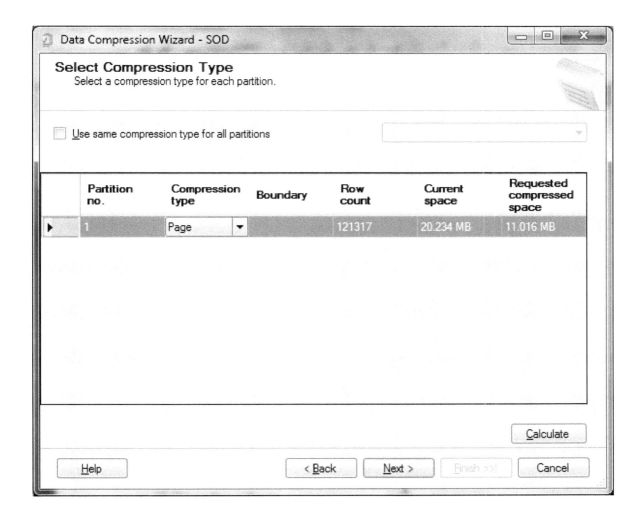

Output Panel Offers Scripting And Execution Options

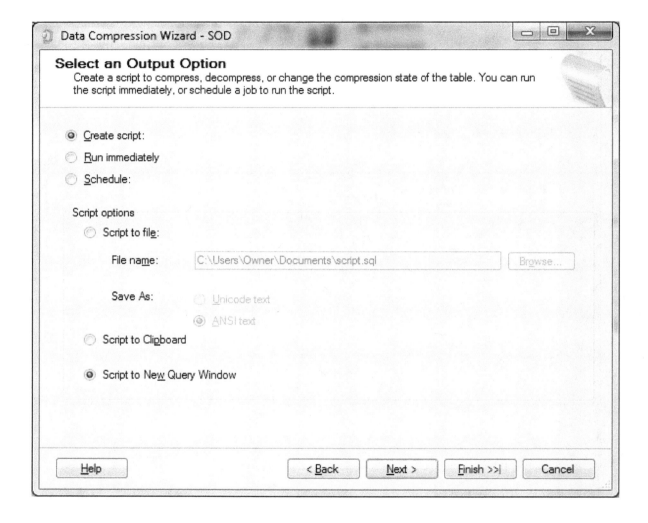

Testing the generated script with the sp_spaceused system stored procedure

Indexes Can Be Compressed With The Wizard As Well

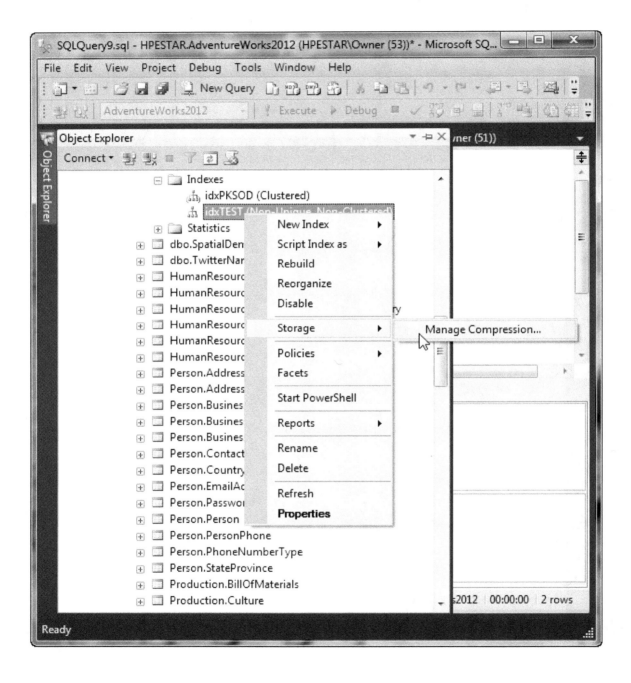

The generated script follows with measurement before and after index compression.

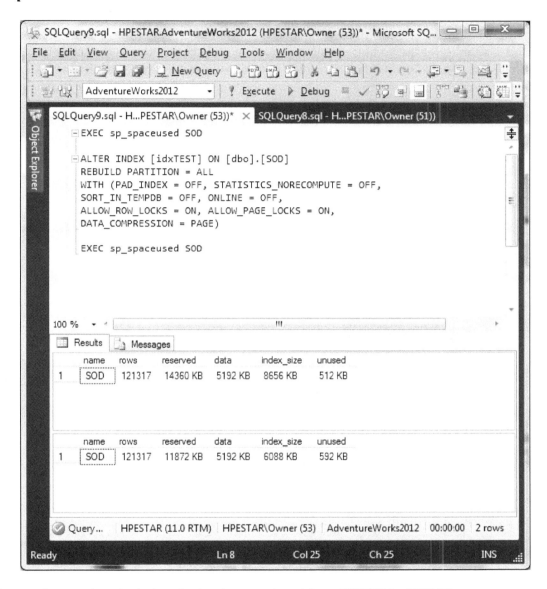

We can observe that the index size has been reduced from 8656KB to 6088 KB.

Articles
Data Compression: Strategy, Capacity Planning and Best Practices
http://msdn.microsoft.com/en-us/library/dd894051(v=sql.100).aspx
Data Compression http://msdn.microsoft.com/en-us/library/cc280449.aspx

CHAPTER 8: Advanced Database Design Concepts

Partitioned Table, Partition Function & Partition Scheme

When data is stored from New York, Chicago, Houston, London and Hong Kong operations in a table, it makes you wonder if the server trips over NYC data when looking for London information. Analogous, 95% of the time in a typical business the last 30 days data may be accessed in a table, yet the dominant storage is for the 5% access of the 5 years prior data. The solution is logical: partition the data according to a usage-based scheme. Partitioning can improve performance, the scalability and manageability of large tables and tables that have varying query access patterns. **Gains with partitioning is not automatic.** Careful design studies are necessary for a successful table partitioning implementation.

In order to carry out a demonstration, first we create a copy of AdventureWorks2012 database from a backup file.

```
/* RESTORE script to create a new copy of AdventureWorks2012
 * Folder  FS1 should exist; FSBeta should not exist; AW12 should exist
 * Folder Backup should exist */
USE [master]
GO
```

```
BACKUP DATABASE [AdventureWorks2012] TO
DISK = N'C:\Data\Backup\AW12.bak'
GO
```

```
RESTORE DATABASE [CopyOfAdventureWorks2012]
FROM  DISK = N'C:\Data\Backup\AW12.bak'
WITH  FILE = 1,  MOVE N'FSAlpha' TO N'F:\data\FS1\FSBeta',
MOVE N'AdventureWorks2012_Data' TO N'F:\AW12\xAdventureWorks2012_Data.mdf',
MOVE N'AdventureWorks2012_Log' TO N'F:\AW12\xAdventureWorks2012_log.ldf',
NOUNLOAD,  STATS = 5
GO
```

We will partition a table with SalesOrderDetail subset information. First a partition function is created.

```
USE CopyOfAdventureWorks2012;
GO
```

```
CREATE PARTITION FUNCTION pfSOD (int)
AS RANGE LEFT FOR VALUES (1, 20000, 40000, 60000, 80000, 150000) ;
GO
```

The next step is to test the partition function to make sure it works as intended.

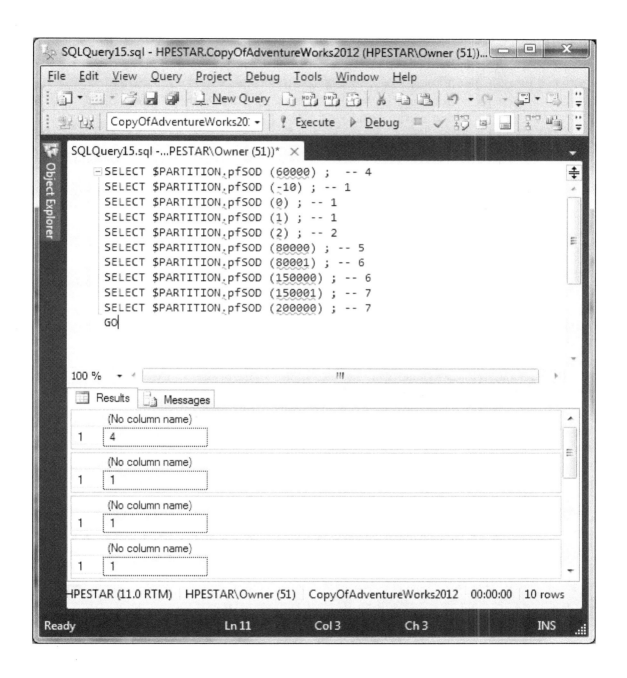

T-SQL scripts to create FILEGROUPs for the partitions

```
USE [master]
GO


ALTER DATABASE [CopyOfAdventureWorks2012] ADD FILEGROUP [Test1FileGroup]
ALTER DATABASE [CopyOfAdventureWorks2012] ADD FILEGROUP [Test2FileGroup]
ALTER DATABASE [CopyOfAdventureWorks2012] ADD FILEGROUP [Test3FileGroup]
ALTER DATABASE [CopyOfAdventureWorks2012] ADD FILEGROUP [Test4FileGroup]
ALTER DATABASE [CopyOfAdventureWorks2012] ADD FILEGROUP [Test5FileGroup]
ALTER DATABASE [CopyOfAdventureWorks2012] ADD FILEGROUP [Test6FileGroup]
ALTER DATABASE [CopyOfAdventureWorks2012] ADD FILEGROUP [Test7FileGroup]
GO


ALTER DATABASE [CopyOfAdventureWorks2012]
ADD FILE ( NAME = N'Test1', FILENAME = N'F:\UTIL\Microsoft\sampledatabases\Test1.ndf' ,
SIZE = 3072KB , FILEGROWTH = 1024KB ) TO FILEGROUP [Test1FileGroup]
ALTER DATABASE [CopyOfAdventureWorks2012]
ADD FILE ( NAME = N'Test2', FILENAME = N'F:\UTIL\Microsoft\sampledatabases\Test2.ndf' ,
SIZE = 3072KB , FILEGROWTH = 1024KB ) TO FILEGROUP [Test2FileGroup]
ALTER DATABASE [CopyOfAdventureWorks2012]
ADD FILE ( NAME = N'Test3', FILENAME = N'F:\UTIL\Microsoft\sampledatabases\Test3.ndf' ,
SIZE = 3072KB , FILEGROWTH = 1024KB ) TO FILEGROUP [Test3FileGroup]
ALTER DATABASE [CopyOfAdventureWorks2012]
ADD FILE ( NAME = N'Test4', FILENAME = N'F:\UTIL\Microsoft\sampledatabases\Test4.ndf' ,
SIZE = 3072KB , FILEGROWTH = 1024KB ) TO FILEGROUP [Test4FileGroup]
ALTER DATABASE [CopyOfAdventureWorks2012]
ADD FILE ( NAME = N'Test5', FILENAME = N'F:\UTIL\Microsoft\sampledatabases\Test5.ndf' ,
SIZE = 3072KB , FILEGROWTH = 1024KB ) TO FILEGROUP [Test5FileGroup]
ALTER DATABASE [CopyOfAdventureWorks2012]
ADD FILE ( NAME = N'Test6', FILENAME = N'F:\UTIL\Microsoft\sampledatabases\Test6.ndf' ,
SIZE = 3072KB , FILEGROWTH = 1024KB ) TO FILEGROUP [Test6FileGroup]
ALTER DATABASE [CopyOfAdventureWorks2012]
ADD FILE ( NAME = N'Test7', FILENAME = N'F:\UTIL\Microsoft\sampledatabases\Test7.ndf' ,
SIZE = 3072KB , FILEGROWTH = 1024KB ) TO FILEGROUP [Test7FileGroup]
GO
```

T-SQL scripts to create a partition scheme, a partitioned table and populate the new table with INSERT SELECT

```
USE CopyOfAdventureWorks2012;
GO

CREATE PARTITION SCHEME psSOD
AS PARTITION pfSOD
TO (Test1FileGroup, Test2FileGroup, Test3FileGroup, Test4FileGroup,
Test5FileGroup, Test6FileGroup, Test7FileGroup) ;
GO

CREATE TABLE SODPartitioned   (col1 int, col2 char(30))  ON psSOD (col1) ;
GO

insert SODPartitioned
select    SalesOrderDetailID, 'Unit Price: '+convert(varchar,UnitPrice)
from AdventureWorks2012.Sales.SalesOrderDetail;
GO

insert SODPartitioned
select SalesOrderDetailID+1,  'Unit Price: '+convert(varchar,UnitPrice+1)
from AdventureWorks2012.Sales.SalesOrderDetail;
GO

insert SODPartitioned select SalesOrderDetailID+2,  'Unit Price: '+convert(varchar,UnitPrice+2)
from AdventureWorks2012.Sales.SalesOrderDetail;
```

CHAPTER 8: Advanced Database Design Concepts

Query To Check The Data Distribution Within The Partitions

A few more counting queries to check entire table and a single partition population

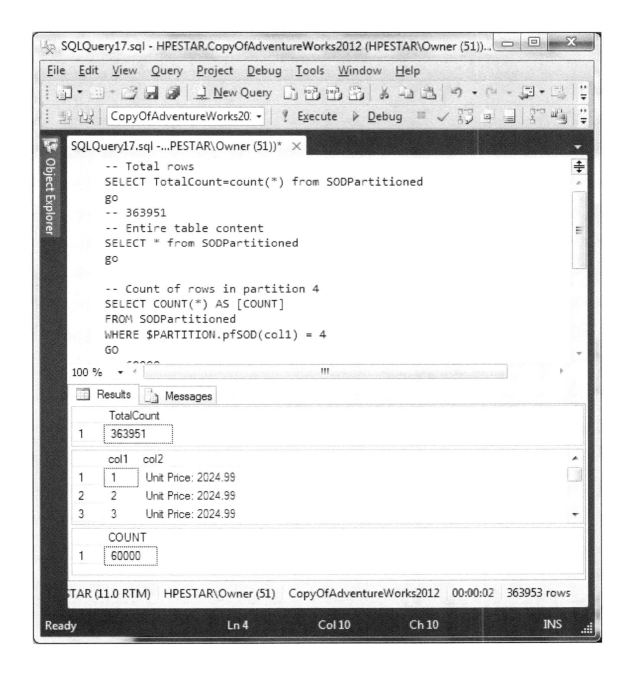

System views with "partition" prefix contain metadata on partitions.

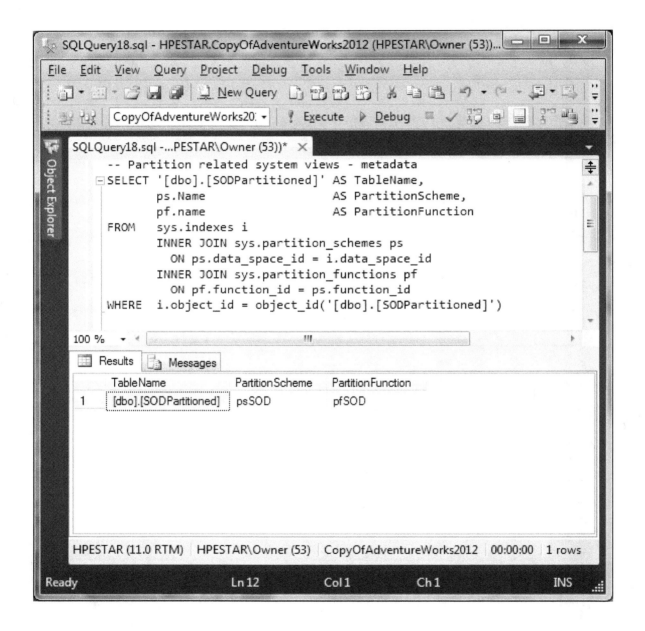

In the following example, we partition for "UK", "US" and other countries.

The GUI Create Partition Wizard

SSMS Object Explorer Create Partition Wizard provides GUI environment for partition design and setup.

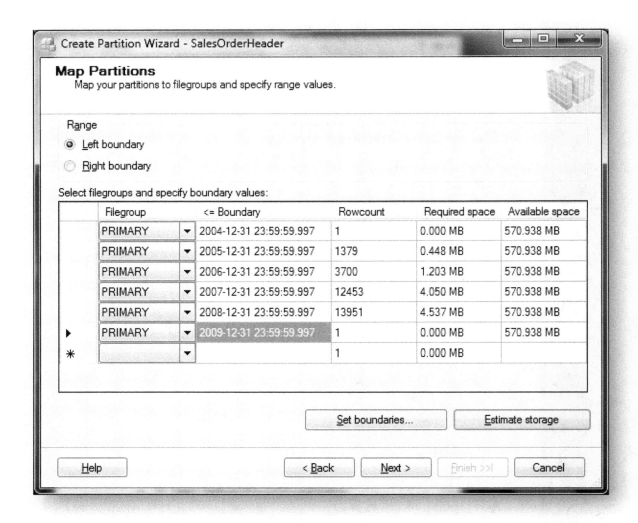

Columnstore Index for Data Warehouse Performance

Columnstore index for static tables, new to SQL Server 2012, is designed for Data Warehouse performance enhancement. The first script is a timing script for a GROUP BY summary query, and the second script is the creation of the columnstore index.

```
-- Timing before creating Columnstore index (5th timing)
USE AdventureWorksDW2012;
dbcc dropcleanbuffers;
declare @start datetime = getdate()
SELECT SalesTerritoryKey, SUM(ExtendedAmount) AS SalesByTerritory
FROM FactResellerSales    GROUP BY SalesTerritoryKey;
select [Timing]=datediff(millisecond, @Start, getdate());
GO 5
-- 190 msec
```

```
CREATE NONCLUSTERED COLUMNSTORE INDEX [idxColStoreResellerSales]
ON [FactResellerSales]
(
    [ProductKey],
    [OrderDateKey],
    [ShipDateKey],
    [EmployeeKey],
    [PromotionKey],
    [CurrencyKey],
    [SalesTerritoryKey],
    [SalesOrderNumber],
    [SalesOrderLineNumber],
    [OrderQuantity],
    [UnitPrice],
    [ExtendedAmount],
    [UnitPriceDiscountPct],
    [DiscountAmount],
    [ProductStandardCost],
    [TotalProductCost],
    [SalesAmount],
    [TaxAmt],
    [Freight],
    [CarrierTrackingNumber],
    [CustomerPONumber],
    [OrderDate],
    [DueDate],
    [ShipDate]
);
```

CHAPTER 8: Advanced Database Design Concepts

Checking the same query after creating the index.

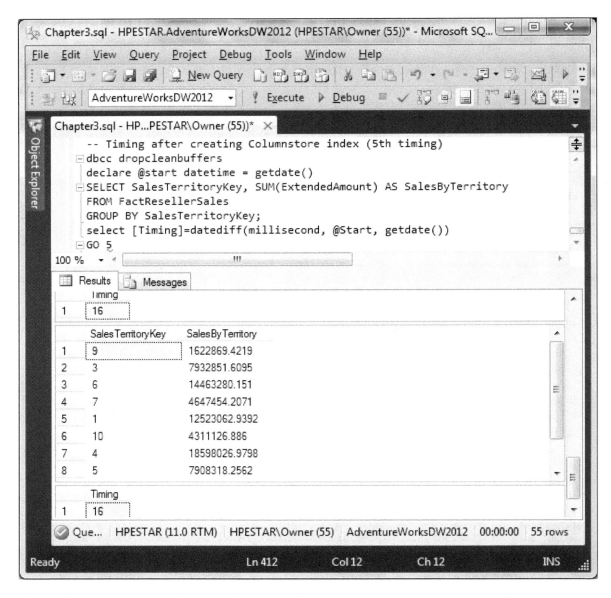

The performance gain on this particular query: from 190 msec to 16 msec. Generally columnstore index leads to significant query performance improvement in Data Warehouse environment.

DATE Data Type Solves Many Problems with DATETIME

DATE columns should be DATE type (3 bytes) not DATETIME type (8 bytes) with exception when time is needed for the record such as credit card or online banking transaction.

Example: Sales.Customer table create with one computed column which has unique index defined.

```
CREATE TABLE Sales.Customer(
        CustomerID int IDENTITY(1,1) PRIMARY KEY,
        PersonID int REFERENCES Person.Person (BusinessEntityID),
        StoreID int REFERENCES Sales.Store (BusinessEntityID),
        TerritoryID int REFERENCES Sales.SalesTerritory (TerritoryID),

        AccountNumber  AS (isnull('AW'+dbo.ufnLeadingZeros(CustomerID),'')) ,

        RowGuid uniqueidentifier ROWGUIDCOL  NOT NULL default (newid()),
        ModifiedDate datetime NOT NULL default (CURRENT_TIMESTAMP));
GO

SELECT TOP 2 * FROM AdventureWorks.Sales.Customer  ORDER BY AccountNumber;
GO
```

CustomerID	TerritoryID	AccountNumber	CustomerType	rowguid	ModifiedDate
1	1	AW00000001	S	3F5AE95E-B87D-4AED-95B4-C3797AFCB74F	2004-10-13 11:15:07.263
2	1	AW00000002	S	E552F657-A9AF-4A7D-A645-C429D6E02491	2004-10-13 11:15:07.263

Pad with Leading Zeros

Padding with leading zeros is a frequent business requirement. The ufnLeadingZeros() scalar-valued user-defined function converts the number into a string and pads it with leading zeros.

```
SELECT [dbo].[ufnLeadingZeros] (999);    -- 00000999

-- T-SQL script to pad with leading zeros
USE AdventureWorks2012;  DECLARE @Len tinyint=8;
SELECT   BusinessEntityID AS EmployeeID,   Rate,
         RIGHT(REPLICATE('0',@Len) + CAST(Rate AS VARCHAR(20)),@Len) AS PaddedRate
FROM   HumanResources.EmployeePayHistory;
```

EmployeeID	Rate	PaddedRate
1	125.50	00125.50
2	63.4615	00063.46
3	43.2692	00043.27

CHAPTER 8: Advanced Database Design Concepts

Database Design & Programming Standards

Standards have multiple purposes:

> ➢ Increase the productivity of the database developer.
> ➢ Increase the productivity of the project team.
> ➢ Decrease future maintenance cost of the RDBMS system.

Standards are about communications among project team members and among future software engineers who will come in contact with the work done presently by the software project team. Software standards are simple ordinary rules which should be followed. It is like when you turn on the left-turn signal in your car, the driver behind you anticipates you slowing down and making the next left turn. The situation is a little bit different though with software standards: there is no enforcing authority like the state authority in case of traffic rules. Many times argument can break out within the project team: "I like it this way", "it is really stupid to do it that way", "database expert Q says to do it this way in a blog" and so on. The following standards are pretty reasonable, and are based on industry acceptance, albeit not universal acceptance. The project manager has to enlist the support of all of the project team members for successful standards implementation. Database Design & Programming Standards to aid in optimal usability of SQL Server schema, scripts and stored procedures, user defined functions developed for applications by defining a reasonable, consistent and effective coding style. The identifier segment of the standard will formalize naming conventions. Without standards, database design, function, stored procedure and script development may become sloppy and unreadable, resulting in diminished productivity, usability, reusability, maintainability and extendibility.

Database Design Standards

Base design is normalized to 3NF or higher. History, log, Data Warehouse and reporting tables, containing second-hand data, need not be normalized. Similar considerations for staging and lookup tables. Each OLTP table has the following layout:

```
TableNameID (PRIMARY KEY) - commonly int identity(1,1) SURROGATE PRIMARY KEY
TableNameAlphaID (FOREIGN KEY if any)
TableNameBetaID (FOREIGN KEY if any)
natural-key column(s)
non-key columns
row maintenance columns
  RowGuid         uniqueidentifier
  IsActive        maintenance flag (bit 0 = not active, 1 = active)
  CreateDate      maintenance date (datetime if necessary)
  ModifiedDate    maintenance date (datetime if necessary)
  ModifiedByUser  last user who modified the record
```

CHAPTER 8: Advanced Database Design Concepts

Identifiers

CamelCase (Pascal case) naming convention: OrderDetail, ShippingCompany

With prefix example: vInvoiceHistory (view - Hungarian naming after Charles Simonyi)

Old-style naming example: sales_order_detail

Space usage is not a good idea in identifier: confusing & forces square brackets or double quotation marks use (delimited identifier).

Using spaces example: [sales order detail]

PREFIX ASSIGNMENT

Primary Key Clustered	pk
Primary Key Nonclustered	pknc
Index Clustered	idxc
Index Nonclustered	idxnc
Foreign Key	fk
Unique Constraint	uq
Check Constraint	chk
Column Default	dflt
Synonym	syn

Passed Parameter @p (input/output parameter) or @ - Example: @pStartDate, @StartDate

Local Variable @ - Example: @WeekOfTransaction

Table   usually no prefix; exception large number of tables

Reporting table	rpt
Log table	log
History table	hist or arch
Date Warehouse table	dw, dim, fact
Common Table Expression	cte
View	v or view
User Defined Scalar Function	udf or fns or ufn or fn
User Defined Table Function	udf or fnt or ufn or fn
Stored Procedure	usp, sproc, or none

CHAPTER 8: Advanced Database Design Concepts

Principles of T-SQL Identifier Architecture

Each word in the naming must be functional. The first word must be the highest level category or action indicator. Examples for stored procedure names:

> uspAccountPayableSummary
> uspInsertAccountPayableTransaction
> uspUpdateStockPrice
> sprocInsertInventoryItem
> sprocAccountReceivableSummary
> AccountReceivableMonthly

Commonly accepted or easily understood abbreviations are allowed. Examples for business abbreviations usage in view naming:

> vAPSummary
> vAPDetail
> vARSummary
> vARMonthly
> vGLTrialBalance

AdventureWorks2012 long stored procedure and view names.

SELECT name, type FROM sys.objects WHERE LEN(name) > 20 AND type in ('V', 'P') ORDER BY name;

name	type
uspGetBillOfMaterials	P
uspGetEmployeeManagers	P
uspGetManagerEmployees	P
uspGetWhereUsedProductID	P
uspSearchCandidateResumes	P
uspUpdateEmployeeHireInfo	P
uspUpdateEmployeeLogin	P
uspUpdateEmployeePersonalInfo	P
vAdditionalContactInfo	V
vEmployeeDepartmentHistory	V
vJobCandidateEducation	V
vJobCandidateEmployment	V
vProductAndDescription	V
vProductModelCatalogDescription	V
vProductModelInstructions	V
vSalesPersonSalesByFiscalYears	V
vStateProvinceCountryRegion	V
vStoreWithDemographics	V

CHAPTER 8: Advanced Database Design Concepts

Stored Procedure Outline

```
use {DatabaseName};
if (objectProperty(object_id('{schema}.{ProcedureName}'),
'IsProcedure') is not null)
    drop procedure {schema}.{ProcedureName}
go

create procedure {schema}.{ProcedureName}
  [{parameter} {data type}]....
as
/****************************************************************
* PROCEDURE: {ProcedureName}
* PURPOSE: {brief procedure description}
* NOTES: {special set up or requirements, etc.}
* CREATED:  {developer name} {date}
* LAST MODIFIED: {developer name} {date}

* DATE        AUTHOR          DESCRIPTION
-----------------------------------------------------------------
* {date}      {developer} {brief modification description}
****************************************************************/
BEGIN
[declare {variable name} {data type}....
[{set session}] e.g. SET NOCOUNT ON
[{initialize variables}]

{body of procedure - comment only what is not obvious}

return (Value if any)

{error handler}
return (Value if any)
END
 go
```

User-Defined Function Outline
Similar to stored procedure outline

How to Create a Database with T-SQL Script

Database can be created by a script (CREATE DATABASE) or in SSMS Object Explorer using GUI. Here is a T-SQL script version.

```
-- SQL CREATE DATABASE
USE master;
GO


-- F:\DB\DATA\ folder should exist

CREATE DATABASE [Finance]
ON  PRIMARY
( NAME = N'Finance_Data',
FILENAME = N'F:\DB\DATA\Finance.mdf' , SIZE = 217152KB ,
MAXSIZE = UNLIMITED, FILEGROWTH = 16384KB )
LOG ON
( NAME = N'Finance_Log',
FILENAME = N'F:\DB\DATA\Finance_1.ldf' ,
SIZE = 67584KB , MAXSIZE = 2048GB , FILEGROWTH = 16384KB )
GO


-- SQL compatibility level 110 is SQL Server 2012
ALTER DATABASE [Finance] SET COMPATIBILITY_LEVEL = 110
GO


USE Finance;
-- SQL select into table create
SELECT * INTO POH
FROM AdventureWorks2012.Purchasing.PurchaseOrderHeader;
GO


 -- SQL select query for 3 random records
SELECT TOP (3) * FROM POH ORDER BY NEWID()
GO
```

PurchaseOrderID	RevisionNumber	Status	EmployeeID	VendorID
3506	1	4	261	1666
233	1	4	257	1578
84	1	3	261	1654

CHAPTER 8: Advanced Database Design Concepts

Adding New Column to a Table with ALTER TABLE

It happens quite often that a table in production for years needs a new column. While adding a new column to a populated table is relatively simple, there is a downside: application software needs to be retested to make sure it still works with the new table. One offending statement is "SELECT * FROM". The application software was programmed, let's say for example, 6 columns, after the addition SELECT * is sending 7 columns which causes error in the application. T-SQL scripts to demonstrate the addition of a new column to a table for sequencing or other purposes.

```
USE AdventureWorks2012;

SELECT NewProductID = ROW_NUMBER()    OVER (  ORDER BY ProductID),
    *
INTO   #Product
FROM   AdventureWorks.Production.Product
GO
-- (504 row(s) affected)

ALTER TABLE #Product ADD CountryOfOrigin nvarchar(32) not null DEFAULT ('USA');
GO
-- Command(s) completed successfully.

SELECT          ProductID,
                Name                        AS ProductName,
                ProductNumber,
                ListPrice,
                COALESCE(Color,'')          AS Color,
                CountryOfOrigin
FROM   #Product
ORDER BY ProductName;
GO
```

ProductID	ProductName	ProductNumber	ListPrice	Color	CountryOfOrigin
1	Adjustable Race	AR-5381	0.00		USA
879	All-Purpose Bike Stand	ST-1401	159.00		USA
712	AWC Logo Cap	CA-1098	8.99	Multi	USA
3	BB Ball Bearing	BE-2349	0.00		USA
2	Bearing Ball	BA-8327	0.00		USA
877	Bike Wash - Dissolver	CL-9009	7.95		USA
316	Blade	BL-2036	0.00		USA
843	Cable Lock	LO-C100	25.00		USA
952	Chain	CH-0234	20.24	Silver	USA
324	Chain Stays	CS-2812	0.00		USA
322	Chainring	CR-7833	0.00	Black	USA
320	Chainring Bolts	CB-2903	0.00	Silver	USA

```
-- Cleanup
DROP TABLE #Product
```

CHAPTER 8: Advanced Database Design Concepts

IDENTITY Column in a Table Variable

Using IDENTITY function for row numbering in new column with table variable. Statements must be in one batch, that is the scope of table variable.

```
DECLARE @Product TABLE
 (
   ID        INT IDENTITY(1, 1),    -- new column
   ProductID  int,
   ProductName varchar(64),
   ListPrice   money,
   Color      varchar(32)
 ) ;

INSERT @Product
    (ProductID,
     ProductName,
     ListPrice,
     Color)
SELECT ProductID,
    Name,
    ListPrice,
    Color
FROM   AdventureWorks2012.Production.Product
WHERE  ListPrice > 0
    AND Color IS NOT NULL
ORDER  BY Name;

SELECT TOP(7) *
FROM   @Product
ORDER  BY ID;
GO
```

ID	ProductID	ProductName	ListPrice	Color
1	712	AWC Logo Cap	8.99	Multi
2	952	Chain	20.24	Silver
3	866	Classic Vest, L	63.50	Blue
4	865	Classic Vest, M	63.50	Blue
5	864	Classic Vest, S	63.50	Blue
6	948	Front Brakes	106.50	Silver
7	945	Front Derailleur	91.49	Silver

Note: the above "GO" (ending the batch) terminated the scope of @Product table variable.

```
SELECT TOP(7) * FROM   @Product ;
/* Msg 1087, Level 15, State 2, Line 1    Must declare the table variable "@Product" */
```

CHAPTER 8: Advanced Database Design Concepts

Partition Data By Country Query

Partition sales data by country and sequence sales staff from best to worst.

NOTE: ROW_NUMBER() only sequencing; to rank use the RANK() function.

```
SELECT CONCAT(LastName,', ', FirstName)              AS SalesPerson,
       CountryRegionName                             AS Country,
       ROW_NUMBER()  OVER(
                      PARTITION BY CountryRegionName
                      ORDER BY SalesYTD DESC)        AS 'Row Number',
       FORMAT( SalesYTD, 'c', 'en-US')               AS SalesYTD
INTO   #SalesPersonRank
FROM   AdventureWorks2012.Sales.vSalesPerson
WHERE  TerritoryName IS NOT NULL
       AND SalesYTD <> 0;
```

```
-- Add new column StarRank, which is 1 "*" for each $1,000,000 of sales
ALTER TABLE #SalesPersonRank ADD StarRank varchar(32) NOT NULL DEFAULT ('');
--Command(s) completed successfully.
```

```
-- New column empty so far, population follows with UPDATE
UPDATE #SalesPersonRank SET StarRank =
REPLICATE ('*', FLOOR(CONVERT(Money, REPLACE(SalesYTD,',',''))  / 1000000.0));
-- (14 row(s) affected)
```

```
SELECT * FROM  #SalesPersonRank  ORDER  BY Country,    [Row Number];
```

SalesPerson	Country	Row Number	SalesYTD	StarRank
Tsoflias, Lynn	Australia	1	$1,421,810.92	*
Saraiva, José	Canada	1	$2,604,540.72	**
Vargas, Garrett	Canada	2	$1,453,719.47	*
Varkey Chudukatil, Ranjit	France	1	$3,121,616.32	***
Valdez, Rachel	Germany	1	$1,827,066.71	*
Pak, Jae	United Kingdom	1	$4,116,871.23	****
Mitchell, Linda	United States	1	$4,251,368.55	****
Blythe, Michael	United States	2	$3,763,178.18	***
Carson, Jillian	United States	3	$3,189,418.37	***
Ito, Shu	United States	4	$2,458,535.62	**
Reiter, Tsvi	United States	5	$2,315,185.61	**
Mensa-Annan, Tete	United States	6	$1,576,562.20	*
Campbell, David	United States	7	$1,573,012.94	*
Ansman-Wolfe, Pamela	United States	8	$1,352,577.13	*

```
DROP TABLE #SalesPersonRank;
```

CHAPTER 8: Advanced Database Design Concepts

Diagram of Sales.SalesPerson & Related Tables

The sales staff is crucial in any business organization. It is reflected on the following diagram.

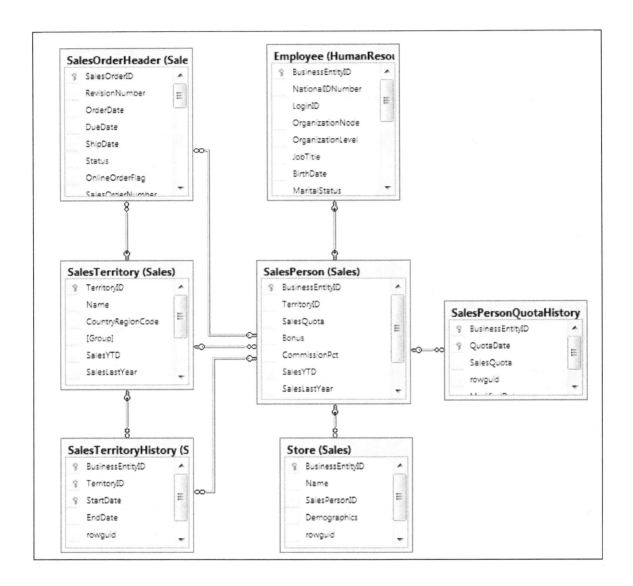

Adding IDENTITY Column To Empty Table

Add IDENTITY column to a table for sequential unique numbering (autonumber).

```
USE tempdb;
CREATE TABLE Department
 (
   Name        varchar(32)  UNIQUE,
   GroupName    varchar(256),
   ModifiedDate date default (CURRENT_TIMESTAMP)
 );
GO -- Command(s) completed successfully.
```

```
-- Add new IDENTITY column
ALTER TABLE Department    ADD DepartmentID smallint IDENTITY(1, 1) PRIMARY KEY;
GO
-- Command(s) completed successfully.
```

```
-- Only one identity column per table
ALTER TABLE Department
 ADD SecondIdentity smallint IDENTITY(1, 1);
GO
/* Msg 2744, Level 16, State 2, Line 1
Multiple identity columns specified for table 'Department'. Only one identity  column per table is allowed.
*/
```

```
INSERT INTO Department ( DepartmentID, Name, Groupname) VALUES (17, 'Student Affairs', 'Executive');
/* Msg 544, Level 16, State 1, Line 1
Cannot insert explicit value for identity column in table 'Department'  when IDENTITY_INSERT is set to
OFF. */
```

SET IDENTITY INSERT tablename ON

```
-- SQL identity insert enabled
SET IDENTITY_INSERT Department ON;

INSERT INTO Department ( DepartmentID, Name, Groupname) VALUES (17, 'Student Affairs', 'Executive');
-- (1 row(s) affected)

-- SQL identity insert disabled (default)
SET IDENTITY_INSERT Department OFF;
GO
```

CHAPTER 8: Advanced Database Design Concepts

DBCC CHECKIDENT Command

DBCC CHECKIDENT can be used to check and reseed IDENTITY parameters.

DBCC CHECKIDENT('Production.Product');
/*Checking identity information: current identity value '999', current column value '999'.
DBCC execution completed. If DBCC printed error messages, contact your system administrator. */

-- SQL reseeding identity column; reset identity column
DBCC CHECKIDENT ("dbo.Department", RESEED, 999);
/*Checking identity information: current identity value '17'.
DBCC execution completed. If DBCC printed error messages, contact your system administrator. */

INSERT INTO Department (Name, Groupname) VALUES ('Alumni Affairs', 'Executive');

SELECT * FROM Department;

Name	GroupName	ModifiedDate	DepartmentID
Student Affairs	Executive	2016-07-19	17
Alumni Affairs	Executive	2016-07-19	1000

-- Add more records to table with INSERT SELECT
INSERT INTO Department (Name, Groupname)
SELECT Name, GroupName FROM AdventureWorks2012.HumanResources.Department;

SELECT * FROM Department ORDER BY DepartmentID;

Name	GroupName	ModifiedDate	DepartmentID
Student Affairs	Executive	2012-07-19	17
Alumni Affairs	Executive	2012-07-19	1000
Engineering	Research and Development	2012-07-19	1001
Tool Design	Research and Development	2012-07-19	1002
Sales	Sales and Marketing	2012-07-19	1003
Marketing	Sales and Marketing	2012-07-19	1004
Purchasing	Inventory Management	2012-07-19	1005
Research and Development	Research and Development	2012-07-19	1006
Production	Manufacturing	2012-07-19	1007
Production Control	Manufacturing	2012-07-19	1008
Human Resources	Executive General and Administration	2012-07-19	1009
Finance	Executive General and Administration	2012-07-19	1010
Information Services	Executive General and Administration	2012-07-19	1011
Document Control	Quality Assurance	2012-07-19	1012
Quality Assurance	Quality Assurance	2012-07-19	1013
Facilities and Maintenance	Executive General and Administration	2012-07-19	1014
Shipping and Receiving	Inventory Management	2012-07-19	1015
Executive	Executive General and Administration	2012-07-19	1016

DROP TABLE tempdb.dbo.Department;

ADD Partitioned Sequence Number to Table

Partition table by subcategory (ProductSubcategoryID) by applying ROW_NUMBER for sequencing within each partition.

```
SELECT ROW_NUMBER()    OVER (  PARTITION BY p.ProductSubcategoryID
                               ORDER BY ProductID)          AS RowID,
       ps.Name                                              AS SubCategory,
       p.Name                                               AS ProductName,
       ProductNumber,
       Color,
       ListPrice
INTO   #ProductsByCategory
FROM   AdventureWorks.Production.Product p
    INNER JOIN AdventureWorks.Production.ProductSubcategory ps
        ON p.ProductSubcategoryID = ps.ProductSubcategoryID ;
GO


-- Add new column for display in currency format
ALTER TABLE #ProductsByCategory ADD Dollar varchar(32) not null DEFAULT ('');
GO
-- Command(s) completed successfully.


-- Populate new column with UPDATE
UPDATE #ProductsByCategory  SET Dollar = FORMAT(ListPrice, 'c', 'en-US');
GO
-- (295 row(s) affected)

SELECT * FROM  #ProductsByCategory  ORDER BY Subcategory,  RowID;
```

RowID	SubCategory	ProductName	ProductNumber	Color	ListPrice	Dollar
1	Bib-Shorts	Men's Bib-Shorts, S	SB-M891-S	Multi	89.99	$89.99
2	Bib-Shorts	Men's Bib-Shorts, M	SB-M891-M	Multi	89.99	$89.99
3	Bib-Shorts	Men's Bib-Shorts, L	SB-M891-L	Multi	89.99	$89.99
1	Bike Racks	Hitch Rack - 4-Bike	RA-H123	NULL	120.00	$120.00
1	Bike Stands	All-Purpose Bike Stand	ST-1401	NULL	159.00	$159.00
1	Bottles and Cages	Water Bottle - 30 oz.	WB-H098	NULL	4.99	$4.99
2	Bottles and Cages	Mountain Bottle Cage	BC-M005	NULL	9.99	$9.99
3	Bottles and Cages	Road Bottle Cage	BC-R205	NULL	8.99	$8.99
1	Bottom Brackets	LL Bottom Bracket	BB-7421	NULL	53.99	$53.99
2	Bottom Brackets	ML Bottom Bracket	BB-8107	NULL	101.24	$101.24
3	Bottom Brackets	HL Bottom Bracket	BB-9108	NULL	121.49	$121.49
1	Brakes	Rear Brakes	RB-9231	Silver	106.50	$106.50
2	Brakes	Front Brakes	FB-9873	Silver	106.50	$106.50
1	Caps	AWC Logo Cap	CA-1098	Multi	8.99	$8.99
1	Chains	Chain	CH-0234	Silver	20.24	$20.24

```
-- Cleanup
DROP TABLE #ProductsByCategory
```

CHAPTER 8: Advanced Database Design Concepts

Add ROW_NUMBER & RANK Columns to Table

Add row number and rank number to SELECT INTO table create without partitioning and rank (dense ranking) high price items to low price items.

```
SELECT ROW_NUMBER()
    OVER(
    ORDER BY Name ASC)                      AS ROWID,
   DENSE_RANK()
    OVER(
    ORDER BY ListPrice DESC)                AS RANKID,
   ListPrice                                AS Price,
    *
INTO  tempdb.dbo.RankedProduct
FROM  AdventureWorks2012.Production.Product
ORDER BY      RANKID,
              ROWID;
GO
-- (504 row(s) affected)


SELECT * FROM  tempdb.dbo.RankedProduct;
GO
-- (504 row(s) affected) - Partial results.
```

ROWID	RANKID	Price	ProductID	Name	ProductNumber	MakeFlag	FinishedGoodsFlag	Color
376	1	3578.27	750	Road-150 Red, 44	BK-R93R-44	1	1	Red
377	1	3578.27	751	Road-150 Red, 48	BK-R93R-48	1	1	Red
378	1	3578.27	752	Road-150 Red, 52	BK-R93R-52	1	1	Red
379	1	3578.27	753	Road-150 Red, 56	BK-R93R-56	1	1	Red
380	1	3578.27	749	Road-150 Red, 62	BK-R93R-62	1	1	Red
332	2	3399.99	771	Mountain-100 Silver, 38	BK-M82S-38	1	1	Silver
333	2	3399.99	772	Mountain-100 Silver, 42	BK-M82S-42	1	1	Silver
334	2	3399.99	773	Mountain-100 Silver, 44	BK-M82S-44	1	1	Silver

```
DROP TABLE tempdb.dbo.RankedProduct;
GO
```

3-Part Name Table Reference

The above script can be executed from any database on this server instance since we are using three-part name as table reference. Referencing a table on a linked server requires 4-part name. Double dot in table reference means default value between dots. Example:

[LONDONPROD1].TranMaster..OnlineOrderDetail is equivalent to
[LONDONPROD1].TranMaster.dbo.OnlineOrderDetail .

CHAPTER 9: The Art of Database Design

The Nature of Connection Between Tables

There is only **one kind of connection between tables** which is defined as FOREIGN KEY **references** the PRIMARY KEY or UNIQUE KEY. Nonetheless, the application functional meaning of the connections can be many, for example, star schema in a data warehouse.

Categorical Relationship

```
USE AdventureWorks2012;

CREATE TABLE Production.ProductSubcategoryTest(
       ProductSubcategoryID int IDENTITY(1,1) PRIMARY KEY,
       ProductCategoryID int NOT NULL
              REFERENCES Production.ProductCategory(ProductCategoryID),
       Name dbo.Name NOT NULL,
       rowguid uniqueidentifier ROWGUIDCOL  NOT NULL DEFAULT( NEWID() ),
       ModifiedDate datetime NOT NULL DEFAULT( CURRENT_TIMESTAMP ));
-- (1 row(s) affected)
```

Based on the naming, with the help of our Human Intelligence, we conclude the connection is **categorization**, from subcategory to (super)category. The example clearly illustrates the importance of good naming in database design. SQL Server would work equally well with Table1 and Table2, but that would make the design practically unreadable.

The connection between Production.Product and Production.ProductSubcategory is also categorization at the bottom level of the Product --> Subcategory --> Category hierarchy.

```
ALTER TABLE Production.Product
       WITH CHECK
       ADD  CONSTRAINT FK_Product_ProductSubcategory_ProductSubcategoryID
       FOREIGN KEY(ProductSubcategoryID)
       REFERENCES Production.ProductSubcategory (ProductSubcategoryID)
GO
```

CHAPTER 9: The Art of Database Design

Information Object Belongs To Relationship

Since we are working with information in the data processing industry, it may not come as a big surprise that frequently we are dealing with information object rather than real world objects. The products in the AdventureWorks2012 database have information objects associated with them: photos, documents and reviews for example. The relationship is many information objects to one product.

.

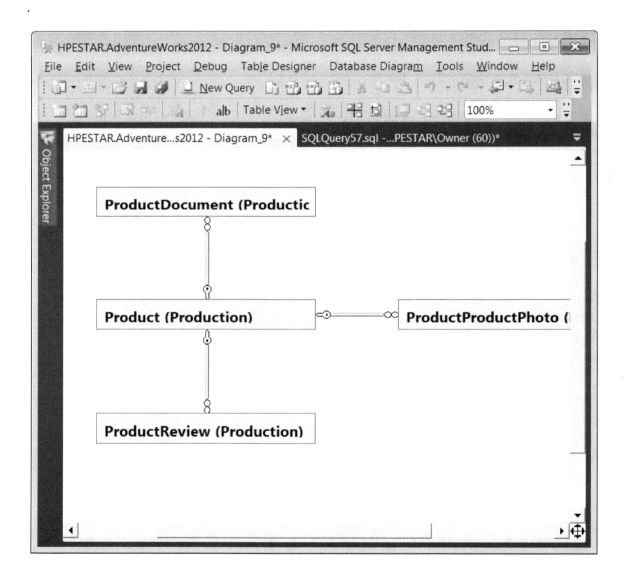

Checking Out Information Objects

Let's take a look at the ProductReview table. The information object is customer review about a product.

```
SELECT  P.Name                          AS ProductName,
        R.ReviewerName,
        LEFT(R.Comments,256)            AS Comments
FROM Production.ProductReview R
        INNER JOIN Production.Product P
            ON P.ProductID = R.ProductID
ORDER BY        ProductName,
                ReviewerName;
GO
```

ProductName	ReviewerName	Comments
HL Mountain Pedal	David	A little on the heavy side, but overall the entry/exit is easy in all conditions. I've used these pedals for more than 3 years and I've never had a problem. Cleanup is easy. Mud and sand don't get trapped. I would like them even better if there was a w
HL Mountain Pedal	Jill	Maybe it's just because I'm new to mountain biking, but I had a terrible time getting use to these pedals. In my first outing, I wiped out trying to release my foot. Any suggestions on ways I can adjust the pedals, or is it just a learning curve thing?
Mountain Bike Socks, M	John Smith	I can't believe I'm singing the praises of a pair of socks, but I just came back from a grueling 3-day ride and these socks really helped make the trip a blast. They're lightweight yet really cushioned my feet all day. The reinforced toe is nearly bulle
Road-550-W Yellow, 40	Laura Norman	The Road-550-W from Adventure Works Cycles is everything it's advertised to be. Finally, a quality bike that is actually built for a woman and provides control and comfort in one neat package. The top tube is shorter, the suspension is weight-tuned and th

CHAPTER 9: The Art of Database Design

The Bike Photo Information Object

The digital bike photo is stored in binary format in the Production.ProductPhoto table. Visualization requires Reporting Services report or external graphics software. SSMS cannot display the image, only the binary content.

```
SELECT          P.Name                              AS ProductName,
                PP.ThumbnailPhotoFilename,
                PP.LargePhotoFilename
FROM Production.ProductProductPhoto PPP
     INNER JOIN Production.Product P
          ON P.ProductID = PPP.ProductID
     INNER JOIN Production.ProductPhoto PP
          ON PPP.ProductPhotoID = PP.ProductPhotoID
WHERE P.Name = 'Road-550-W Yellow, 40'
ORDER BY        ProductName;
GO
```

ProductName	ThumbnailPhotoFilename	LargePhotoFilename
Road-550-W Yellow, 40	racer02_yellow_f_small.gif	racer02_yellow_f_large.gif

The photo of the yellow road bike.

XML Diagram Object

The AdventureWorks2012 sample database includes a number of XML data type columns. These columns cannot be displayed in a formatted fashion using Management Studio, rather they require special software for formatting or visualization.

SELECT Diagram FROM AdventureWorks2012.Production.Illustration WHERE IllustrationID = 4;
-- Partial results

```
<Canvas>
    <!-- Layer 1/<Path> -->
    <Path StrokeThickness="0.500000" Stroke="#ff656565" StrokeMiterLimit="1.000000" Fill="#ff656565" Data="F1 M
111.049805,46.655762 L 114.526367,48.509766 L 112.671875,52.911621 L 109.694336,51.374512 L 111.049805,46.655762 Z" />
    <!-- Layer 1/<Path> -->
    <Path StrokeThickness="1.202600" Stroke="#ff989898" StrokeMiterLimit="1.000000" Data="F1 M 155.380859,314.981934" />
    <!-- Layer 1/<Path> -->
    <Path StrokeThickness="1.000000" Stroke="#ff000000" StrokeMiterLimit="1.000000" Data="F1 M 88.621094,132.691406 C
88.621094,132.691406 89.542969,135.905762 88.029785,130.630371 C 86.841797,126.486328 88.501953,126.418457
91.141113,125.661621 C 93.777832,124.904785 116.826172,118.705566 120.486328,117.249512 C 124.144531,115.791504
125.061523,117.566406 125.819336,120.205566 C 126.576172,122.842285 126.205078,121.554688 126.205078,121.554688 L
122.169922,123.121582 L 164.131836,264.715332 L 161.495117,268.324707 L 163.008789,273.599121 L 141.530273,279.757324 L
139.910156,274.105957 L 134.900391,272.280762 L 93.264160,131.816406 L 88.621094,132.691406 Z">
      <Path.Fill>
        <LinearGradientBrush MappingMode="Absolute" StartPoint="87.639160,198.240234" EndPoint="164.131836,198.240234">
          <LinearGradientBrush.GradientStops>
            <GradientStop Offset="0.000000" Color="#ffffffff" />
            <GradientStop Offset="0.258800" Color="#fffcfcfc" />
            <GradientStop Offset="0.396200" Color="#fff4f4f4" />
```

The diagram can be visualized by special XAML software.

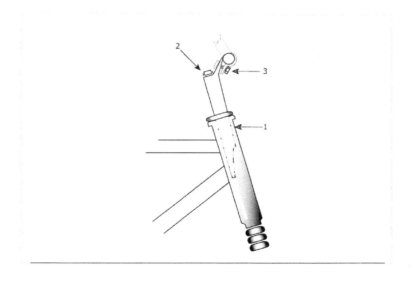

Exporting & Presenting XML Data from Production.ProductModel

XML columns contain semi-structured data. There is no general software which can make the XML data presentable. Each XML data requires specialized software for presentation. The Production.ProductModel table contains 2 XML columns. We export one cell from the first XML column, CatalogDescription, using bcp into an xhtml fil.

```
bcp "SELECT CatalogDescription FROM AdventureWorks2012.Production.ProductModel WHERE ProductModelID=19" queryout f:\data\xml\Product19.xhtml -c -t -S yourserver -T
```

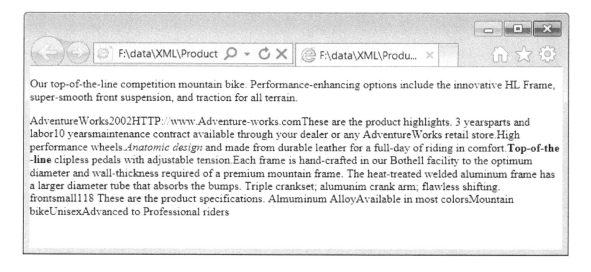

When we double click on the new .xhtml file, the information appears in a presentable format without the XML tags.

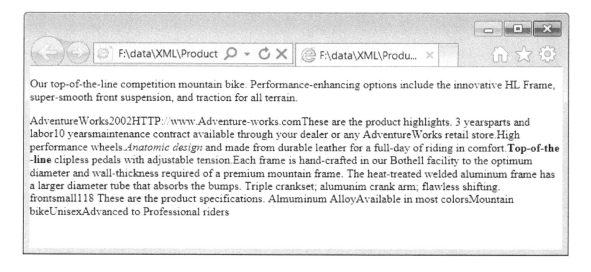

CHAPTER 9: The Art of Database Design

Product, ProductPhoto & ProductProductPhoto Tables Diagram

The ProductProductPhoto is a junction table representing many to many relationship between the Product and ProductPhoto. A product may have many photos and a photo may belong to many products.

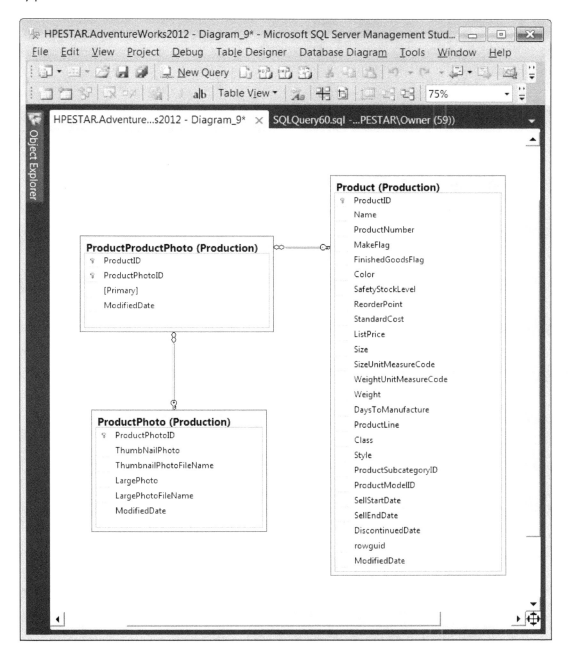

Graphical Query Design Using the Product & Photo Tables

The good database design lends itself to easy query building with Query Designer. To alias a table requires right click on the table and setting the Alias property.

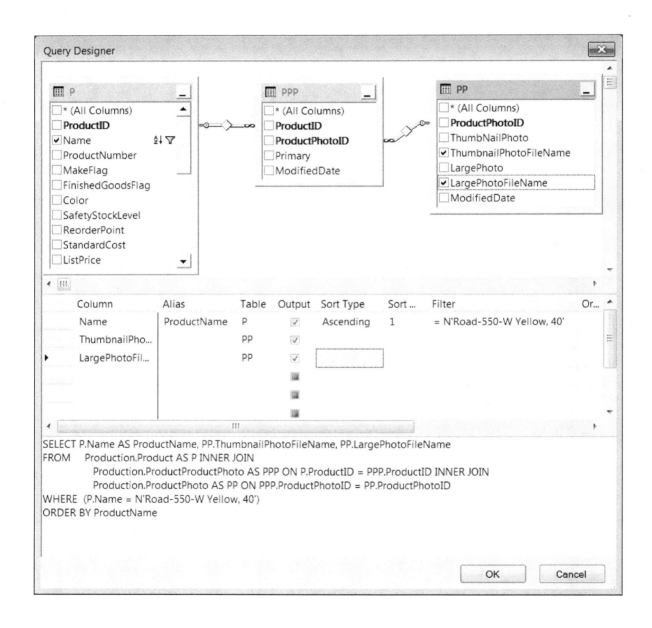

Company Received an Order Relationship

Vendor is a company supplying parts or finished product to AdventureWorks Cycles. Here is the relationship diagram. The purchase order to vendor FOREIGN KEY means a sale for the vendor. The detail to header FOREIGN KEY means the detail belongs to the header.

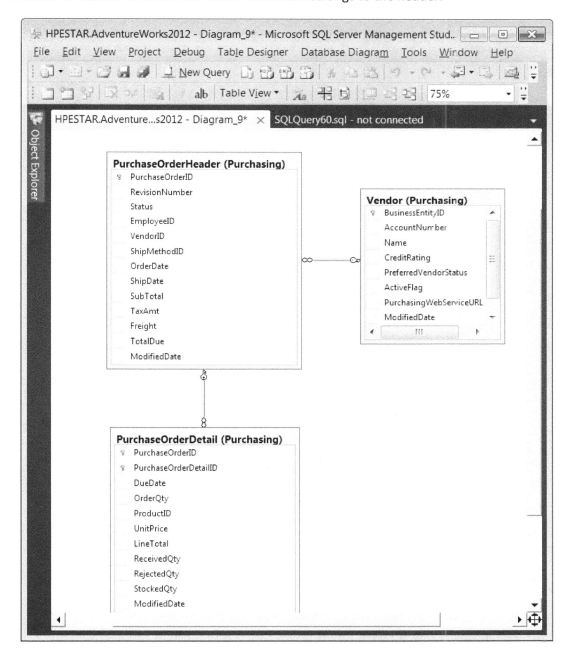

Querying the Vendor & Purchase Order Tables

The query list all purchase orders issued by AdventureWorks Cycles on a particular day.

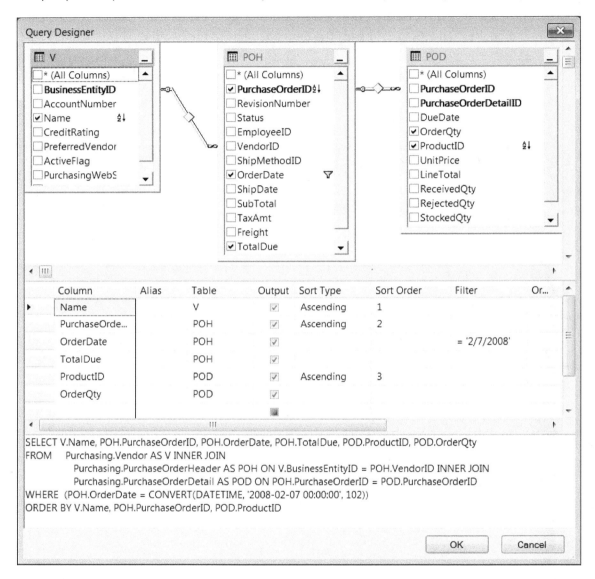

Upon execution the query returns 34 rows. Partial results.

Name	PurchaseOrderID	OrderDate	TotalDue	ProductID	OrderQty
Advanced Bicycles	1641	2008-02-07 00:00:00.000	555.9106	369	3
Allenson Cycles	1642	2008-02-07 00:00:00.000	9776.2665	530	550
American Bicycles and Wheels	1643	2008-02-07 00:00:00.000	189.0395	4	3

Type Relationship

A very frequent FOREIGN KEY representing an attribute of an object. For example a celebrity is a singer, actor, fashion model, writer, talk show host, sports figure and so on.

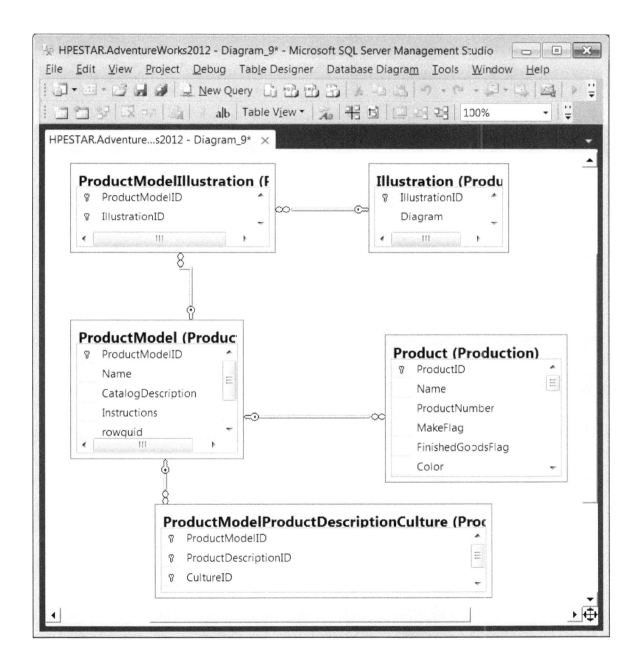

Obtaining Model Information for a Bike

We use the graphical query designer to see Model information for high-priced bikes.

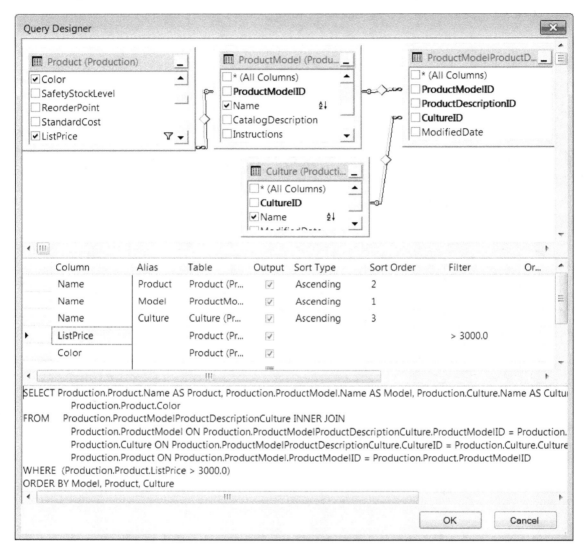

Partial results from the generated query.

Product	Model	Culture	ListPrice	Color
Mountain-100 Silver, 48	Mountain-100	English	3399.99	Silver
Mountain-100 Silver, 48	Mountain-100	French	3399.99	Silver
Mountain-100 Silver, 48	Mountain-100	Hebrew	3399.99	Silver
Mountain-100 Silver, 48	Mountain-100	Thai	3399.99	Silver
Road-150 Red, 44	Road-150	Arabic	3578.27	Red
Road-150 Red, 44	Road-150	Chinese	3578.27	Red

CHAPTER 9: The Art of Database Design

When to Use & Not to Use Composite PRIMARY KEYs

A composite PRIMARY KEY can be used in a junction table if it is unlikely that FOREIGN KEY reference needed from other tables. AdventureWorks2012 example of composite PRIMARY KEY with 4 columns in a junction table.

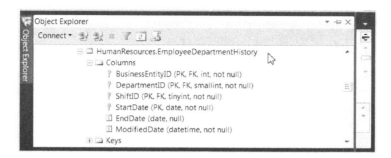

Composite PRIMARY KEY should not be used if FOREIGN KEY reference is necessary today or in the future: ineffective to have FOREIGN KEYs consisting of multiple columns & subtle violation of 3NF rules by duplication of PK table content in other tables as FKs**. The bottom line: COMPOSITE PRIMARY KEYs should not be used in regular tables.** Instead of the composite PRIMARY KEY design:

CREATE TABLE AlbumSong(
  AlbumTitle NVARCHAR(64) not null,
  DiskNo INTEGER not null,
  TrackNo INTEGER not null,
  PRIMARY KEY (AlbumTitle, DiskNo, TrackNo),
  Song NVARCHAR(128) not null,
  ModifiedDate DATE default(CURRENT_TIMESTAMP));

Design with **SURROGATE PRIMARY KEY** and apply composite **UNIQUE KEY** constraint:

CREATE TABLE AlbumSong(
  AlbumSongID INT IDENTITY(1,1) PRIMARY KEY NONCLUSTERED,
  AlbumTitle NVARCHAR(64) not null,
  DiskNo INTEGER not null,
  TrackNo INTEGER not null,
  UNIQUE CLUSTERED (AlbumTitle, DiskNo, TrackNo),
  Song NVARCHAR(128) not null,
  ModifiedDate DATE default(CURRENT_TIMESTAMP));

Where to place the clustered index should be based on performance considerations.

CHAPTER 9: The Art of Database Design

How To Design a Table

It is very important that we follow in order. Rules are with reference to the Celebrity table.

> ➢ Identify the NATURAL KEY column(s) (LastName, FirstName) & set it as UNIQUE (KEY)
> ➢ Design the non-key columns (BirthDate, BirthPlace, NameAtBirth)
> ➢ Design the row maintenance columns (CreatedDate)
> ➢ Configure the FOREIGN KEY(s) (CountryID)
> ➢ Configure the IDENTITY SURROGATE PRIMARY KEY (CelebrityID)

```
CREATE TABLE Profession (
    ProfessionID TINYINT IDENTITY(1,1) PRIMARY KEY,
    Name varchar(50) NOT NULL UNIQUE,
    CreatedDate DATETIME DEFAULT(CURRENT_TIMESTAMP) );
```

```
CREATE TABLE Country (
    ID TINYINT IDENTITY(1,1) PRIMARY KEY,
    Name varchar(128) NOT NULL UNIQUE,
    CreatedDate DATETIME DEFAULT(CURRENT_TIMESTAMP) );
```

```
CREATE TABLE Celebrity(
    CelebrityID SMALLINT IDENTITY(1,1) PRIMARY KEY nonclustered,
    CountryID TINYINT REFERENCES Country(ID),
    LastName nvarchar(40) NOT NULL CHECK( LEN(LastName) > 4),
    FirstName nvarchar(40),
    UNIQUE clustered (LastName, FirstName),
    BirthDate DATE NOT NULL,
    BirthPlace nvarchar(50),
    NameAtBirth nvarchar(60),
    CreatedDate DATETIME DEFAULT(CURRENT_TIMESTAMP) );
```

```
CREATE TABLE CelebrityProfessionXref(
    CelebrityID SMALLINT NOT NULL REFERENCES Celebrity(CelebrityID),
    ProfessionID TINYINT NOT NULL REFERENCES Profession(ProfessionID),
    PRIMARY KEY (CelebrityID, ProfessionID),
    CreatedDate DATETIME DEFAULT(CURRENT_TIMESTAMP) );
```

Without NATURAL KEY we don't have a table. The NATURAL KEY can be set as UNIQUE KEY or PRIMARY KEY. We can tentatively move the clustered index away from the PRIMARY KEY (default), however, final decision point is when we identify the business critical queries. Clustered index is helpful with range query performance.

Table-Related Database Objects

Table is the content object in a database. It has a number of supporting objects to keep the content accurate and accessible. The list of database object types in sys.objects system view.

```
SELECT SeqNo=ROW_NUMBER() OVER (ORDER BY type_desc),
    *
FROM ( SELECT DISTINCT type, type_desc
            FROM sys.objects ) x
ORDER BY SeqNo;
```

SeqNo	type	type_desc
1	C	CHECK_CONSTRAINT
2	D	DEFAULT_CONSTRAINT
3	F	FOREIGN_KEY_CONSTRAINT
4	IT	INTERNAL_TABLE
5	PK	PRIMARY_KEY_CONSTRAINT
6	SO	SEQUENCE_OBJECT
7	SQ	SERVICE_QUEUE
8	IF	SQL_INLINE_TABLE_VALUED_FUNCTION
9	FN	SQL_SCALAR_FUNCTION
10	P	SQL_STORED_PROCEDURE
11	TF	SQL_TABLE_VALUED_FUNCTION
12	TR	SQL_TRIGGER
13	S	SYSTEM_TABLE
14	TT	TYPE_TABLE
15	UQ	UNIQUE_CONSTRAINT
16	U	USER_TABLE
17	V	VIEW

Indexes have their own system view.

```
SELECT      OBJECT_NAME(object_ID)      AS TableName,
            name                        AS IndexName,
             index_id,
             type_desc
FROM AdventureWorks2012.sys.indexes  ORDER BY TableName, index_id;
-- (333 row(s) affected) - Partial Results
```

TableName	IndexName	index_id	type_desc
Address	PK_Address_AddressID	1	CLUSTERED
Address	AK_Address_rowguid	2	NONCLUSTERED
Address	IX_Address_AddressLine1_AddressLine2_City_StateProvinceID_PostalCode	3	NONCLUSTERED
Address	IX_Address_StateProvinceID	4	NONCLUSTERED

CHAPTER 9: The Art of Database Design

Listing All PRIMARY KEYs

Getting database object information can start in sys.objects system view.

```
SELECT  SCHEMA_NAME(schema_id)              AS SchemaName,
            OBJECT_NAME(parent_object_id)       AS TableName,
            name                                AS PKName
FROM AdventureWorks2012.sys.objects WHERE type = 'PK'
ORDER BY SchemaName, TableName;
GO
```

SchemaName	TableName	PKName
dbo	AWBuildVersion	PK_AWBuildVersion_SystemInformationID
dbo	DatabaseLog	PK_DatabaseLog_DatabaseLogID
dbo	ErrorLog	PK_ErrorLog_ErrorLogID
HumanResources	Department	PK_Department_DepartmentID
HumanResources	Employee	PK_Employee_BusinessEntityID
HumanResources	EmployeeDepartmentHistory	PK_EmployeeDepartmentHistory_BusinessEntityID_StartDate_DepartmentID
HumanResources	EmployeePayHistory	PK_EmployeePayHistory_BusinessEntityID_RateChangeDate
HumanResources	JobCandidate	PK_JobCandidate_JobCandidateID
HumanResources	Shift	PK_Shift_ShiftID
Person	Address	PK_Address_AddressID
Person	AddressType	PK_AddressType_AddressTypeID
Person	BusinessEntity	PK_BusinessEntity_BusinessEntityID
Person	BusinessEntityAddress	PK_BusinessEntityAddress_BusinessEntityID_AddressID_AddressTypeID
Person	BusinessEntityContact	PK_BusinessEntityContact_BusinessEntityID_PersonID_ContactTypeID
Person	ContactType	PK_ContactType_ContactTypeID
Person	CountryRegion	PK_CountryRegion_CountryRegionCode
Person	EmailAddress	PK_EmailAddress_BusinessEntityID_EmailAddressID
Person	Password	PK_Password_BusinessEntityID
Person	Person	PK_Person_BusinessEntityID
Person	PersonPhone	PK_PersonPhone_BusinessEntityID_PhoneNumber_PhoneNumberTypeID
Person	PhoneNumberType	PK_PhoneNumberType_PhoneNumberTypeID
Person	StateProvince	PK_StateProvince_StateProvinceID
Production	BillOfMaterials	PK_BillOfMaterials_BillOfMaterialsID
Production	Culture	PK_Culture_CultureID
Production	Document	PK_Document_DocumentNode
Production	Illustration	PK_Illustration_IllustrationID
Production	Location	PK_Location_LocationID
Production	Product	PK_Product_ProductID
Production	ProductCategory	PK_ProductCategory_ProductCategoryID
Production	ProductCostHistory	PK_ProductCostHistory_ProductID_StartDate
Production	ProductDescription	PK_ProductDescription_ProductDescriptionID
Production	ProductDocument	PK_ProductDocument_ProductID_DocumentNode
Production	ProductInventory	PK_ProductInventory_ProductID_LocationID
Production	ProductListPriceHistory	PK_ProductListPriceHistory_ProductID_StartDate
Production	ProductModel	PK_ProductModel_ProductModelID
Production	ProductModelIllustration	PK_ProductModelIllustration_ProductModelID_IllustrationID
Production	ProductModelProductDescriptionCulture	PK_ProductModelProductDescriptionCulture_ProductModelID_ProductDescriptionID_CultureID
Production	ProductPhoto	PK_ProductPhoto_ProductPhotoID
Production	ProductProductPhoto	PK_ProductProductPhoto_ProductID_ProductPhotoID
Production	ProductReview	PK_ProductReview_ProductReviewID
Production	ProductSubcategory	PK_ProductSubcategory_ProductSubcategoryID
Production	ScrapReason	PK_ScrapReason_ScrapReasonID
Production	TransactionHistory	PK_TransactionHistory_TransactionID
Production	TransactionHistoryArchive	PK_TransactionHistoryArchive_TransactionID
Production	UnitMeasure	PK_UnitMeasure_UnitMeasureCode
Production	WorkOrder	PK_WorkOrder_WorkOrderID
Production	WorkOrderRouting	PK_WorkOrderRouting_WorkOrderID_ProductID_OperationSequence
Purchasing	ProductVendor	PK_ProductVendor_ProductID_BusinessEntityID
Purchasing	PurchaseOrderDetail	PK_PurchaseOrderDetail_PurchaseOrderID_PurchaseOrderDetailID
Purchasing	PurchaseOrderHeader	PK_PurchaseOrderHeader_PurchaseOrderID
Purchasing	ShipMethod	PK_ShipMethod_ShipMethodID
Purchasing	Vendor	PK_Vendor_BusinessEntityID
Sales	CountryRegionCurrency	PK_CountryRegionCurrency_CountryRegionCode_CurrencyCode
Sales	CreditCard	PK_CreditCard_CreditCardID

CHAPTER 9: The Art of Database Design

Sales	Currency	PK_Currency_CurrencyCode
Sales	CurrencyRate	PK_CurrencyRate_CurrencyRateID
Sales	Customer	PK_Customer_CustomerID
Sales	PersonCreditCard	PK_PersonCreditCard_BusinessEntityID_CreditCardID
Sales	SalesOrderDetail	PK_SalesOrderDetail_SalesOrderID_SalesOrderDetailID
Sales	SalesOrderHeader	PK_SalesOrderHeader_SalesOrderID
Sales	SalesOrderHeaderSalesReason	PK_SalesOrderHeaderSalesReason_SalesOrderID_SalesReasonID
Sales	SalesPerson	PK_SalesPerson_BusinessEntityID
Sales	SalesPersonQuotaHistory	PK_SalesPersonQuotaHistory_BusinessEntityID_QuotaDate
Sales	SalesReason	PK_SalesReason_SalesReasonID
Sales	SalesTaxRate	PK_SalesTaxRate_SalesTaxRateID
Sales	SalesTerritory	PK_SalesTerritory_TerritoryID
Sales	SalesTerritoryHistory	PK_SalesTerritoryHistory_BusinessEntityID_StartDate_TerritoryID
Sales	ShoppingCartItem	PK_ShoppingCartItem_ShoppingCartItemID
Sales	SpecialOffer	PK_SpecialOffer_SpecialOfferID
Sales	SpecialOfferProduct	PK_SpecialOfferProduct_SpecialOfferID_ProductID
Sales	Store	PK_Store_BusinessEntityID

UNIQUEIDENTIFIER As PRIMARY KEY

For most applications INT IDENTITY(1,1) (SURROGATE) PRIMARY KEY is the perfect choice. However, some enterprise applications require the generation of a random rowid without any reference to a database. For those, UNIQUEIDENTIFIER can be used with NEWID() or NEWSEQUENTIALID() fill. **The latter is faster but not completely random therefore should not be used for secure applications.** INT IDENTITY() is fastest of the three (not in following test).

```
USE tempdb; SET NOCOUNT ON;
DECLARE @MaxCount Int = 100000,@START DATETIME,@END DATETIME, @i INT
CREATE TABLE TESTID ( ID UNIQUEIDENTIFIER DEFAULT NEWID() PRIMARY KEY,
-- CREATE TABLE TESTID ( ID UNIQUEIDENTIFIER DEFAULT NEWSEQUENTIALID() PRIMARY KEY,
COL1 CHAR(256) DEFAULT 'Everglades', COL2 CHAR(256) DEFAULT 'Everglades',
COL3 CHAR(256) DEFAULT 'Everglades', COL4 CHAR(256) DEFAULT 'Everglades',
COL5 CHAR(256) DEFAULT 'Everglades', COL6 CHAR(256) DEFAULT 'Everglades',
COL7 CHAR(256) DEFAULT 'Everglades', COL8 CHAR(256) DEFAULT 'Everglades',
COL9 CHAR(256) DEFAULT 'Everglades', COL10 CHAR(256) DEFAULT 'Everglades');
SELECT TOP(0) * INTO #Result FROM TESTID;
DBCC DROPCLEANBUFFERS;  SET @START = GETDATE(); SET @i = 1;
WHILE (@i < @MaxCount)
BEGIN INSERT TESTID DEFAULT VALUES; SET @i += 1; END
INSERT #Result SELECT t1.* FROM TESTID t1 INNER JOIN TESTID t2 ON t1.ID=t2.ID
SELECT  DATEDIFF(ms,@START,GETDATE());  DROP TABLE #Result; DROP TABLE TESTID;


-- Test with newid(): 22,436 msec
-- Test with newid(): 14,866 msec
-- Test with newid(): 14,576 msec


-- Test with newsequentialid(): 12,126 msec
-- Test with newsequentialid(): 11,290 msec
-- Test with newsequentialid(): 10,713 msec
```

CHAPTER 9: The Art of Database Design

List All PK & FK Columns in the Database

We can use INFORMATION_SCHEMA metadata system views for the task. The position indicates the placement of the column within a composite key.

```
USE AdventureWorks2012;
SELECT k.table_schema              AS SchemaName,
        k.table_name               AS  TableName,
        k.column_name              AS ColumnName,
        k.ordinal_position         AS Position,
        c.constraint_type          AS KeyConstraint
FROM   information_schema.table_constraints c
    INNER JOIN information_schema.key_column_usage k
      ON c.table_name = k.table_name
        AND c.constraint_name = k.constraint_name
ORDER BY SchemaName, TableName, KeyConstraint DESC, Position, ColumnName;
GO
-- (194 row(s) affected) - Partial results
```

SchemaName	TableName	ColumnName	Position	KeyConstraint
HumanResources	Department	DepartmentID	1	PRIMARY KEY
HumanResources	Employee	BusinessEntityID	1	PRIMARY KEY
HumanResources	Employee	BusinessEntityID	1	FOREIGN KEY
HumanResources	EmployeeDepartmentHistory	BusinessEntityID	1	PRIMARY KEY
HumanResources	EmployeeDepartmentHistory	StartDate	2	PRIMARY KEY
HumanResources	EmployeeDepartmentHistory	DepartmentID	3	PRIMARY KEY
HumanResources	EmployeeDepartmentHistory	ShiftID	4	PRIMARY KEY
HumanResources	EmployeeDepartmentHistory	BusinessEntityID	1	FOREIGN KEY
HumanResources	EmployeeDepartmentHistory	DepartmentID	1	FOREIGN KEY
HumanResources	EmployeeDepartmentHistory	ShiftID	1	FOREIGN KEY
HumanResources	EmployeePayHistory	BusinessEntityID	1	PRIMARY KEY
HumanResources	EmployeePayHistory	RateChangeDate	2	PRIMARY KEY
HumanResources	EmployeePayHistory	BusinessEntityID	1	FOREIGN KEY
HumanResources	JobCandidate	JobCandidateID	1	PRIMARY KEY
HumanResources	JobCandidate	BusinessEntityID	1	FOREIGN KEY
HumanResources	Shift	ShiftID	1	PRIMARY KEY
Person	Address	AddressID	1	PRIMARY KEY
Person	Address	StateProvinceID	1	FOREIGN KEY
Person	AddressType	AddressTypeID	1	PRIMARY KEY
Person	BusinessEntity	BusinessEntityID	1	PRIMARY KEY
Person	BusinessEntityAddress	BusinessEntityID	1	PRIMARY KEY
Person	BusinessEntityAddress	AddressID	2	PRIMARY KEY
Person	BusinessEntityAddress	AddressTypeID	3	PRIMARY KEY
Person	BusinessEntityAddress	AddressID	1	FOREIGN KEY
Person	BusinessEntityAddress	AddressTypeID	1	FOREIGN KEY
Person	BusinessEntityAddress	BusinessEntityID	1	FOREIGN KEY
Person	BusinessEntityContact	BusinessEntityID	1	PRIMARY KEY
Person	BusinessEntityContact	PersonID	2	PRIMARY KEY
Person	BusinessEntityContact	ContactTypeID	3	PRIMARY KEY
Person	BusinessEntityContact	BusinessEntityID	1	FOREIGN KEY
Person	BusinessEntityContact	ContactTypeID	1	FOREIGN KEY
Person	BusinessEntityContact	PersonID	1	FOREIGN KEY
Person	ContactType	ContactTypeID	1	PRIMARY KEY

CHAPTER 9: The Art of Database Design

How to Get Database Object Definition Information

There are alternate ways of getting object definition metadata.

Scripting Object CREATE Definitions

This is the easiest and most reliable way. Start with a right click on the object in Object Explorer.

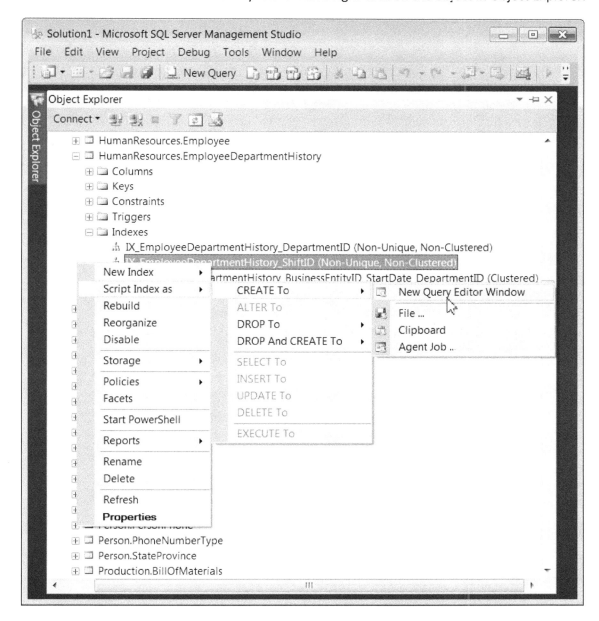

Single Object CREATE & Other Scripts from SSMS Object Explorer

Some of the scripts are generated complete. Others are just templates which require completion and testing.

Index CREATE Script

```
USE [AdventureWorks2012]
GO
```

```
/****** Object:  Index [IX_EmployeeDepartmentHistory_ShiftID]    Script Date: .... ******/
CREATE NONCLUSTERED INDEX [IX_EmployeeDepartmentHistory_ShiftID]
ON [HumanResources].[EmployeeDepartmentHistory]
(
        [ShiftID] ASC
)
WITH (PAD_INDEX = OFF, STATISTICS_NORECOMPUTE = OFF, SORT_IN_TEMPDB = OFF,
DROP_EXISTING = OFF, ONLINE = OFF, ALLOW_ROW_LOCKS = ON, ALLOW_PAGE_LOCKS = ON,
FILLFACTOR = 85) ON [PRIMARY]
GO
```

```
EXEC sys.sp_addextendedproperty @name=N'MS_Description',
@value=N'Nonclustered index.' ,
@level0type=N'SCHEMA',@level0name=N'HumanResources',
@level1type=N'TABLE',@level1name=N'EmployeeDepartmentHistory',
@level2type=N'INDEX',@level2name=N'IX_EmployeeDepartmentHistory_ShiftID'
GO
```

Index DROP Script

```
/****** Object:  Index [IX_EmployeeDepartmentHistory_ShiftID]    Script Date: ..... ******/
DROP INDEX [IX_EmployeeDepartmentHistory_ShiftID] ON
[HumanResources].[EmployeeDepartmentHistory]
GO
```

View DELETE Script

```
USE [AdventureWorks2012]
GO

DELETE FROM [Person].[vStateProvinceCountryRegion]
      WHERE <Search Conditions,,>
GO
```

CHAPTER 9: The Art of Database Design

View UPDATE Script

```
USE [AdventureWorks2012]
GO
UPDATE [Production].[vProductAndDescription]
  SET [ProductID] = <ProductID, int,>
    ,[Name] = <Name, Name,>
    ,[ProductModel] = <ProductModel, Name,>
    ,[CultureID] = <CultureID, nchar(6),>
    ,[Description] = <Description, nvarchar(400),>
 WHERE <Search Conditions,,>
GO
```

Inline Table-Valued User-Defined Function ALTER Script

```
USE [AdventureWorks2012]
GO
/****** Object:  UserDefinedFunction [Sales].[ufnStaffSalesByFiscalYear]    Script Date: ...... ******/
SET ANSI_NULLS ON
GO
SET QUOTED_IDENTIFIER ON
GO
ALTER FUNCTION [Sales].[ufnStaffSalesByFiscalYear] (@OrderYear INT)
RETURNS TABLE  AS
RETURN
SELECT
    CONVERT(date, soh.OrderDate)                                    AS OrderDate
    ,CONCAT(p.FirstName, ' ', COALESCE(p.MiddleName, ''), ' ', p.LastName)    AS FullName
    ,e.JobTitle
    ,st.Name                                                        AS SalesTerritory
    ,FORMAT(soh.SubTotal, 'c', 'en-US')                             AS SalesAmount
    ,YEAR(DATEADD(mm, 6, soh.OrderDate))                            AS FiscalYear
FROM Sales.SalesPerson sp
    INNER JOIN Sales.SalesOrderHeader soh
        ON sp.BusinessEntityID = soh.SalesPersonID
    INNER JOIN Sales.SalesTerritory st
        ON sp.TerritoryID = st.TerritoryID
    INNER JOIN HumanResources.Employee e
        ON soh.SalesPersonID = e.BusinessEntityID
    INNER JOIN Person.Person p
        ON p.BusinessEntityID = sp.BusinessEntityID
WHERE           soh.OrderDate >= datefromparts(@OrderYear, 1, 1)
        AND soh.OrderDate < dateadd(yy,1, datefromparts(@OrderYear, 1, 1));
GO
```

Searching for Database Objects in Object Explorer Details

We start by positioning on AdventureWorks2012 in Object Explorer. We activate the Object Explorer Details window from the Views tab. Enter the keyword or wildcard in the search box and press the Enter key.

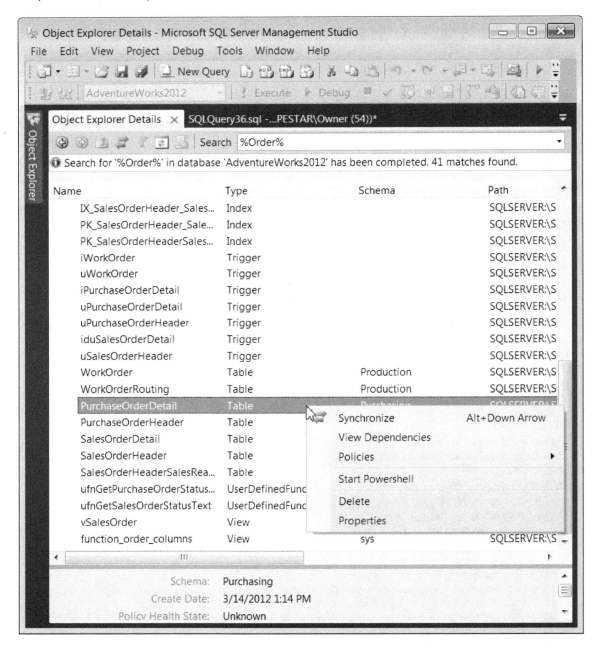

OBJECT_DEFINITION() Function for Getting Source Code

The OBJECT_DEFINITIION() function can be used to retrieve the database object definition source text for some objects such as view, stored procedure, trigger & function.

SELECT OBJECT_DEFINITION(object_id('INFORMATION_SCHEMA.TABLES'));

```
CREATE VIEW INFORMATION_SCHEMA.TABLES
AS
SELECT
        DB_NAME()                        AS TABLE_CATALOG,
        s.name                           AS TABLE_SCHEMA,
        o.name                           AS TABLE_NAME,
        CASE o.type
                WHEN 'U' THEN 'BASE TABLE'
                WHEN 'V' THEN 'VIEW'
        END                              AS TABLE_TYPE
FROM
        sys.objects o LEFT JOIN sys.schemas s
        ON s.schema_id = o.schema_id
WHERE
                o.type IN ('U', 'V')
```

SELECT OBJECT_DEFINITION(object_id('Sales.vSalesPersonSalesByFiscalYears'));

```
CREATE VIEW [Sales].[vSalesPersonSalesByFiscalYears] AS
SELECT    pvt.[SalesPersonID]
  ,pvt.[FullName]
  ,pvt.[JobTitle]
  ,pvt.[SalesTerritory]
  ,pvt.[2006]
  ,pvt.[2007]
  ,pvt.[2008]
FROM (SELECT     soh.[SalesPersonID]
    ,p.[FirstName] + ' ' + COALESCE(p.[MiddleName], '') + ' ' + p.[LastName] AS [FullName]
    ,e.[JobTitle]
    ,st.[Name] AS [SalesTerritory]
    ,soh.[SubTotal]
    ,YEAR(DATEADD(m, 6, soh.[OrderDate])) AS [FiscalYear]
  FROM [Sales].[SalesPerson] sp
    INNER JOIN [Sales].[SalesOrderHeader] soh
    ON sp.[BusinessEntityID] = soh.[SalesPersonID]
    INNER JOIN [Sales].[SalesTerritory] st
    ON sp.[TerritoryID] = st.[TerritoryID]
    INNER JOIN [HumanResources].[Employee] e
    ON soh.[SalesPersonID] = e.[BusinessEntityID]
                INNER JOIN [Person].[Person] p
                ON p.[BusinessEntityID] = sp.[BusinessEntityID]  ) AS soh
PIVOT (
  SUM([SubTotal])
  FOR [FiscalYear]
  IN ([2006], [2007], [2008])
) AS pvt;
```

CHAPTER 9: The Art of Database Design

Scripting Database Objects with PowerShell

PowerShell script can be used to script database object including tables. Scripting tables in the Purchasing schema of AdventureWorks2012 sample database. In all Command Prompt scripts the lines must be without carriage return or new line breaks (CR/NL).

```
sqlps
Set-Location SQLSERVER:\SQL\HPESTAR\DEFAULT\Databases\AdventureWorks2012\Tables;
ForEach ($item in Get-ChildItem | Where-Object { $_.Schema -eq "Purchasing" })
{$item.Script()}
```

```
Command Prompt - sqlps

C:\Users\Owner>sqlps
Microsoft SQL Server PowerShell
Version 11.0.2100.60
Microsoft Corp. All rights reserved.

PS SQLSERVER:\> Set-Location SQLSERVER:\SQL\HPESTAR\DEFAULT\Databases\AdventureW
orks2012\Tables;
PS SQLSERVER:\SQL\HPESTAR\DEFAULT\Databases\AdventureWorks2012\Tables> ForEach (
$item in Get-ChildItem | Where-Object { $_.Schema -eq "Purchasing" }) ($item.Sc
ript())
SET ANSI_NULLS ON
SET QUOTED_IDENTIFIER ON
CREATE TABLE [Purchasing].[ProductVendor](
        [ProductID] [int] NOT NULL,
        [BusinessEntityID] [int] NOT NULL,
        [AverageLeadTime] [int] NOT NULL,
        [StandardPrice] [money] NOT NULL,
        [LastReceiptCost] [money] NULL,
        [LastReceiptDate] [datetime] NULL,
        [MinOrderQty] [int] NOT NULL,
        [MaxOrderQty] [int] NOT NULL,
        [OnOrderQty] [int] NULL,
        [UnitMeasureCode] [nchar](3) COLLATE SQL_Latin1_General_CP1_CI_AS NOT NU
LL,
        [ModifiedDate] [datetime] NOT NULL
```

Instead of the console the scripting output can be piped to a .sql file.

```
ForEach ($item in Get-ChildItem | Where-Object { $_.Schema -eq "Purchasing" }) {$item.Script()
| Out-File "f:data\sql\PurchasingTables.sql" -Append }
```

System Views since SQL Server 2005

SQL Server 2005 has introduced a large collection, 400 in SS 2012, of system views providing detail metadata and operational data which was not available before. As an example, the full-text index & full-text search functionalities have a number of supporting system views. The system tables are no longer accessible. System views cannot be altered or updated. **System views are read only**. The head of systems views list.

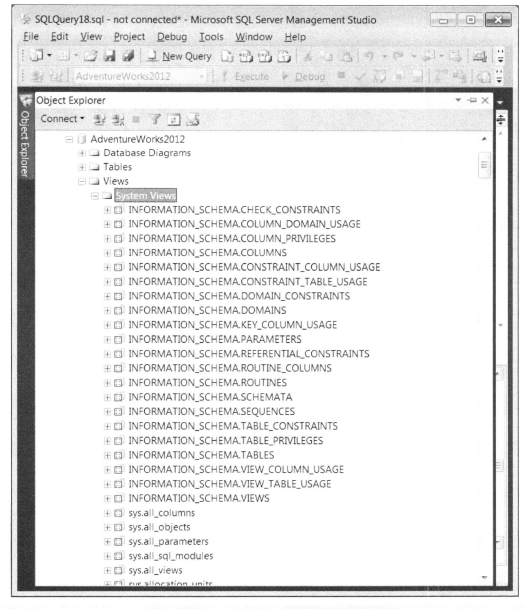

CHAPTER 9: The Art of Database Design

Querying Systems Views

Querying system views is not a trivial task. Frequently a group of tables involved and a Dynamic Management Function (DMF) CROSS APPLY may be necessary for useful results.

> Download site for SQL Server 2008 R2 System Views Map:
> *http://www.microsoft.com/en-us/download/details.aspx?id=722* .

```
USE AdventureWorks2012;
SELECT ReferencedObject = CONCAT(SCHEMA_NAME(o2.schema_id), '.',
                        ed.referenced_entity_name),
       ReferencedObjectType = o2.type,
       ReferencingObjectType = o1.type,
       ReferencingObject = CONCAT(SCHEMA_NAME(o1.schema_id), '.', o1.name)
FROM   sys.sql_expression_dependencies ed
    INNER JOIN sys.objects o1
        ON ed.referencing_id = o1.object_id
    INNER JOIN sys.objects o2
        ON ed.referenced_id = o2.object_id
WHERE  o1.type IN ( 'P', 'TR', 'V', 'TF' )
ORDER  BY      ReferencedObjectType, ReferencedObject, ReferencingObject;
-- (163 row(s) affected) - Partial results
```

ReferencedObject	ReferencedObjectType	ReferencingObjectType	ReferencingObject
HumanResources.Department	U	V	HumanResources.vEmployeeDepartment
HumanResources.Department	U	V	HumanResources.vEmployeeDepartmentHistory
HumanResources.Employee	U	TF	dbo.ufnGetContactInformation
HumanResources.Employee	U	P	dbo.uspGetEmployeeManagers
HumanResources.Employee	U	P	dbo.uspGetManagerEmployees
HumanResources.Employee	U	P	HumanResources.uspUpdateEmployeeHireInfo
HumanResources.Employee	U	P	HumanResources.uspUpdateEmployeeLogin
HumanResources.Employee	U	P	HumanResources.uspUpdateEmployeePersonalInfo
HumanResources.Employee	U	V	HumanResources.vEmployee
HumanResources.Employee	U	V	HumanResources.vEmployeeDepartment
HumanResources.Employee	U	V	HumanResources.vEmployeeDepartmentHistory
HumanResources.Employee	U	V	Sales.vSalesPerson
HumanResources.Employee	U	V	Sales.vSalesPersonSalesByFiscalYears
HumanResources.EmployeeDepartmentHistory	U	V	HumanResources.vEmployeeDepartment
HumanResources.EmployeeDepartmentHistory	U	V	HumanResources.vEmployeeDepartmentHistory
HumanResources.EmployeePayHistory	U	P	HumanResources.uspUpdateEmployeeHireInfo
HumanResources.JobCandidate	U	P	dbo.uspSearchCandidateResumes
HumanResources.JobCandidate	U	V	HumanResources.vJobCandidate
HumanResources.JobCandidate	U	V	HumanResources.vJobCandidateEducation
HumanResources.JobCandidate	U	V	HumanResources.vJobCandidateEmployment

CHAPTER 9: The Art of Database Design

Listing All System Views

Since SQL Server 2005 system tables are off limits, replaced by system views, 400 in SS 2012.

```
;WITH cteTableList  AS (        SELECT CONCAT(SCHEMA_NAME(schema_id), '.', name)            AS  TableName,
    (( ROW_NUMBER() OVER( ORDER BY CONCAT(SCHEMA_NAME(schema_id),'.', name)) ) % 3)      AS  Remainder,
    (( ROW_NUMBER() OVER( ORDER BY CONCAT(SCHEMA_NAME(schema_id),'.', name)) - 1 )/ 3)   AS  Quotient
                        FROM AdventureWorks2012.sys.system_views),
CTE AS (SELECT TableName, CASE WHEN Remainder=0 THEN 3 ELSE Remainder END AS Remainder, Quotient
        FROM cteTableList)
SELECT    MAX(CASE WHEN Remainder = 1 THEN TableName END),
          MAX(CASE WHEN Remainder = 2 THEN TableName END),
          MAX(CASE WHEN Remainder = 3 THEN TableName END)
FROM  CTE GROUP  BY Quotient ORDER  BY Quotient;
```

INFORMATION_SCHEMA.CHECK_CONSTRAINTS	INFORMATION_SCHEMA.COLUMN_DOMAIN_USAGE	INFORMATION_SCHEMA.COLUMN_PRIVILEGES
INFORMATION_SCHEMA.COLUMNS	INFORMATION_SCHEMA.CONSTRAINT_COLUMN_USAGE	INFORMATION_SCHEMA.CONSTRAINT_TABLE_USAGE
INFORMATION_SCHEMA.DOMAIN_CONSTRAINTS	INFORMATION_SCHEMA.DOMAINS	INFORMATION_SCHEMA.KEY_COLUMN_USAGE
INFORMATION_SCHEMA.PARAMETERS	INFORMATION_SCHEMA.REFERENTIAL_CONSTRAINTS	INFORMATION_SCHEMA.ROUTINE_COLUMNS
INFORMATION_SCHEMA.ROUTINES	INFORMATION_SCHEMA.SCHEMATA	INFORMATION_SCHEMA.SEQUENCES
INFORMATION_SCHEMA.TABLE_CONSTRAINTS	INFORMATION_SCHEMA.TABLE_PRIVILEGES	INFORMATION_SCHEMA.TABLES
INFORMATION_SCHEMA.VIEW_COLUMN_USAGE	INFORMATION_SCHEMA.VIEW_TABLE_USAGE	INFORMATION_SCHEMA.VIEWS
sys.all_columns	sys.all_objects	sys.all_parameters
sys.all_sql_modules	sys.all_views	sys.allocation_units
sys.assemblies	sys.assembly_files	sys.assembly_modules
sys.assembly_references	sys.assembly_types	sys.asymmetric_keys
sys.availability_databases_cluster	sys.availability_group_listener_ip_addresses	sys.availability_group_listeners
sys.availability_groups	sys.availability_groups_cluster	sys.availability_read_only_routing_lists
sys.availability_replicas	sys.backup_devices	sys.certificates
sys.change_tracking_databases	sys.change_tracking_tables	sys.check_constraints
sys.column_store_dictionaries	sys.column_store_segments	sys.column_type_usages
sys.column_xml_schema_collection_usages	sys.columns	sys.computed_columns
sys.configurations	sys.conversation_endpoints	sys.conversation_groups
sys.conversation_priorities	sys.credentials	sys.crypt_properties
sys.cryptographic_providers	sys.data_spaces	sys.database_audit_specification_details
sys.database_audit_specifications	sys.database_files	sys.database_filestream_options
sys.database_mirroring	sys.database_mirroring_endpoints	sys.database_mirroring_witnesses
sys.database_permissions	sys.database_principals	sys.database_recovery_status

CHAPTER 9: The Art of Database Design

sys.database_role_members	sys.databases	sys.default_constraints
sys.destination_data_spaces	sys.dm_audit_actions	sys.dm_audit_class_type_map
sys.dm_broker_activated_tasks	sys.dm_broker_connections	sys.dm_broker_forwarded_messages
sys.dm_broker_queue_monitors	sys.dm_cdc_errors	sys.dm_cdc_log_scan_sessions
sys.dm_clr_appdomains	sys.dm_clr_loaded_assemblies	sys.dm_clr_properties
sys.dm_clr_tasks	sys.dm_cryptographic_provider_properties	sys.dm_database_encryption_keys
sys.dm_db_file_space_usage	sys.dm_db_fts_index_physical_stats	sys.dm_db_index_usage_stats
sys.dm_db_log_space_usage	sys.dm_db_mirroring_auto_page_repair	sys.dm_db_mirroring_connections
sys.dm_db_mirroring_past_actions	sys.dm_db_missing_index_details	sys.dm_db_missing_index_group_stats
sys.dm_db_missing_index_groups	sys.dm_db_partition_stats	sys.dm_db_persisted_sku_features
sys.dm_db_script_level	sys.dm_db_session_space_usage	sys.dm_db_task_space_usage
sys.dm_db_uncontained_entities	sys.dm_exec_background_job_queue	sys.dm_exec_background_job_queue_stats
sys.dm_exec_cached_plans	sys.dm_exec_connections	sys.dm_exec_procedure_stats
sys.dm_exec_query_memory_grants	sys.dm_exec_query_optimizer_info	sys.dm_exec_query_resource_semaphores
sys.dm_exec_query_stats	sys.dm_exec_query_transformation_stats	sys.dm_exec_requests
sys.dm_exec_sessions	sys.dm_exec_trigger_stats	sys.dm_filestream_file_io_handles
sys.dm_filestream_file_io_requests	sys.dm_filestream_non_transacted_handles	sys.dm_fts_active_catalogs
sys.dm_fts_fdhosts	sys.dm_fts_index_population	sys.dm_fts_memory_buffers
sys.dm_fts_memory_pools	sys.dm_fts_outstanding_batches	sys.dm_fts_population_ranges
sys.dm_fts_semantic_similarity_population	sys.dm_hadr_auto_page_repair	sys.dm_hadr_availability_group_states
sys.dm_hadr_availability_replica_cluster_nodes	sys.dm_hadr_availability_replica_cluster_states	sys.dm_hadr_availability_replica_states
sys.dm_hadr_cluster	sys.dm_hadr_cluster_members	sys.dm_hadr_cluster_networks
sys.dm_hadr_database_replica_cluster_states	sys.dm_hadr_database_replica_states	sys.dm_hadr_instance_node_map
sys.dm_hadr_name_id_map	sys.dm_io_backup_tapes	sys.dm_io_cluster_shared_drives
sys.dm_io_pending_io_requests	sys.dm_logpool_hashentries	sys.dm_logpool_stats
sys.dm_os_buffer_descriptors	sys.dm_os_child_instances	sys.dm_os_cluster_nodes
sys.dm_os_cluster_properties	sys.dm_os_dispatcher_pools	sys.dm_os_dispatchers
sys.dm_os_hosts	sys.dm_os_latch_stats	sys.dm_os_loaded_modules
sys.dm_os_memory_allocations	sys.dm_os_memory_broker_clerks	sys.dm_os_memory_brokers
sys.dm_os_memory_cache_clock_hands	sys.dm_os_memory_cache_counters	sys.dm_os_memory_cache_entries
sys.dm_os_memory_cache_hash_tables	sys.dm_os_memory_clerks	sys.dm_os_memory_node_access_stats
sys.dm_os_memory_nodes	sys.dm_os_memory_objects	sys.dm_os_memory_pools
sys.dm_os_nodes	sys.dm_os_performance_counters	sys.dm_os_process_memory
sys.dm_os_ring_buffers	sys.dm_os_schedulers	sys.dm_os_server_diagnostics_log_configurations
sys.dm_os_spinlock_stats	sys.dm_os_stacks	sys.dm_os_sublatches
sys.dm_os_sys_info	sys.dm_os_sys_memory	sys.dm_os_tasks

CHAPTER 9: The Art of Database Design

sys.dm_os_threads	sys.dm_os_virtual_address_dump	sys.dm_os_wait_stats
sys.dm_os_waiting_tasks	sys.dm_os_windows_info	sys.dm_os_worker_local_storage
sys.dm_os_workers	sys.dm_qn_subscriptions	sys.dm_repl_articles
sys.dm_repl_schemas	sys.dm_repl_tranhash	sys.dm_repl_traninfo
sys.dm_resource_governor_configuration	sys.dm_resource_governor_resource_pool_affinity	sys.dm_resource_governor_resource_pools
sys.dm_resource_governor_workload_groups	sys.dm_server_audit_status	sys.dm_server_memory_dumps
sys.dm_server_registry	sys.dm_server_services	sys.dm_tcp_listener_states
sys.dm_tran_active_snapshot_database_transactions	sys.dm_tran_active_transactions	sys.dm_tran_commit_table
sys.dm_tran_current_snapshot	sys.dm_tran_current_transaction	sys.dm_tran_database_transactions
sys.dm_tran_locks	sys.dm_tran_session_transactions	sys.dm_tran_top_version_generators
sys.dm_tran_transactions_snapshot	sys.dm_tran_version_store	sys.dm_xe_map_values
sys.dm_xe_object_columns	sys.dm_xe_objects	sys.dm_xe_packages
sys.dm_xe_session_event_actions	sys.dm_xe_session_events	sys.dm_xe_session_object_columns
sys.dm_xe_session_targets	sys.dm_xe_sessions	sys.endpoint_webmethods
sys.endpoints	sys.event_notification_event_types	sys.event_notifications
sys.events	sys.extended_procedures	sys.extended_properties
sys.filegroups	sys.filetable_system_defined_objects	sys.filetables
sys.foreign_key_columns	sys.foreign_keys	sys.fulltext_catalogs
sys.fulltext_document_types	sys.fulltext_index_catalog_usages	sys.fulltext_index_columns
sys.fulltext_index_fragments	sys.fulltext_indexes	sys.fulltext_languages
sys.fulltext_semantic_language_statistics_database	sys.fulltext_semantic_languages	sys.fulltext_stoplists
sys.fulltext_stopwords	sys.fulltext_system_stopwords	sys.function_order_columns
sys.http_endpoints	sys.identity_columns	sys.index_columns
sys.indexes	sys.internal_tables	sys.key_constraints
sys.key_encryptions	sys.linked_logins	sys.login_token
sys.master_files	sys.master_key_passwords	sys.message_type_xml_schema_collection_usages
sys.messages	sys.module_assembly_usages	sys.numbered_procedure_parameters
sys.numbered_procedures	sys.objects	sys.openkeys
sys.parameter_type_usages	sys.parameter_xml_schema_collection_usages	sys.parameters
sys.partition_functions	sys.partition_parameters	sys.partition_range_values
sys.partition_schemes	sys.partitions	sys.plan_guides
sys.procedures	sys.registered_search_properties	sys.registered_search_property_lists
sys.remote_logins	sys.remote_service_bindings	sys.resource_governor_configuration
sys.resource_governor_resource_pool_affinity	sys.resource_governor_resource_pools	sys.resource_governor_workload_groups
sys.routes	sys.schemas	sys.securable_classes
sys.sequences	sys.server_assembly_modules	sys.server_audit_specification_details
sys.server_audit_specifications	sys.server_audits	sys.server_event_notifications
sys.server_event_session_actions	sys.server_event_session_events	sys.server_event_session_fields

CHAPTER 9: The Art of Database Design

sys.server_event_session_targets	sys.server_event_sessions	sys.server_events
sys.server_file_audits	sys.server_permissions	sys.server_principal_credentials
sys.server_principals	sys.server_role_members	sys.server_sql_modules
sys.server_trigger_events	sys.server_triggers	sys.servers
sys.service_broker_endpoints	sys.service_contract_message_usages	sys.service_contract_usages
sys.service_contracts	sys.service_message_types	sys.service_queue_usages
sys.service_queues	sys.services	sys.soap_endpoints
sys.spatial_index_tessellations	sys.spatial_indexes	sys.spatial_reference_systems
sys.sql_dependencies	sys.sql_expression_dependencies	sys.sql_logins
sys.sql_modules	sys.stats	sys.stats_columns
sys.symmetric_keys	sys.synonyms	sys.sysaltfiles
sys.syscacheobjects	sys.syscharsets	sys.syscolumns
sys.syscomments	sys.sysconfigures	sys.sysconstraints
sys.syscurconfigs	sys.syscursorcolumns	sys.syscursorrefs
sys.syscursors	sys.syscursortables	sys.sysdatabases
sys.sysdepends	sys.sysdevices	sys.sysfilegroups
sys.sysfiles	sys.sysforeignkeys	sys.sysfulltextcatalogs
sys.sysindexes	sys.sysindexkeys	sys.syslanguages
sys.syslockinfo	sys.syslogins	sys.sysmembers
sys.sysmessages	sys.sysobjects	sys.sysoledbusers
sys.sysopentapes	sys.sysperfinfo	sys.syspermissions
sys.sysprocesses	sys.sysprotects	sys.sysreferences
sys.sysremotelogins	sys.sysservers	sys.system_columns
sys.system_components_surface_area_configuration	sys.system_internals_allocation_units	sys.system_internals_partition_columns
sys.system_internals_partitions	sys.system_objects	sys.system_parameters
sys.system_sql_modules	sys.system_views	sys.systypes
sys.sysusers	sys.table_types	sys.tables
sys.tcp_endpoints	sys.trace_categories	sys.trace_columns
sys.trace_event_bindings	sys.trace_events	sys.trace_subclass_values
sys.traces	sys.transmission_queue	sys.trigger_event_types
sys.trigger_events	sys.triggers	sys.type_assembly_usages
sys.types	sys.user_token	sys.via_endpoints
sys.views	sys.xml_indexes	sys.xml_schema_attributes
sys.xml_schema_collections	sys.xml_schema_component_placements	sys.xml_schema_components
sys.xml_schema_elements	sys.xml_schema_facets	sys.xml_schema_model_groups
sys.xml_schema_namespaces	sys.xml_schema_types	sys.xml_schema_wildcard_namespaces
sys.xml_schema_wildcards	NULL	NULL

CHAPTER 9: The Art of Database Design

List of System Tables Prior to SQL Server 2005

Some of the system tables were updatable in SQL Server 2000 and previous versions. SS 2005 introduced system views which are not updatable and barred access to system tables.

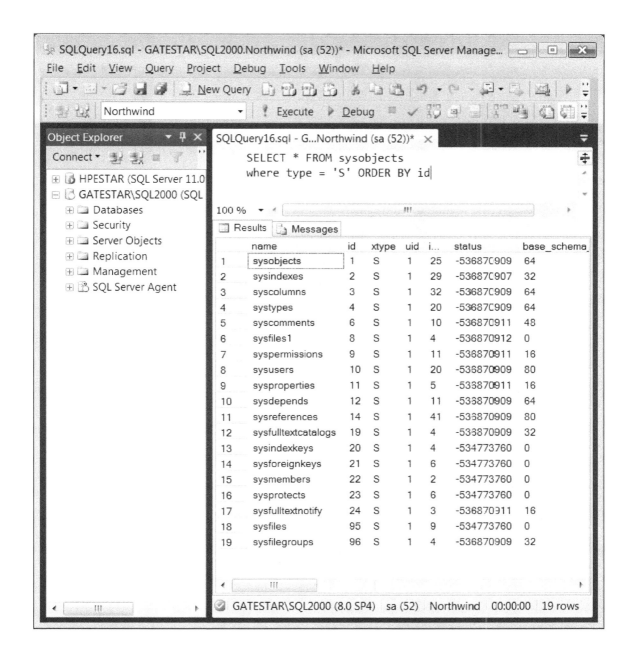

Other Methods of Metadata Access

Graphical Dependency Information

Object dependencies can be launched by a right click on the object.

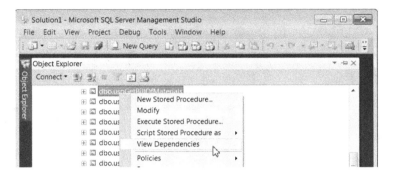

The dependency chart for the uspGetBillOfMaterials stored procedure.

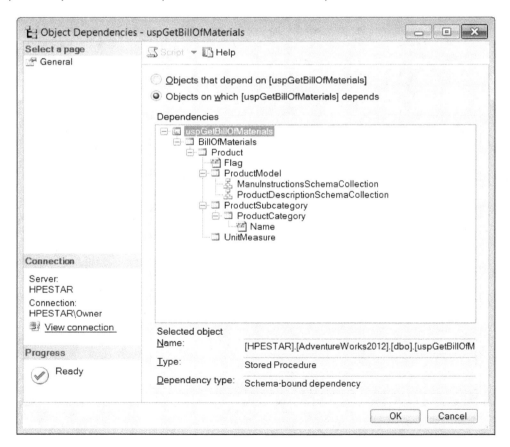

Scripting GUI Object Change

Most of the dialog panels have scripting options. In fact we don't even have to perform the action, we can just script it and execute the script in a (new) connection. The advantage of this approach that the generated script can be modified and saved for future use or reference. We start an index change with right click and properties.

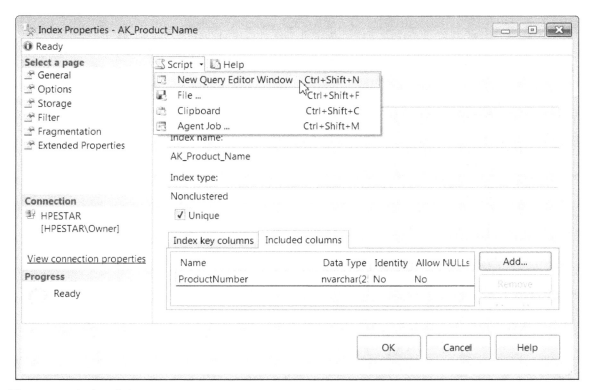

The generated script.

```
USE [AdventureWorks2012]
GO
SET ANSI_PADDING ON
GO
CREATE UNIQUE NONCLUSTERED INDEX [AK_Product_Name] ON [Production].[Product] (
[Name] ASC )
INCLUDE (      [ProductNumber]) WITH (PAD_INDEX = OFF, STATISTICS_NORECOMPUTE = OFF,
SORT_IN_TEMPDB = OFF,
IGNORE_DUP_KEY = OFF, DROP_EXISTING = ON, ONLINE = OFF, ALLOW_ROW_LOCKS = ON,
ALLOW_PAGE_LOCKS = ON, FILLFACTOR = 85) ON [PRIMARY]
GO
```

CHAPTER 9: The Art of Database Design

The sp_helpdb System Procedure

The sp_helpdb system procedure returns information on all or a specified database.

```
EXEC sp_helpdb;
-- Partial results
```

| Accounting | 3.88 MB | HPESTAR\Owner | 17 | May 24 2012 | Status=ONLINE, Updateability=READ_WRITE, UserAccess=MULTI_USER, Recovery=FULL, Version=706, Collation=SQL_Latin1_General_CP1_CI_AS, SQLSortOrder=52, IsAutoCreateStatistics, IsAutoUpdateStatistics, IsFullTextEnabled | 110 |
| AdventureWorks | 213.94 MB | HPESTAR\Owner | 16 | May 24 2012 | Status=ONLINE, Updateability=READ_WRITE, UserAccess=MULTI_USER, Recovery=SIMPLE, Version=706, Collation=SQL_Latin1_General_CP1_CI_AS, SQLSortOrder=52, IsAnsiNullsEnabled, IsAnsiPaddingEnabled, IsAnsiWarningsEnabled, IsArithmeticAbortEnabled, IsAutoCreateStatistics, IsAutoUpdateStatistics, IsFullTextEnabled, IsNullConcat, IsQuotedIdentifiersEnabled, IsRecursiveTriggersEnabled | 90 |

```
EXEC sp_helpdb AdventureWorks2012;
```

name	db_size	owner	dbid	created	status	compatibility_level
AdventureWorks2012	3118.38 MB	sa	7	May 19 2012	Status=ONLINE, Updateability=READ_WRITE, UserAccess=MULTI_USER, Recovery=SIMPLE, Version=706, Collation=SQL_Latin1_General_CP1_CI_AS, SQLSortOrder=52, IsAnsiNullsEnabled, IsAnsiPaddingEnabled, IsAnsiWarningsEnabled, IsArithmeticAbortEnabled, IsAutoCreateStatistics, IsAutoUpdateStatistics, IsFullTextEnabled, IsNullConcat, IsQuotedIdentifiersEnabled	110

The sp_help and sp_helptext System Procedures

The sp_help and sp_helptext provides database metadata in various formats including multiple result sets.

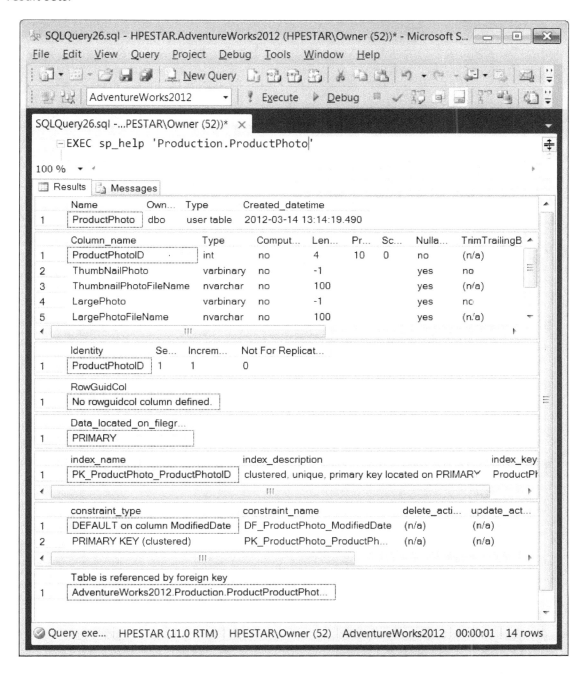

Using sp_helptext for Obtaining Definition

sp_helptext works only for some database objects. Table definition cannot be obtained by command, any command.

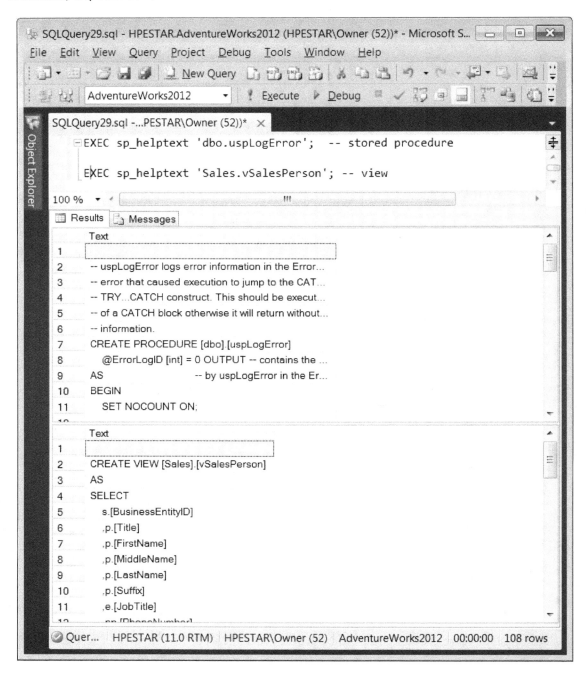

Partial List of sp_helpx System Procedures
The following list is from the master database System Stored Procedures.

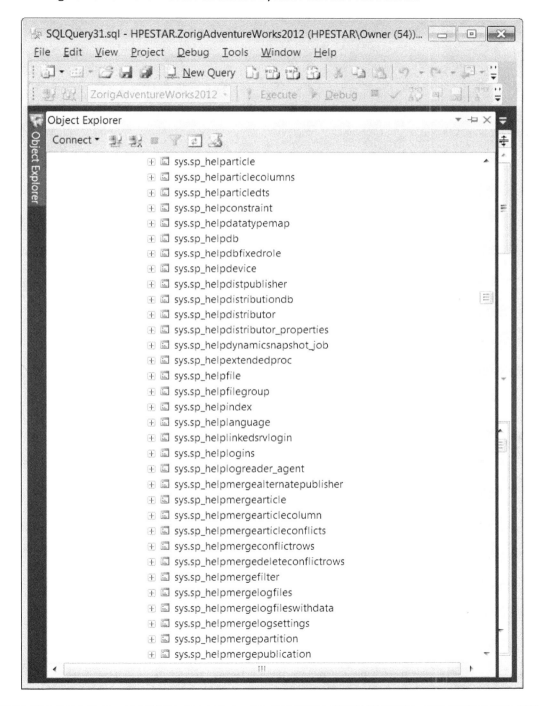

Listing All CHECK Constraints in a Database

We can use INFORMATION_SCHEMA views to perform this task.

```
USE AdventureWorks2012;
GO


SELECT        cc.CONSTRAINT_SCHEMA            AS SCHEMA_NAME,
              TABLE_NAME,
              COLUMN_NAME,
              CHECK_CLAUSE,
              cc.CONSTRAINT_NAME
FROM    INFORMATION_SCHEMA.CHECK_CONSTRAINTS cc
          INNER JOIN INFORMATION_SCHEMA.CONSTRAINT_COLUMN_USAGE c
              ON cc.CONSTRAINT_NAME = c.CONSTRAINT_NAME
ORDER BY      SCHEMA_NAME,
              TABLE_NAME,
              COLUMN_NAME;
-- (105 row(s) affected) - Partial results.
```

SCHEMA_NAME	TABLE_NAME	COLUMN_NAME	CHECK_CLAUSE	CONSTRAINT_NAME
HumanResources	Employee	BirthDate	([BirthDate]>='1930-01-01' AND [BirthDate]<=dateadd(year,(-18),getdate()))	CK_Employee_BirthDate
HumanResources	Employee	Gender	(upper([Gender])='F' OR upper([Gender])='M')	CK_Employee_Gender
HumanResources	Employee	HireDate	([HireDate]>='1996-07-01' AND [HireDate]<=dateadd(day,(1),getdate()))	CK_Employee_HireDate
HumanResources	Employee	MaritalStatus	(upper([MaritalStatus])='S' OR upper([MaritalStatus])='M')	CK_Employee_MaritalStatus
HumanResources	Employee	SickLeaveHours	([SickLeaveHours]>=(0) AND [SickLeaveHours]<=(120))	CK_Employee_SickLeaveHours
HumanResources	Employee	VacationHours	([VacationHours]>=(-40) AND [VacationHours]<=(240))	CK_Employee_VacationHours
HumanResources	EmployeeDepartmentHistory	EndDate	([EndDate]>=[StartDate] OR [EndDate] IS NULL)	CK_EmployeeDepartmentHistory_EndDate
HumanResources	EmployeeDepartmentHistory	StartDate	([EndDate]>=[StartDate] OR [EndDate] IS NULL)	CK_EmployeeDepartmentHistory_EndDate
HumanResources	EmployeePayHistory	PayFrequency	([PayFrequency]=(2) OR [PayFrequency]=(1))	CK_EmployeePayHistory_PayFrequency
HumanResources	EmployeePayHistory	Rate	([Rate]>=(6.50) AND [Rate]<=(200.00))	CK_EmployeePayHistory_Rate
Person	Person	EmailPromotion	([EmailPromotion]>=(0) AND [EmailPromotion]<=(2))	CK_Person_EmailPromotion

CHAPTER 9: The Art of Database Design

Creating a UDF CHECK Constraint

UDF CHECK constraint relies on a user-defined function for logic rather than the simple constraint expression. Demonstration script creates a test table with UDF check constraint.

```
USE tempdb;
SELECT TOP 10  P.BusinessEntityID, FirstName, LastName,        -- Create test table
            Email=convert(varchar(64),EmailAddress)
INTO Person FROM AdventureWorks2012.Person.Person P
            INNER JOIN AdventureWorks2012.Person.EmailAddress E
                ON E.BusinessEntityID = P.BusinessEntityID;
GO
-- Create user-defined function (UDF) for checking
CREATE FUNCTION ufnEmailValidityCheck (@Email varchar(64))
RETURNS BIT  AS
BEGIN
IF EXISTS(SELECT 1 WHERE
    CHARINDEX('.',@Email,CHARINDEX('@',@Email))-CHARINDEX('@',@Email)>1
    AND CHARINDEX('.',REVERSE(LTRIM(RTRIM(@Email)))) > 2
    AND CHARINDEX('@',LTRIM(@Email)) > 2) RETURN(1)
RETURN (0)
END;
GO
  -- Create UDF check constraint
ALTER TABLE [dbo].[Person]  WITH CHECK
ADD CONSTRAINT [EmailCheck] CHECK (   dbo.ufnEmailValidityCheck (Email) = 1);
GO
 -- SQL check constraint violated missing . (period)
INSERT Person (BusinessEntityID, FirstName, LastName, Email)
VALUES (100000, 'Elvis', 'Presley', 'elvispresley@thekingcom');
/*  Msg 547, Level 16, State 0, Line 5
The INSERT statement conflicted with the CHECK constraint "EmailCheck". The conflict occurred
in database "tempdb", table "dbo.Person", column 'Email'.*/
 -- SQL check constraint met
INSERT Person (BusinessEntityID, FirstName, LastName, Email)
VALUES (100000, 'Elvis', 'Presley', 'elvispresley@theking.com');
GO   -- (1 row(s) affected)
 SELECT * FROM Person ORDER BY Email;  -- Partial results.
```

BusinessEntityID	FirstName	LastName	Email
8	Diane	Margheim	diane1@adventure-works.com
7	Dylan	Miller	dylan0@adventure-works.com
100000	Elvis	Presley	elvispresley@theking.com

CHAPTER 9: The Art of Database Design

List All DEFAULT Constraint Definitions

We can use system views to carry out the task.

USE AdventureWorks2012;


```
SELECT
    SCHEMA_NAME(o.schema_id)        AS SchemaName,
    o.name                          AS TableName,
    c.name                          AS ColumnName,
    d.definition                    AS DefaultDefinition,
    d.name                          AS ConstraintName
FROM sys.default_constraints d
        INNER JOIN sys.columns c
                ON d.parent_object_id = c.object_id
                AND d.parent_column_id = c.column_id
        INNER JOIN sys.objects o
                ON o.object_id = c.object_id
ORDER BY SchemaName, TableName, ColumnName;
-- (152 row(s) affected) - Partial results.
```

SchemaName	TableName	ColumnName	DefaultDefinition	ConstraintName
dbo	AWBuildVersion	ModifiedDate	(getdate())	DF_AWBuildVersion_ModifiedDate
dbo	ErrorLog	ErrorTime	(getdate())	DF_ErrorLog_ErrorTime
HumanResources	Department	ModifiedDate	(getdate())	DF_Department_ModifiedDate
HumanResources	Employee	CurrentFlag	((1))	DF_Employee_CurrentFlag
HumanResources	Employee	ModifiedDate	(getdate())	DF_Employee_ModifiedDate
HumanResources	Employee	rowguid	(newid())	DF_Employee_rowguid
HumanResources	Employee	SalariedFlag	((1))	DF_Employee_SalariedFlag
HumanResources	Employee	SickLeaveHours	((0))	DF_Employee_SickLeaveHours
HumanResources	Employee	VacationHours	((0))	DF_Employee_VacationHours
HumanResources	EmployeeDepartmentHistory	ModifiedDate	(getdate())	DF_EmployeeDepartmentHistory_ModifiedDate
HumanResources	EmployeePayHistory	ModifiedDate	(getdate())	DF_EmployeePayHistory_ModifiedDate
HumanResources	JobCandidate	ModifiedDate	(getdate())	DF_JobCandidate_ModifiedDate
HumanResources	Shift	ModifiedDate	(getdate())	DF_Shift_ModifiedDate
Person	Address	ModifiedDate	(getdate())	DF_Address_ModifiedDate
Person	Address	rowguid	(newid())	DF_Address_rowguid
Person	AddressType	ModifiedDate	(getdate())	DF_AddressType_ModifiedDate
Person	AddressType	rowguid	(newid())	DF_AddressType_rowguid
Person	BusinessEntity	ModifiedDate	(getdate())	DF_BusinessEntity_ModifiedDate
Person	BusinessEntity	rowguid	(newid())	DF_BusinessEntity_rowguid
Person	BusinessEntityAddress	ModifiedDate	(getdate())	DF_BusinessEntityAddress_ModifiedDate
Person	BusinessEntityAddress	rowguid	(newid())	DF_BusinessEntityAddress_rowguid
Person	BusinessEntityContact	ModifiedDate	(getdate())	DF_BusinessEntityContact_ModifiedDate
Person	BusinessEntityContact	rowguid	(newid())	DF_BusinessEntityContact_rowguid
Person	ContactType	ModifiedDate	(getdate())	DF_ContactType_ModifiedDate
Person	CountryRegion	ModifiedDate	(getdate())	DF_CountryRegion_ModifiedDate

Database Object-Definition from sys.sql_modules System View

The sys.sql_modules systems view contains definition for stored procedures, triggers, functions and views. Prior to SQL Server 2005 the sys.syscomments table was used to obtain object definition source code.

```
USE AdventureWorks2012;
GO

SELECT object_id, LEFT(definition,64) AS DefinitionPrefix
FROM sys.SQL_Modules ORDER BY object_id;
GO
-- (52 row(s) affected) - Partial results.
```

object_id	DefinitionPrefix
7671075	CREATE VIEW [Sales].[vStoreWithContacts] AS SELECT s.[
23671132	CREATE VIEW [Sales].[vStoreWithAddresses] AS SELECT s.
39671189	CREATE VIEW [Purchasing].[vVendorWithContacts] AS SELECT
55671246	CREATE VIEW [Purchasing].[vVendorWithAddresses] AS SELECT
71671303	CREATE FUNCTION [dbo].[ufnGetAccountingStartDate]() RETURNS [
87671360	CREATE FUNCTION [dbo].[ufnGetAccountingEndDate]() RETURNS [da
103671417	CREATE FUNCTION [dbo].[ufnGetContactInformation](@PersonID int
119671474	CREATE FUNCTION [dbo].[ufnGetProductDealerPrice](@ProductI
135671531	CREATE FUNCTION [dbo].[ufnGetProductListPrice](@ProductID [int
151671588	CREATE FUNCTION [dbo].[ufnGetProductStandardCost](@ProductID [

CHAPTER 9: The Art of Database Design

Retrieving the Full Definition of a Stored Procedure

```
SELECT          schema_name(schema_id)              AS SchemaName,
                object_Name(m.object_ID)            AS ObjectName,
                definition                          AS ObjectDefinition
FROM   sys.SQL_Modules m
  INNER JOIN sys.objects o       ON m.object_id=o.object_id
WHERE  object_Name(m.object_ID) = 'uspGetBillOfMaterials'
GO
```

```
SchemaName          ObjectName           ObjectDefinition
dbo                 uspGetBillOfMaterials   CREATE PROCEDURE [dbo].[uspGetBillOfMaterials]
  @StartProductID [int],
  @CheckDate [datetime]
AS
BEGIN
  SET NOCOUNT ON;

  -- Use recursive query to generate a multi-level Bill of Material (i.e. all level 1
  -- components of a level 0 assembly, all level 2 components of a level 1 assembly)
  -- The CheckDate eliminates any components that are no longer used in the product on this date.
  WITH [BOM_cte]([ProductAssemblyID], [ComponentID], [ComponentDesc], [PerAssemblyQty], [StandardCost], [ListPrice],
[BOMLevel], [RecursionLevel]) -- CTE name and columns
  AS (
    SELECT b.[ProductAssemblyID], b.[ComponentID], p.[Name], b.[PerAssemblyQty], p.[StandardCost], p.[ListPrice], b.[BOMLevel],
0 -- Get the initial list of components for the bike assembly
    FROM [Production].[BillOfMaterials] b
      INNER JOIN [Production].[Product] p
      ON b.[ComponentID] = p.[ProductID]
    WHERE b.[ProductAssemblyID] = @StartProductID
      AND @CheckDate >= b.[StartDate]
      AND @CheckDate <= ISNULL(b.[EndDate], @CheckDate)
    UNION ALL
    SELECT b.[ProductAssemblyID], b.[ComponentID], p.[Name], b.[PerAssemblyQty], p.[StandardCost], p.[ListPrice], b.[BOMLevel],
[RecursionLevel] + 1 -- Join recursive member to anchor
    FROM [BOM_cte] cte
      INNER JOIN [Production].[BillOfMaterials] b
      ON b.[ProductAssemblyID] = cte.[ComponentID]
      INNER JOIN [Production].[Product] p
      ON b.[ComponentID] = p.[ProductID]
    WHERE @CheckDate >= b.[StartDate]
      AND @CheckDate <= ISNULL(b.[EndDate], @CheckDate)
    )
  -- Outer select from the CTE
  SELECT b.[ProductAssemblyID], b.[ComponentID], b.[ComponentDesc], SUM(b.[PerAssemblyQty]) AS [TotalQuantity] ,
b.[StandardCost], b.[ListPrice], b.[BOMLevel], b.[RecursionLevel]
  FROM [BOM_cte] b
  GROUP BY b.[ComponentID], b.[ComponentDesc], b.[ProductAssemblyID], b.[BOMLevel], b.[RecursionLevel], b.[StandardCost],
b.[ListPrice]
  ORDER BY b.[BOMLevel], b.[ProductAssemblyID], b.[ComponentID]     OPTION (MAXRECURSION 25)
END;
```

Snowflake Schema Data Warehouse Design

If the following DW design were Star Schema, the DimProduct would be a flat dimension including DimProductSubcategory and DimProductCategory. In Snowflake Schema the dimension tables follow 3NF relational design.

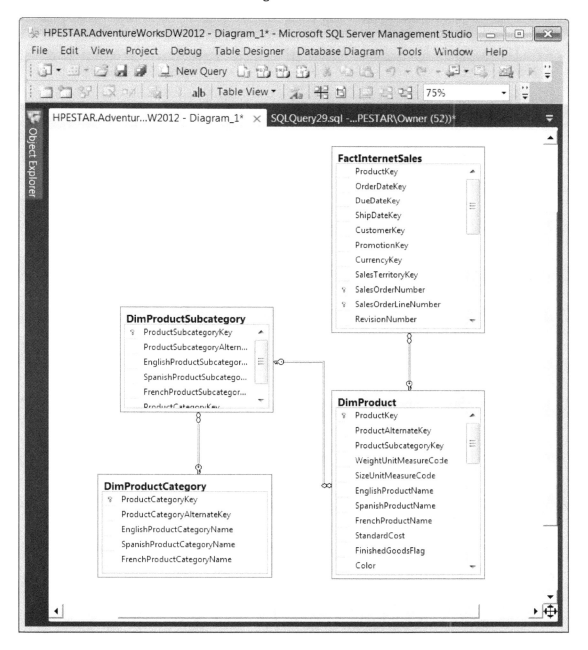

Object Explorer Table Editor

A table editor is available for directly editing data in a table. It is designed for limited use. First we create a test table, Department, then we launch the editor.

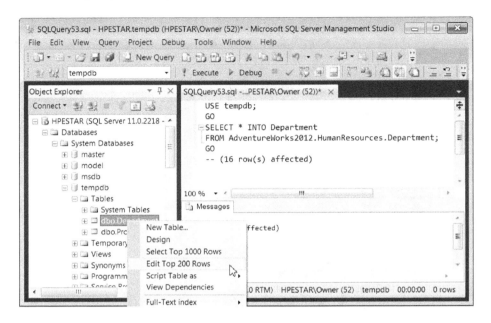

We added row 17 just by typing it in, then investigated the right click drop-down menu.

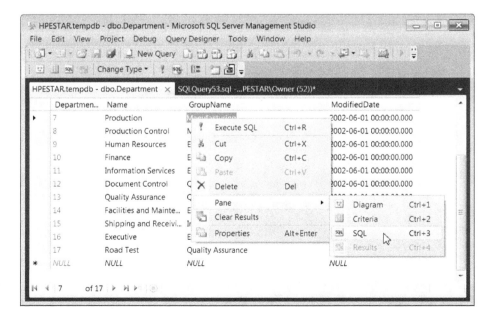

All Tables Row Count without the COUNT() Function

Here is quick way to get a row count, not exact like COUNT(*) but really fast.

USE AdventureWorks2012;

```
SELECT  CONCAT(SCHEMA_NAME(schema_id),'.',o.name )        AS TableName,
        FORMAT(max(i.rows),'###,###,###')                 AS Rows
FROM    sys.sysobjects o
    INNER JOIN sys.sysindexes i
      ON o.id = i.id
    INNER JOIN sys.objects oo
      ON o.id = oo.object_id
WHERE   xtype = 'u'
    AND OBJECTPROPERTY(o.id,N'IsUserTable') = 1
GROUP BY schema_id, o.name
ORDER BY max(i.rows) DESC, TableName;
GO
-- (71 row(s) affected)  -- Partial results.
```

TableName	Rows
Sales.SalesOrderDetail	121,317
Production.TransactionHistory	113,443
Production.TransactionHistoryArchive	89,253
Production.WorkOrder	72,591
Production.WorkOrderRouting	67,131
Sales.SalesOrderHeader	31,465
Sales.SalesOrderHeaderSalesReason	27,647
Person.BusinessEntity	20,777
Person.EmailAddress	19,972
Person.Password	19,972
Person.Person	19,972
Person.PersonPhone	19,972
Sales.Customer	19,820
Person.Address	19,614
Person.BusinessEntityAddress	19,614
Sales.CreditCard	19,118
Sales.PersonCreditCard	19,118
Sales.CurrencyRate	13,532
Purchasing.PurchaseOrderDetail	8,845
Purchasing.PurchaseOrderHeader	4,012
Production.BillOfMaterials	2,679
dbo.DatabaseLog	1,597
Production.ProductInventory	1,069
Person.BusinessEntityContact	909
Production.ProductDescription	762

CHAPTER 9: The Art of Database Design

Column Properties Page in Object Explorer

Object Explorer right click on a column launches the column properties page.
Production.Product table ProductNumber column properties. No changes can be performed on
this page. To change the table, we have to launch the table designer.

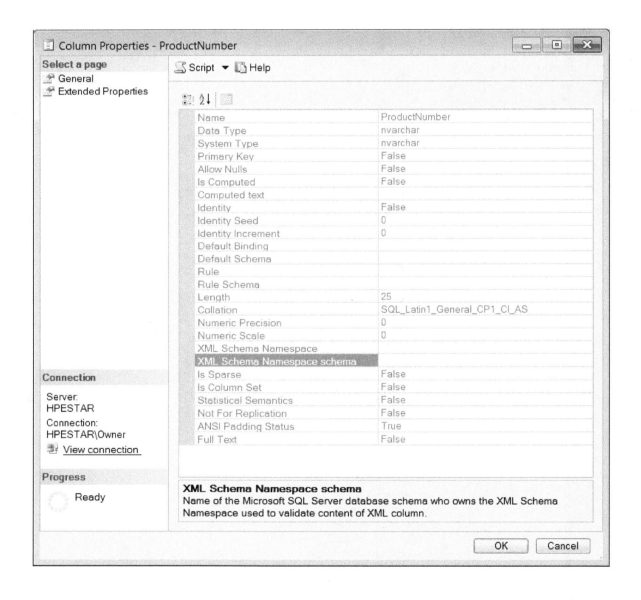

Listing All Columns with PK, FK & IDENTITY Properties

There are various ways for retrieving column properties including the COLUMNPROPERTY() function.

```
USE AdventureWorks2012;

SELECT c.TABLE_CATALOG                                          AS DatabaseName,
    c.TABLE_SCHEMA                                              AS SchemaName,
    c.TABLE_NAME                                                AS TableName,
    c.COLUMN_NAME                                               AS ColumnName,
    Columnproperty(Object_id(CONCAT(c.TABLE_SCHEMA,'.',c.TABLE_NAME)),
                   c.COLUMN_NAME, 'ISIDENTITY')                 AS IsIdentity,
    CASE
      WHEN CONSTRAINT_NAME IN (SELECT NAME
              FROM   sys.objects
              WHERE  TYPE = 'PK') THEN 1
      ELSE 0   END                                              AS IsPrimaryKey,
    CASE
      WHEN CONSTRAINT_NAME IN (SELECT NAME
              FROM   sys.objects
              WHERE  TYPE = 'F') THEN 1
      ELSE 0   END                                              AS IsForeignKey
FROM   INFORMATION_SCHEMA.TABLES t
    INNER JOIN INFORMATION_SCHEMA.COLUMNS c
        ON c.TABLE_CATALOG = t.TABLE_CATALOG
        AND c.TABLE_SCHEMA = t.TABLE_SCHEMA
        AND c.TABLE_NAME = t.TABLE_NAME
    LEFT JOIN INFORMATION_SCHEMA.KEY_COLUMN_USAGE u
        ON c.TABLE_CATALOG = u.TABLE_CATALOG
        AND c.TABLE_SCHEMA = u.TABLE_SCHEMA
        AND c.TABLE_NAME = u.TABLE_NAME
        AND c.COLUMN_NAME = u.COLUMN_NAME
WHERE  TABLE_TYPE = 'BASE TABLE'
ORDER  BY SchemaName,   TableName,   c.ORDINAL_POSITION;
GO
-- (534 row(s) affected) - Partial results.
```

DatabaseName	SchemaName	TableName	ColumnName	IsIdentity	IsPrimaryKey	IsForeignKey
AdventureWorks2012	Person	EmailAddress	BusinessEntityID	0	0	1
AdventureWorks2012	Person	EmailAddress	BusinessEntityID	0	1	0
AdventureWorks2012	Person	EmailAddress	EmailAddressID	1	1	0
AdventureWorks2012	Person	EmailAddress	EmailAddress	0	0	0

CHAPTER 9: The Art of Database Design

The Collation Column Property & the COLLATE Clause

Each text column requires the collation property. The server & databases also have collation property as defaults only. When the database collation is changed, the actual column collations remain the same. New table columns will inherit the database default collation. New databases inherit the server collation. A column collation can be changed with ALTER TABLE. To change all text collations in a database may prove to be a big task.

```
USE tempdb;

SELECT * INTO Product FROM AdventureWorks2012.Production.Product;
-- (504 row(s) affected)

ALTER TABLE Product ALTER COLUMN Name nvarchar(50)
        COLLATE SQL_Latin1_General_CP1_CS_AS null;
-- Command(s) completed successfully.
```

Text operations with different collations result in error.

```
SELECT COUNT(*) FROM Product p
        INNER JOIN AdventureWorks2012.Production.Product aw12
        ON p.Name = aw12.Name;
GO
```

```
/*  Msg 468, Level 16, State 9, Line 3
Cannot resolve the collation conflict between "SQL_Latin1_General_CP1_CI_AS" and
"SQL_Latin1_General_CP1_CS_AS" in the equal to operation.   */
```

We can correct it in the query with the COLLATE clause. We can use a specific collation on one side of the expression, or the easy to remember DATABASE_DEFAULT.

```
SELECT COUNT(*) FROM Product p
        INNER JOIN AdventureWorks2012.Production.Product aw12
        ON p.Name = aw12.Name COLLATE DATABASE_DEFAULT;
-- 504
```

Restoring the original column collation.

```
ALTER TABLE Product alter column ProductName varchar(40)
        COLLATE SQL_Latin1_General_CP1_CI_AS null;
```

CHAPTER 9: The Art of Database Design

Listing All Database & Server Collations

Database collations can be enumerated by a query, while there is special function for server collations. QUOTENAME() function forms proper object names.

```
USE AdventureWorks2012;
GO

SELECT CONCAT(QUOTENAME(s.name), '.', QUOTENAME(t.name),
            '.', QUOTENAME(c.name))                  AS ColumnName,
            c.collation_name                         AS Collation
FROM sys.schemas s
  INNER JOIN sys.tables t
    ON t.schema_id = s.schema_id
  INNER JOIN sys.columns c
    ON c.object_id = t.object_id
WHERE collation_name is not null
ORDER BY ColumnName;
-- (104 row(s) affected) - Partial results.
```

ColumnName	Collation
[HumanResources].[Employee].[NationalIDNumber]	SQL_Latin1_General_CP1_CI_AS
[HumanResources].[Shift].[Name]	SQL_Latin1_General_CP1_CI_AS
[Person].[Address].[AddressLine1]	SQL_Latin1_General_CP1_CI_AS
[Person].[Address].[AddressLine2]	SQL_Latin1_General_CP1_CI_AS

All server collations can be obtained from a table-valued system function.

```
use master;
select   name                               AS Name,
         COLLATIONPROPERTY(name, 'CodePage') AS CodePage,
         LEFT(description,80)                AS Description
from sys.fn_HelpCollations() order by Name;
-- (3885 row(s) affected) - Partial results;
```

Name	CodePage	Description
Modern_Spanish_CS_AS_KS_WS	1252	Modern-Spanish, case-sensitive, accent-sensitive, kanatype-sensitive, width-sens
Modern_Spanish_CS_AS_WS	1252	Modern-Spanish, case-sensitive, accent-sensitive, kanatype-insensitive, width-se
Mohawk_100_BIN	1252	Mohawk-100, binary sort
Mohawk_100_BIN2	1252	Mohawk-100, binary code point comparison sort
Mohawk_100_CI_AI	1252	Mohawk-100, case-insensitive, accent-insensitive, kanatype-insensitive, width-in

CHAPTER 9: The Art of Database Design

Designing Table for Multi-Language Support with UNICODE

Let's script the DimProductSubcategory table from AdventureWorks2012 to demonstrate multi-language support. nvarchar data type is for UNICODE data with each character 2 bytes. It has sufficient capacity to hold even Chinese, Japanese and Korean letters among others.

```
CREATE TABLE dbo.DimProductSubcategory(
        ProductSubcategoryKey int IDENTITY(1,1) NOT NULL,
        ProductSubcategoryAlternateKey int NULL,
        EnglishProductSubcategoryName nvarchar(50) NOT NULL,
        SpanishProductSubcategoryName nvarchar(50) NOT NULL,
        FrenchProductSubcategoryName nvarchar(50) NOT NULL,
        ProductCategoryKey int NULL,
        CONSTRAINT PK_DimProductSubcategory_ProductSubcategoryKey
                PRIMARY KEY CLUSTERED (ProductSubcategoryKey ASC),
        CONSTRAINT AK_DimProductSubcategory_ProductSubcategoryAlternateKey
                UNIQUE NONCLUSTERED (ProductSubcategoryAlternateKey ASC ) );
```

Since there are no COLLATE clauses for the English, Spanish & French names, the collation is the database default. The DATABASEPROPERTYEX() function can be used to retrieve it.

```
SELECT DATABASEPROPERTYEX('AdventureWorksDW2012', 'Collation');
-- SQL_Latin1_General_CP1_CI_AS
```

To get a Spanish language sort, we have to add the COLLATE clause to the ORDER BY clause.

```
SELECT * FROM DimProductSubcategory
ORDER BY SpanishProductSubcategoryName COLLATE Modern_Spanish_CI_AS_WS;
-- (37 row(s) affected) - Partial results.
```

ProductSubcateg oryKey	ProductSubcategoryAlte rnateKey	EnglishProductSubcateg oryName	SpanishProductSubcateg oryName	FrenchProductSubcateg oryName	ProductCatego ryKey
4	4	Handlebars	Barra	Barre d'appui	2
2	2	Road Bikes	Bicicleta de carretera	Vélo de route	1
1	1	Mountain Bikes	Bicicleta de montaña	VTT	1
3	3	Touring Bikes	Bicicleta de paseo	Vélo de randonnée	1
8	8	Cranksets	Bielas	Pédalier	2
36	36	Pumps	Bomba	Pompe	4

Find all collations for a culture.

```
SELECT name, description = LEFT(description, 60) FROM   sys.fn_HelpCollations()
WHERE  name LIKE '%german%' ORDER BY name;  -- (52 row(s) affected)
```

CHAPTER 9: The Art of Database Design

CHAPTER 10: Basic SELECT Statement Syntax & Examples

Simple SELECT Statement Variations

SELECT is the most famous statement in the SQL language. It is used to query tables, and generate reports for users. Although SQL Server Reporting Services and other 3rd party packages available for reporting purposes, frequently reports are generated straight from the database with SELECT queries. The next query returns all rows, all columns sorted on DepartmentID.

USE AdventureWorks2012;

SELECT * FROM HumanResources.Department ORDER BY DepartmentID;
-- (16 row(s) affected)

DepartmentID	Name	GroupName	ModifiedDate
1	Engineering	Research and Development	1998-06-01 00:00:00.000
2	Tool Design	Research and Development	1998-06-01 00:00:00.000
3	Sales	Sales and Marketing	1998-06-01 00:00:00.000
4	Marketing	Sales and Marketing	1998-06-01 00:00:00.000
5	Purchasing	Inventory Management	1998-06-01 00:00:00.000
6	Research and Development	Research and Development	1998-06-01 00:00:00.000
7	Production	Manufacturing	1998-06-01 00:00:00.000
8	Production Control	Manufacturing	1998-06-01 00:00:00.000
9	Human Resources	Executive General and Administration	1998-06-01 00:00:00.000
10	Finance	Executive General and Administration	1998-06-01 00:00:00.000
11	Information Services	Executive General and Administration	1998-06-01 00:00:00.000
12	Document Control	Quality Assurance	1998-06-01 00:00:00.000
13	Quality Assurance	Quality Assurance	1998-06-01 00:00:00.000
14	Facilities and Maintenance	Executive General and Administration	1998-06-01 00:00:00.000
15	Shipping and Receiving	Inventory Management	1998-06-01 00:00:00.000
16	Executive	Executive General and Administration	1998-06-01 00:00:00.000

Since the time part of ModifiedDate is not being used, and that makes business sense, we can format it just as date.

SELECT TOP (3) DepartmentID, Name, GroupName, CONVERT(DATE, ModifiedDate) AS ModifiedDate
FROM HumanResources.Department ORDER BY DepartmentID;
-- (16 row(s) affected)

DepartmentID	Name	GroupName	ModifiedDate
1	Engineering	Research and Development	1998-06-01
2	Tool Design	Research and Development	1998-06-01
3	Sales	Sales and Marketing	1998-06-01

CHAPTER 10: Basic SELECT Statement Syntax & Examples

SELECT query with sort on EnglishProductName in DESCending order
ASCending sort is the default.

```
USE AdventureWorksDW2012
GO


SELECT  *
FROM    DimProduct
ORDER BY EnglishProductName DESC
GO
-- (606 row(s) affected) - Partial results.
```

EnglishProductName	SpanishProductName	FrenchProductName	StandardCost
Women's Tights, S	Mallas para mujer, P	Collants pour femmes, taille S	30.9334
Women's Tights, M	Mallas para mujer, M	Collants pour femmes, taille M	30.9334
Women's Tights, L	Mallas para mujer, G	Collants pour femmes, taille L	30.9334
Women's Mountain Shorts, S			26.1763
Women's Mountain Shorts, M			26.1763
Women's Mountain Shorts, L			26.1763
Water Bottle - 30 oz.			1.8663
Touring-Panniers, Large	Cesta de paseo, grande	Sacoches de vélo de randonnée, grande capacité	51.5625
Touring-3000 Yellow, 62	Paseo: 3000, amarilla, 62	Vélo de randonnée 3000 jaune, 62	461.4448
Touring-3000 Yellow, 58	Paseo: 3000, amarilla, 58	Vélo de randonnée 3000 jaune, 58	461.4448

The next query sorts on the SpanishProductName column in ascending order.

```
SELECT  *
FROM    DimProduct
ORDER BY SpanishProductName ASC
GO
-- (606 row(s) affected) - Partial results.
```

EnglishProductName	SpanishProductName
HL Crankset	Bielas GA
LL Crankset	Bielas GB
ML Crankset	Bielas GM
Mountain Pump	Bomba de montaña
Cable Lock	Cable antirrobo
Chain	Cadena
Mountain Bike Socks,	Calcetines para bicicleta de montaña, G

Sorting on FrenchProductName, if empty, use EnglishProductName.

```
SELECT  * FROM    DimProduct ORDER BY FrenchProductName, EnglishProductName;
GO
```

CHAPTER 10: Basic SELECT Statement Syntax & Examples

Using the TOP Clause in SELECT Queries

The TOP clause limits the number of rows returned as specified in the TOP expression according the sorted order if any. In the following query, the sorting is based on a major key (LastName) and a minor key (FirstName).

```
USE AdventureWorks2012
GO

SELECT   TOP 100 *
FROM     Person.Person ORDER BY LastName, FirstName
-- (100 row(s) affected) - Partial results.
```

BusinessEntityID	PersonType	Title	FirstName	LastName	EmailPromotion
285	SP	Mr.	Syed	Abbas	0
293	SC	Ms.	Catherine	Abel	1
295	SC	Ms.	Kim	Abercrombie	0
2170	GC	NULL	Kim	Abercrombie	2
38	EM	NULL	Kim	Abercrombie	2
211	EM	NULL	Hazem	Abolrous	0
2357	GC	NULL	Sam	Abolrous	1
297	SC	Sr.	Humberto	Acevedo	2
291	SC	Mr.	Gustavo	Achong	2
299	SC	Sra.	Pilar	Ackerman	0

The total population of the Person.Person table is 19,972 rows.

```
SELECT  * FROM    Person.Person ORDER BY LastName, FirstName
-- (19972 row(s) affected)
```

We can also count the rows applying the COUNT function.

```
SELECT  RowsCount = count(*)  FROM    Person.Person
-- 19972
```

When counting, it is safe to count the PRIMARY KEY (ProductID) values.

```
SELECT  RowsCount = count(ProductID)   FROM    Production.Product;
-- 504
```

```
SELECT  RowsCount = count(Color)   FROM    Production.Product;      -- 256
```

Using the WHERE Clause in SELECT Queries

The WHERE clause filters the rows to be returned according the one or more predicates. The next T-SQL scripts demonstrate simple WHERE clause predicates, including multiple WHERE conditions.

```
-- Last name starts with S
SELECT *
FROM    Person.Person
WHERE   LEFT(LastName,1) = 'S'
ORDER BY LastName;
-- (2130 row(s) affected)
```

```
-- First name is Shelly
SELECT  *
FROM    Person.Person
WHERE   FirstName = 'Shelly'
ORDER BY LastName;
-- (1 row(s) affected)
```

```
-- First name is John
SELECT  *
FROM    Person.Person
WHERE   FirstName = 'John'
ORDER BY LastName;
-- (58 row(s) affected)
```

```
-- First name John, last name starts with S - Multiple WHERE conditions
SELECT  *
FROM    Person.Person
WHERE   FirstName = 'John'
    AND LEFT(LastName,1) = 'S'
ORDER BY LastName ;
-- (2 row(s) affected)
```

```
-- Last name starts with S OR first name starts with J
SELECT  *
FROM    Person.Person
WHERE   LEFT(FirstName,1) = 'J'  OR LEFT(LastName,1) = 'S'
ORDER BY LastName;
-- (4371 row(s) affected)
```

```
-- Last name starts with S AND first name starts with J
SELECT  *
FROM    Person.Person  WHERE   LEFT(FirstName,1) = 'J'   AND LEFT(LastName,1) = 'S'
ORDER BY LastName;   -- (221 row(s) affected)
```

CHAPTER 10: Basic SELECT Statement Syntax & Examples

Using Literals in SELECT Queries

Literals or constants are used commonly in T-SQL queries, also as defaults for columns, local variables, and parameters. The format of a literal depends on the data type of the value it represents. The database engine may perform implicit conversion to match data types. Explicit conversion of literals can be achieved with the CONVERT or CAST functions. T-SQL scripts demonstrate literal use in WHERE clause predicates.

```
USE AdventureWorks2012;
-- Integer literal  in WHERE clause predicate
SELECT * FROM Production.Product
WHERE ProductID = 800;
-- (1 row(s) affected)
```

```
-- String literal in WHERE clause predicate
SELECT * FROM Production.Product WHERE Color = 'Blue';
-- (26 row(s) affected)
```

```
USE AdventureWorksDW2012;
-- UNICODE (2 bytes per character) string literal
SELECT * FROM DimProduct
WHERE SpanishProductName = N'Jersey clásico de manga corta, G';
-- (1 row(s) affected)
```

```
-- UNICODE string literal
SELECT * FROM DimProduct
WHERE FrenchProductName = N'Roue arrière de vélo de randonnée';
-- (1 row(s) affected)
```

```
USE AdventureWorks2012;
-- Money literal in WHERE clause predicate
SELECT * FROM Production.Product
WHERE ListPrice > = $2000.0;
-- (35 row(s) affected)
```

```
-- Floating point literal with implicit conversion to MONEY
SELECT * FROM Production.Product  WHERE ListPrice > = 2.000E+3;
-- (35 row(s) affected)
```

```
-- Hex (binary) literal
SELECT * FROM Production.Product  WHERE rowguid >= 0x23D89CEE9F444F3EB28963DE6BA2B737
-- (302 row(s) affected)
```

```
-- The rest of the 504 products
SELECT * FROM Production.Product  WHERE rowguid < 0x23D89CEE9F444F3EB28963DE6BA2B737
-- (202 row(s) affected)
```

CHAPTER 10: Basic SELECT Statement Syntax & Examples

Date & Time Literals in SELECT Queries

Date and time literals appear to come from an infinite pool. Every country has tens of string date & time variations. Despite the many external string representation, **date, datetime, datetime, time, smalldatetime** and other temporal data types have unique, well-defined representation within the database engine.

ymd date literal format is the cleanest. There is eternal confusion about the North American mdy string date format and the European dmy string date format. The date and time format with "T" separator (last one) is the ISO date time format literal. ANSI Date literal - YYYYMMDD - the best choice since it work in any country.

CONVERT or CAST Date Time Literal	Result
SELECT [Date] = CAST('20160228' AS date)	2016-02-28
SELECT [Datetime] = CAST('20160228' AS datetime)	2016-02-28 00:00:00.000
SELECT [SmallDatetime] = CAST('20160228' AS smalldatetime)	2016-02-28 00:00:00
SELECT [Datetime] = CONVERT(datetime,'2016-02-28')	2016-02-28 00:00:00.000
SELECT [Datetime2] = CONVERT(datetime2,'2016-02-28')	2016-02-28 00:00:00.0000000
SELECT [Datetime] = CONVERT(datetime, '20160228')	2016-02-28 00:00:00.000
SELECT [Datetime2] = CONVERT(datetime2,'20160228')	2016-02-28 00:00:00.0000000
SELECT [Datetime] = CAST('Mar 15, 2016' AS datetime)	2016-03-15 00:00:00.000
SELECT [Datetime2] = CAST('Mar 15, 2016' AS datetime2)	2016-03-15 00:00:00.0000000
SELECT [Date] = CAST('Mar 15, 2016' AS date)	2016-03-15
SELECT CAST('16:40:31' AS datetime)	1900-01-01 16:40:31.000
SELECT CAST('16:40:31' AS time)	16:40:31.0000000
SELECT [Datetime] = CAST('Mar 15, 2016 12:07:34.444' AS datetime)	2016-03-15 12:07:34.443
SELECT [Datetime2] = CAST('Mar 15, 2016 12:07:34.4445555' AS datetime2)	2016-03-15 12:07:34.4445555
SELECT [Datetime] = CAST('2016-03-15T12:07:34.513' AS datetime)	2016-03-15 12:07:34.513

CHAPTER 10: Basic SELECT Statement Syntax & Examples

ymd, dmy & mdy String Date Format Literals

Date and time string literals are the least understood part of the T-SQL language by database developers. It is a constant source of confusion and frustration, in addition huge economic cost of lost programmer's productivity. ymd, dmy & mdy are the main string date formats. Some countries use ydm format. Setting dateformat overrides the implicit setting by language.

The basic principles:

➢ **There is only one DATETIME data type internal format**, independent where SQL Server is operated: New York, London, Amsterdam, Berlin, Moscow, Hong Kong, Singapore, Tokyo, Melbourne or Rio de Janeiro.
➢ There are hundreds of national string date & time formats which have nothing to do with SQL Server.
➢ String date must be properly converted to DATETIME format.

```
SET DATEFORMAT ymd
SELECT convert(datetime,'16/05/08')           -- 2016-05-08 00:00:00.000


-- Setting DATEFORMAT to UK-Style (European)
SET DATEFORMAT dmy
SELECT convert(datetime,'20/05/16')           -- 2016-05-20 00:00:00.000


-- Setting DATEFORMAT to US-Style
SET DATEFORMAT mdy
SELECT convert(datetime,'05/20/16')           -- 2016-05-20 00:00:00.000
SELECT convert(datetime,'05/20/2016')         -- 2016-05-20 00:00:00.000
```
Interestingly we can achieve the same implicit conversion action by setting language.

```
-- Setting DATEFORMAT ymd  via language
SET LANGUAGE Japanese;  SELECT convert(datetime,'16/05/08') ;      -- 2016-05-08 00:00:00.000


-- Setting DATEFORMAT to UK-Style (European) via language
SET LANGUAGE British;  SELECT convert(datetime,'20/05/16');        -- 2016-05-20 00:00:00.000
SELECT convert(datetime,'05/20/16');
/* Msg 242, Level 16, State 3, Line 3
The conversion of a varchar data type to a datetime data type resulted in an out-of-range value.  */


-- Setting DATEFORMAT to US-Style via language
SET LANGUAGE English;  SELECT convert(datetime,'05/20/16');        -- 2016-05-20 00:00:00.000
SELECT convert(datetime,'05/20/2016');             -- 2016-05-20 00:00:00.000
SELECT convert(datetime,'20/05/2016');
/* Msg 242, Level 16, State 3, Line 4
The conversion of a varchar data type to a datetime data type resulted in an out-of-range value.  */
```

CHAPTER 10: Basic SELECT Statement Syntax & Examples

Setting DATEFIRST with Literal

DATEFIRST indicates the first day of the week which may vary by country, culture or business. The next T-SQL script demonstrates how it can be set by integer literal 1-7. It overrides the implicit setting by language. @@DATEFIRST is a system (SQL Server database engine) variable.

```
SET DATEFIRST 7  -- Sunday as first day of the week
SELECT DATEPART(dw, '20160315');            -- 3
SELECT DATENAME(dw, '20160315');            -- Tuesday
SELECT @@DATEFIRST                          -- 7


SET DATEFIRST 1  -- Monday as first day of the week
SELECT DATEPART(dw, '20160315');            -- 2
SELECT DATENAME(dw, '20160315');            -- Tuesday
SELECT @@DATEFIRST                          -- 1
```

Language Setting - SET LANGUAGE

DATEFIRST is tied to the language setting, just the like the date format (ymd, dmy, or mdy).

```
SET LANGUAGE us_english
SELECT DATEPART(dw, '20160315');            -- 3
SELECT DATENAME(dw, '20160315');            -- Tuesday
SELECT @@DATEFIRST                          -- 7


SET LANGUAGE german
SELECT DATEPART(dw, '20160315');            -- 2
SELECT DATENAME(dw, '20160315');            -- Dienstag
SELECT @@DATEFIRST                          -- 1


SET LANGUAGE british
SELECT DATEPART(dw, '20160315');            -- 2
SELECT DATENAME(dw, '20160315');            -- Tuesday
SELECT @@DATEFIRST                          -- 1


SET LANGUAGE hungarian
SELECT DATEPART(dw, '20160315');            -- 2
SELECT DATENAME(dw, '20160315');            -- kedd
SELECT @@DATEFIRST                          -- 1


SET LANGUAGE spanish
SELECT DATEPART(dw, '20160315');            -- 2
SELECT DATENAME(dw, '20160315');            -- Martes
SELECT @@DATEFIRST                          -- 1
```

The sys.syslanguages System View

The syslanguages table contains not only language related information, but date related settings as well.

```
SELECT
        langid,
        dateformat,
        datefirst,
        name                            AS native_language,
        alias                           AS english,
        left(shortmonths, 15)           AS shortmonths,
        left(days,15)                   AS days
FROM AdventureWorks2012.sys.syslanguages
ORDER BY langid;
GO
-- (34 row(s) affected)  -  Partial results.
```

langid	dateformat	datefirst	native_language	english	shortmonths	days
0	mdy	7	us_english	English	Jan,Feb,Mar,Apr	Monday,Tuesday,
1	dmy	1	Deutsch	German	Jan,Feb,Mär,Apr	Montag,Dienstag
2	dmy	1	Français	French	janv,févr,mars,	lundi,mardi,mer
3	ymd	7	日本語	Japanese	01,02,03,04,05,	月曜日,火曜日,水曜日,木曜日
4	dmy	1	Dansk	Danish	jan,feb,mar,apr	mandag,tirsdag,
5	dmy	1	Español	Spanish	Ene,Feb,Mar,Abr	Lunes,Martes,Mi
6	dmy	1	Italiano	Italian	gen,feb,mar,apr	lunedì,martedì,
7	dmy	1	Nederlands	Dutch	jan,feb,mrt,apr	maandag,dinsdag
8	dmy	1	Norsk	Norwegian	jan,feb,mar,apr	mardag,tirsdag,
9	dmy	7	Português	Portuguese	jan,fev,mar,abr	segunda-feira,t
10	dmy	1	Suomi	Finnish	tammi,helmi,maa	maanantai,tiist
11	ymd	1	Svenska	Swedish	jan,feb,mar,apr	mårdag,tisdag,o
12	dmy	1	čeština	Czech	I,II,III,IV,V,V	pondělí,úterý,s
13	ymd	1	magyar	Hungarian	jan,febr,márc,á	hétfő,kedd,szer
14	dmy	1	polski	Polish	I,II,III,IV,V,V	pon edziałek,wt
15	dmy	1	română	Romanian	Ian,Feb,Mar,Apr	luni,marţi,mier
16	ymd	1	hrvatski	Croatian	sij,vel,ožu,tra	ponedjeljak,uto
17	dmy	1	slovenčina	Slovak	I,II,III,IV,V,V	pondelok,utorok
18	dmy	1	slovenski	Slovenian	jan,feb,mar,apr	ponedelje<,tore
19	dmy	1	ελληνικά	Greek	Ιαν,Φεβ,Μαρ,Απρ	Δευτέρα,Τρίτη,Τ
20	dmy	1	български	Bulgarian	януари,февруари	понеделник,втор
21	dmy	1	русский	Russian	янв,фев,мар,апр	понедельник,вто
22	dmy	1	Türkçe	Turkish	Oca,Şub,Mar,Nis	Pazartesi,Salı,
23	dmy	1	British	British English	Jan,Feb,Mar,Apr	Monday,Tuesday,
24	dmy	1	eesti	Estonian	jaan,veebr,märt	esmaspäev,teisi
25	ymd	1	latviešu	Latvian	jan,feb,mar,apr	pirmdiena,otrdi
26	ymd	1	lietuvių	Lithuanian	sau,vas,kov,bal	pirmadienis,ant
27	dmy	7	Português (Brasil)	Brazilian	Jan,Fev,Mar,Abr	Segunda-Feira,T
28	ymd	7	繁體中文	Traditional Chinese	01,02,03,04,05,	星期一,星期二,星期三,星期四
29	ymd	7	한국어	Korean	01,02,03,04,05,	월요일,화요일,수요일,목요일
30	ymd	7	简体中文	Simplified Chinese	01,02,03,04,05,	星期一,星期二,星期三,星期四
31	dmy	1	Arabic	Arabic	Jan,Feb,Mar,Apr	Monday,Tuesday,
32	dmy	7	ไทย	Thai	ม.ค.,ก.พ.,มี.ค.	จันทร์,อังคาร,พ
33	dmy	1	norsk (bokmål)	Bokmål	jan,feb,mar,apr	mandag,tirsdag,

CHAPTER 10: Basic SELECT Statement Syntax & Examples

DBCC USEROPTIONS

The DBCC USEROPTIONS command displays some of the connection (session) settings. As we have seen these settings play an important part on how date literals are interpreted by the system such as dateformat.

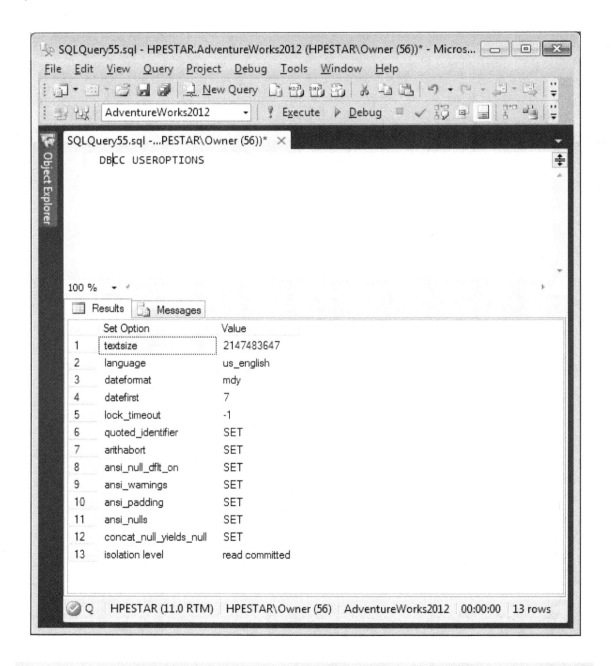

Easy SELECT Queries for Fun & Learning

T-SQL scripts to demonstrate simple, easy-to-read SELECT query variations. Important note: alias column names cannot be reused in successive computed columns by expressions or anywhere else in the query except the ORDER BY clause.

```
-- Datetime range with string literal date
SELECT  *  FROM    Person.Person
WHERE   ModifiedDate <= '2002-08-09 00:00:00.000'  ORDER BY LastName;
-- (38 row(s) affected)
```

> **NOTE**
> The string literal above looks like datetime, but it is not. It is only a string literal. The database engine will try to convert it to datetime data type at runtime (implicit conversion), and if successful the query will be executed.
> The syntax of the following query is OK, however, it will fail at execution time.
> SELECT * FROM   Person.Person WHERE   ModifiedDate <= 'New York City' ORDER BY LastName;
> /* Msg 241, Level 16, State 1, Line 1 Conversion failed when converting date and/or time from character string. */

```
-- Complimentary (remaining) datetime range specified again with string literal
SELECT *  FROM    Person.Person  WHERE    ModifiedDate > '2002-08-09 00:00:00.000'  ORDER BY
LastName;
-- (19934 row(s) affected)
```

```
-- Total rows in Person.Person
SELECT ( 38 + 19934 ) AS TotalRows;    -- 19972
```

```
SELECT count(* ) FROM   Person.Person -- 19972
```

```
SELECT TableRows = count(* ),  Calc = 38 + 19934  FROM   Person.Person; -- 19972     19972
```

```
-- Get prefix left of comma or entire string if there is no comma present
SELECT TOP 4                                                               ProductNumber,
       LEFT(Name, COALESCE(NULLIF(CHARINDEX(',',Name)-1,-1),LEN(Name)))    AS NamePrefix,
       Name                                                                AS ProductName
FROM AdventureWorks2012.Production.Product   WHERE CHARINDEX(',',Name) > 0
ORDER BY ProductName;
```

ProductNumber	NamePrefix	ProductName
VE-C304-L	Classic Vest	Classic Vest, L
VE-C304-M	Classic Vest	Classic Vest, M
VE-C304-S	Classic Vest	Classic Vest, S
GL-F110-L	Full-Finger Gloves	Full-Finger Gloves, L

CHAPTER 10: Basic SELECT Statement Syntax & Examples

NULL refers to no information available. Note: "=" and "!=" operators are not used with NULL; "IS" or "IS NOT" operators are applicable.

```
SELECT *
FROM    Person.Person
WHERE    AdditionalContactInfo IS NOT NULL
ORDER BY LastName;
-- (10 row(s) affected)
```

```
SELECT *
FROM    Person.Person
WHERE    AdditionalContactInfo IS NULL
ORDER BY LastName;
-- (19962 row(s) affected)
```

```
SELECT   DISTINCT FirstName
FROM    Person.Person
ORDER BY FirstName;      -- (1018 row(s) affected)
```

```
-- Summary revenue by product, interesting sort
USE AdventureWorks2012;
GO
SELECT  TOP 10 p.Name                                        AS ProductName,
  FORMAT(SUM(((OrderQty * UnitPrice) * (1.0 - UnitPriceDiscount)))),'c','en-US') AS SubTotal
FROM Production.Product AS p
INNER JOIN Sales.SalesOrderDetail AS sod
ON p.ProductID = sod.ProductID
GROUP BY p.Name
ORDER BY REVERSE(p.Name);
```

ProductName	SubTotal
Water Bottle - 30 oz.	$28,654.16
Hydration Pack - 70 oz.	$105,826.42
LL Mountain Frame - Black, 40	$1,198.99
ML Mountain Frame - Black, 40	$14,229.41
Mountain-300 Black, 40	$501,648.88
Mountain-500 Black, 40	$101,734.12
LL Mountain Frame - Silver, 40	$69,934.28
ML Mountain Frame-W - Silver, 40	$195,826.39
Mountain-500 Silver, 40	$145,089.43
Mountain-400-W Silver, 40	$323,703.82

DISTINCT & GROUP BY operations are generally "expensive".

```
SELECT   DISTINCT LastName FROM    Person.Person ORDER BY LastName;  -- (1206 row(s) affected)

-- LastName popularity descending
SELECT LastName,     Frequency = count(* )
FROM    Person.Person
GROUP BY LastName
ORDER BY Frequency DESC;
GO
```

LastName	Frequency
Diaz	211
Hernandez	188
Sanchez	175
Martinez	173
Torres	172
Martin	171
Perez	170
Gonzalez	169
Lopez	168
Rodriguez	166

```
-- Sort on column not in SELECT list - Note: demo only, confusing to end user
SELECT   LastName
FROM    Person.Person
ORDER BY FirstName;
-- (19972 row(s) affected)

-- Sort on column not in SELECT list
SELECT   Name = CONCAT(LastName, ', ', FirstName )
FROM    Person.Person
ORDER BY LastName;
-- (19972 row(s) affected)

-- Sort on column alias
SELECT   Name = CONCAT(LastName, ', ', FirstName )
FROM    Person.Person
ORDER BY Name;
-- (19972 row(s) affected)

SELECT   CONCAT(LastName, ', ', FirstName ) AS FullName
FROM    Person.Person
WHERE    LastName >= 'K' ORDER BY LastName;
-- (12057 row(s) affected)
```

CHAPTER 10: Basic SELECT Statement Syntax & Examples

The NULLIF Function Actually Creates A NULL

```
SELECT   CONCAT(LastName, ', ', FirstName )  AS FullName
FROM    Person.Person  WHERE    LastName < 'K'  ORDER BY LastName;
-- (7915 row(s) affected)
```

```
-- Cardinality check
SELECT Difference= ((count(*)) - (12057 + 7915)) FROM  Person.Person; -- 0
```

```
-- Using the NULLIF function in counting
-- Count of all list prices - no NULLs in column
SELECT COUNT(ListPrice) FROM   AdventureWorks2012.Production.Product
-- 504
```

```
-- Counts only when ListPrice != 0 - does not count NULLs (ListPrice = 0.0)
SELECT COUNT(NULLIF(ListPrice,0.0)) FROM   AdventureWorks2012.Production.Product
-- 304
```

```
SELECT COUNT(ListPrice)  FROM  AdventureWorks2012.Production.Product  WHERE ListPrice = 0;
-- 200
```

Cardinality of DISTINCT & GROUP BY Clauses

The cardinality of DISTINCT and the cardinality of GROUP BY are the same with the same column(s).

```
-- FirstName by popularity descending
SELECT FirstName,
        Freq = count(* )
FROM    Person.Person
GROUP BY FirstName
ORDER BY Freq DESC;
-- (1018 row(s) affected)
```

FirstName	Freq
Richard	103
Katherine	99
Marcus	97
James	97
Jennifer	96
Dalton	93
Lucas	93
Alexandra	93
Morgan	92
Seth	92

```
SELECT   DISTINCT FirstName  FROM    Person.Person  ORDER BY FirstName;  -- (1018 row(s) affected)
```

CHAPTER 10: Basic SELECT Statement Syntax & Examples

Column Alias Can only Be Used in ORDER BY

Column aliases cannot be used in other computed columns (expressions), neither in the WHERE clause or GROUP BY clause.

```
SELECT  TableRows = count(* ),
        Calculated = 38 + 19934,
        Difference = (count(*) - 38 - 19934)
FROM  Person.Person;
```

TableRows	Calculated	Difference
19972	19972	0

Workarounds for Column Alias Use Restriction

There is a simple workaround for recycling column aliases in other clauses than just the ORDER BY: make the query into a derived table (x) and include it in an outer query. Similarly, CTEs can be used instead of derived tables.

```
-- Derived table workaround
SELECT TableRows, Calculated, Difference = TableRows - Calculated
FROM (
        SELECT  TableRows = count(* ),     Calculated = 38 + 19934,
        FROM  Person.Person
        ) x ;  -- Derived table
GO
```

TableRows	Calculated	Difference
19972	19972	0

```
-- CTE workaround
;WITH CTE AS (
        SELECT  TableRows = count(* ),     Calculated = 38 + 19934
        FROM  Person.Person)
-- Outer query
SELECT TableRows, Calculated, Difference = TableRows - Calculated
FROM CTE;
```

TableRows	Calculated	Difference
19972	19972	0

CHAPTER 10: Basic SELECT Statement Syntax & Examples

When the Clock Strikes Midnight: datetime Behaviour

This is one of the most troublesome issues in T-SQL programming (midnight bug, Cinderella syndrom): the predicate YYYYMMDD (date string literal) = DatetimeColumn does not include the entire day, only records with time at midnight: 00:00:00.000 .

```
USE AdventureWorks2012;

-- Note: only midnight 2003-08-09 included
-- Even a second after midnight is not included like 2003-08-09 00:00:01.000
SELECT  *
FROM    Person.Person
WHERE     ModifiedDate BETWEEN '2002-08-09 00:00:00.000'
          AND '2003-08-09 00:00:00.000'
ORDER BY LastName;
GO
-- (396 row(s) affected)


-- Entire day of 2003-08-09 included
-- The count same as before because no records after midnight 2003-08-09
SELECT  *
FROM    Person.Person
WHERE     ModifiedDate >= '2002-08-09 00:00:00.000'
          AND ModifiedDate < '2003-08-10 00:00:00.000'
ORDER BY LastName;
GO
-- (396 row(s) affected)
```

LEFT(), RIGHT() & SUBSTRING() String Functions

```
SELECT  FirstCharOfFirstName = LEFT(FirstName,1),              -- column alias
        FirstCharOfLastName  = LEFT(LastName,1),               -- column alias
        LastCharOfLastName  = RIGHT(LastName,1),               -- column alias
        FullName = CONCAT(FirstName, SPACE(1), LastName) ,     -- column alias
        *                                                      -- wild card, all columns
FROM    Person.Person
WHERE   SUBSTRING(FirstName,1,1) = 'J'
    AND SUBSTRING (LastName,1,1) = 'S'
    AND (RIGHT(LastName,1) = 'H' OR RIGHT(LastName,1) = 'Z')
ORDER BY LastName;
-- (59 row(s) affected) - Partial result.
```

FirstCharOfFirstName	FirstCharOfLastName	LastCharOfLastName	FullName	BusinessEntityID
J	S	z	Jacqueline Sanchez	8975
J	S	z	Jada Sanchez	9499
J	S	z	Jade Sanchez	9528
J	S	z	Janelle Sanchez	18590
J	S	z	Jared Sanchez	15265
J	S	z	Jarrod Sanchez	2948
J	S	z	Jay Sanchez	10293
J	S	z	Jennifer Sanchez	20440
J	S	z	Jeremiah Sanchez	15292
J	S	z	Jermaine Sanchez	8040

```
-- Sort on first column
SELECT BusinessEntityID, JobTitle, SUBSTRING(JobTitle, 5, 7)  AS MiddleOfJobTitle
FROM   HumanResources.Employee
WHERE  BirthDate <= '1960/12/31'    -- date literal (constant)
ORDER BY 1;
-- (27 row(s) affected) - Partial results.
```

BusinessEntityID	JobTitle	MiddleOfJobTitle
5	Design Engineer	gn Engi
6	Design Engineer	gn Engi
12	Tool Designer	Design
15	Design Engineer	gn Engi
23	Marketing Specialist	eting S
27	Production Supervisor - WC60	uction

```
-- String functions usage in formatting
DECLARE @SSN char(9) = '123456789';
SELECT SSN=CONCAT(LEFT(@SSN,3),'-', SUBSTRING(@SSN,4,2),'-', RIGHT(@SSN,4));
-- 123-45-6789
```

CHAPTER 10: Basic SELECT Statement Syntax & Examples

ASCII value range is 0-127. Extended ASCII: 128-255. Size is 8-bit, one byte.

```
SELECT TOP 5     ProductNumber,
                 SUBSTRING(ProductNumber,9,1)            AS MiddleSubstring,
                 ASCII(SUBSTRING(ProductNumber,9,1))     AS ASCIIValue
FROM AdventureWorks2008.Production.Product
WHERE LEN(ProductNumber) > 8
ORDER BY Name;                          - OK syntax, but does not make sense
```

ProductNumber	MiddleSubstring	ASCIIValue
VE-C304-L	L	76
VE-C304-M	M	77
VE-C304-S	S	83
GL-F110-L	L	76
GL-F110-M	M	77

NOTE
Table columns and columns by expressions (computed) can be mixed in a query at will.

```
-- Computed (expressions) & table columns
SELECT FirstCharOfFirstName = LEFT(FirstName,1),        -- string expression
       FirstCharOfLastName  = LEFT(LastName,1),         -- string expression
       FullName = CONCAT(LastName, ', ', FirstName ),   -- string expression
       SquareOfID = SQUARE(BusinessEntityID),           -- math expression
       *                                                -- wild card, all table columns
FROM    Person.Person
WHERE   LEFT(FirstName,1) = 'J'
    AND LEFT(LastName,2) = 'Sm'
ORDER BY FullName;
-- (14 row(s) affected)  - Partial results.
```

FirstCharOfFirstName	FirstCharOfLastName	FullName	SquareOfID	BusinessEntityID
J	S	Smith, Jacob	348680929	18673
J	S	Smith, James	308986084	17578
J	S	Smith, Jasmine	129572689	11383
J	S	Smith, Jeff	3139984	1772
J	S	Smith, Jennifer	122699929	11077
J	S	Smith, Jeremiah	20511841	4529
J	S	Smith, Jessica	145829776	12076
J	S	Smith, John	332041284	18222
J	S	Smith, Jonathan	312228900	17670
J	S	Smith, Jose	300710281	17341
J	S	Smith, Joseph	357474649	18907
J	S	Smith, Joshua	351825049	18757
J	S	Smith, Julia	121616784	11028
J	S	Smith, Justin	324900625	18025

CHAPTER l0: Basic SELECT Statement Syntax & Examples

Transact-SQL Reserved Keywords

List of reserved keywords in SQL Server 2012 Transact-SQL. Keywords can only be used as delimited identifiers such as [Inner] or "Order".

ADD	EXTERNAL	PROCEDURE
ALL	FETCH	PUBLIC
ALTER	FILE	RAISERROR
AND	FILLFACTOR	READ
ANY	FOR	READTEXT
AS	FOREIGN	RECONFIGURE
ASC	FREETEXT	REFERENCES
AUTHORIZATION	FREETEXTTABLE	REPLICATION
BACKUP	FROM	RESTORE
BEGIN	FULL	RESTRICT
BETWEEN	FUNCTION	RETURN
BREAK	GOTO	REVERT
BROWSE	GRANT	REVOKE
BULK	GROUP	RIGHT
BY	HAVING	ROLLBACK
CASCADE	HOLDLOCK	ROWCOUNT
CASE	IDENTITY	ROWGUIDCOL
CHECK	IDENTITY_INSERT	RULE
CHECKPOINT	IDENTITYCOL	SAVE
CLOSE	IF	SCHEMA
CLUSTERED	IN	SECURITYAUDIT
COALESCE	INDEX	SELECT
COLLATE	INNER	SEMANTICKEYPHRASETABLE
COLUMN	INSERT	SEMANTICSIMILARITYDETAILSTABLE
COMMIT	INTERSECT	SEMANTICSIMILARITYTABLE
COMPUTE	INTO	SESSION_USER
CONSTRAINT	IS	SET
CONTAINS	JOIN	SETUSER
CONTAINSTABLE	KEY	SHUTDOWN
CONTINUE	KILL	SOME
CONVERT	LEFT	STATISTICS
CREATE	LIKE	SYSTEM_USER
CROSS	LINENO	TABLE
CURRENT	LOAD	TABLESAMPLE
CURRENT_DATE	MERGE	TEXTSIZE
CURRENT_TIME	NATIONAL	THEN
CURRENT_TIMESTAMP	NOCHECK	TO
CURRENT_USER	NONCLUSTERED	TOP
CURSOR	NOT	TRAN
DATABASE	NULL	TRANSACTION
DBCC	NULLIF	TRIGGER
DEALLOCATE	OF	TRUNCATE
DECLARE	OFF	TRY_CONVERT
DEFAULT	OFFSETS	TSEQUAL
DELETE	ON	UNION
DENY	OPEN	UNIQUE
DESC	OPENDATASOURCE	UNPIVOT
DISK	OPENQUERY	UPDATE
DISTINCT	OPENROWSET	UPDATETEXT
DISTRIBUTED	OPENXML	USE
DOUBLE	OPTION	USER
DROP	OR	VALUES
DUMP	ORDER	VARYING
ELSE	OUTER	VIEW
END	OVER	WAITFOR
ERRLVL	PERCENT	WHEN
ESCAPE	PIVOT	WHERE
EXCEPT	PLAN	WHILE
EXEC	PRECISION	WITH
EXECUTE	PRIMARY	WITHIN GROUP
EXISTS	PRINT	WRITETEXT
EXIT	PROC	

CHAPTER 10: Basic SELECT Statement Syntax & Examples

Case Sensitive Sort with Latin1_General_CS_AI

For case sensitive sort on a column with case insensitive collation, we have use a case sensitive (CS) collation such as Latin1_General_CS_AI.

```
-- CASE INSENSITIVE sort using default collation
SELECT lname FROM
        (SELECT TOP 5 UPPER (LastName) AS lname FROM Person.Person ORDER BY FirstName) x
UNION ALL    SELECT lname FROM
        (SELECT TOP 5 LOWER (LastName) AS lname FROM Person.Person ORDER BY FirstName) y
ORDER BY lname;
-- ADAMS, adams, alexander, ALEXANDER, leonetti, LEONETTI, WRIGHT, WRIGHT, wright, wright
```

```
-- CASE SENSITIVE sort using %CS% collation
SELECT lname FROM ( SELECT lname FROM
  (SELECT TOP 5 UPPER (LastName) AS lname FROM Person.Person ORDER BY FirstName) x
  UNION ALL  SELECT lname FROM
  (SELECT TOP 5 LOWER (LastName) AS lname FROM Person.Person ORDER BY FirstName) y  ) z
ORDER BY lname COLLATE Latin1_General_CS_AI;
-- adams,ADAMS,alexander,ALEXANDER,leonetti,LEONETTI,wright,wright,WRIGHT,WRIGHT
```

CHAPTER 10: Basic SELECT Statement Syntax & Examples

The ORDER BY Clause for Sorting Query Results

The ORDER BY clause is located at the very end of the query. In fact the sorting itself takes place after the query executed and generated **an unordered result set**. Although frequently, especially for small sets, the results appear to be sorted, **only an ORDER BY clause can guarantee proper sorting**. INSERT, UPDATE, DELETE & MERGE statement do not support sorting, **the database engine performs all set operations unordered**. T-SQL scripts demonstrate the many variations of the ORDER BY clause.

```
USE AdventureWorks2012;
GO


-- A column can be used for sorting even though not explicitly used in the SELECT list
SELECT *
FROM   Production.Product
ORDER  BY Name ASC;
GO


-- Sort on the second column, whatever it may be
SELECT *
FROM   Production.Product
ORDER  BY 2 DESC;
GO


-- ASCending is the default sort order, it is not necessary to use
SELECT  Name AS ProductName,
        *
FROM   Production.Product
ORDER  BY ProductName ASC;
GO


SELECT  TOP (10) Name AS ProductName,          *
FROM   Production.Product   ORDER  BY 1 ASC;
```

ProductName	ProductID	Name	ProductNumber	MakeFlag	FinishedGoodsFlag	Color	SafetyStockLevel
Adjustable Race	1	Adjustable Race	AR-5381	0	0	NULL	1000
All-Purpose Bike Stand	879	All-Purpose Bike Stand	ST-1401	0	1	NULL	4
AWC Logo Cap	712	AWC Logo Cap	CA-1098	0	1	Multi	4
BB Ball Bearing	3	BB Ball Bearing	BE-2349	1	0	NULL	800
Bearing Ball	2	Bearing Ball	BA-8327	0	0	NULL	1000
Bike Wash - Dissolver	877	Bike Wash - Dissolver	CL-9009	0	1	NULL	4
Blade	316	Blade	BL-2036	1	0	NULL	800
Cable Lock	843	Cable Lock	LO-C100	0	1	NULL	4
Chain	952	Chain	CH-0234	0	1	Silver	500
Chain Stays	324	Chain Stays	CS-2812	1	0	NULL	1000

CHAPTER 10: Basic SELECT Statement Syntax & Examples

Using Column Alias in the ORDER BY Clause

Column alias can be used in an ORDER BY clause. In fact, it should be used to make the query more readable.

```
-- ProductName is a column alias, it can only be used in the ORDER BY clause, not anywhere before
SELECT ProductName = Name, *
FROM Production.Product
WHERE ProductName like '%glove%'
ORDER BY ProductName ASC ;
GO
/* ERROR
Msg 207, Level 16, State 1, Line 3
Invalid column name 'ProductName'.
*/
```

```
-- The TOP clause uses the ORDER BY sorting to select the 5 rows
SELECT TOP (5) ProductName = Name, *
FROM Production.Product
WHERE Name like '%glove%'
ORDER BY ProductName ASC ;
```

ProductName	ProductID	Name	ProductNumber	MakeFlag	FinishedGoodsFlag	Color	SafetyStockLevel
Full-Finger Gloves, L	863	Full-Finger Gloves, L	GL-F110-L	0	1	Black	4
Full-Finger Gloves, M	862	Full-Finger Gloves, M	GL-F110-M	0	1	Black	4
Full-Finger Gloves, S	861	Full-Finger Gloves, S	GL-F110-S	0	1	Black	4
Half-Finger Gloves, L	860	Half-Finger Gloves, L	GL-H102-L	0	1	Black	4
Half-Finger Gloves, M	859	Half-Finger Gloves, M	GL-H102-M	0	1	Black	4

```
-- Descending sort on name which is string data type
SELECT TOP (10) ProductName = Name, *
FROM Production.Product
WHERE Name like '%road%'
ORDER BY ProductName DESC ;
```

ProductName	ProductID	Name	ProductNumber	MakeFlag	FinishedGoodsFlag	Color	SafetyStockLevel
Road-750 Black, 58	977	Road-750 Black, 58	BK-R19B-58	1	1	Black	100
Road-750 Black, 52	999	Road-750 Black, 52	BK-R19B-52	1	1	Black	100
Road-750 Black, 48	998	Road-750 Black, 48	BK-R19B-48	1	1	Black	100
Road-750 Black, 44	997	Road-750 Black, 44	BK-R19B-44	1	1	Black	100
Road-650 Red, 62	761	Road-650 Red, 62	BK-R50R-62	1	1	Red	100
Road-650 Red, 60	760	Road-650 Red, 60	BK-R50R-60	1	1	Red	100
Road-650 Red, 58	759	Road-650 Red, 58	BK-R50R-58	1	1	Red	100
Road-650 Red, 52	764	Road-650 Red, 52	BK-R50R-52	1	1	Red	100
Road-650 Red, 48	763	Road-650 Red, 48	BK-R50R-48	1	1	Red	100
Road-650 Red, 44	762	Road-650 Red, 44	BK-R50R-44	1	1	Red	100

Using Table Alias in the ORDER BY Clause
Unlike the column alias, table alias can be used anywhere in the query within the scope of the alias.

```
-- Using table alias in ORDER BY
SELECT P.*
FROM   Production.Product P
ORDER  BY P.Name ASC;
GO
```

ProductID	Name	ProductNumber	MakeFlag	FinishedGoodsFlag	Color	SafetyStockLevel
958	Touring-3000 Blue, 54	BK-T18U-54	1	1	Blue	100
959	Touring-3000 Blue, 58	BK-T18U-58	1	1	Blue	100
960	Touring-3000 Blue, 62	BK-T18U-62	1	1	Blue	100
961	Touring-3000 Yellow, 44	BK-T18Y-44	1	1	Yellow	100
962	Touring-3000 Yellow, 50	BK-T18Y-50	1	1	Yellow	100
963	Touring-3000 Yellow, 54	BK-T18Y-54	1	1	Yellow	100
964	Touring-3000 Yellow, 58	BK-T18Y-58	1	1	Yellow	100
965	Touring-3000 Yellow, 62	BK-T18Y-62	1	1	Yellow	100
842	Touring-Panniers, Large	PA-T100	0	1	Grey	4
870	Water Bottle - 30 oz.	WB-H098	0	1	NULL	4
869	Women's Mountain Shorts, L	SH-W890-L	0	1	Black	4
868	Women's Mountain Shorts, M	SH-W890-M	0	1	Black	4
867	Women's Mountain Shorts, S	SH-W890-S	0	1	Black	4
854	Women's Tights, L	TG-W091-L	0	1	Black	4
853	Women's Tights, M	TG-W091-M	0	1	Black	4
852	Women's Tights, S	TG-W091-S	0	1	Black	4

```
-- Specific column list instead of all (*)
SELECT   Name,
         ProductNumber,
         ListPrice AS PRICE
FROM   Production.Product  P
ORDER  BY P.Name ASC;
GO


SELECT          Name,
                ProductNumber,
                ListPrice AS PRICE
FROM   Production.Product  P
ORDER  BY P.ListPrice DESC;


-- Equivalent to above with column alias usage
SELECT          Name,
                ProductNumber,
                ListPrice AS PRICE
FROM   Production.Product  P ORDER  BY PRICE DESC;
```

Easy ORDER BY Queries for Exercises

T-SQL scripts demonstrate easily readable queries with sorted result sets.

```
USE pubs ;
```

```
SELECT TYPE,  AvgPrice=FORMAT(AVG(price) , 'c', 'en-US')
FROM  titles WHERE  royalty = 10 GROUP  BY TYPE ORDER  BY TYPE ;
```

TYPE	AvgPrice
business	$17.31
popular_comp	$20.00
psychology	$14.14
trad_cook	$17.97

```
SELECT         type = type,
               AvgPrice = FORMAT(AVG(price),'c', 'en-US')
FROM  titles  WHERE  royalty = 10  GROUP  BY type  ORDER  BY AvgPrice;
```

type	AvgPrice
psychology	$14.14
business	$17.31
trad_cook	$17.97
popular_comp	$20.00

```
SELECT  type                        AS [type],
        FORMAT(AVG(price),'c', 'en-US')    AS AvgPrice
FROM  titles  GROUP  BY [type]  ORDER  BY [type] desc;
```

type	AvgPrice
UNDECIDED	NULL
trad_cook	$15.96
psychology	$13.50
popular_comp	$21.48
mod_cook	$11.49
business	$13.73

An Aggregate Function Can Be Used in an ORDER BY Clause

The NULL related warning message can be turned off: SET ANSI_WARNINGS OFF; alternately ISNULL function can be used in the query.

```
SELECT TYPE, AVG(price) Avg FROM titles  GROUP  BY TYPE ORDER  BY AVG(price);
/* Warning: Null value is eliminated by an aggregate or other SET operation.
(6 row(s) affected) */
```

CHAPTER 10: Basic SELECT Statement Syntax & Examples

Eliminate NULL in result with COALESCE or ISNULL functions

```
SELECT [type] = type,
       AvgPrice = COALESCE(FORMAT(AVG(price),'c', 'en-US') ,'')
FROM   titles  GROUP  BY [type]  ORDER  BY [type] desc;
```

type	AvgPrice
UNDECIDED	
trad_cook	$15.96
psychology	$13.50
popular_comp	$21.48
mod_cook	$11.49
business	$13.73

```
SELECT          pub_name                          Publisher,
                FORMAT(AVG(price),'c', 'en-US')    AvgPrice
FROM   titles
    INNER JOIN publishers
      ON  titles.pub_id = publishers.pub_id
GROUP  BY pub_name
ORDER  BY pub_name;
```

Publisher	AvgPrice
Algodata Infosystems	$18.98
Binnet & Hardley	$15.41
New Moon Books	$9.78

```
SELECT TOP(3) * FROM   titles ORDER  BY title;
```

title_id	title	type	pub_id	price	advance	royalty	ytd_sales	notes	pubdate
PC1035	But Is It User Friendly?	popular_comp	1389	22.95	7000.00	16	8780	A survey of software for the naive user, focusing on the 'friendliness' of each.	1991-06-30 00:00:00.000
PS1372	Computer Phobic AND Non-Phobic Individuals: Behavior Variations	psychology	0877	21.59	7000.00	10	375	A must for the specialist, this book examines the difference between those who hate and fear computers and those who don't.	1991-10-21 00:00:00.000
BU1111	Cooking with Computers: Surreptitious Balance Sheets	business	1389	11.95	5000.00	10	3876	Helpful hints on how to use your electronic resources to the best advantage.	1991-06-09 00:00:00.000

```
SELECT TOP(3) * FROM   publishers  ORDER  BY pub_name;
```

pub_id	pub_name	city	state	country
1389	Algodata Infosystems	Berkeley	CA	USA
0877	Binnet & Hardley	Washington	DC	USA
1622	Five Lakes Publishing	Chicago	IL	USA

CHAPTER 10: Basic SELECT Statement Syntax & Examples

Sorting Products by Attributes

USE Northwind;

SELECT   UnitsInStock,
                ProductID,
                ProductName,
                QuantityPerUnit,
                FORMAT(UnitPrice, 'c', 'en-US') AS UnitPrice -- Column alias is same as column
FROM   Northwind.dbo.Products WHERE UnitsInStock BETWEEN 15 AND 25 ORDER BY
UnitsInStock;

UnitsInStock	ProductID	ProductName	QuantityPerUnit	UnitPrice
15	7	Uncle Bob's Organic Dried Pears	12 - 1 lb pkgs.	$30.00
15	26	Gumbär Gummibärchen	100 - 250 g bags	$31.23
15	48	Chocolade	10 pkgs.	$12.75
15	70	Outback Lager	24 - 355 ml bottles	$15.00
17	38	Côte de Blaye	12 - 75 cl bottles	$263.50
17	43	Ipoh Coffee	16 - 500 g tins	$46.00
17	62	Tarte au sucre	48 pies	$49.30
17	2	Chang	24 - 12 oz bottles	$19.00
19	60	Camembert Pierrot	15 - 300 g rounds	$34.00
20	24	Guaraná Fantástica	12 - 355 ml cans	$4.50
20	35	Steeleye Stout	24 - 12 oz bottles	$18.00
20	51	Manjimup Dried Apples	50 - 300 g pkgs.	$53.00
21	54	Tourtière	16 pies	$7.45
21	56	Gnocchi di nonna Alice	24 - 250 g pkgs.	$38.00
22	11	Queso Cabrales	1 kg pkg.	$21.00
22	64	Wimmers gute Semmelknödel	20 bags x 4 pieces	$33.25
24	13	Konbu	2 kg box	$6.00
24	63	Vegie-spread	15 - 625 g jars	$43.90
25	19	Teatime Chocolate Biscuits	10 boxes x 12 pieces	$9.20

-- A second key is necessary for unique ordering
SELECT TOP(8) UnitsInStock,
                ProductID,
                ProductName,
                QuantityPerUnit,
                FORMAT(UnitPrice, 'c', 'en-US') AS UnitPrice
FROM   Northwind.dbo.Products
WHERE UnitsInStock BETWEEN 15 AND 25 ORDER BY UnitsInStock, ProductName;

UnitsInStock	ProductID	ProductName	QuantityPerUnit	UnitPrice
15	48	Chocolade	10 pkgs.	$12.75
15	26	Gumbär Gummibärchen	100 - 250 g bags	$31.23
15	70	Outback Lager	24 - 355 ml bottles	$15.00
15	7	Uncle Bob's Organic Dried Pears	12 - 1 lb pkgs.	$30.00
17	2	Chang	24 - 12 oz bottles	$19.00
17	38	Côte de Blaye	12 - 75 cl bottles	$263.50
17	43	Ipoh Coffee	16 - 500 g tins	$46.00
17	62	Tarte au sucre	48 pies	$49.30

CHAPTER 10: Basic SELECT Statement Syntax & Examples

Changing WHERE condition changes the cardinality of result set

```
SELECT          UnitsInStock,
                ProductID,
                ProductName,
                QuantityPerUnit,
                FORMAT( UnitPrice, 'c', 'en-US')              AS UnitPrice
FROM   Northwind.dbo.Products
WHERE  UnitsInStock = 15 or UnitsInStock = 25  -- same as UnitsInStock IN (15, 25)
ORDER  BY UnitsInStock, ProductName;
```

UnitsInStock	ProductID	ProductName	QuantityPerUnit	UnitPrice
15	48	Chocolade	10 pkgs.	$12.75
15	26	Gumbär Gummibärchen	100 - 250 g bags	$31.23
15	70	Outback Lager	24 - 355 ml bottles	$15.00
15	7	Uncle Bob's Organic Dried Pears	12 - 1 lb pkgs.	$30.00
25	19	Teatime Chocolate Biscuits	10 boxes x 12 pieces	$9.20

```
SELECT   TOP(7)  UnitsInStock,
                ProductID,
                ProductName,
                QuantityPerUnit,
                FORMAT( UnitPrice, 'c', 'en-US')              AS UnitPrice
FROM   Northwind.dbo.Products  ORDER  BY UnitsInStock DESC, ProductName ASC;
```

UnitsInStock	ProductID	ProductName	QuantityPerUnit	UnitPrice
125	75	Rhönbräu Klosterbier	24 - 0.5 l bottles	$7.75
123	40	Boston Crab Meat	24 - 4 oz tins	$18.40
120	6	Grandma's Boysenberry Spread	12 - 8 oz jars	$25.00
115	55	Pâté chinois	24 boxes x 2 pies	$24.00
113	61	Sirop d'érable	24 - 500 ml bottles	$28.50
112	33	Geitost	500 g	$2.50
112	36	Inlagd Sill	24 - 250 g jars	$19.00

```
SELECT   TOP(5)  UnitsInStock, ProductID, ProductName,       QuantityPerUnit,
                FORMAT( UnitPrice, 'c', 'en-US') AS UnitPrice
FROM   Northwind.dbo.Products
WHERE  UnitsInStock > 15  AND UnitsInStock < 25  ORDER  BY UnitsInStock DESC, ProductName ASC;
```

UnitsInStock	ProductID	ProductName	QuantityPerUnit	UnitPrice
24	13	Konbu	2 kg box	$6.00
24	63	Vegie-spread	15 - 625 g jars	$43.90
22	11	Queso Cabrales	1 kg pkg.	$21.00
22	64	Wimmers gute Semmelknödel	20 bags x 4 pieces	$33.25
21	56	Gnocchi di nonna Alice	24 - 250 g pkgs.	$38.00

The "Tricky" BETWEEN & NOT BETWEEN Operators
They are very English-like, but results should be verified to make sure they work as intended.

```
SELECT  TOP(5)  UnitsInStock, ProductID, ProductName,     QuantityPerUnit,
                FORMAT( UnitPrice, 'c', 'en-US') AS UnitPrice
FROM  Northwind.dbo.Products
WHERE  UnitsInStock BETWEEN 15 AND 25
ORDER  BY UnitsInStock DESC, ProductName ASC;
GO
```

UnitsInStock	ProductID	ProductName	QuantityPerUnit	UnitPrice
25	19	Teatime Chocolate Biscuits	10 boxes x 12 pieces	$9.20
24	13	Konbu	2 kg box	$6.00
24	63	Vegie-spread	15 - 625 g jars	$43.90
22	11	Queso Cabrales	1 kg pkg.	$21.00
22	64	Wimmers gute Semmelknödel	20 bags x 4 pieces	$33.25

```
SELECT  TOP(5)  UnitsInStock, ProductID, ProductName,     QuantityPerUnit,
                FORMAT( UnitPrice, 'c', 'en-US') AS UnitPrice
FROM  Northwind.dbo.Products
WHERE  UnitsInStock NOT BETWEEN 15 AND 25
ORDER  BY UnitsInStock DESC, ProductName ASC;
```

UnitsInStock	ProductID	ProductName	QuantityPerUnit	UnitPrice
125	75	Rhönbräu Klosterbier	24 - 0.5 l bottles	$7.75
123	40	Boston Crab Meat	24 - 4 oz tins	$18.40
120	6	Grandma's Boysenberry Spread	12 - 8 oz jars	$25.00
115	55	Pâté chinois	24 boxes x 2 pies	$24.00
113	61	Sirop d'érable	24 - 500 ml bottles	$28.50

```
SELECT        Orders.OrderID,
              Shippers.*
FROM  Shippers
   INNER JOIN Orders
   ON ( Shippers.ShipperID = Orders.ShipVia )
ORDER  BY Orders.OrderID;
GO
-- (830 row(s) affected) - Partial results.
```

OrderID	ShipperID	CompanyName	Phone
10248	3	Federal Shipping	(503) 555-9931
10249	1	Speedy Express	(503) 555-9831
10250	2	United Package	(503) 555-3199
10251	1	Speedy Express	(503) 555-9831
10252	2	United Package	(503) 555-3199
10253	2	United Package	(503) 555-3199

CHAPTER 10: Basic SELECT Statement Syntax & Examples

A second key is frequently required in sorting exception is PRIMARY KEY column.

```
SELECT  OrderID,
        ProductID,
        FORMAT( UnitPrice, 'c', 'en-US')            AS UnitPrice,
        Quantity,
        Discount
FROM  [Order Details]  ORDER  BY OrderID ASC, ProductID ASC;
GO
-- (2155 row(s) affected) - Partial results.
```

OrderID	ProductID	UnitPrice	Quantity	Discount
10248	11	$14.00	12	0
10248	42	$9.80	10	0
10248	72	$34.80	5	0
10249	14	$18.60	9	0
10249	51	$42.40	40	0
10250	41	$7.70	10	0
10250	51	$42.40	35	0.15
10250	65	$16.80	15	0.15

```
-- Sort keys are different from expression column EmployeeName
SELECT  CONCAT(LastName,', ', FirstName)  AS EmployeeName ,
        Title, City, Country
FROM  Northwind.dbo.Employees ORDER  BY LastName,  FirstName ASC;
```

EmployeeName	Title	City	Country
Buchanan, Steven	Sales Manager	London	UK
Callahan, Laura	Inside Sales Coordinator	Seattle	USA
Davolio, Nancy	Sales Representative	Seattle	USA
Dodsworth, Anne	Sales Representative	London	UK
Fuller, Andrew	Vice President, Sales	Tacoma	USA
King, Robert	Sales Representative	London	UK
Leverling, Janet	Sales Representative	Kirkland	USA
Peacock, Margaret	Sales Representative	Redmond	USA
Suyama, Michael	Sales Representative	London	UK

```
-- Equivalent sort
SELECT TOP(3)    CONCAT(LastName,', ', FirstName) AS EmployeeName ,    Title, City, Country
FROM  Northwind.dbo.Employees  ORDER  BY EmployeeName ASC;
```

EmployeeName	Title	City	Country
Buchanan, Steven	Sales Manager	London	UK
Callahan, Laura	Inside Sales Coordinator	Seattle	USA
Davolio, Nancy	Sales Representative	Seattle	USA

CHAPTER 10: Basic SELECT Statement Syntax & Examples

Using Multiple Keys in the ORDER BY Clause

If a single sort key does not result in unique ordering, multiple keys can be used. In the next example the Price (major) key is based on a column which is not unique. If we add Name as a second (minor) key, unique ordering will be guaranteed since Name is a unique column, it has a unique index and not null. It's worth noting if Name would allow nulls, we would need a third key for unique ordering.

```
-- Single key sort
SELECT   P.Name,
         P.ProductNumber,
         P.ListPrice              AS PRICE
FROM   Production.Product  P
WHERE  P.ProductLine = 'R'   AND P.DaysToManufacture < 4    ORDER  BY  P. ListPrice DESC;
```

Name	ProductNumber	PRICE
HL Road Frame - Black, 58	FR-R92B-58	1431.50
HL Road Frame - Red, 58	FR-R92R-58	1431.50
HL Road Frame - Red, 62	FR-R92R-62	1431.50
HL Road Frame - Red, 44	FR-R92R-44	1431.50
HL Road Frame - Red, 48	FR-R92R-48	1431.50
HL Road Frame - Red, 52	FR-R92R-52	1431.50
HL Road Frame - Red, 56	FR-R92R-56	1431.50
HL Road Frame - Black, 62	FR-R92B-62	1431.50
HL Road Frame - Black, 44	FR-R92B-44	1431.50
HL Road Frame - Black, 48	FR-R92B-48	1431.50
HL Road Frame - Black, 52	FR-R92B-52	1431.50
ML Road Frame-W - Yellow, 40	FR-R72Y-40	594.83

```
-- Double key sort - PRICE is the major key, Name is the minor key
SELECT   P.Name,
         P.ProductNumber,
         P.ListPrice              AS PRICE
FROM   Production.Product  P
WHERE  P.ProductLine = 'R'   AND P.DaysToManufacture < 4  ORDER  BY  PRICE DESC, Name;
```

Name	ProductNumber	PRICE
HL Road Frame - Black, 44	FR-R92B-44	1431.50
HL Road Frame - Black, 48	FR-R92B-48	1431.50
HL Road Frame - Black, 52	FR-R92B-52	1431.50
HL Road Frame - Black, 58	FR-R92B-58	1431.50
HL Road Frame - Black, 62	FR-R92B-62	1431.50
HL Road Frame - Red, 44	FR-R92R-44	1431.50
HL Road Frame - Red, 48	FR-R92R-48	1431.50
HL Road Frame - Red, 52	FR-R92R-52	1431.50
HL Road Frame - Red, 56	FR-R92R-56	1431.50
HL Road Frame - Red, 58	FR-R92R-58	1431.50
HL Road Frame - Red, 62	FR-R92R-62	1431.50
ML Road Frame - Red, 44	FR-R72R-44	594.83

CHAPTER 10: Basic SELECT Statement Syntax & Examples

ORDER BY in Complex Queries

An ORDER BY can be in a complex query and/or ORDER BY can be complex itself. T-SQL scripts demonstrate complex ORDER BY usage.

```
-- We cannot tell just by query inspection if the second key is sufficient for unique ordering or not
-- If we inspect the result set it becomes obvious that we need a third key at least (SalesOrderID unsorted)
SELECT   ProductName          = P.Name,
         NonDiscountSales      = ( OrderQty * UnitPrice ),
         Discounts            = ( ( OrderQty * UnitPrice ) * UnitPriceDiscount ) ,
         SalesOrderID
FROM   Production.Product P
    INNER JOIN Sales.SalesOrderDetail SOD
       ON P.ProductID = SOD.ProductID
ORDER  BY      ProductName DESC,
               NonDiscountSales DESC;
GO
```

ProductName	NonDiscountSales	Discounts	SalesOrderID
Women's Tights, S	1049.86	104.986	47355
Women's Tights, S	824.89	41.2445	46987
Women's Tights, S	783.6455	39.1823	47400
Women's Tights, S	742.401	37.1201	50206
Women's Tights, S	701.1565	35.0578	46993
Women's Tights, S	701.1565	35.0578	46671
Women's Tights, S	701.1565	35.0578	50688
Women's Tights, S	701.1565	35.0578	49481
Women's Tights, S	659.912	32.9956	48295
Women's Tights, S	659.912	32.9956	46967
Women's Tights, S	618.6675	30.9334	46652
Women's Tights, S	608.9188	12.1784	46672
Women's Tights, S	608.9188	12.1784	47365
Women's Tights, S	565.4246	11.3085	47004
Women's Tights, S	565.4246	11.3085	50663

NOTE
Even though SELECT DISTINCT results may appear to be sorted, **only ORDER BY clause can guarantee sort**. This holds true for any kind of SELECT statement, simple or complex.

```
SELECT DISTINCT JobTitle   FROM   HumanResources.Employee ;

SELECT DISTINCT JobTitle   FROM   HumanResources.Employee ORDER  BY JobTitle;
```

CHAPTER 10: Basic SELECT Statement Syntax & Examples

ORDER BY with ROW_NUMBER()

T-SQL queries demonstrate sorting with not matching and matching ROW_NUMBER() sequence number.

```
SELECT
  ROW_NUMBER() OVER( PARTITION BY CountryRegionName  ORDER BY SalesYTD ASC) AS SeqNo,
  CountryRegionName AS Country,  FirstName, LastName,  JobTitle,
  FORMAT(SalesYTD, 'c', 'en-US') AS SalesYTD,
  FORMAT(SalesLastYear, 'c', 'en-US') AS SalesLastYear
FROM  Sales.vSalesPerson          ORDER BY JobTitle,  SalesYTD DESC;
```

SeqNo	Country	FirstName	LastName	JobTitle	SalesYTD	SalesLastYear
2	United States	Amy	Alberts	European Sales Manager	$519,905.93	$0.00
3	United States	Stephen	Jiang	North American Sales Manager	$559,697.56	$0.00
1	United States	Syed	Abbas	Pacific Sales Manager	$172,524.45	$0.00
11	United States	Linda	Mitchell	Sales Representative	$4,251,368.55	$1,439,156.03
1	United Kingdom	Jae	Pak	Sales Representative	$4,116,871.23	$1,635,823.40
10	United States	Michael	Blythe	Sales Representative	$3,763,178.18	$1,750,406.48
9	United States	Jillian	Carson	Sales Representative	$3,189,418.37	$1,997,186.20
1	France	Ranjit	Varkey Chudukatil	Sales Representative	$3,121,616.32	$2,396,539.76
2	Canada	José	Saraiva	Sales Representative	$2,604,540.72	$2,038,234.65
8	United States	Shu	Ito	Sales Representative	$2,458,535.62	$2,073,506.00
7	United States	Tsvi	Reiter	Sales Representative	$2,315,185.61	$1,849,640.94
1	Germany	Rachel	Valdez	Sales Representative	$1,827,066.71	$1,307,949.79
6	United States	Tete	Mensa-Annan	Sales Representative	$1,576,562.20	$0.00
5	United States	David	Campbell	Sales Representative	$1,573,012.94	$1,371,635.32
1	Canada	Garrett	Vargas	Sales Representative	$1,453,719.47	$1,620,276.90
1	Australia	Lynn	Tsoflias	Sales Representative	$1,421,810.92	$2,278,548.98
4	United States	Pamela	Ansman-Wolfe	Sales Representative	$1,352,577.13	$1,927,059.18

```
-- ROW_NUMBER() ORDER BY in synch with sort ORDER BY
SELECT  ROW_NUMBER() OVER( ORDER BY JobTitle, SalesYTD DESC) AS SeqNo,
   CountryRegionName AS Country,  FirstName, LastName,  JobTitle,
   FORMAT(SalesYTD, 'c', 'en-US') AS SalesYTD, FORMAT(SalesLastYear, 'c', 'en-US') AS SalesLastYear
FROM  Sales.vSalesPerson ORDER BY       SeqNo;
```

SeqNo	Country	FirstName	LastName	JobTitle	SalesYTD	SalesLastYear
1	United States	Amy	Alberts	European Sales Manager	$519,905.93	$0.00
2	United States	Stephen	Jiang	North American Sales Manager	$559,697.56	$0.00
3	United States	Syed	Abbas	Pacific Sales Manager	$172,524.45	$0.00
4	United States	Linda	Mitchell	Sales Representative	$4,251,368.55	$1,439,156.03
5	United Kingdom	Jae	Pak	Sales Representative	$4,116,871.23	$1,635,823.40
6	United States	Michael	Blythe	Sales Representative	$3,763,178.18	$1,750,406.48
7	United States	Jillian	Carson	Sales Representative	$3,189,418.37	$1,997,186.20
8	France	Ranjit	Varkey Chudukatil	Sales Representative	$3,121,616.32	$2,396,539.76
9	Canada	José	Saraiva	Sales Representative	$2,604,540.72	$2,038,234.65
10	United States	Shu	Ito	Sales Representative	$2,458,535.62	$2,073,506.00
11	United States	Tsvi	Reiter	Sales Representative	$2,315,185.61	$1,849,640.94
12	Germany	Rachel	Valdez	Sales Representative	$1,827,066.71	$1,307,949.79
13	United States	Tete	Mensa-Annan	Sales Representative	$1,576,562.20	$0.00
14	United States	David	Campbell	Sales Representative	$1,573,012.94	$1,371,635.32
15	Canada	Garrett	Vargas	Sales Representative	$1,453,719.47	$1,620,276.90
16	Australia	Lynn	Tsoflias	Sales Representative	$1,421,810.92	$2,278,548.98
17	United States	Pamela	Ansman-Wolfe	Sales Representative	$1,352,577.13	$1,927,059.18

ORDER BY Clause with CASE Conditional Expression

Sort by LastName, MiddleName if exists else FirstName, and FirstName in case MiddleName is used.

```
USE AdventureWorks;

SELECT          FirstName,
                COALESCE(MiddleName, '')        AS MName,  -- ISNULL can also be used
                LastName,
                AddressLine1,
                COALESCE(AddressLine2, '')      AS Addr2,
                City,
                SP.Name                         AS [State],
                CR.Name                         AS Country,
                I.CustomerID
FROM   Person.Contact AS C
    INNER JOIN Sales.Individual AS I
        ON C.ContactID = I.ContactID
    INNER JOIN Sales.CustomerAddress AS CA
        ON CA.CustomerID = I.CustomerID
    INNER JOIN Person.[Address] AS A
        ON A.AddressID = CA.AddressID
    INNER JOIN Person.StateProvince SP
        ON SP.StateProvinceID = A.StateProvinceID
    INNER JOIN Person.CountryRegion CR
        ON CR.CountryRegionCode = SP.CountryRegionCode
ORDER  BY LastName,
    CASE
      WHEN MiddleName != '' THEN MiddleName
      ELSE FirstName
    END,
    FirstName;
-- (18508 row(s) affected) -Partial results.
```

FirstName	MName	LastName	AddressLine1	Addr2	City	State	Country	CustomerID
Chloe	A	Adams	3001 N. 48th Street		Marysville	Washington	United States	19410
Eduardo	A	Adams	4283 Meaham Drive		San Diego	California	United States	25292
Kaitlyn	A	Adams	3815 Berry Dr.		Westminster	British Columbia	Canada	11869
Mackenzie	A	Adams	9639 Ida Drive		Langford	British Columbia	Canada	14640
Sara	A	Adams	7503 Hill Drive		Milwaukie	Oregon	United States	16986
Adam		Adams	9381 Bayside Way		Newport Beach	California	United States	13323
Amber		Adams	9720 Morning Glory Dr.		Brisbane	Queensland	Australia	26746
Angel		Adams	9556 Lyman Rd.		Burlingame	California	United States	18504
Aaron	B	Adams	4116 Stanbridge Ct.		Downey	California	United States	28866
Noah	B	Adams	6738 Wallace Dr.		El Cajon	California	United States	16977
Bailey		Adams	1817 Adobe Drive		Kirkland	Washington	United States	13280
Ben		Adams	1534 Land Ave		Bremerton	Washington	United States	28678
Alex	C	Adams	237 Bellwood Dr.		Lake Oswego	Oregon	United States	21139
Courtney	C	Adams	6089 Santa Fe Dr.		Torrance	California	United States	18075
Ian	C	Adams	7963 Elk Dr	#4	Versailles	Yveline	France	29422

Special Sorting, Like United States On Top Of The Country Pop-Up List
It requires CASE or IIF conditional expression.

```
-- Major sort key is Color if not null, else product name
-- Minor sort on ProductNumber
SELECT ProductID,
    ProductNumber,
    Name AS ProductName,
    FORMAT(ListPrice, 'c', 'en-US')  AS ListPrice,
    Color
FROM   Production.Product
WHERE  Name LIKE ( '%Road%' )
ORDER  BY        CASE
                    WHEN Color IS NULL THEN Name
                    ELSE Color
                END,
                ProductNumber DESC;
-- (103 row(s) affected) - Partial results.
```

ProductID	ProductNumber	ProductName	ListPrice	Color
768	BK-R50B-44	Road-650 Black, 44	$782.99	Black
977	BK-R19B-58	Road-750 Black, 58	$539.99	Black
999	BK-R19B-52	Road-750 Black, 52	$539.99	Black
998	BK-R19B-48	Road-750 Black, 48	$539.99	Black
997	BK-R19B-44	Road-750 Black, 44	$539.99	Black
813	HB-R956	HL Road Handlebars	$120.27	NULL
512	RM-R800	HL Road Rim	$0.00	NULL
519	SA-R522	HL Road Seat Assembly	$196.92	NULL
913	SE-R995	HL Road Seat/Saddle	$52.64	NULL
933	TI-R982	HL Road Tire	$32.60	NULL
811	HB-R504	LL Road Handlebars	$44.54	NULL
510	RM-R436	LL Road Rim	$0.00	NULL
517	SA-R127	LL Road Seat Assembly	$133.34	NULL
911	SE-R581	LL Road Seat/Saddle	$27.12	NULL
931	TI-R092	LL Road Tire	$21.49	NULL
812	HB-R720	ML Road Handlebars	$61.92	NULL
511	RM-R600	ML Road Rim	$0.00	NULL
518	SA-R430	ML Road Seat Assembly	$147.14	NULL
912	SE-R908	ML Road Seat/Saddle	$39.14	NULL
932	TI-R628	ML Road Tire	$24.99	NULL
717	FR-R92R-62	HL Road Frame - Red, 62	$1,431.50	Red
706	FR-R92R-58	HL Road Frame - Red, 58	$1,431.50	Red
721	FR-R92R-56	HL Road Frame - Red, 56	$1,431.50	Red

T-SQL queries demonstrate complex sorting with the CASE expression usage.
CASE expression returns a SINGLE SCALAR VALUE of the same data type.

```
SELECT  SellStartDate,
        SellEndDate,
        *
FROM   Production.Product
WHERE  Name LIKE ( '%mountain%' )
ORDER  BY CASE
                WHEN SellEndDate IS NULL THEN SellStartDate
                ELSE SellEndDate
        END DESC, Name;
GO
-- (94 row(s) affected) -Partial results.
```

SellStartDate	SellEndDate	ProductID	Name	ProductNumber
2007-07-01 00:00:00.000	NULL	986	Mountain-500 Silver, 44	BK-M18S-44
2007-07-01 00:00:00.000	NULL	987	Mountain-500 Silver, 48	BK-M18S-48
2007-07-01 00:00:00.000	NULL	988	Mountain-500 Silver, 52	BK-M18S-52
2007-07-01 00:00:00.000	NULL	869	Women's Mountain Shorts, L	SH-W890-L
2007-07-01 00:00:00.000	NULL	868	Women's Mountain Shorts, M	SH-W890-M
2007-07-01 00:00:00.000	NULL	867	Women's Mountain Shorts, S	SH-W890-S
2006-07-01 00:00:00.000	2007-06-30 00:00:00.000	817	HL Mountain Front Wheel	FW-M928
2006-07-01 00:00:00.000	2007-06-30 00:00:00.000	825	HL Mountain Rear Wheel	RW-M928
2006-07-01 00:00:00.000	2007-06-30 00:00:00.000	815	LL Mountain Front Wheel	FW-M423
2006-07-01 00:00:00.000	2007-06-30 00:00:00.000	823	LL Mountain Rear Wheel	RW-M423
2006-07-01 00:00:00.000	2007-06-30 00:00:00.000	814	ML Mountain Frame - Black, 38	FR-M63B-38
2006-07-01 00:00:00.000	2007-06-30 00:00:00.000	830	ML Mountain Frame - Black, 40	FR-M63B-40

```
-- 2 keys descending sort
SELECT          PRODUCTNAME  = P.Name,
                SALETOTAL       = ( OrderQty * UnitPrice ),
                NETSALETOTAL  = ( ( OrderQty - RejectedQty ) * UnitPrice )
FROM   Production.Product P
    INNER JOIN Purchasing.PurchaseOrderDetail SOD
        ON P.ProductID = SOD.ProductID
ORDER  BY PRODUCTNAME  DESC,  SALETOTAL DESC;

-- Column alias sorting of GROUP BY aggregation results
SELECT [YEAR]=YEAR(OrderDate), Orders = COUNT(*)
FROM AdventureWorks2012.Sales.SalesOrderHeader
GROUP BY YEAR(OrderDate)  ORDER BY [YEAR];
```

YEAR	Orders
2005	1379
2006	3692
2007	12443
2008	13951

ORDER BY Clause with IIF Conditional Function

Sort by LastName, MiddleName if exists else FirstName, and FirstName in case MiddleName is used.

```
USE AdventureWorks;

SELECT          FirstName,
                COALESCE(MiddleName, '')        AS MName,  -- ISNULL can also be used
                LastName,
                AddressLine1,
                COALESCE(AddressLine2, '')      AS Addr2,
                City,
                SP.Name                         AS [State],
                CR.Name                         AS Country,
                I.CustomerID
FROM   Person.Contact AS C
    INNER JOIN Sales.Individual AS I
        ON C.ContactID = I.ContactID
    INNER JOIN Sales.CustomerAddress AS CA
        ON CA.CustomerID = I.CustomerID
    INNER JOIN Person.[Address] AS A
        ON A.AddressID = CA.AddressID
    INNER JOIN Person.StateProvince SP
        ON SP.StateProvinceID = A.StateProvinceID
    INNER JOIN Person.CountryRegion CR
        ON CR.CountryRegionCode = SP.CountryRegionCode
ORDER  BY       LastName,
                IIF( MiddleName != '',
                        MiddleName,             -- TRUE condition return value
                        FirstName),             -- FALSE condition return value
                FirstName;
GO
-- (18508 row(s) affected) -Partial results.
```

FirstName	MName	LastName	AddressLine1	Addr2	City	State	Country	CustomerID
Chloe	A	Adams	3001 N. 48th Street		Marysville	Washington	United States	19410
Eduardo	A	Adams	4283 Meaham Drive		San Diego	California	United States	25292
Kaitlyn	A	Adams	3815 Berry Dr.		Westminster	British Columbia	Canada	11869
Mackenzie	A	Adams	9639 Ida Drive		Langford	British Columbia	Canada	14640
Sara	A	Adams	7503 Hill Drive		Milwaukie	Oregon	United States	16986
Adam		Adams	9381 Bayside Way		Newport Beach	California	United States	13323
Amber		Adams	9720 Morning Glory Dr.		Brisbane	Queensland	Australia	26746
Angel		Adams	9556 Lyman Rd.		Burlingame	California	United States	18504
Aaron	B	Adams	4116 Stanbridge Ct.		Downey	California	United States	28866
Noah	B	Adams	6738 Wallace Dr.		El Cajon	California	United States	16977
Bailey		Adams	1817 Adobe Drive		Kirkland	Washington	United States	13280
Ben		Adams	1534 Land Ave		Bremerton	Washington	United States	28678
Alex	C	Adams	237 Bellwood Dr.		Lake Oswego	Oregon	United States	21139
Courtney	C	Adams	6089 Santa Fe Dr.		Torrance	California	United States	18075
Ian	C	Adams	7963 Elk Dr	#4	Versailles	Yveline	France	29422

ORDER BY Clause with the RANK() Function

T-SQL query demonstrates the combination of CASE expression and RANK() function in an ORDER BY clause. Note that while such a complex sort is technically impressive, ultimately it has to make sense to the user, the Business Intelligence consumer.

```
-- SQL complex sorting
USE AdventureWorks;

SELECT          ContactID,
                FirstName,
                LastName,
                COALESCE(Title, '')  AS Title
FROM   Person.Contact
WHERE  LEFT(FirstName, 1) = 'M'
ORDER  BY CASE
                WHEN LEFT(LastName, 1) = 'A' THEN RANK()
                        OVER( ORDER BY CONCAT(FirstName, SPACE(1), LastName))
                WHEN LEFT(LastName, 1) = 'M' THEN RANK()
                        OVER( ORDER BY CONCAT(LastName,', ', FirstName), Title)
                WHEN LEFT(LastName, 1) = 'U' THEN RANK()
                        OVER( ORDER BY CONCAT(LastName,', ', FirstName)  DESC)
                ELSE RANK()
                        OVER( ORDER BY LastName ASC, FirstName DESC)
        END;
```

ContactID	FirstName	LastName	Title
9500	Mackenzie	Adams	
10144	Mackenzie	Allen	
10128	Madeline	Allen	
11708	Madison	Alexander	
11527	Madison	Anderson	
19872	Morgan	Bailey	
8059	Michelle	Bailey	
8080	Melissa	Bailey	
18291	Megan	Bailey	
8070	Mariah	Bailey	
2432	Maria	Bailey	
14378	Marcus	Bailey	
8063	Makayla	Bailey	
8032	Mackenzie	Bailey	
9521	Morgan	Baker	
3320	Miguel	Baker	
15437	Mason	Baker	
9546	Mary	Baker	
1082	Mary	Baker	
9539	Maria	Baker	

ORDER BY Clause with Custom Mapped Sort Sequence

Typically we rely on alphabets or numbers for sorting. What if, for example, we don't want United States way down on a website drop-down menu, rather than on the top with Canada and United Kingdom just above "lucky" Australia? We have to do custom mapping for such a sort in the ORDER BY clause.

```
USE AdventureWorks;
SELECT          AddressLine1,
                City,
                SP.StateProvinceCode            AS State,
                PostalCode,
                CR.Name                         AS  Country
FROM   Person.[Address] A
   INNER JOIN Person.StateProvince SP           ON A.StateProvinceID = SP.StateProvinceID
   INNER JOIN Person.CountryRegion CR           ON SP.CountryRegionCode = CR.CountryRegionCode
ORDER  BY (     CASE    WHEN CR.Name = 'United States' THEN 0
                        WHEN CR.Name = 'Canada' THEN 1
                        WHEN CR.Name = 'United Kingdom' THEN 2   ELSE 3  END ),
                Country,
                City
                AddressLine1;
-- (19614 row(s) affected) - Partial results.
```

AddressLine1	City	State	PostalCode	Country
9355 Armstrong Road	York	ENG	YO15	United Kingdom
939 Vista Del Diablo	York	ENG	YO15	United Kingdom
9458 Flame Drive	York	ENG	YO15	United Kingdom
9557 Steven Circle	York	ENG	Y03 4TN	United Kingdom

Sorting on the Last Word of a String

```
USE tempdb;
SELECT BusinessEntityID, FULLNAME = CONCAT(FirstName , SPACE(1), LastName )
INTO   People FROM   AdventureWorks2012.Person.Person ORDER  BY BusinessEntityID ;

SELECT *  FROM   People
ORDER  BY REVERSE(LEFT(REVERSE(FullName), charindex(' ', REVERSE(FullName) + ' '  ) - 1)),
        FullName ;
GO -- (19972 row(s) affected) - Partial results.
```

BusinessEntityID	FULLNAME
285	Syed Abbas
293	Catherine Abel
295	Kim Abercrombie

ORDER BY Clause with Custom Alphanumeric Sort Sequence

A frequent requirement is custom sorting on alphanumeric field (column). The next T-SQL query demonstrates special alphanumeric sorting.

```
USE AdventureWorks;

SELECT AddressLine1,
            isnull(AddressLine2, '')      AS Addressline2,
            City,
            SP.StateProvinceCode      AS State,
            PostalCode,
            CR.Name                   AS Country
FROM   Person.[Address] A
    INNER JOIN Person.StateProvince SP
    ON A.StateProvinceID = SP.StateProvinceID
    INNER JOIN Person.CountryRegion CR
    ON SP.CountryRegionCode = CR.CountryRegionCode
ORDER  BY (     CASE
                    WHEN Ascii([AddressLine1]) BETWEEN 65 AND 90 THEN 0 -- Upper case alpha
                    WHEN Ascii([AddressLine1]) BETWEEN 48 AND 57 THEN 1 -- Digits
                    ELSE 2
                END ),
            AddressLine1,
            City;
GO
-- (19614 row(s) affected) - Partial results.
```

AddressLine1	Addressline2	City	State	PostalCode	Country
Zur Lindung 46		Leipzig	NW	04139	Germany
Zur Lindung 6		Saarlouis	SL	66740	Germany
Zur Lindung 6		Solingen	NW	42651	Germany
Zur Lindung 609		Sulzbach Taunus	SL	66272	Germany
Zur Lindung 7		Berlin	HE	14129	Germany
Zur Lindung 7		Neunkirchen	SL	66578	Germany
Zur Lindung 764		Paderborn	HH	33041	Germany
Zur Lindung 78		Berlin	HH	10791	Germany
Zur Lindung 787		München	NW	80074	Germany
00, rue Saint-Lazare		Dunkerque	59	59140	France
02, place de Fontenoy		Verrieres Le Buisson	91	91370	France
035, boulevard du Montparnasse		Verrieres Le Buisson	91	91370	France
081, boulevard du Montparnasse		Saint-Denis	93	93400	France
081, boulevard du Montparnasse		Seattle	WA	98104	United States
084, boulevard du Montparnasse		Les Ulis	91	91940	France
1 Corporate Center Drive		Miami	FL	33127	United States
1 Mt. Dell Drive		Portland	OR	97205	United States
1 Smiling Tree Court	Space 55	Los Angeles	CA	90012	United States
1, allée des Princes		Courbevoie	92	92400	France

Working with Synonyms

A synonym is a shorthand name for a longer name including multi-part names. **While prefix like "sn" or "syn" is not required, it is a good practice since otherwise a synonym can be confused with a (real) table for example, leading to loss of DBA or developer productivity.**

```
USE tempdb;
GO


-- Create synonyms for a 3-part names
CREATE SYNONYM snCustomerAW  FOR AdventureWorks.Sales.Customer;
CREATE SYNONYM snCustomerAW12  FOR AdventureWorks2012.Sales.Customer;


-- Create a synonym for 4-part name linked server
CREATE SYNONYM snCustomerLDNAW12  FOR
        [LONDONPROD8].AdventureWorks2012.Sales.Customer;
GO -- Command(s) completed successfully.


-- Query the Customer tables by using the synonyms
SELECT * FROM snCustomerAW ORDER BY AccountNumber;    -- (19185 row(s) affected)
SELECT * FROM snCustomerAW12 ORDER BY AccountNumber; -- (19820 row(s) affected)
GO


-- Delete a synonym
DROP SYNONYM snCustomerAW;  -- Command(s) completed successfully.
GO


-- Enumerating all synonyms in database
SELECT  name                              AS "Name"
        ,base_object_name                 AS "Definition"
        ,PARSENAME(base_object_name, 4)   AS "Server"
        ,PARSENAME(base_object_name, 3)   AS "Database"
        ,PARSENAME(base_object_name, 2)   AS "Schema"
        ,PARSENAME(base_object_name, 1)   AS "Object"
FROM sys.synonyms ORDER BY Definition;
```

Name	Definition	Server	Database	Schema	Object
CustomerAW12	[AdventureWorks2012].[Sales].[Customer]	NULL	AdventureWorks2012	Sales	Customer
CustomerLNDAW12	[LONDONPROD8].[AdventureWorks2012].[Sales].[Customer]	LONDONPROD8	AdventureWorks2012	Sales	Customer

Date & Time Conversion To / From String

While there are only a few internal representation of date and time, string representations are many, even not deterministic since they may change from one country to another such as weekday and month names.   T-SQL scripts demonstrate the myriad of date and time conversion possibilities.

The CONVERT() Function with Style Number Parameter

```
-- String source  format: mon dd yyyy hh:mmAM (or PM)
-- 100 is the style number parameter for CONVERT
SELECT [Date&Time] = convert(datetime, 'Oct 23 2020 11:01AM', 100)
```

```
        Date&Time
        2020-10-23 11:01:00.000
```

```
-- Default without style number
SELECT convert(datetime, 'Oct 23 2020 11:01AM')                    -- 2020-10-23 11:01:00.000
```

```
-- Without century (yy) string date conversion with style number 0
-- Input format: mon dd yy hh:mmAM (or PM)
SELECT [Date&Time] = convert(datetime, 'Oct 23 20 11:01AM', 0)
```

```
        Date&Time
        2020-10-23 11:01:00.000
```

```
-- Default without style number
SELECT convert(datetime, 'Oct 23 20 11:01AM')                      -- 2020-10-23 11:01:00.000
```

 Convert string date & time to datetime (8-bytes internal representation) data type.

```
SELECT convert(datetime, '10/23/2016', 101)           -- mm/dd/yyyy
```

```
SELECT convert(datetime, '2016.10.23', 102)              -- yyyy.mm.dd ANSI date with century
```

```
SELECT convert(datetime, '23/10/2016', 103)              -- dd/mm/yyyy
```

```
SELECT convert(datetime, '23.10.2016', 104)-- dd.mm.yyyy
```

```
SELECT convert(datetime, '23-10-2016', 105)              -- dd-mm-yyyy
```

```
-- mon (month) types are nondeterministic conversions, dependent on language setting.
SELECT convert(datetime, '23 OCT 2016', 106)             -- dd mon yyyy
```

CHAPTER 10: Basic SELECT Statement Syntax & Examples

String Datetime Formats With "Mon" Are Nondeterministic, Language Dependent

SELECT [Date&Time] = convert(datetime, 'Oct 23, 2016', 107) -- mon dd, yyyy

> Date&Time
> 2016-10-23 00:00:00.000

SELECT [Date&Time]=convert(datetime, '20:10:44', 108)   -- hh:mm:ss

> Date&Time
> 1900-01-01 20:10:44.000

SELECT [Date&Time]=convert(datetime, 'Oct 23 2016 11:02:44:013AM', 109) -- mon dd yyyy hh:mm:ss:mmmAM (or PM)

> Date&Time
> 2016-10-23 11:02:44.013

SELECT convert(datetime, '10-23-2016', 110)   -- mm-dd-yyyy
SELECT convert(datetime, '2016/10/23', 111)   -- yyyy/mm/dd

-- YYYYMMDD ISO date format works at any language setting - international standard
SELECT [Date&Time]=convert(datetime, '20161023')

> Date&Time
> 2016-10-23 00:00:00.000

SELECT [Date&Time]=convert(datetime, '20161023', 112)   -- ISO yyyymmdd

> Date&Time
> 2016-10-23 00:00:00.000

SELECT [Date&Time]=convert(datetime, '23 Oct 2016 11:02:07:577', 113) -- dd mon yyyy hh:mm:ss:mmm

> Date&Time
> 2016-10-23 11:02:07.577

SELECT [Date&Time]=convert(datetime, '20:10:25:300', 114)   -- hh:mm:ss:mmm(24h)

> Date&Time
> 1900-01-01 20:10:25.300

SELECT [Date&Time]=convert(datetime, '2016-10-23 20:44:11', 120)   -- yyyy-mm-dd hh:mm:ss(24h)
> Date&Time
> 2016-10-23 20:44:11.000

CHAPTER 10: Basic SELECT Statement Syntax & Examples

Style 126 Is ISO 8601 Format: International Standard; Works With Any Language Setting

SELECT [Date&Time]=convert(datetime, '2018-10-23T18:52:47.513', 126) -- yyyy-mm-ddThh:mm:ss(.mmm)

>   Date&Time
>   2018-10-23 18:52:47.513

SELECT [Date&Time]=convert(datetime, '2016-10-23 20:44:11.500', 121)   – yyyy-mm-dd hh:mm:ss.mmm

>   Date&Time
>   2016-10-23 20:44:11.500

-- Islamic / Hijri date conversion

SELECT CONVERT(nvarchar(32), convert(datetime,'2016-10-23'), 130);
-- 22 محرم 1438 12:00:00:000AM

SELECT [Date&Time]=convert(datetime, N'23 شوال 1441 6:52:47:513PM', 130)

>   Date&Time
>   2020-06-14 18:52:47.513

SELECT [Date&Time]=convert(datetime, '23/10/1441 6:52:47:513PM',   131)

>   Date&Time
>   2020-06-14 18:52:47.513

-- Convert DDMMYYYY format to datetime with intermediate conversion using STUFF().

SELECT STUFF(STUFF('31012016',3,0,'-'),6,0,'-');
-- 31-01-2016

SELECT [Date&Time]=convert(datetime, STUFF(STUFF('31012016',3,0,'-'),6,0,'-'), 105)

>   Date&Time
>   2016-01-31 00:00:00.000

-- Equivalent
SELECT STUFF(STUFF('31012016',3,0,'/'),6,0,'/');   -- 31/01/2016
SELECT [Date&Time]=convert(datetime, STUFF(STUFF('31012016',3,0,'/'),6,0,'/'), 103)

CHAPTER 10: Basic SELECT Statement Syntax & Examples

String to Datetime Conversion Without Century

String to datetime conversion without century - some exceptions.   Nondeterministic means language setting (also regional setting) dependent such as Mar/Mär/mars/márc .

SELECT [Date&Time]=convert(datetime, 'Oct 23 16 11:02:44AM')   -- Default

Date&Time
2016-10-23 11:02:44.000

SELECT convert(datetime, '10/23/16', 1)	mm/dd/yy	U.S.
SELECT convert(datetime, '16.10.23', 2)	yy.mm.dd	ANSI
SELECT convert(datetime, '23/10/16', 3)	dd/mm/yy	UK/FR
SELECT convert(datetime, '23.10.16', 4)	dd.mm.yy	German
SELECT convert(datetime, '23-10-16', 5)	dd-mm-yy	Italian
SELECT convert(datetime, '23 OCT 16', 6)	dd mon yy	non-det.
SELECT convert(datetime, 'Oct 23, 16', 7)	mon dd, yy	non-det.
SELECT convert(datetime, '20:10:44', 8)	hh:mm:ss	
SELECT convert(datetime, 'Oct 23 16 11:02:44:013AM', 9)	Default with msec	
SELECT convert(datetime, '10-23-16', 10)	mm-dd-yy	U.S.
SELECT convert(datetime, '16/10/23', 11)	yy/mm/dd	Japan
SELECT convert(datetime, '161023', 12)	yymmdd	ISO
SELECT convert(datetime, '23 Oct 16 11:02:07:577', 13)	dd mon yy hh:mm:ss:mmm EU dflt	
SELECT convert(datetime, '20:10:25:300', 14)	hh:mm:ss:mmm(24h)	
SELECT convert(datetime, '2016-10-23 20:44:11',20)	yyyy-mm-dd hh:mm:ss(24h) ODBC can.	
SELECT convert(datetime, '2016-10-23 20:44:11.500', 21)	yyyy-mm-dd hh:mm:ss.mmm ODBC	

Combine Date & Time String into Datetime

```
DECLARE @DateTimeValue varchar(32), @DateValue char(8), @TimeValue char(6)
 SELECT @DateValue = '20200718',          @TimeValue = '211920'
SELECT          @DateTimeValue =
               CONCAT(
               convert(varchar, convert(datetime, @DateValue), 111),
                ' ', substring(@TimeValue, 1, 2) , ':', substring(@TimeValue, 3, 2) , ' ',
substring(@TimeValue, 5, 2)  )

SELECT   DateInput = @DateValue, TimeInput = @TimeValue,  DateTimeOutput = @DateTimeValue;
GO
```

DateInput	TimeInput	DateTimeOutput
20200718	211920	2020/07/18 21:19:20

```
SELECT DATETIMEFROMPARTS (2020, 07, 1, 21, 01, 20, 700)          -- New in SQL Server 2012
```

Date and Time Internal Storage Format

DATETIME 8 bytes internal storage structure:

- ➤ 1st 4 bytes: number of days after the base date 1900-01-01
- ➤ 2nd 4 bytes: number of clock-ticks (3.33 milliseconds) since midnight

```
SELECT CONVERT(binary(8), CURRENT_TIMESTAMP);
```

```
Hex
0x0000A09C00F23CE1
```

DATE 3 bytes internal storage structure:

- ➤ 3 bytes integer: number of days after the first date 0001-01-01
- ➤ Note: hex byte order reversed

SMALLDATETIME 4 bytes internal storage structure

- ➤ 1st 2 bytes: number of days after the base date 1900-01-01
- ➤ 2nd 2 bytes: number of minutes since midnight

```
SELECT Hex=CONVERT(binary(4), convert(smalldatetime, getdate()));
```

```
Hex
0xA09C0375
```

CHAPTER 10: Basic SELECT Statement Syntax & Examples

Date & Time Operations Using System Operators & Functions

```
-- Conversion from hex (binary) to datetime value
DECLARE @dtHex binary(8)= 0x00009966002d3344;  DECLARE @dt datetime = @dtHex;
SELECT @dt;   -- 2007-07-09 02:44:34.147
```

```
-- SQL convert seconds to HH:MM:SS -
DECLARE  @Seconds INT;  SET @Seconds = 20000 ;
SELECT HH = @Seconds / 3600, MM = (@Seconds%3600) / 60, SS = (@Seconds%60) ;
```

HH	MM	SS
5	33	20

Extract Date Only from DATETIME Data Type

```
DECLARE @Now datetime = CURRENT_TIMESTAMP -- getdate()

SELECT  DateAndTime      = @Now     -- Date portion and Time portion
        ,DateString             = REPLACE(LEFT(CONVERT (varchar, @Now, 112),10),' ','-')
        ,[Date]                 = CONVERT(DATE, @Now)  -- SQL Server 2008 and on - date part
        ,Midnight1              = dateadd(day, datediff(day,0, @Now), 0)
        ,Midnight2              = CONVERT(DATETIME,CONVERT(int, @Now))
        ,Midnight3              = CONVERT(DATETIME,CONVERT(BIGINT,@Now) &
(POWER(Convert(bigint,2),32)-1));
```

DateAndTime	DateString	Date	Midnight1	Midnight2	Midnight3
2020-07-28 15:01:51.960	20200728	2020-07-28	2020-07-28 00:00:00.000	2020-07-29 00:00:00.000	2020-07-29 00:00:00.000

```
-- Compare today with database dates
SELECT          TOP (10)  OrderDate = CONVERT(date, OrderDate),
                Today = CONVERT(date, getdate()),
                DeltaDays = DATEDIFF(DD, OrderDate, getdate())
FROM AdventureWorks2012.Sales.SalesOrderHeader  ORDER BY NEWID(); -- random sort
```

OrderDate	Today	DeltaDays
2008-01-15	2012-08-10	1669
2006-07-14	2012-08-10	2219
2008-07-05	2012-08-10	1497
2008-03-01	2012-08-10	1623
2007-10-01	2012-08-10	1775
2007-01-15	2012-08-10	2034
2008-05-27	2012-08-10	1536
2008-04-18	2012-08-10	1575
2008-04-25	2012-08-10	1568
2006-12-17	2012-08-10	2063

CHAPTER 10: Basic SELECT Statement Syntax & Examples

String Date Formats Without Time

```
-- String date format yyyy/mm/dd from datetime
SELECT CONVERT(VARCHAR(10), GETDATE(), 111) AS [YYYY/MM/DD] ;
```

> YYYY/MM/DD
> 2012/07/28

```
SELECT CONVERT(VARCHAR(10), GETDATE(), 112) AS [YYYYMMDD];
```

> YYYYMMDD
> 20120728

```
SELECT REPLACE(CONVERT(VARCHAR(10), GETDATE(), 111),'/',' ') AS [YYYY MM DD];
```

> YYYY MM DD
> 2020 07 28

```
-- Converting to special (non-standard) date formats: DD-MMM-YY
SELECT UPPER(REPLACE(CONVERT(VARCHAR,GETDATE(),6),' ','-')) AS CustomDate;
```

> CustomDate
> 28-JUL-20

```
-- SQL convert date string to datetime - time set to 00:00:00.000 or 12:00AM

PRINT CONVERT(datetime,'07-10-2020',110) ;       -- Jul 10 2020 12:00AM
PRINT CONVERT(datetime,'2020/07/10',111) ;       -- Jul 10 2020 12:00AM
PRINT CONVERT(datetime,'20200710',  112);        -- Jul 10 2020 12:00AM
GO
```

```
-- SQL Server cast string to date / datetime
DECLARE @DateValue char(8) = '20200718'

SELECT [Date] = CAST (@DateValue AS datetime);
GO
```

> Date
> 2020-07-18 00:00:00.000

CHAPTER 10: Basic SELECT Statement Syntax & Examples

String date to string date conversion with nested CONVERT

SELECT CONVERT(varchar, CONVERT(datetime, '20140508'), 100) AS StringDate;

StringDate
May 8 2014 12:00AM

```
-- T-SQL convert date to integer
DECLARE @Date datetime;  SET @Date = getdate();
SELECT DateAsInteger = CAST (CONVERT(varchar,@Date,112) as INT);
GO
```

DateAsInteger
20120728

```
-- SQL Server convert integer to datetime
DECLARE @iDate int = 20151225;
SELECT IntegerToDatetime = CAST(convert(varchar,@iDate) as datetime)
GO
```

IntegerToDatetime
2015-12-25 00:00:00.000

```
-- Alternates: date-only datetime values

SELECT [DATE-ONLY]=CONVERT(DATETIME, FLOOR(CONVERT(FLOAT, GETDATE())));

SELECT [DATE-ONLY]=CONVERT(DATETIME, FLOOR(CONVERT(MONEY, GETDATE())));

SELECT [DATE-ONLY]=CONVERT(DATETIME, CONVERT(DATE, GETDATE()));

-- CAST string to datetime
-- String date preparation, length is 10 characters
SELECT CONVERT(varchar, GETDATE(), 101), LEN (CONVERT(varchar, GETDATE(), 101))
--       07/28/2018      10

SELECT [DATE-ONLY]=CAST(CONVERT(varchar, GETDATE(), 101) AS DATETIME);
```

DATE-ONLY
2018-07-28 00:00:00.000

DATEADD() and DATEDIFF() Functions

```
-- T-SQL strip time from date
SELECT getdate() AS [DateTime], dateadd(dd, datediff(dd, 0, getdate()), 0) [DateOnly];
```

DateTime	DateOnly
2012-07-28 17:24:07.300	2012-07-28 00:00:00.000

```
-- First day of current month
SELECT dateadd(month, datediff(month, 0, getdate()), 0)  AS FirstDayOfCurrentMonth;
SELECT dateadd(dd,1, EOMONTH(getdate(),-1));  -- New to SQL Server 2012
```

FirstDayOfCurrentMonth
2020-07-01 00:00:00.000

```
 -- 15th day of current month
SELECT dateadd(day,14,dateadd(month, datediff(month,0,getdate()),0))
                                                    AS MiddleOfCurrentMonth;
SELECT dateadd(dd,15, EOMONTH(getdate(),-1));  -- New to SQL Server 2012
```

MiddleOfCurrentMonth
2012-07-15 00:00:00.000

```
-- First Monday of current month
SELECT  dateadd(day, (9-datepart(weekday,
        dateadd(month, datediff(month, 0, getdate()), 0)))%7,
        dateadd(month, datediff(month, 0, getdate()), 0))  AS [First Monday Cf Current Month];
GO
```

First Monday Of Current Month
2012-07-02 00:00:00.000

```
-- Next Monday calculation from the reference date which was a Monday
DECLARE @Now datetime = GETDATE();
DECLARE @NextMonday datetime = dateadd(dd, ((datediff(dd, '19000101 , @Now)
            / 7) * 7) + 7, '19000101');
SELECT [Now]=@Now, [Next Monday]=@NextMonday;
GO
```

Now	Next Monday
2012-07-28 17:35:29.657	2012-07-30 00:00:00.000

CHAPTER 10: Basic SELECT Statement Syntax & Examples

Last Date & First Date Calculations

```
-- Last Friday of current month

SELECT   dateadd(day, -7+(6-datepart(weekday,

         dateadd(month, datediff(month, 0, getdate())+1, 0)))%7,

         dateadd(month, datediff(month, 0, getdate())+1, 0)) ;

-- First day of next month

SELECT dateadd(month, datediff(month, 0, getdate())+1, 0) ;

-- 15th of next month

SELECT dateadd(day,14, dateadd(month, datediff(month, 0, getdate())+1, 0));

-- First Monday of next month

SELECT   dateadd(day, (9-datepart(weekday,
         dateadd(month, datediff(month, 0, getdate())+1, 0)))%7,
         dateadd(month, datediff(month, 0, getdate())+1, 0));


-- Next 12 months start & end - EOMONTH is new to SQL Server 2012
SELECT TOP 12
         DATEADD(DD,1, EOMONTH(getdate(),number-1))     AS Start,
         EOMONTH(getdate(),number)                      AS [End]
FROM master.dbo.spt_values   -- get integer sequence
WHERE type='P'  ORDER BY number;
GO
```

Start	End
2016-08-01	2016-08-31
2016-09-01	2016-09-30
2016-10-01	2016-10-31
2016-11-01	2016-11-30
2016-12-01	2016-12-31
2017-01-01	2017-01-31
2017-02-01	2017-02-28
2017-03-01	2017-03-31
2017-04-01	2017-04-30
2017-05-01	2017-05-31
2017-06-01	2017-06-30
2017-07-01	2017-07-31

BETWEEN Operator for Date Range

Date time range SELECT using the using >= and < operators. Count Sales Orders for date range 2007 OCT-NOV.

```
DECLARE  @StartDate DATETIME,  @EndDate DATETIME
SET @StartDate = convert(DATETIME,'10/01/2007',101)
SET @EndDate   = convert(DATETIME,'11/30/2007',101)
SELECT @StartDate, @EndDate
-- 2007-10-01 00:00:00.000  2007-11-30 00:00:00.000
SELECT dateadd(DAY,1,@EndDate),    dateadd(ms,-3,dateadd(DAY,1,@EndDate))
-- 2007-12-01 00:00:00.000  2007-11-30 23:59:59.997

SELECT [Sales Orders for 2007 OCT-NOV] = COUNT(* )
FROM   AdventureWorks2012.Sales.SalesOrderHeader
WHERE  OrderDate >= @StartDate
        AND OrderDate < dateadd(DAY,1,@EndDate)
```

```
        Sales Orders for 2007 OCT-NOV
        3668
```

Equivalent date range query using BETWEEN comparison. It requires a bit of trick programming. 23.59.59.997 is the last available time in a day.

```
SELECT [Sales Orders for 2007 OCT-NOV] = COUNT(* )
FROM   AdventureWorks2012.Sales.SalesOrderHeader
WHERE   OrderDate BETWEEN @StartDate
        AND dateadd(ms,-3, dateadd(DAY, 1, @EndDate))
GO
```

```
        Sales Orders for 2007 OCT-NOV
        3668
```

The BETWEEN operator can be used with string dates as well. Note: anything after midnight on 2004-02-10 is not included.

```
USE AdventureWorks;
SELECT POs=COUNT(*) FROM Purchasing.PurchaseOrderHeader
WHERE OrderDate BETWEEN '20040201' AND '20040210'
GO
```

```
    POs
    108
```

BETWEEN Dates Without Time: Entire 2004-02-10 Day Included This Fashion

```
SELECT POs=COUNT(*) FROM Purchasing.PurchaseOrderHeader
WHERE datediff(dd,0,OrderDate)
        BETWEEN datediff(dd,0,'20040201 12:11:39') AND datediff(dd,0,'20040210 14:33:19')
```

POs
108

The datetime range BETWEEN is equivalent to >=...AND....<= operators.

```
SELECT POs=COUNT(*) FROM Purchasing.PurchaseOrderHeader
WHERE OrderDate  BETWEEN '2004-02-01 00:00:00.000' AND '2004-02-10  00:00:00.000'
```

POs
108

Orders with datetime OrderDate-s of

'2004-02-10 00:00:01.000'	1 second after midnight (start of day at 12:00AM)
'2004-02-10 00:01:00.000'	1 minute after midnight
'2004-02-10 01:00:00.000'	1 hour after midnight
'2004-02-10 23:00:00.000'	23 hours after midnight

would not included in the preceding two queries. Only datetime OrderDate of '2004-02-10 00:00:00.000' would be included. That would be OK if the time part is not used. But even in that case and order can be entered accidentally with a time part, that would throw off the count.

To include the entire day of 2004-02-10, move the day up by one and use the < operator:

```
SELECT POs=COUNT(*) FROM Purchasing.PurchaseOrderHeader
WHERE OrderDate >= '20040201' AND OrderDate < '20040211';
```

POs
108

The reason we cannot detect a difference is due to lack of data passed midnight on 2004-02-11.

```
SELECT  [PurchaseOrderID], [RevisionNumber], [Status],
        [EmployeeID], [VendorID], [ShipMethodID], [OrderDate]
FROM [AdventureWorks].[Purchasing].[PurchaseOrderHeader] WHERE PurchaseOrderID = 1665;
```

PurchaseOrderID	RevisionNumber	Status	EmployeeID	VendorID	ShipMethodID	OrderDate
1665	0	4	261	43	5	2004-02-10 00:00:00.000

CHAPTER IO: Basic SELECT Statement Syntax & Examples

Advance the datetime one second from midnight, the BETWEEN datetime query is not going to count it

```
UPDATE [AdventureWorks].[Purchasing].[PurchaseOrderHeader]
      SET OrderDate = '2004-02-10 00:00:01.000'
WHERE PurchaseOrderID = 1665;  -- (1 row(s) affected)
```

This is the current value for OrderDate datetime.

PurchaseOrderID	RevisionNumber	Status	EmployeeID	VendorID	ShipMethodID	OrderDate
1665	0	4	261	43	5	2004-02-10 00:00:01.000

The following queries are not going to count this passed midnight record any more.

```
SELECT POs=COUNT(*) FROM Purchasing.PurchaseOrderHeader
WHERE OrderDate BETWEEN '2004-02-01 00:00:00.000' AND '2004-02-10  00:00:00.C00'
```

```
POs
107
```

```
USE AdventureWorks; SELECT POs=COUNT(*) FROM Purchasing.PurchaseOrderHeader
WHERE OrderDate BETWEEN '20040201' AND '20040210'
```

```
POs
107
```

While the query we designed specifically for a case like this will count it correctly.

```
SELECT POs=COUNT(*) FROM Purchasing.PurchaseOrderHeader
WHERE OrderDate >= '20040201' AND OrderDate < '20040211'
```

```
POs
108
```

We restore the data to its original value.

```
UPDATE [AdventureWorks].[Purchasing].[PurchaseOrderHeader]
      SET OrderDate = '2004-02-10 00:00:00.000'
WHERE PurchaseOrderID = 1665;    -- (1 row(s) affected)
```

CHAPTER 10: Basic SELECT Statement Syntax & Examples

Date Validation Function ISDATE()

```
DECLARE @StringDate varchar(32);
SET @StringDate = '2011-03-15 18:50';
IF EXISTS( SELECT * WHERE ISDATE(@StringDate) = 1)
  PRINT 'VALID DATE: ' + @StringDate
ELSE
  PRINT 'INVALID DATE: ' + @StringDate;
```

```
VALID DATE: 2011-03-15 18:50
```

```
DECLARE @StringDate varchar(32) ;
SET @StringDate = '20112-03-15 18:50';
IF EXISTS( SELECT * WHERE ISDATE(@StringDate) = 1)
  PRINT 'VALID DATE: ' + @StringDate
ELSE  PRINT 'INVALID DATE: ' + @StringDate;
GO
```

```
INVALID DATE: 20112-03-15 18:50
```

First and Last Day of Date Periods
Calculating date periods markers is a very important task in T-SQL programming, especially related to reporting queries.

```
DECLARE @Date DATE = '20161023'; SELECT ReferenceDate  = @Date;

SELECT FirstDayOfYear  = CONVERT(DATE, dateadd(yy, datediff(yy,0, @Date),0));

SELECT LastDayOfYear   = CONVERT(DATE, dateadd(yy, datediff(yy,0, @Date)+1,-1));

SELECT FDofSemester = CONVERT(DATE, dateadd(qq,((datediff(qq,0,@Date)/2)*2),0));

SELECT LastDayOfSemester  = CONVERT(DATE, dateadd(qq,((datediff(qq,0,@Date)/2)*2)+2,-1));

SELECT FirstDayOfQuarter  = CONVERT(DATE, dateadd(qq, datediff(qq,0, @Date),0));

SELECT LastDayOfQuarter = CONVERT(DATE, dateadd(qq, datediff(qq,0,@Date)+1,-1));
```

LastDayOfQuarter
2016-12-31

The brand-new EOMonth() function simplifies month start/end formulas

```
SELECT LastDayOfMonth = EOMonth (@Date);  -- New in SQL Server 2012

SELECT FirstDayOfMonth = CONVERT(DATE, dateadd(mm, datediff(mm,0, @Date),0));

SELECT LastDayOfMonth  = CONVERT(DATE, dateadd(mm, datediff(mm,0, @Date)+1,-1));

SELECT FirstDayOfWeek  = CONVERT(DATE, dateadd(wk, datediff(wk,0, @Date),0));

SELECT LastDayOfWeek   = CONVERT(DATE, dateadd(wk, datediff(wk,0, @Date)+1,-1));
GO
```

Month Sequence Generator

Sometimes date based data may have gaps missing months. For reporting purposes we may want to include all months from start date to end date. To do that we have to generate a continuous sequence of months, and use it to fill in the gaps. Calendar table can also be used for such a task.

```
DECLARE @Date date = '2000-01-01'
SELECT MonthStart=dateadd(MM, number, @Date)
FROM  master.dbo.spt_values
WHERE type='P' AND  dateadd(MM, number, @Date) <= CURRENT_TIMESTAMP
ORDER BY MonthStart;    -- (151 row(s) affected) - Partial results.
```

MonthStart
2000-01-01
2000-02-01
2000-03-01
2000-04-01
2000-05-01
2000-06-01
2000-07-01
2000-08-01
2000-09-01
2000-10-01
2000-11-01
2000-12-01
2001-01-01
2001-02-01
2001-03-01
2001-04-01

Selected U.S. & International Date Styles

The U.S. date style is m/d/y.

```
DECLARE @DateTimeValue varchar(32) = '10/23/2016';

SELECT StringDate=@DateTimeValue,  [SSMS-Style] = CONVERT(datetime, @DatetimeValue);

SELECT @DateTimeValue = '10/23/2016 23:01:05';

SELECT StringDate = @DateTimeValue,  [SSMS-Style] = CONVERT(datetime, @DatetimeValue);
GO
```

StringDate	SSMS-Style
10/23/2016	2016-10-23 00:00:00.000

StringDate	SSMS-Style
10/23/2016 23:01:05	2016-10-23 23:01:05.000

The UK or British/French style is dmy.

```
DECLARE @DateTimeValue varchar(32) = '23/10/16 23:01:05';

SELECT StringDate = @DateTimeValue,  [SSMS-Style] = CONVERT(datetime, @DatetimeValue, 3);

 SELECT @DateTimeValue = '23/10/2016 04:01 PM';

SELECT StringDate = @DateTimeValue,  [SSMS-Style] = CONVERT(datetime, @DatetimeValue, 103);
GO
```

The German style is dmy as well with a new twist to it: period instead of slash.

```
DECLARE @DateTimeValue varchar(32)  = '23.10.16 23:01:05';
SELECT StringDate = @DateTimeValue,  [SSMS -Style] = CONVERT(datetime, @DatetimeValue, 4);
 SELECT @DateTimeValue = '23.10.2016 04:01 PM';
SELECT StringDate = @DateTimeValue,  [SSMS -Style] = CONVERT(datetime, @DatetimeValue, 104);
GO
```

```
-- Nondeterministic month name (mon)
SET LANGUAGE Spanish; SELECT CONVERT(varchar, getdate(), 100);        -- Ago 10 2018  4:43PM
SET LANGUAGE Turkish; SELECT CONVERT(varchar, getdate(), 100);        -- Agu 10 2018  4:44PM
SET LANGUAGE Polish; SELECT CONVERT(varchar, getdate(), 100);         -- VIII 10 2018  4:46PM
SET LANGUAGE Hungarian; SELECT CONVERT(varchar, getdate(), 100);      -- aug 10 2018  4:46PM
SET LANGUAGE Russian; SELECT CONVERT(nvarchar, getdate(), 100);       -- авг 10 2018  4:47PM
```

The DATEPART() Function to Decompose a Date

The DATEPART() function returns a part of a date.

```
DECLARE @dt datetime = getdate();
SELECT DATEPART(YEAR, @dt)          AS YYYY,
       DATEPART(MONTH, @dt)         AS MM,
       DATEPART(DAY, @dt)           AS DD;
```

YYYY	MM	DD
2016	7	29

```
SELECT  *  FROM Northwind.dbo.Orders
WHERE DATEPART(YEAR, OrderDate)          = '1996'  AND
      DATEPART(MONTH,OrderDate)          = '07'    AND
      DATEPART(DAY, OrderDate)           = '10'
```

```
/*OrderID        CustomerID       EmployeeID       OrderDate         RequiredDate         ShippedDate
    ShipVia  Freight  ShipName       Shipaddress         ShipCity ShipRegion          ShipPostalCode
    ShipCountry
10253   HANAR  3          1996-07-10 00:00:00.000 1996-07-24 00:00:00.000 1996-07-16 00:00:00.000
    2       58.17    Hanari Carnes    Rua do Paço, 67  Rio de Janeiro   RJ        05454-876
    Brazil  */
```

Alternate syntax for DATEPART.

```
SELECT * FROM Northwind.dbo.Orders
WHERE       YEAR(OrderDate)    = 1996      AND
            MONTH(OrderDate)   = 07        AND
            DAY(OrderDate)     = 10
GO
```

```
-- Additional datepart parameters including Julian date
DECLARE @dt datetime = getdate();
SELECT DATEPART(DAY, @dt)           AS DD,
       DATEPART(WEEKDAY, @dt)       AS WD,
       DATEPART(DAYOFYEAR, @dt)     AS JulianDate,
       DATEPART(WEEK, @dt)          AS Week,
       DATEPART(ISO_WEEK, @dt)      AS ISOWeek,
       DATEPART(HOUR, @dt)          AS HH;
```

DD	WD	JulianDate	Week	ISOWeek	HH
10	5	223	33	32	17

CHAPTER 10: Basic SELECT Statement Syntax & Examples

The DATENAME() Function to Get Date Part Names
The DATENAME() function can be used to find out the words for months and weekdays.

```
SELECT DayName=DATENAME(weekday, OrderDate), SalesPerWeekDay = COUNT(*)
FROM AdventureWorks2008.Sales.SalesOrderHeader
GROUP BY DATENAME(weekday, OrderDate), DATEPART(weekday,OrderDate)
ORDER BY DATEPART(weekday,OrderDate);
```

DayName	SalesPerWeekDay
Sunday	4482
Monday	4591
Tuesday	4346
Wednesday	4244
Thursday	4483
Friday	4444
Saturday	4875

DATENAME application for month names

```
SELECT MonthName=DATENAME(month, OrderDate), SalesPerMonth = COUNT(*)
FROM AdventureWorks2008.Sales.SalesOrderHeader
GROUP BY DATENAME(month, OrderDate), MONTH(OrderDate) ORDER BY MONTH(OrderDate);
```

MonthName	SalesPerMonth
January	2483
February	2686
March	2750
April	2740
May	3154
June	3079
July	2094
August	2411
September	2298
October	2282
November	2474
December	3014

```
SELECT DATENAME(MM,dateadd(MM,7,-1))  -- July  - Month name from month number
```

CHAPTER 10: Basic SELECT Statement Syntax & Examples

Extract Date from Text with PATINDEX Pattern Matching

```
USE tempdb;
go

CREATE TABLE InsiderTransaction (
    InsiderTransactionID int identity primary key,
    TradeDate datetime,
    TradeMsg varchar(256),
    ModifiedDate datetime default (getdate())  );

-- Populate table with dummy data
INSERT InsiderTransaction (TradeMsg)
VALUES ('INSIDER TRAN QABC Hammer, Bruce D. CSO 09-02-08 Buy 2,000 6.10');
INSERT InsiderTransaction (TradeMsg)
VALUES ('INSIDER TRAN QABC Schmidt, Steven CFO 08-25-08 Buy 2,500 6.70') ;
INSERT InsiderTransaction (TradeMsg)
VALUES ('INSIDER TRAN QABC  Hammer, Bruce D. CSO  08-20-08 Buy 3,000 8.59');
INSERT InsiderTransaction (TradeMsg)
VALUES ('INSIDER TRAN QABC Walters,  Jeff CTO 08-15-08  Sell 5,648 8.49');
INSERT InsiderTransaction (TradeMsg)
VALUES  ('INSIDER TRAN  QABC  Walters, Jeff CTO   08-15-08 Option Exercise 5,648 2.15');
INSERT InsiderTransaction (TradeMsg)
VALUES('INSIDER TRAN QABC Hammer, Bruce D. CSO 07-31-08  Buy 5,000 8.05');
INSERT InsiderTransaction (TradeMsg)
VALUES('INSIDER TRAN QABC Lennot, Mark  Director  08-31-07 Buy 1,500 9.97');
INSERT InsiderTransaction (TradeMsg)
VALUES('INSIDER TRAN QABC O''Neal, Linda COO  08-01-08 Sell 5,000 6.50');
```

Pattern match for MM-DD-YY using the PATINDEX string function to extract dates from stock trade message text.

```
SELECT   InsiderTransactionID ,      substring(TradeMsg,
       patindex('%[01][0-9]-[0123][0-9]-[0-9][0-9]%', TradeMsg),8) AS TradeDate
FROM InsiderTransaction  WHERE  patindex('%[01][0-9]-[0123][0-9]-[0-9][0-9]%', TradeMsg) > 0;
```

InsiderTransactionID	TradeDate
1	09-02-08
2	08-25-08
3	08-20-08
4	08-15-08
5	08-15-08
6	07-31-08
7	08-31-07
8	08-01-08

CHAPTER 10: Basic SELECT Statement Syntax & Examples

Valid Ranges for Date & Time Data Types

➢ DATE (3 bytes) date range:

➢ January 1, 1 through December 31, 9999 A.D.

➢ SMALLDATETIME (4 bytes) date range:

➢ January 1, 1900 through June 6, 2079

➢ DATETIME (8 bytes) date range:

➢ January 1, 1753 through December 31, 9999

➢ DATETIME2 (6-8 bytes) date range:

➢ January 1, 1 A.D. through December 31, 9999 A.D.

Smalldatetime has limited range. The statement below will give a date range error.

```
SELECT CONVERT(smalldatetime, '2110-01-01')
/* Msg 242, Level 16, State 3, Line 1
The conversion of a varchar data type to a smalldatetime data type
resulted in an out-of-range value. */
```

```
-- Date Columbus discovers America
SELECT CONVERT(datetime, '14921012');
/* Msg 242, Level 16, State 3, Line 2
The conversion of a varchar data type to a datetime data type resulted in an out-of-range value. */
```

```
SELECT CONVERT(datetime2, '14921012');    -- 1492-10-10 00:00:00.0000000
```

```
SELECT CONVERT(date, '14921012');                    -- 1492-10-12
```

CHAPTER 10: Basic SELECT Statement Syntax & Examples

Last Week Calculations

```
-- SQL last Friday - Implied string to datetime conversions in dateadd & datediff
DECLARE @BaseFriday CHAR(8), @LastFriday datetime, @LastMonday datetime;
SET @BaseFriday = '19000105';
SELECT   @LastFriday = dateadd(dd,
         (datediff (dd, @BaseFriday, CURRENT_TIMESTAMP) / 7) * 7, @BaseFriday) ;
SELECT [Last Friday] = @LastFriday ;
```

Last Friday
2012-07-27 00:00:00.000

```
-- Last Monday (last week's Monday)
SELECT   @LastMonday=dateadd(dd,  (datediff (dd, @BaseFriday,
         CURRENT_TIMESTAMP) / 7) * 7 - 4, @BaseFriday)
SELECT [Last Monday]= @LastMonday;
```

Last Monday
2012-07-23 00:00:00.000

```
-- Last week - SUN - SAT
SELECT          [Last Week] = CONCAT(CONVERT(varchar,dateadd(day, -1, @LastMonday), 101), ' - ',
                CONVERT(varchar, dateadd(day, 1,  @LastFriday), 101))
```

Last Week
07/22/2012 - 07/28/2012

```
-- Next 10 weeks including this one; SUN - SAT
SELECT   TOP 10   [ Week] = CONCAT(CONVERT(varchar,dateadd(day, -1+number*7, @LastMonday), 101),
         ' - ',     CONVERT(varchar, dateadd(day, 1+number*7,  @LastFriday), 101))
FROM master.dbo.spt_values  WHERE type = 'P';
```

Week
08/05/2012 - 08/11/2012
08/12/2012 - 08/18/2012
08/19/2012 - 08/25/2012
08/26/2012 - 09/01/2012
09/02/2012 - 09/08/2012
09/09/2012 - 09/15/2012
09/16/2012 - 09/22/2012
09/23/2012 - 09/29/2012
09/30/2012 - 10/06/2012
10/07/2012 - 10/13/2012

CHAPTER 10: Basic SELECT Statement Syntax & Examples

Specific Day Calculations

```
-- First day of current month
SELECT dateadd(month, datediff(month, 0, getdate()), 0);


 -- 15th day of current month
SELECT dateadd(day,14,dateadd(month,datediff(month,0,getdate()),0));


-- First Monday of current month
SELECT   dateadd(day, (9-datepart(weekday,
         dateadd(month, datediff(month, 0, getdate()), 0)))%7,
         dateadd(month, datediff(month, 0, getdate()), 0)) ;


-- Next Monday calculation from the reference date which was a Monday
DECLARE @Now datetime = GETDATE();
DECLARE @NextMonday datetime = dateadd(dd, ((datediff(dd, '19000101', @Now)  / 7) * 7) + 7,
'19000101');
SELECT [Now]=@Now, [Next Monday]=@NextMonday;


-- Last Friday of current month
SELECT   dateadd(day, -7+(6-datepart(weekday,
         dateadd(month, datediff(month, 0, getdate())+1, 0)))%7,
         dateadd(month, datediff(month, 0, getdate())+1, 0)) ;


-- First day of next month
SELECT dateadd(month, datediff(month, 0, getdate())+1, 0);


-- 15th of next month
SELECT dateadd(day,14, dateadd(month, datediff(month, 0, getdate())+1, 0));


-- First Monday of next month
SELECT   dateadd(day, (9-datepart(weekday,
         dateadd(month, datediff(month, 0, getdate())+1, 0)))%7,
          dateadd(month, datediff(month, 0, getdate())+1, 0))  AS NextMonthMonday;
```

NextMonthMonday
2012-08-06 00:00:00.000

CHAPTER 10: Basic SELECT Statement Syntax & Examples

CHAPTER 11: Maintaining Data Integrity in the Enterprise

Why is Data Integrity Paramount

A business or organization can only operate efficiently with good quality data. Computers were the real engine of economic progress since the 1950-s. Without computers, we would pretty much be at post Second World War level. Computers work with data and produce data. As the saying goes: garbage in, garbage out. Therefore it is our job as database designers, database developers and database administrators to ensure the data integrity in a database. What are the sources of the bad data? They can be data feeds received from various sources,   data entry by people, and bugs in database or application programming. The best way to minimize bugs is putting each piece of new software through rigorous quality assurance (QA) process. To prevent bad data getting into the database there are a number of possibilities: table design, constraints, stored procedures, triggers and application software.

At the lowest level, constraints make up the guarding force over data integrity. The default constraint is different from the rest: it provides predefined default value if no value is provided for a cell (a column in a row), it does not give an error message.

```
USE AdventureWorks2012;
SELECT          ConstraintType = type_desc,   [Count] = COUNT(*)
FROM sys.objects
WHERE type_desc in      (
                'CHECK_CONSTRAINT',
                'DEFAULT_CONSTRAINT',
                'FOREIGN_KEY_CONSTRAINT',
                'PRIMARY_KEY_CONSTRAINT',
                'UNIQUE_CONSTRAINT'
                )
GROUP BY type_desc ORDER BY type_desc;
```

ConstraintType	Count
CHECK_CONSTRAINT	89
DEFAULT_CONSTRAINT	152
FOREIGN_KEY_CONSTRAINT	90
PRIMARY_KEY_CONSTRAINT	71
UNIQUE_CONSTRAINT	1

CHAPTER 11: Maintaining Data Integrity in the Enterprise

Entity Integrity

Entity Integrity defines a row as a unique entity for a particular table. The main enforcing mechanisms are: NOT NULL constraint and unique index. PRIMARY KEY implies not null, and unique index automatically created. In the Production.Product table ProductID is the INT IDENTITY PRIMARY KEY, Name & ProductNumber are NATURAL KEYs and rowguid is a system generated unique key. All four keys are not null and all have unique index defined. The implication is that we can use any of 4 columns for row identification. However, ProductID INT (4 bytes) column is the most efficient row (record) identifier.

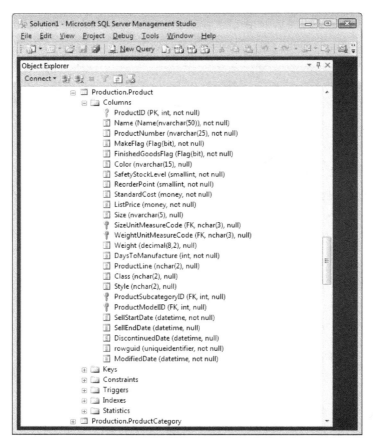

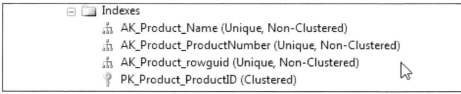

How to Remove Duplicates in a Table

The best way to prevent duplicates is by placing a UNIQUE KEY or unique index on the unique column(s). PRIMARY KEY & UNIQUE KEY constraints automatically create a unique index on the key column(s). If the entire row is a duplicate, removal is real simple with the DISTINCT clause.

```
SELECT DISTINCT * INTO T2 FROM T1;
GO
```

If duplicates are only in one or more columns, then duplicates removal is fairly easy with the ROW_NUMBER method, it is more involved with the GROUP BY method (prior to SQL Server 2005).

```
-- Create test table
USE tempdb;
SELECT          ProductID=CONVERT(int, ProductID),
                ProductName = Name,  ProductNumber,
                ListPrice = ListPrice + 1.00
INTO Product
FROM AdventureWorks2012.Production.Product    WHERE ListPrice > 0.0;
GO  -- (304 row(s) affected)
```

```
-- Unique index prevents duplicates
CREATE UNIQUE INDEX idxProd ON Product(ProductName, ProductNumber);
GO
```

```
 -- Try to insert  duplicates on ProductName & ProductNumber
INSERT INTO Product
SELECT          TOP (100) ProductID=CONVERT(int, ProductID) + 1000,
                ProductName = Name, ProductNumber,
                ListPrice = ListPrice + 2.00
FROM AdventureWorks2008.Production.Product
WHERE ListPrice > 0.0 ORDER BY NEWID();
GO
/*  Msg 2601, Level 14, State 1, Line 2
Cannot insert duplicate key row in object 'dbo.Product' with unique index 'idxProd'.
The duplicate key value is (Fender Set - Mountain, FE-6654).
The statement has been terminated.  */
```

```
DROP INDEX Product.idxProd;
GO
```

Rows with Duplicates Can Be Numbered in Ordered or Random Manner

```
-- Insert 100 duplicates on ProductName & ProductNumber
INSERT INTO Product
SELECT          TOP (100) ProductID=CONVERT(int, ProductID) + 1000,
                ProductName = Name, ProductNumber,   ListPrice = ListPrice + 2.00
FROM AdventureWorks2008.Production.Product
WHERE ListPrice > 0.0
ORDER BY NEWID();
GO
```

```
-- Quantify duplicates with GROUP BY query
SELECT ProductName, ProductNumber, [Count] = count(*)
FROM Product
GROUP BY ProductName, ProductNumber
      HAVING count(*) > 1
ORDER BY ProductName, ProductNumber;
GO -- (100 row(s) affected) - Partial results.
```

ProductName	ProductNumber	Count
Bike Wash - Dissolver	CL-9009	2
Classic Vest, L	VE-C304-L	2
Classic Vest, S	VE-C304-S	2
Front Brakes	FB-9873	2
Full-Finger Gloves, M	GL-F110-M	2

```
-- Quantify duplicates with ROW_NUMBER OVER - we don't care about duplicates ordering
;WITH CTE AS (
   SELECT RN=ROW_NUMBER() OVER (PARTITION BY ProductName, ProductNumber
   ORDER BY NEWID() ),  ProductName, ProductNumber
   FROM Product)
SELECT * FROM CTE WHERE RN > 1
ORDER BY ProductName, ProductNumber;
GO -- (100 row(s) affected) - Partial results.
```

RN	ProductName	ProductNumber
2	Bike Wash - Dissolver	CL-9009
2	Classic Vest, L	VE-C304-L
2	Classic Vest, S	VE-C304-S
2	Front Brakes	FB-9873
2	Full-Finger Gloves, M	GL-F110-M

CHAPTER II: Maintaining Data Integrity in the Enterprise

Remove Duplicates with CTE & ROW_NUMBER OVER PARTITION BY

```
-- To removal of duplicates is real easy with CTE & ROW_NUMBER
;WITH CTE AS (
    SELECT RN=ROW_NUMBER() OVER (PARTITION BY ProductName, ProductNumber
    ORDER BY NEWID()),  ProductName, ProductNumber   FROM Product)
DELETE CTE  WHERE RN > 1;
GO -- (100 row(s) affected)


-- Test for duplicates again
SELECT ProductName, ProductNumber, [Count] = count(*)
FROM Product  GROUP BY ProductName, ProductNumber  HAVING count(*) > 1
ORDER BY ProductName, ProductNumber;
GO -- (0 row(s) affected)


SELECT COUNT(*) FROM Product;  -- 304
GO
```

Remove Duplicates with GROUP BY

```
-- Insert  duplicates on ProductName & ProductNumber
INSERT INTO Product    SELECT     TOP (100) ProductID=CONVERT(int, ProductID) + 1000,
                ProductName = Name, ProductNumber,    ListPrice = ListPrice + 2.00
FROM AdventureWorks2008.Production.Product  WHERE ListPrice > 0.0  ORDER BY NEWID();
GO


-- Sample of conflicting data - It is a business decision what to keep
SELECT TOP (4) * FROM Product WHERE ProductNumber IN
   ( SELECT ProductNumber FROM Product   GROUP BY ProductNumber HAVING count(*) > 1   )
ORDER BY ProductNumber;
```

ProductID	ProductName	ProductNumber	ListPrice
992	Mountain-500 Black, 48	BK-M18B-48	540.9900
1992	Mountain-500 Black, 48	BK-M18B-48	541.9900
993	Mountain-500 Black, 52	BK-M18B-52	540.9900
1993	Mountain-500 Black, 52	BK-M18B-52	541.9900

```
-- Assume it does not matter which duplicate to keep: any ProductID and any ListPrice OK
SELECT ProductID=MIN(ProductID), ProductName, ProductNumber, ListPrice=MIN(ListPrice)
INTO Product1 FROM Product GROUP BY ProductName, ProductNumber ORDER BY ProductID;
GO  -- (304 row(s) affected)
```

CHAPTER 11: Maintaining Data Integrity in the Enterprise

Domain Integrity

A domain defines the possible values for a column. Domain Integrity rules enforce the validity
data in a column:

Data type	table design
Data length	table design
Nullability	table design
Collation	table design
Allowable values	check constraints - table design
Default value	default constraints - table design

CHECK constraint is used for simple rules such as OrderQty > 0. UDF CHECK constraints can be
used for complex rules. In addition, at the development phase, triggers, stored procedures and
client-side application software can be developed to enforce Domain Integrity.

Server-side CHECK constraints are the most desirable. Client-side Domain Integrity enforcement
is the least desirable. However, it may happen that there is no database expert on the project
and developers feel more confident programming data validity rules in the application software.
Ultimately what counts is valid data in the database. Usually big-budget projects can do
everything the right way due to the availability of expert-level resources in all areas of the
software development project. Basic table definition data from INFORMATION_SCHEMA views.

```
SELECT          COLUMN_NAME, ORDINAL_POSITION, DATA_TYPE, IS_NULLABLE,
                CHARACTER_MAXIMUM_LENGTH, COLLATION_NAME, COLUMN_DEFAULT
FROM INFORMATION_SCHEMA.COLUMNS WHERE TABLE_NAME = 'SalesOrderHeader';
```

COLUMN_NAME	ORDINAL_POSITION	DATA_TYPE	IS_NULLABLE	CHARACTER_MAXIMUM_LENGTH	COLLATION_NAME	COLUMN_DEFAULT
SalesOrderID	1	int	NO	NULL	NULL	NULL
RevisionNumber	2	tinyint	NO	NULL	NULL	((0))
OrderDate	3	datetime	NO	NULL	NULL	(getdate())
DueDate	4	datetime	NO	NULL	NULL	NULL
ShipDate	5	datetime	YES	NULL	NULL	NULL
tatus	6	tinyint	NO	NULL	NULL	((1))
OnlineOrderFlag	7	bit	NO	NULL	NULL	((1))
SalesOrderNumber	8	nvarchar	NO	25	SQL_Latin1_General_CP1_CI_AS	NULL
PurchaseOrderNumber	9	nvarchar	YES	25	SQL_Latin1_General_CP1_CI_AS	NULL
AccountNumber	10	nvarchar	YES	15	SQL_Latin1_General_CP1_CI_AS	NULL
CustomerID	11	int	NO	NULL	NULL	NULL
SalesPersonID	12	int	YES	NULL	NULL	NULL
TerritoryID	13	int	YES	NULL	NULL	NULL
BillToAddressID	14	int	NO	NULL	NULL	NULL
ShipToAddressID	15	int	NO	NULL	NULL	NULL
ShipMethodID	16	int	NO	NULL	NULL	NULL
CreditCardID	17	int	YES	NULL	NULL	NULL
CreditCardApprovalCode	18	varchar	YES	15	SQL_Latin1_General_CP1_CI_AS	NULL
CurrencyRateID	19	int	YES	NULL	NULL	NULL
SubTotal	20	money	NO	NULL	NULL	((0.00))
TaxAmt	21	money	NO	NULL	NULL	((0.00))
Freight	22	money	NO	NULL	NULL	((0.00))
TotalDue	23	money	NO	NULL	NULL	NULL
Comment	24	nvarchar	YES	128	SQL_Latin1_General_CP1_CI_AS	NULL
rowguid	25	uniqueidentifier	NO	NULL	NULL	(newid())
ModifiedDate	26	datetime	NO	NULL	NULL	(getdate())

Domain Integrity Summary Display with sp_help

The sp_help system procedure provides a convenient way to display a summary of Domain Integrity definitions for a table.

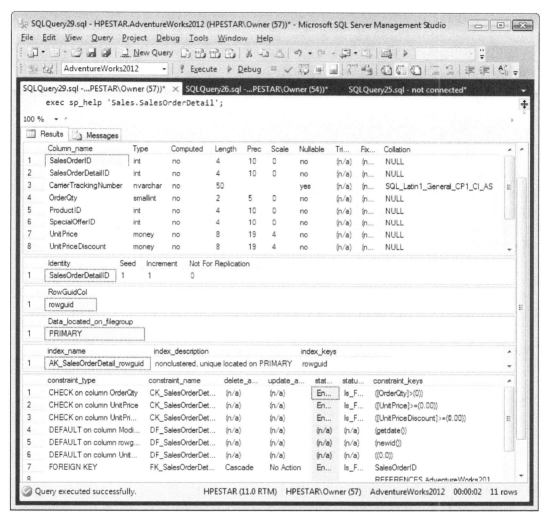

We can query "sys" system views metadata for column definition as well.

SELECT * FROM sys.columns
WHERE object_name(object_id) = 'PurchaseOrderHeader' ORDER BY column_id;
-- (13 row(s) affected) - Partial results.

object_id	name	column_id	system_type_id	user_type_id	max_length	precision	scale	collation_name
946102411	PurchaseOrderID	1	56	56	4	10	0	NULL

CHAPTER II: Maintaining Data Integrity in the Enterprise

THE COLUMNPROPERTY() Function

The COLUMNPROPERTY() function can be used for programmatic discovery of column properties. Script to generate SELECT queries for all properties.

```
USE AdventureWorks2012;
GO


DECLARE @Parms TABLE (Property varchar(32))
INSERT  @Parms VALUES
('AllowsNull'), ('ColumnId'),
('FullTextTypeColumn'), ('IsComputed'),
('IsCursorType'), ('IsDeterministic'),
('IsFulltextIndexed'), ('IsIdentity'),
('IsIdNotForRepl'), ('IsIndexable'),
('IsOutParam'), ('IsPrecise'),
('IsRowGuidCol'), ('IsSystemVerified'),
('IsXmlIndexable'), ('Precision'),
('Scale'), ('StatisticalSemantics'),
('SystemDataAccess'), ('UserDataAccess'),
('UsesAnsiTrim'), ('IsSparse'),
('IsColumnSet')
SELECT CONCAT('SELECT COLUMNPROPERTY( OBJECT_ID("Person.Person"), "LastName", "',
                Property, '") AS [', Property, '];')
FROM @Parms
GO  -- Partial results.
```

```
SELECT COLUMNPROPERTY( OBJECT_ID('Person.Person'), 'LastName', 'AllowsNull') AS [AllowsNull];
SELECT COLUMNPROPERTY( OBJECT_ID('Person.Person'), 'LastName', 'ColumnId') AS [ColumnId];
SELECT COLUMNPROPERTY( OBJECT_ID('Person.Person'), 'LastName', 'FullTextTypeColumn') AS [FullTextTypeColumn];
SELECT COLUMNPROPERTY( OBJECT_ID('Person.Person'), 'LastName', 'IsComputed') AS [IsComputed];
SELECT COLUMNPROPERTY( OBJECT_ID('Person.Person'), 'LastName', 'IsCursorType') AS [IsCursorType];
```

Executing the queries, the column properties are returned one by one.

	AllowsNull
1	0

	ColumnId
1	7

	FullTextTypeColumn
1	0

	IsComputed
1	0

	IsCursorType
1	0

Column List Using System Views & Data Dictionary

We can combine sys. system views with data dictionary description to get a valuable list when working with domain integrity.

```
USE AdventureWorks2012;
SELECT SCHEMA_NAME(T.schema_id)    AS SchemaName,
    T.name                         AS TableName,
    C.name                         AS ColumnName,
    TP.name                        AS ColumnType,
    C.max_length                   AS ColumnLength,
    COALESCE(EP.value, Space(1))   AS ColumnDesc
FROM   sys.tables AS T
    INNER JOIN sys.columns AS C
        ON T.object_id = C.object_id
    INNER JOIN sys.types AS TP
        ON  C.system_type_id = TP.user_type_id
    LEFT JOIN sys.extended_properties AS EP
        ON EP.major_id = T.object_id
            AND EP.minor_id = C.column_id
ORDER  BY SchemaName,  TableName,  ColumnName;
GO  -- (643 row(s) affected) - Partial Results.
```

Purchasing	PurchaseOrderHeader	EmployeeID	int	4	Employee who created the purchase order. Foreign key to Employee.BusinessEntityID.
Purchasing	PurchaseOrderHeader	Freight	money	8	Shipping cost.
Purchasing	PurchaseOrderHeader	ModifiedDate	datetime	8	Date and time the record was last updated.
Purchasing	PurchaseOrderHeader	OrderDate	datetime	8	Purchase order creation date.
Purchasing	PurchaseOrderHeader	PurchaseOrderID	int	4	Primary key.
Purchasing	PurchaseOrderHeader	PurchaseOrderID	int	4	Clustered index created by a primary key constraint.
Purchasing	PurchaseOrderHeader	RevisionNumber	tinyint	1	Incremental number to track changes to the purchase order over time.
Purchasing	PurchaseOrderHeader	RevisionNumber	tinyint	1	Nonclustered index.
Purchasing	PurchaseOrderHeader	ShipDate	datetime	8	Estimated shipment date from the vendor.
Purchasing	PurchaseOrderHeader	ShipMethodID	int	4	Shipping method. Foreign key to ShipMethod.ShipMethodID.
Purchasing	PurchaseOrderHeader	Status	tinyint	1	Order current status. 1 = Pending; 2 = Approved; 3 = Rejected; 4 = Complete
Purchasing	PurchaseOrderHeader	Status	tinyint	1	Nonclustered index.
Purchasing	PurchaseOrderHeader	SubTotal	money	8	Purchase order subtotal. Computed as SUM(PurchaseOrderDetail.LineTotal)for the appropriate PurchaseOrder D.
Purchasing	PurchaseOrderHeader	TaxAmt	money	8	Tax amount.
Purchasing	PurchaseOrderHeader	TotalDue	money	8	Total due to vendor. Computed as Subtotal + TaxAmt + Freight.
Purchasing	PurchaseOrderHeader	VendorID	int	4	Vendor with whom the purchase order is placed. Foreign key to Vendor.BusinessEntityID.

Declarative Referential Integrity

Referential Integrity refers to ensuring that relationships between tables remain consistent. Declarative means it is part of table setup, not in programming objects like stored procedure. When one table attempts to create a FOREIGN KEY to another (PK) table, Referential Integrity requires that the primary key value exists in the referenced (PK) table. The optional cascading update & cascading delete ensure that changes made to the primary table are reflected in the linked referencing (FK) table. For example, if a row is deleted in the primary table, then all referencing rows are automatically deleted in the linked (FK) table when ON DELETE CASCADE is set. All three Referential Integrity constraint actions are demonstrated by the following script.

```
USE tempdb;

-- Create 2 test tables with PK-FK relationship
CREATE TABLE Product (
       ProductID INT PRIMARY KEY,
       ProductName varchar(50) UNIQUE,
       ProductNumber varchar(20) UNIQUE,
       ListPrice MONEY);
GO

-- First we test without the DELETE CASCADE action
CREATE TABLE OrderDetail (
       SalesOrderID INT,
       SalesOrderDetailID INT,
       PRIMARY KEY (SalesOrderID, SalesOrderDetailID),
       OrderQty INT ,
       ProductID INT REFERENCES Product(ProductID)  -- ON DELETE CASCADE  );
GO
```

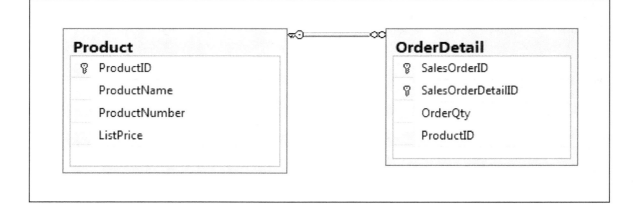

FOREIGN KEY Constraint Protects Two Ways

```
-- Populate test tables
INSERT Product
SELECT ProductID, Name, ProductNumber, ListPrice
FROM AdventureWorks2012.Production.Product
ORDER BY ProductID;
GO
--(504 row(s) affected)


INSERT OrderDetail
SELECT          SalesOrderID,
                SalesOrderDetailID,
                OrderQty,
                ProductID
FROM AdventureWorks2012.Sales.SalesOrderDetail
ORDER BY SalesOrderID, SalesOrderDetailID;
GO
-- (121317 row(s) affected)
```

-- Attempting to insert into FK table a reference to a non-existing (PK) ProductID
```
INSERT OrderDetail
SELECT          SalesOrderID = 100000,
                SalesOrderDetailID = 1000000,
                OrderQty = 5,
                ProductID = 2000
GO
/* Msg 547, Level 16, State 0, Line 1
The INSERT statement conflicted with the FOREIGN KEY constraint
"FK__OrderDeta__Produ__59FA5E80". The conflict occurred in database "tempdb", table
"dbo.Product", column 'ProductID'.
The statement has been terminated.   */
```

-- Attempting to delete from PK table a ProductID which is referenced from the FK table
```
DELETE Product WHERE ProductID = 800;
GO
/* Msg 547, Level 16, State 0, Line 1
The DELETE statement conflicted with the REFERENCE constraint
"FK__OrderDeta__Produ__59FA5E80". The conflict occurred in database "tempdb", table
"dbo.OrderDetail", column 'ProductID'.
The statement has been terminated.  */
```

ON DELETE CASCADE Action Causes DELETE Chain Reaction

```
-- Change FOREIGN KEY: specify ON DELETE CASCADE option
-- Lookup FK constraints name
SELECT * FROM INFORMATION_SCHEMA.REFERENTIAL_CONSTRAINTS;
```

CONSTRAINT_ CATALOG	CONSTRAINT _SCHEMA	CONSTRAINT_NAME	UNIQUE_CONSTRAI NT_CATALOG	UNIQUE_CONSTRAI NT_SCHEMA	UNIQUE_CONSTRAIN T_NAME	MATCH_ OPTION	UPDATE _RULE	DELETE _RULE
tempdb	dbo	FK__OrderDeta__Prod u__0A9D95DB	tempdb	dbo	PK__Product__B40CC 6ED66641298	SIMPLE	NO ACTION	NO ACTION

```
BEGIN TRANSACTION
GO
ALTER TABLE dbo.OrderDetail  DROP CONSTRAINT FK__OrderDeta__Produ__0A9D95DB;
GO
ALTER TABLE dbo.Product SET (LOCK_ESCALATION = TABLE)
GO
COMMIT TRANSACTION -- Command(s) completed successfully.


BEGIN TRANSACTION;
GO
ALTER TABLE dbo.OrderDetail  ADD CONSTRAINT FK__OrderDeta__Produ__0A9D95DB
FOREIGN KEY (ProductID)  REFERENCES dbo.Product (ProductID) ON DELETE CASCADE;
GO
ALTER TABLE dbo.OrderDetail SET (LOCK_ESCALATION = TABLE);
GO
COMMIT TRANSACTION;  -- Command(s) completed successfully.

SELECT * FROM INFORMATION_SCHEMA.REFERENTIAL_CONSTRAINTS;
```

CONSTRAINT_ CATALOG	CONSTRAINT _SCHEMA	CONSTRAINT_NAME	UNIQUE_CONSTRAI NT_CATALOG	UNIQUE_CONSTRAI NT_SCHEMA	UNIQUE_CONSTRAIN T_NAME	MATCH_ OPTION	UPDATE _RULE	DELETE _RULE
tempdb	dbo	FK__OrderDeta__Prod u__0A9D95DB	tempdb	dbo	PK__Product__B40CC 6ED66641298	SIMPLE	NO ACTION	CASCAD E

```
SELECT COUNT(*) FROM OrderDetail;
GO  -- 121317


-- Cascading DELETE: first DELETE all referencing FK records, then DELETE PK record
DELETE Product WHERE ProductID = 800;
GO
-- (1 row(s) affected)

SELECT COUNT(*) FROM OrderDetail;
GO  -- 120822
```

CHAPTER 11: Maintaining Data Integrity in the Enterprise

FOREIGN KEY Constraints Represent the Only Connections Among Tables

While we talk about linked tables in functional terms such as master/header-detail, parent-child, dimension-fact, junction, etc., **there is only a single way to connect tables: FOREIGN KEY references PRIMARY KEY in another table**. We are going to demonstrate it in a grand manner: we will create 290 tables with the names of all the employees of AdventureWorks Cycles (fictional) company in a new test database. We shall connect all of them with FOREIGN KEY constraints: employee (FK table) references manager (PK table).

```
USE master;
GO
CREATE DATABASE AWOrgChart;
GO
USE AWOrgChart;
GO

DECLARE @SQL NVARCHAR(max) = '';

WITH CTE (ID, Emp, Mgr, MgrNode)  -- CTE with column names
    AS
(    SELECT E.BusinessEntityID,
         Emp=CONCAT(P.FirstName, SPACE(1), P.LastName),
         NULL,
         NULL
    FROM   AdventureWorks2012.HumanResources.Employee E
        INNER JOIN AdventureWorks2012.Person.Person P
            ON E.BusinessEntityID = P.BusinessEntityID
    WHERE  E.OrganizationNode = 0x                        -- Root node
    UNION
    SELECT E.BusinessEntityID,
        CONCAT(P.FirstName, SPACE(1), P.LastName)              AS Emp,
        CONCAT(PP.FirstName, SPACE(1), PP.LastName)            AS Mgr,
        E.OrganizationNode.GetAncestor(1)                      AS SuperNode
    FROM   AdventureWorks2012.HumanResources.Employee E
        INNER JOIN AdventureWorks2012.Person.Person P
            ON E.BusinessEntityID = P.BusinessEntityID
        INNER JOIN AdventureWorks2012.HumanResources.Employee EE
            ON ( EE.OrganizationNode = E.OrganizationNode.GetAncestor(1) )
        INNER JOIN AdventureWorks2012.Person.Person PP
            ON EE.BusinessEntityID = PP.BusinessEntityID)
```

```
SELECT @SQL = CONCAT(@SQL, CONCAT('CREATE TABLE ', QUOTENAME(Emp),
              '( ID INT PRIMARY KEY ,',
                 ' MgrID INT ',
                      CASE
           WHEN Mgr IS NOT NULL THEN CONCAT(' REFERENCES ',
                      QUOTENAME(Mgr),   '(ID)')
           ELSE ''   END, '); '))
FROM   CTE;

PRINT @SQL;  -- Partial text.
```

```
CREATE TABLE [Ken Sánchez]( ID INT PRIMARY KEY , MgrID INT );
CREATE TABLE [Terri Duffy]( ID INT PRIMARY KEY , MgrID INT  REFERENCES [Ken Sánchez](ID));
CREATE TABLE [Roberto Tamburello]( ID INT PRIMARY KEY ,
MgrID INT  REFERENCES [Terri Duffy](ID));
CREATE TABLE [Rob Walters]( ID INT PRIMARY KEY ,
MgrID INT  REFERENCES [Roberto Tamburello](ID));
CREATE TABLE [Gail Erickson]( ID INT PRIMARY KEY ,
MgrID INT  REFERENCES [Roberto Tamburello](ID));
CREATE TABLE [Jossef Goldberg]( ID INT PRIMARY KEY ,
MgrID INT  REFERENCES [Roberto Tamburello](ID));
CREATE TABLE [Dylan Miller]( ID INT PRIMARY KEY ,
MgrID INT  REFERENCES [Roberto Tamburello](ID));
CREATE TABLE [Diane Margheim]( ID INT PRIMARY KEY ,
MgrID INT  REFERENCES [Dylan Miller](ID));
CREATE TABLE [Gigi Matthew]( ID INT PRIMARY KEY , MgrID INT  REFERENCES [Dylan Miller](ID));
CREATE TABLE [Michael Raheem]( ID INT PRIMARY KEY ,
MgrID INT  REFERENCES [Dylan Miller](ID));
CREATE TABLE [Ovidiu Cracium]( ID INT PRIMARY KEY ,
MgrID INT  REFERENCES [Roberto Tamburello](ID));
CREATE TABLE [Thierry D'Hers]( ID INT PRIMARY KEY ,
MgrID INT  REFERENCES [Ovidiu Cracium](ID));
```

The functional meaning of Terry Duffy "references" Ken Sanchez: Duffy reports to Sanchez.

```
EXEC sp_executeSQL @SQL;  -- Dynamic SQL execution: create 290 linked tables
GO
```

```
-- USE master;
DROP DATABASE AWOrgChart;
```

CHAPTER II: Maintaining Data Integrity in the Enterprise

Diagram Tool Can Be Used for Organizational Charts

We can use the diagram tool in the AWOrgChart database as an orgchart tool. We add a chosen table to the diagram, for example, [Ken Sanchez]. With the right click menu, we add related tables, set view to table name only & arrange selection. The result is orgchart with the CEO and executive managers.

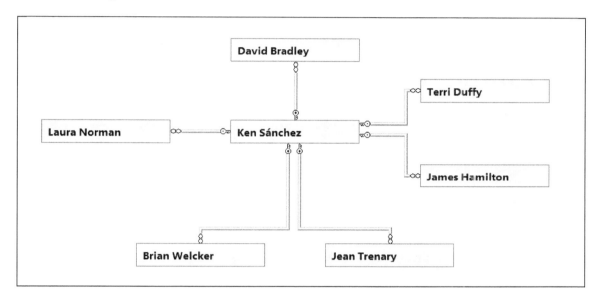

Orgchart starting with [David Hamilton]. Hamilton reports to Krebs (Gold Key).

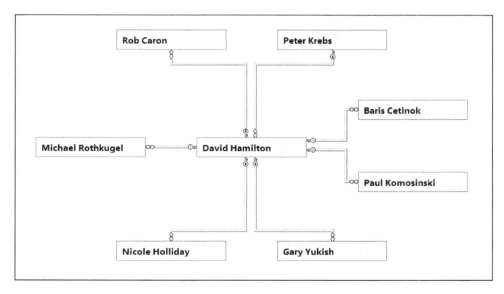

CHAPTER 11: Maintaining Data Integrity in the Enterprise

Enterprise-Level Business Rules Enforcement

Enterprise-Level Business Rules can be enforced by stored procedures & triggers on the server-side and application programs on the client-side. While stored procedures & application programs can be used to implement a complex set of business rules, they can only effect the current application. Stored procedure or application cannot catch an UPDATE transaction, for example, coming from a legacy application nobody dares to touch at the IT department. In a way stored procedure can be configured to perform after-the-fact near-real-time updates for recently posted data: configure the stored procedure as SQL Server Agent job and schedule it to run each minute.

Special Role of Triggers

Triggers, on the other hand, can catch, for example, an INSERT to the ProductPrice table, wherever it is coming from; current in-house application software, old in-house application, another profit-center of the enterprise application or 3rd party software package. An example for an enterprise business rule: convert foreign currency pricing to USD in the INSERT record to ProductPrice using the latest conversion rates from the ForeignExchange table. A constraint cannot be used to implement such a rule, a trigger can. Trigger code almost as flexible as stored procedure code. Triggers can also be used for cross-database referential integrity enforcement. While triggers are compiled into one database, they can access tables in another database. Because of their omnipotent nature, triggers are frequently misapplied as fix-it-all tools.

WARNING
Triggers are high maintenance database objects. Triggers are not for junior staff. Dropped/disabled triggers do not "COMPLAIN": stealth behavior.

Triggers are just like silent workhorses. They can be forgotten after months of operation since they don't have to be called explicitly from the client-side application programs, they are event launched on the server-side. DDL trigger can be applied to guard DML triggers, but then someone or something has to guard the DDL trigger as well. On the other hand, a dropped stored procedure causes user error ("complains"). Dropped trigger can cause user error also, but the error cannot easily be traced back the trigger.

The following update trigger will prevent last name update from new software, old software, other department's software or even 3rd party software package.

```
CREATE TRIGGER trgEmployee  ON Employee FOR UPDATE AS
   IF (UPDATE(LastName))              BEGIN
      RAISERROR ('Last name cannot be changed', 16, 1);  ROLLBACK TRAN;  RETURN;   END
GO
```

CHAPTER 11: Maintaining Data Integrity in the Enterprise

Product Reorder Trigger

The UPDATE trigger is attached to the Products table. It fires whenever there is an UPDATE for the table, no matter what kind of software application from what part of the world executed the UPDATE statement. **A trigger should never return a result set**. However, there is no error if we try to return a result set with a SELECT statement just like in a stored procedure. For testing & debugging purposes we can return results.

```
USE Northwind
GO


-- Logging table for product reorder notices
CREATE TABLE Reorder (
        ID INT IDENTITY(1,1) PRIMARY KEY,
        Message varchar(256),
        CreateDate datetime default (CURRENT_TIMESTAMP));
GO


IF EXISTS (select * from sys.objects where type='TR' and name = 'trgProductReorder')
        DROP TRIGGER trgProductReorder
GO


CREATE TRIGGER trgProductReorder
ON Products FOR UPDATE
AS
  BEGIN
    SET NOCOUNT ON;
    DECLARE @MsgText    varchar(128),    @QtyOnHand   int, @ReorderLevel int;
    SELECT @MsgText = CONCAT('Please place a reorder  for ', Rtrim(ProductName))
    FROM   inserted;

    SELECT @QtyOnHand = UnitsInStock,   @ReorderLevel = ReorderLevel  FROM   inserted;

    IF @QtyOnHand < @ReorderLevel
        INSERT Reorder  (Message)        SELECT @MsgText;

  --select * from deleted -- for testing &debugging only
  --select * from inserted
  --select @MsgText
  END
GO
```

A Trigger Should Never Return A Result Set Like A Stored Procedure

Check Data Manipulation Language (DML) trigger existence with sp_helptrigger system procedure.

```
EXEC sp_helptrigger Products ;
GO
```

trigger_name	trigger_owner	isupdate	isdelete	isinsert	isafter	isinsteadof	trigger_schema
trgProductReorder	dbo	1	0	0	1	0	dbo

```
-- Test trigger
/* For demonstration purposes, the debugging statements in trigger were uncommented */
UPDATE Products
        SET   UnitsInStock = 10
        WHERE  ProductID = 77;
GO
```

SQL Server UPDATE is implemented as complete deleted (old) and inserted (new) rows. Even if 1 byte updated, a complete row deleted and complete row inserted generated for logging.

deleted table row:

Product ID	ProductName	Supplier ID	Category ID	QuantityPer Unit	UnitPrice	**UnitsInStock**	UnitsOnOrder	ReorderLevel	Discontinued
77	Original Frankfurter grüne Soße	12	2	12 boxes	13.00	**50**	0	15	0

inserted table row:

Product ID	ProductName	Supplier ID	Category ID	QuantityPer Unit	UnitPrice	**UnitsInStock**	UnitsOnOrder	ReorderLevel	Discontinued
77	Original Frankfurter grüne Soße	12	2	12 boxes	13.00	**10**	0	15	0

```
SELECT * FROM   Reorder;
GO
```

ID	Message	CreateDate
1	Please place a reorder for Original Frankfurter grüne Soße	2016-11-25 06:06:45.043

```
DROP TRIGGER trgProductReorder;
DROP TABLE Reorder;
```

Trigger Examples In AdventureWorks2012

List of triggers in the sample database. parent_object_id is the object_id of the trigger parent table. SELF-JOIN is required to get the parent information.

```
USE AdventureWorks2012;
SELECT
    o.name                                          AS TriggerName,
    SCHEMA_NAME(po.schema_id)                        AS TableSchema,
    OBJECT_NAME(o.parent_object_id)                  AS TableName,
    OBJECTPROPERTY( o.object_id, 'ExecIsUpdateTrigger')    AS [isupdate],
    OBJECTPROPERTY( o.object_id, 'ExecIsDeleteTrigger')    AS [isdelete],
    OBJECTPROPERTY( o.object_id, 'ExecIsInsertTrigger')    AS [isinsert],
    OBJECTPROPERTY( o.object_id, 'ExecIsAfterTrigger')     AS [isafter],
    OBJECTPROPERTY( o.object_id, 'ExecIsInsteadOfTrigger') AS [isinsteadof],
    OBJECTPROPERTY( o.object_id, 'ExecIsTriggerDisabled')  AS [disabled]
FROM sys.objects AS o
        INNER JOIN sys.objects AS po    ON o.parent_object_id = po.object_id
WHERE o.[type] = 'TR'  ORDER BY TableSchema, TableName, TriggerName;
```

TriggerName	TableSchema	TableName	isupdate	isdelete	isinsert	isafter	isinsteadof	disabled
dEmployee	HumanResources	Employee	0	1	0	0	1	0
iuPerson	Person	Person	1	0	1	1	0	0
iWorkOrder	Production	WorkOrder	0	0	1	1	0	0
uWorkOrder	Production	WorkOrder	1	0	0	1	0	0
iPurchaseOrderDetail	Purchasing	PurchaseOrderDetail	0	0	1	1	0	0
uPurchaseOrderDetail	Purchasing	PurchaseOrderDetail	1	0	0	1	0	0
uPurchaseOrderHeader	Purchasing	PurchaseOrderHeader	1	0	0	1	0	0
dVendor	Purchasing	Vendor	0	1	0	0	1	0
iduSalesOrderDetail	Sales	SalesOrderDetail	1	1	1	1	0	0
uSalesOrderHeader	Sales	SalesOrderHeader	1	0	0	1	0	0

Alternate method of obtaining all triggers information.

```
SELECT * FROM sys.triggers ORDER BY name; -- Partial results.
```

name	object_id	parent_class	parent_class_desc	parent_id	type	type_desc
ddlDatabaseTriggerLog	261575970	0	DATABASE	0	TR	SQL_TRIGGER
dEmployee	1739153241	1	OBJECT_OR_COLUMN	1237579447	TR	SQL_TRIGGER
dVendor	1851153640	1	OBJECT_OR_COLUMN	766625774	TR	SQL_TRIGGER
iduSalesOrderDetail	1819153526	1	OBJECT_OR_COLUMN	1154103152	TR	SQL_TRIGGER
iPurchaseOrderDetail	1771153355	1	OBJECT_OR_COLUMN	850102069	TR	SQL_TRIGGER
iuPerson	1755153298	1	OBJECT_OR_COLUMN	1765581328	TR	SQL_TRIGGER
iWorkOrder	1867153697	1	OBJECT_OR_COLUMN	846626059	TR	SQL_TRIGGER
uPurchaseOrderDetail	1787153412	1	OBJECT_OR_COLUMN	850102069	TR	SQL_TRIGGER
uPurchaseOrderHeader	1803153469	1	OBJECT_OR_COLUMN	946102411	TR	SQL_TRIGGER
uSalesOrderHeader	1835153583	1	OBJECT_OR_COLUMN	1266103551	TR	SQL_TRIGGER
uWorkOrder	1883153754	1	OBJECT_OR_COLUMN	846626059	TR	SQL_TRIGGER

Trigger Can Be Modified in Object Explorer

When the Modify Trigger option is picked, Object Explorer loads it as ALTER TRIGGER script.

Programmatic way to get trigger definition.

SELECT OBJECT_DEFINITION(object_id('Person.iuPerson'));

```
CREATE TRIGGER [Person].[iuPerson] ON [Person].[Person]
AFTER INSERT, UPDATE NOT FOR REPLICATION AS
BEGIN
    DECLARE @Count int;
    SET @Count = @@ROWCOUNT;
    IF @Count = 0       RETURN;
    SET NOCOUNT ON;
    IF UPDATE([BusinessEntityID]) OR UPDATE([Demographics])
```

CHAPTER 11: Maintaining Data Integrity in the Enterprise

Business Intelligence in the Enterprise

SQL Server Analysis Services (SSAS), SQL Server Integration Services (SSIS) & SQL Server Reporting Services (SSRS) are the server side Business Intelligence software components. Easy to remember associations: SSAS: OLAP cubes and more, SSIS: ETL (extract, transform, load) data transfer system & SSRS: traditional reports, interactive & OLAP reports. SQL Server Data Tools (SSDT) provides 3 customized templates as design environments.

SSRS: Designing Complex Interactive Reports

SSDT report design environment: product catalog in the report design editor.

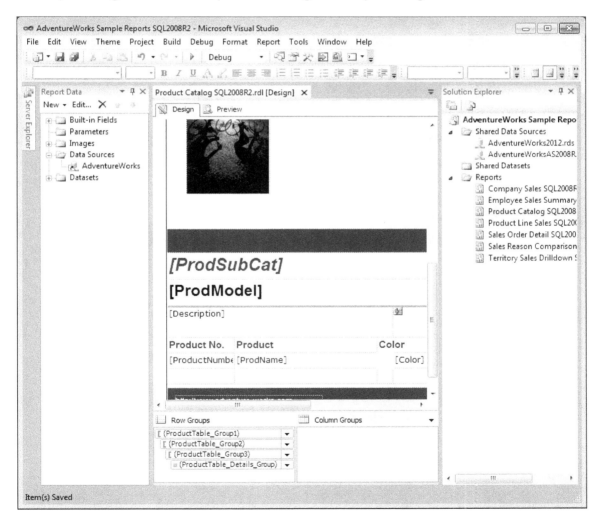

Previewing the Report Design

The product catalog is interactive with a drill down directory on the left which is based on the Production.ProductCategory and Production.ProductSubcategory tables. The Product, ProductSubcategory & ProductCategory tables form a hierarchy which is neatly exploited in the product catalog report. What makes the report design environment extremely powerful that you can try the look & feel of a report just by clicking a tab and staying in the studio environment. The product images are from the ProductPhoto table(in Management Studio we cannot see the images, only the binary code).

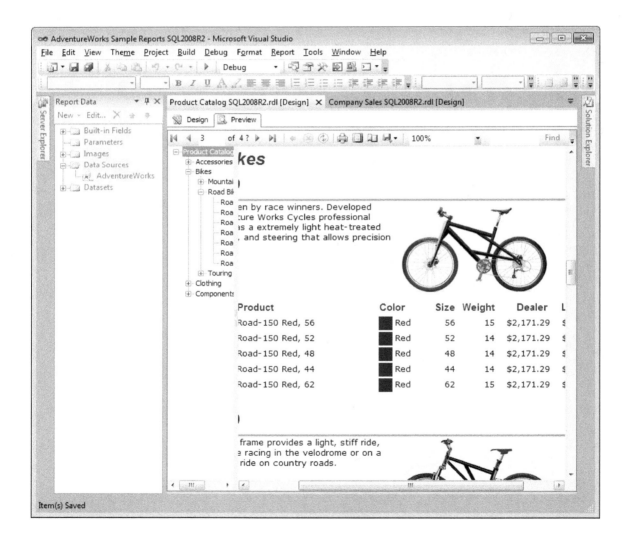

Detailed Preview of AWC Product Catalog

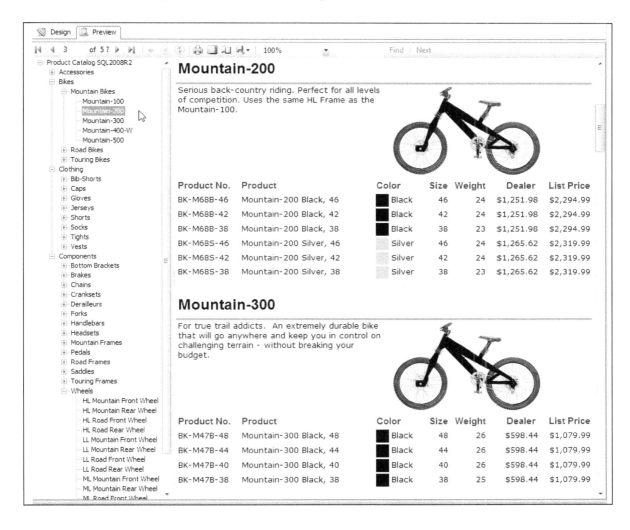

CHAPTER 11: Maintaining Data Integrity in the Enterprise

SSAS: Designing Multi-Dimensional Cubes

SSAS cubes contain millions of pre-calculated answers just waiting for the question like: what was the net revenue in Florida for the 3rd Quarter of 2016? Since the answer is ready, the response time is sub-second. AS cubes are derived from dimension tables and fact tables in a data warehouse database.

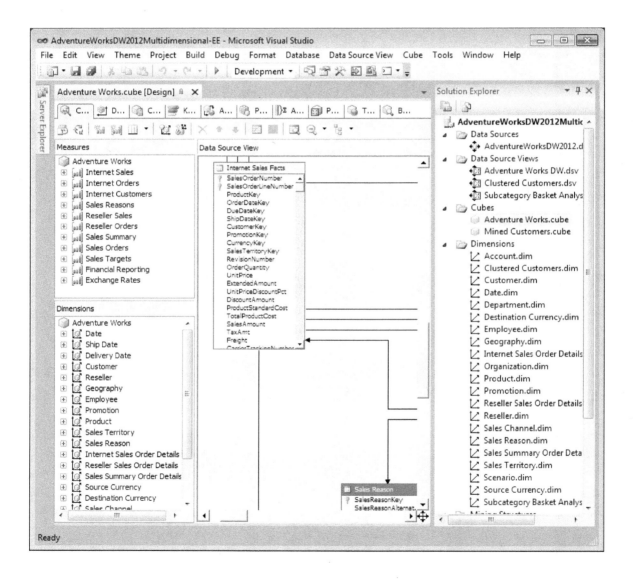

Test OLAP Analysis Services Cube Design with Browser

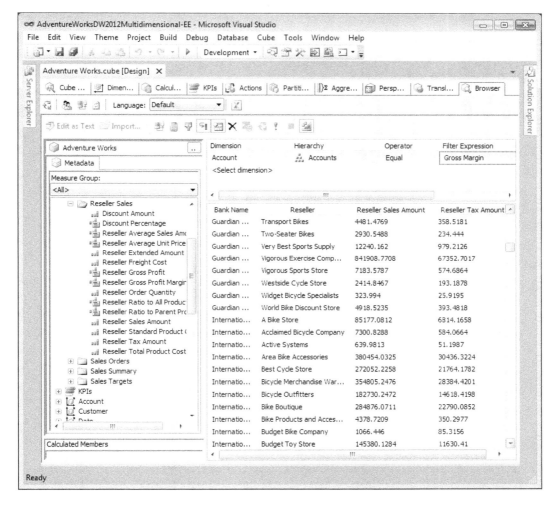

Dimension Usage Display

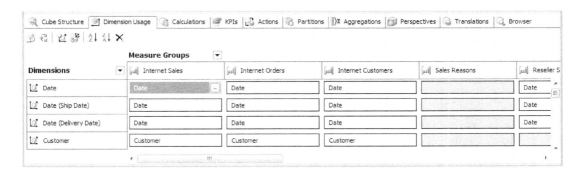

CHAPTER II: Maintaining Data Integrity in the Enterprise

Browsing Multidimensional Cube in Management Explorer

In Object Explorer we can connect to Analysis Server and browse the available multidimensional cubes.

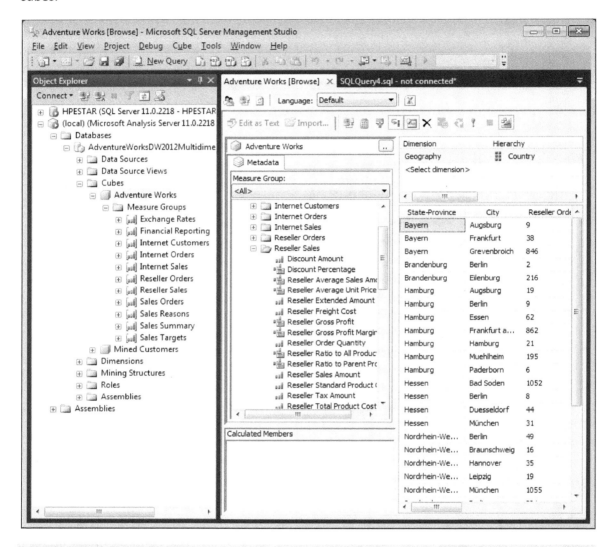

```
USE AdventureWorksDW2012;
-- Searching data warehouse database metadata for table objects
SELECT  CONCAT(schema_name(O.schema_id),'.', O.NAME) AS ObjectName,
        O.TYPE AS ObjectType,      C.NAME AS ColumnName
FROM sys.objects O INNER JOIN sys.columns C ON O.OBJECT_ID = C.OBJECT_ID
WHERE  O.type='U' AND O.NAME LIKE '%sales%' AND C.NAME LIKE '%price%'
ORDER BY ObjectName, ColumnName;   -- Partial results.
-- dbo.FactInternetSales    U          UnitPrice
```

CHAPTER 11: Maintaining Data Integrity in the Enterprise

Excel PivotTable Report Using AS Cube Datasource

Excel can use as datasource SQL Server database and Analysis Services database(bottom image). Actually PivotTable is a very good match for browsing multidimensional cubes since the underlying concepts are very similar: summary data tabulations by dimensions.

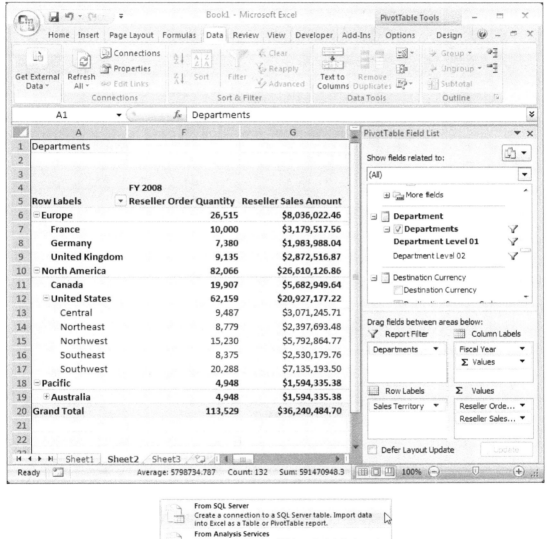

Sales Reason Comparison Report Based on AS Cube

The Sales Reason Comparison report (converted to 2012) is based on the multidimensional AdventureWorksAS AS cube. Design mode and report segment in preview mode.

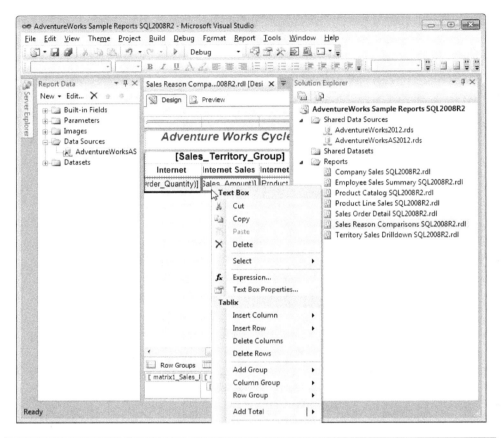

SSIS: Enterprise Level Data Integration

SSIS is an enterprise level data integration and data transformation software tool. Transmit (clean, transformed) data from different data sources to the database and vice versa. The Data Flow editor in SSDT for an SSIS sample project.

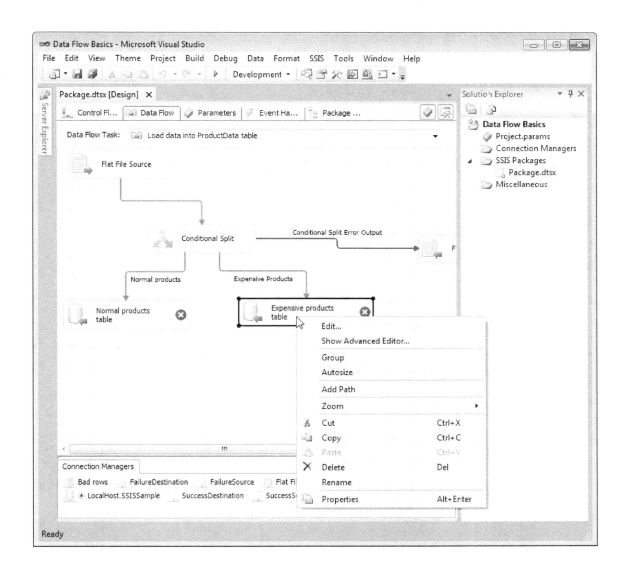

SSAS, SSIS, SSRS in Configuration Manager

SSIS is shared for all instances. SSAS & SSRS are per instance. MSSQLSERVER means the default instance, HPESTAR. SQL12 means the names instance HPESTAR\SQL12.

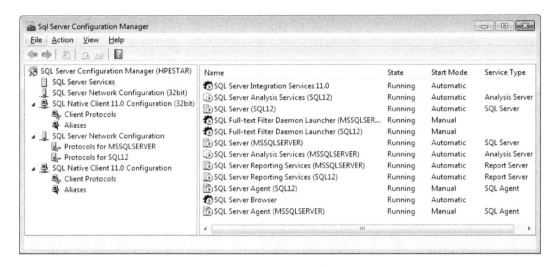

ReportServer & ReportServerTempDB Databases

Each Reporting Services instance is supported by two databases.

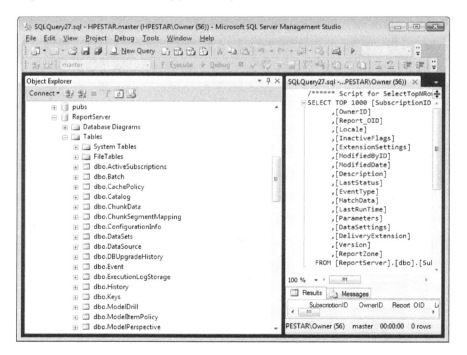

Full-Text Index & Full-Text Search

Full-Text Search in SQL Server 2012 allows users and application programs, such as C#, to execute Full-Text Search queries against text-based data in SQL Server 2012 tables. Prior to running full-text search queries on a table, full-text catalog and full-text indexes on table text column(s) must be created.

```
USE AdventureWorks2012;
SELECT * INTO dbo.JobCandidate FROM HumanResources.JobCandidate; ; -- (13 row(s) affected)
GO
CREATE UNIQUE INDEX idxHRJC ON JobCandidate(JobCandidateID);
CREATE FULLTEXT CATALOG HRFullText AS DEFAULT;
CREATE FULLTEXT INDEX ON JobCandidate(Resume) KEY INDEX idxHRJC WITH STOPLIST = SYSTEM;
GO

SELECT JobCandidateID FROM JobCandidate WHERE CONTAINS(Resume, ' "production line ' ');       -- 2

SELECT JobCandidateID FROM JobCandidate WHERE CONTAINS(Resume, ' "C#" ');                     -- 3

SELECT JobCandidateID FROM JobCandidate WHERE CONTAINS (Resume, ' "machin*" ' );              -- 1, 7

SELECT * FROM CONTAINSTABLE(JobCandidate, Resume, 'ISABOUT ("mach*",
    tool WEIGHT(0.9),  automatic WEIGHT(0.1)   ) ' );
```

KEY	RANK
1	51
7	22

```
SELECT jc.JobCandidateID, x.* FROM JobCandidate jc
        INNER JOIN  CONTAINSTABLE(JobCandidate, Resume, 'ISABOUT ("mach*",
                tool WEIGHT(0.9),  automatic WEIGHT(0.1)  ) ' ) x  ON x.[KEY] = jc.JobCandicateID;
```

JobCandidateID	KEY	RANK
1	1	51
7	7	22

```
SELECT JobCandidateID FROM JobCandidate WHERE CONTAINS(Resume, '(ingénierie NEAR expérimenté)'); -- 7

SELECT JobCandidateID FROM JobCandidate WHERE CONTAINS(Resume, '(visual and basic)');  -- 3

SELECT JobCandidateID FROM JobCandidate WHERE CONTAINS(Resume, '(visual or basic)'); -- 2, 3

SELECT JobCandidateID FROM JobCandidate WHERE CONTAINS (Resume,'FORMSOF(INFLECTIONAL,"computer")'); -- 1
GO

DROP TABLE dbo.JobCandidate;
DROP FULLTEXT CATALOG HRFullText;
GO
```

CHAPTER 11: Maintaining Data Integrity in the Enterprise

SQL Azure - Enterprise in the Clouds

Microsoft Windows Azure account is available at:

http://www.windowsazure.com/en-us/ .

There is a 90-day free trial package available which includes an SQL database. Credit card is required for an Azure account. One form of verification: a code is sent to your mobile phone.

Creating an SQL database in the "clouds".

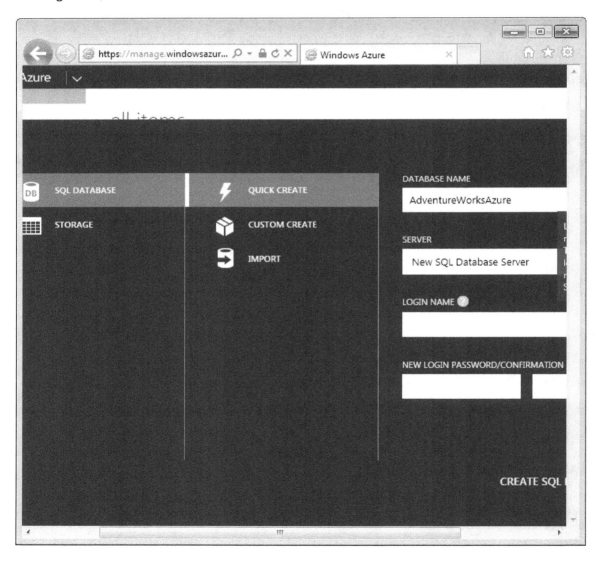

Getting Started with SQL Azure Database

Basic configuration has to be done online such as setting SQL Azure server login & password, and setting up firewall rules so you can use Management Studio and other client software from your computer. The configuration processes are automated to a large degree and user-friendly. The best part: once you are finished with configuration, you can continue with the "friendly skies" from the friendly Management Studio environment.

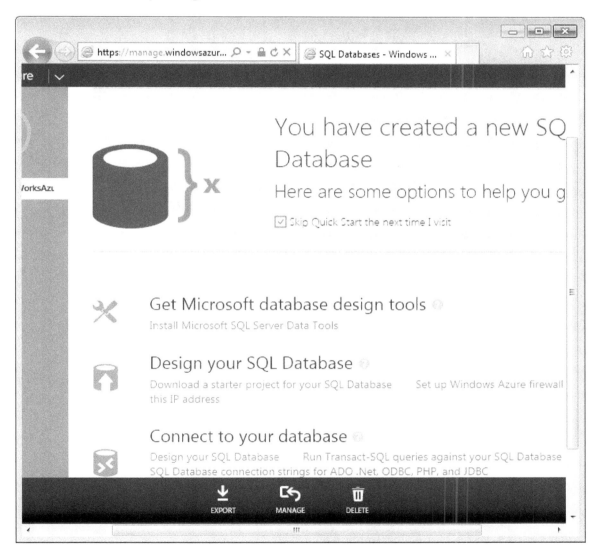

Connecting Azure SQL Server from Management Studio

You can connect to the Azure SQL Server after setting up a firewall rule for your computer IP using the regular dialog box with SQL Server authentication. The server name is: yourazureserver.database.windows.net. The login & password is what you configured on Azure. Some server & login information has been blanked out on the following screenshot. The Azure T-SQL is different from SQL Server 2012 T-SQL

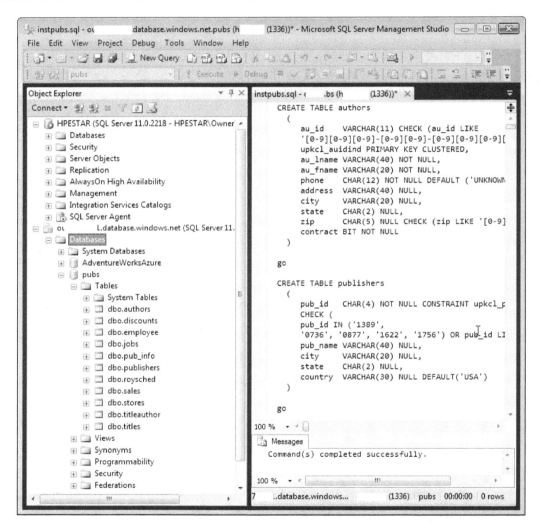

We can get SQL Azure version information by a SELECT:

select @@version -- Microsoft SQL Azure (RTM) - 11.0.2065.0 Aug 29 2012 18:41:07

This page is intentionally left blank.

This page is intentionally left blank.

APPENDIX A: Job Interview Questions

Selected Database Design Questions

D1. What is your approach to database design?

D2. Some of our legacy databases are far from 3NF. Can you work in such an environment?

D3. Can UNIQUE KEY be used instead of PRIMARY KEY?

D4. Can a FOREIGN KEY be NULL?

D5. Can a PRIMARY KEY be NULL?

D6. Can a PRIMARY KEY be based on non-clustered unique index?

D7. Do you implement OrderQty > 0 condition as a CHECK constraint or in the application software?

D8. What is a heap?

D9. Can a table have 2 IDENTITY columns, 2 FOREIGN KEYs, 2 PRIMARY KEYs and 2 clustered indexes?

D10. Should each table have a NATURAL KEY or is INT IDENTITY PK sufficient?

D11. How can you prevent entry of "U.S", "USA", etc. instead of "United States" into Country column?

D12. How would you implement ManagerID in an Employee table with EmployeeID as PRIMARY KEY?

D13. How would you implement the relationship between OrderMaster and OrderDetail tables?

D14. Product table has the Color column. Would you create a Color table & change column to ColorID FK?

D15. Can you insert directly into an IDENTITY column?

D16. Which one is better? Composite PRIMARY KEY on NATURAL KEY, or INT IDENTITY PRIMARY KEY & UNIQUE KEY on NATURAL KEY?

D17. What is the lifetime of a regular table created in tempdb?

D18. How many different ways can you connect tables in a database?

D19. How would you connect the Vehicle and Owner tables?

D20. Can you have the same table names in different schemas?

Selected Database Programming Questions

P1. Write a query to list all departments with employee count based on the Department column of Employee table.

P2. Same as above but the Employee table has the DepartmentID column.

P3. Write an INSERT statement for a new "Social Technology" department with GroupName "Sales & Marketing".

P4. Same query es in P2, but the new department should be included even though no employees yet.

P5. Write a query to generate 1000 sequential numbers without a table.

P6. Write a query with SARGable predicate to list all orders from OrderMaster received on 2016-10-23. OrderDate is datetime.

P7. Write a query to add a header record DEPARTMENTNAME to the departments listing from the Department table. If there are 20 departments, the result set should have 21 records.

P8. Make the previous query a derived table in an outer SELECT * query

P9. Write an ORDER BY clause for the previous query with CASE expression to sort DEPARTMENTNAME as first record and alphabetically descending from there on.

P10. Same as above with the IIF conditional.

P11. The table-valued dbo.ufnSplitCSV splits a comma delimited string (input parameter). The Product table has some ProductName-s with comma(s). Write a CROSS APPLY query to return ProductName-s with comma and each split string value from the UDF as separate line. ProductName should repeat for each split part.

ProductName	SplitPart
Full-Finger Gloves, L	Full-Finger Gloves
Full-Finger Gloves, L	L

P12. You need the inserted lines count 10 lines down following the INSERT statement. What should be the statement immediately following the INSERT statement?

P13. What is the result of the second query? What is it called?

SELECT COUNT_BIG(*) FROM Sales.SalesOrderDetail;   -- 121317

SELECT COUNT_BIG(*) FROM Sales.SalesOrderDetail x, Sales.SalesOrderDetail y;

P14. Declare & Assign the string variable @Text varchar(32) the literal '2016/10/23 10:20:12' without the "/" and ":".

P15. You want to add a parameter to a frequently used view. What is the workaround?

P16. When converting up to 40 characters string, can you use varchar instead of varchar(40)?

P17. Can you roll back IDENTITY seeds and table variables with ROLLBACK TRANSACTION?

P18. How do you decide where to place the clustered index?

P19. What is the simplest solution for the collation error: "Cannot resolve collation conflict..."?

P20. Which system table can be used for integer sequence up to 2^12 values?

This page is intentionally left blank.

This page is intentionally left blank.

APPENDIX B: Job Interview Answers

Selected Database Design Answers

D1. I prefer 3NF design due to high database developer productivity and low maintenance cost.

D2. I did have such projects in the past. I can handle them. Hopefully, introduce some improvements.

D3. Partially yes since UNIQUE KEYs can be FK referenced, fully no. Every table should a PRIMARY KEY.

D4. Yes.

D5. No.

D6. Yes. The default is clustered unique index. Only unique index is required.

D7. CHECK constraint. A server-side object solution is more reliable than code in application software.

D8. A table without clustered index. Database engine generally works better if a table has clustered index.

D9. No, yes, no, no.

D10. A table should be designed with NATURAL KEY(s). INT IDENTITY PK is not a replacement for NK.

D11. Lookup table with UDF CHECK Constraint. UDF checks the Lookup table for valid entries.

D12. ManagerID as a FOREIGN KEY referencing the PRIMARY KEY of the same table; self-referencing.

D13. OrderID PRIMARY KEY of OrderMaster. OrderID & LineItemID composit on PK of OrderDetail. OrderID of OrderDetail FK to OrderID of OderMaster.

D14. Yes. It makes sense for color to be in its own table.

D15. No. Only if you SET IDENTITY_INSERT tablename ON.

D16. Meaningless INT IDENTITY PRIMARY KEY with UNIQUE KEY ON NATURAL KEY is better.

D17. Until SQL Server restarted. tempdb starts empty as copy of model database.

D18. There is only one way: FOREIGN KEY constraint.

D19. With the OwnerVehicleXref junction table reflecting many-to-many relationship.

D20. Yes. A table is identified by SchemaName.TableName . dbo is the default schema.

Selected Database Programming Answers

P1. SELECT Department, Employees=COUNT(*) FROM Employee
   GROUP BY Department ORDER BY Department;

P2. SELECT d.Department, Employees = COUNT(EmployeeID) FROM Employee e
   INNER JOIN Department d ON e.DepartmentID = d.DepartmentID
   GROUP BY d.Department ORDER BY Department;

P3. INSERT Department (Name, GroupName) VALUES ('Social Technology', 'Sales & Marketing');

P4. SELECT d.Department, Employees = COUNT(EmployeeID) FROM Employee e
   RIGHT JOIN Department d ON e.DepartmentID = d.DepartmentID
   GROUP BY d.Department ORDER BY Department;

P5. ;WITH Seq AS (SELECT SeqNo = 1 UNION ALL SELECT SeqNo+1 FROM Seq WHERE SeqNo < 100)
   SELECT * FROM Seq;

P6. SELECT * FROM OrderMaster WHERE OrderDate >='20161023'
   AND OrderDate < DATEADD(DD,1,'20161023');

P7. SELECT AllDepartments = 'DEPARTMENTNAME' UNION SELECT Department FROM Department;

P8. SELECT * FROM (SELECT AllDepartments = 'DEPARTMENTNAME' UNION SELECT Name
    FROM HumanResources.Department) x

P9. ORDER BY CASE WHEN AllDepartments = 'DEPARTMENTNAME' THEN 1 ELSE 2 END,
   AllDepartments DESC;

P10. ORDER BY IIF(AllDepartments = 'DEPARTMENTNAME', 1 , 2), AllDepartments DESC;

P11. SELECT ProductName, S.SplitPart FROM Product P CROSS APPLY dbo.ufnSplitCSV (Name) S
    WHERE ProductName like '%,%';

P12. DECLARE @InsertedCount INT = @@ROWCOUNT;

P13. 121317*121317; Cartesian product.

P14. DECLARE @Text varchar(32) =
     REPLACE(REPLACE ('2016/10/23 10:20:12', '/', SPACE(0)), ':', SPACE(0));

P15. Table-valued INLINE user-defined function.

P16. varchar(40). It is a good idea to specify the length always. The default is 30.

P17. No. ROLLBACK has no effect on IDENTITY seeds or table variables. If an INSERT advanced the
IDENTITY seed by 5 during the rollbacked transaction, it will stay that way after the ROLLBACK. It means a
gap in the IDENTITY sequence.

P18. Business critical queries are the determining factor in placing the clustered index. Clustered index
speeds up range queries.

P19. Place "COLLATE DATABASE_DEFAULT" on the right side of the expression.

P20. spt_values table.
SELECT N = number FROM master.dbo.spt_values WHERE type='P' ORDER BY N;

This page is intentionally left blank.

APPENDIX B: Job Interview Answers

This page is intentionally left blank.

INDEX of SQL Server 2012 Database Design

Index of the Most Important Topics

D

This page is intentionally left blank.

www.ingramcontent.com/pod-product-compliance
Lightning Source LLC
LaVergne TN
LVHW062300060326
832902LV00013B/1981